TROJAN-HORSE AID

D1739098

Trojan-Horse Aid

Seeds of Resistance and Resilience in the Bolivian Highlands and Beyond

SUSAN WALSH

McGill-Queen's University Press
Montreal & Kingston • London • Ithaca

© McGill-Queen's University Press 2014
ISBN 978-0-7735-4433-8 (cloth)
ISBN 978-0-7735-4434-5 (paper)
ISBN 978-0-7735-9661-0 (ePDF)
ISBN 978-0-7735-9662-7 (ePUB)

Legal deposit fourth quarter 2014
Bibliothèque nationale du Québec

Printed in Canada on acid-free paper that is 100% ancient forest
free (100% post-consumer recycled), processed chlorine free.

McGill-Queen's University Press acknowledges the support of
the Canada Council for the Arts for our publishing program.
We also acknowledge the financial support of the Government
of Canada through the Canada Book Fund for our publishing
activities.

Library and Archives Canada Cataloguing in Publication

Walsh, Susan, 1955–, author
    Trojan-horse aid : seeds of resistance and resilience in the
Bolivian highlands and beyond / Susan Walsh.

Includes bibliographical references and index.
Issued in print and electronic formats.
ISBN 978-0-7735-4433-8 (bound). – ISBN 978-0-7735-4434-5 (pbk.). –
ISBN 978-0-7735-9661-0 (ePDF). – ISBN 978-0-7735-9662-7 (ePUB)

    1. Agricultural assistance – Bolivia – Potosí (Department).
2. Agriculture – Bolivia – Potosí (Department). 3. Quechua Indians
– Agriculture – Bolivia – Potosí (Department). 4. Peasants – Bolivia
– Potosí (Department). I. Title.

HD1870.P6W24 2014   338.1'81098414   C2014-905359-2
                                                C2014-905360-6

This book was typeset by True to Type in 10.5/13 Sabon

To my mother, the late Jo Walsh;
my daughter, Kelsey Walsh;
my best friend, Krista Paznokaitis;
and my husband, Pat Mooney.
Their courage in facing the unexpected
has been a source of deep inspiration.

Contents

Acknowledgments

When balancing full-time employment and family responsibilities, writing a book requires a good measure of pigheadedness and a still greater measure of excitement about the subject matter. I seem to have had both, but even this was not enough to get the job done. This completed book is also a testament to the enormous support I received from a number of thoughtful and generous people.

First and foremost, my special thanks go to the Jalq'a people of Chimpa Rodeo and Mojón, Bolivia. They not only put up with a *gringa* peering into their lives, they also shared their time, traditions, and points of view to a degree well beyond my expectations.

My colleagues and research associates within Instituto Politecnico Toma Katari's (IPTK) Ravelo field station also deserve a deep bow of appreciation. There were hard working, committed, amazingly open, and respectful in their interactions with farmers. Our conversations, sometimes lasting well into the night, deepened my understanding of their world and the world of the Indigenous peoples they worked alongside. Although I am critical of some of the development strategies they were asked to implement, I left Ravelo with a great deal of admiration for their skilled handling of their demanding assignments. Several *colegos* deserve a special note of thanks, including Gunnar Rodriguez, Alberto Choque, and Cornelio Puma; the latter two offered direct research assistance that was well beyond the call of duty. IPTK Directors Frans Barrios, Eduardo Barrios, Grover Linares, and Ramiro Arancibia, as well as Sucre-based staff Patricia Duran, Amelia Espada, and Mirtha Castro, always made me feel welcomed and free to probe as I wished. I do not think that I have ever encountered an organization quite as open as IPTK.

Thanks as well to staff members of Food for the Hungry International (FHI), the United Nations' Children's Fund (UNICEF), the United Nations Fund on Population Activities (UNFPA), and the International Potato Center (CIP). While I did not establish a close working relationship with these organizations, their staffs were generally very obliging when I knocked on their doors.

My Andean-based, Canadian Lutheran World Relief colleagues in 2000, Judith O'Campo, Martin Blum, Pedro Veilz, and Jaime Bravo, also offered important insights. Jaime also kept me sane during the more stressful early days in Sucre. Agronomist Regis Cepeda volunteered his time to help me understand technical matters related to the genetic diversity of the potato crops in Ravelo. Lia Vargas de Argondoña and Marta Miranda greatly facilitated our family's settlement in Sucre. The Gomez and Ramiro families offered friendship to Kelsey and our family that we will always treasure.

Academic supporters at the University of Manitoba who were critical to the success of this endeavour include Raymond Wiest, John Loxley, William Koolage, and Fikret Berkes. Dr Weist was an especially adept supervisor, who led me to the right people and resources. Dr Loxley's gifts as a lecturer made the field of economics make sense. Dr Koolage introduced me to a fascinating body of literature about Canada's Northern peoples and Dr Berkes' teachings on resilience theory represented a turning point in my research and in my career. Warm thanks as well to June Nash, distinguished professor emeritus at CUNY, for inspiring me to think about the notion of paradox and contradiction, and to historian Veronica Strong-Boag of the University of British Columbia, who taught me both to assert myself as a woman scholar and to write clearly. Dr Melaku Worede of Addis Ababa, Ethiopia mentored my thinking about the centrality of agricultural biodiversity for our planet's survival. I continue to see him as one the world's best thinkers on this subject. I thank the Social Sciences and Humanities Research Council of Canada (SSHRC) and the Graduate Studies Department of the University of Manitoba for their generous research grants.

I also could not have succeeded without the support of my two key employers in 2000 and today: Canadian Lutheran World Relief (CLWR) and USC Canada. They both understood the value of deeper reflection about the development assignment. Thanks to CLWR's Sophie Gebreyes for her help with my work-writing balance. Especially warm thanks to USC Board Chair Mark Austin for his encouragement and patient read through the first draft and to my executive assistant, Marie Dulude, for her friendship and amazing ability to help me juggle competing roles. My McGill-Queen's University Press editor, Mark Abley, was also an extremely helpful critic and patient advocate. Thanks as well to Harold Otto for his copy edit, Jessica Howarth for her meticulous work on the manuscript, and Tim Pearson for a thorough index.

Finally, a special word of warm thanks goes to book publisher, editor, and writer Douglas Gibson. On hearing me give a talk a few years back about my experience in Bolivia, he suggested that I write this book.

Then there is that essential family support, without which a task like this would be far too daunting. My husband, Patrick Mooney, the first to get me thinking about literacy's mixed blessings, and my first and foremost guide on the politics of plant genetic resources, helped keep the fort in order in Sucre, in Winnipeg, and in Ottawa. He also remained confident about this book, when I was not. At 10 years of age, my daughter Kelsey braved departure from familiar territory to follow her mom into a strange new world. Her courage was an inspiration. Extended visits from my step-children Robin, Kate, Jeff, and Nick Mooney and my sisters Sheilagh Walsh and Anne Charron as well as my brother-in-law Luc Charron, offered family experience that enormously enriched our Bolivian adventure. My since-deceased mother Jo Walsh, Aditi Walsh, and Sarah Mooney were unable to visit but were there in spirit.

Approaching Ravelo. All photos by Susan Walsh, unless otherwise noted.

Welcome to Ravelo

Just above 2700 meters approaching Ravelo

Chimpa Rodeo, March 2011

Mojón, March 2011

Organic potato fields nearing harvest, Chimpa Rodeo, March 2011

Potato Seeds, March 2011

Members of Mojón Weavers' Group, March 2011

Don Gregorio and baby daughter, Mojón, March 2011

Don Domingo and Don Leandro, Chimpa Rodeo Leaders, March 2011

Doña
Desideria,
my Chimpa
Rodeo host,
March 2011

My friend, Doña Lucilla, widowed
mother of four, Chimpa Rodeo,
March 2011

Mojón Weavers, March 2011

Mojón with UNICEF Latrines, March 2011

A Mojón farmer prepares the field to plant his potato tubers, November 2000

Author with Mojón friends, March 2005. Photo by Awgetchew Teshome

TROJAN-HORSE AID

When Making Other Plans

True knowledge is full of politics and dreams and actually arises from
rebellious struggles to change the world and ourselves ...

Paulo Freire[1]

MARCH 2011: RETURN TO SUCRE

We are about to land. I am peering through holes in a blanket of white
at row on row of hunchback peaks and ridges with attitude. They don't
look very welcoming to the farmers who are the majority of people in
this country. But now, as we dip below the clouds, I see valley bottoms
and mountain hillsides green with produce that will soon be harvested.
Rivers that seemed completely dry a minute ago have thin streams that
shimmer like silver. They make me think about the veins of shiny ore
that once made this region Bolivia's wealthiest. Didn't I read a quote
recently about how enough silver was pulled out of these highlands to
build a solid bridge from here to Madrid?[2] Self-interest dressed in development apparel has an all too extensive history in these magnificent
highlands. Plus ça change, plus c'est la même chose!

The wheels of the airplane drop down and we land smoothly. As I
descend the small set of stairs to the tarmac, the smell of the crisp
mountain air immediately draws me back to my life here a decade ago. I
am happy to be back in *la Ciudad Blanca* – a colonial city dressed in
white. The airport has not changed one iota. We crowd around a small
conveyer belt and within just a few minutes watch a stocky baggage han-
dler as he manually pulls a full cart to the baggage area. There's my suitcase, stuffed and strained at the zipper like most of the others. Travelling
light has never been my forte.

I leave the airport and see a young man hovering near the exit, hoping
to become a taxi driver for a day. His offer is 20 Bolivianos (three dollars),

cheaper than the going rate. I peek at his car nearby. The tires have
treads. He looks at me hopefully and in I go. I have forgotten the name
of the street that my hostel is on and my reservation letter is buried deep
in my suitcase. With the help of my smart phone, we find it in the city
centre. The trip from Ottawa has been incredibly straightforward, no
delays, so unlike our family journey here in 2000.

JANUARY 2000: GETTING TO SUCRE
On the fifteenth day of the new millennium, my husband, Pat, and ten-
year-old daughter, Kelsey, and I had landed in La Paz. We were tired after
a sleepless overnight flight from Miami but eager to start our yearlong
adventure. For Pat – researcher and activist on issues ranging from farmers' rights to the politics of new technologies – and Kelsey, a grade five
student, it would be work and school as usual, or at least a variation on
that theme. For me, the year was a break in a sixteen-year career in international development. I was about to embark on anthropological
research among Indigenous potato farmers in the highlands of Potosí's
Chayanta province.

At 5:35 am we were bleary eyed but excited. Our enthusiasm was soon
dampened, however, with news that our on-going flight to Sucre had
been cancelled. We were told to return early the next morning. Our eyes
shifted to our 22 bags and to our slightly dazed Golden Retriever, Pepe,
in his oversized cage. The ticket agent seemed not to catch our alarm.
How would we ever find a hotel that, at the last minute, would accommodate not only a small family but also a big dog and a year's worth of
belongings? "Perhaps there are lockers or a storage room?" we asked. "No
señora," we were told, still with no demonstrable sympathy. Several
phone calls later; we remained stranded, grouchier by the minute. A desperate call to my work colleague in Santa Cruz, Jaime Bravo, produced
the name of an eco-hotel on the edge of the city, spacious and possibly
more open to the dog. There was indeed room at the inn! Jaime saved
the day, as he was to do time and again that year.

Finding a taxi to load our family entourage proved another challenge.
When our first potential drivers took a good look at our load, even the
offer of a heftier fee was declined. Two drivers with roof racks finally
took pity on us. They successfully crammed us and our luggage into and
onto two used Toyota Corolla station wagons, built for the Japanese
market and for right-hand drive. One of the first things we noticed was
the gaping hole in the passenger-side dashboard. Like Canadians, Boli-

vians drive on the right-hand side of the road. A good deal is a good deal, however; so ingenuity kicked in and the Japanese steering wheels had been transferred to the left side. Pepe was in the front seat with Pat, half on his feet, half on his lap, his tail dipping into the dashboard hole, his tongue nervously trying to lick Pat's face, his cage on the roof, filled with luggage. Kelsey was on my lap in the back, jammed suitcases rubbing both her and my left shoulder. We headed on the downward journey, a zigzag ride from El Alto, just over 4,000 meters above sea level, into a huge bowl, a city unlike any other on this planet. Our La Paz refuge was down on the South side at about 3,600 meters. With each curve, "Mommy, I feel sick," added to the stress!

The hotel owners, a Swiss man and a Bolivian woman, welcomed us with open arms. The only wrench in the works was the need to make sure our dog would not upset the family's two pet *llamas*. They were passive creatures, we were assured, but up for a good long and hefty spit when frightened. The hotel turned out to be in a magical spot, with clear mountain vistas and lots of green in an otherwise stone and concrete city. Pepe did provoke a spit when taken for a quick stroll in the dark of a moonless night. His sleepy owner fortunately avoided the spray from the llama.

Our unexpected day of rest turned into a two-day retreat. After heading to the airport bright and early on day two, we were informed that the flight was once again cancelled. The airline was close to bankruptcy, and so anxious to cut costs. My fighting spirit kicked in at that point. I was the Spanish speaker of our party of three, and thus the negotiator. I cajoled politely, and then insisted strongly, in my best, assertive Spanish that they rebook us with another airline, English expletives under my breath. All flights were overbooked and that was that. I lost the battle. We were back to stuffing ourselves, the dog, and our suitcases, into and onto taxis and back down the twisting road to our now-beloved hotel. The owners were again obliging. The sun was warm and strong. We ate a tasty bowl of quinoa soup – Bolivia's super food – threw our hands up in surrender and just relaxed, albeit still with a nagging worry about whether we would ever get to Sucre. In hindsight, the eco-hotel was a wonderful place to rest before the start of our new lives in Sucre.

The next day family, dog, and twenty-two bags (we counted and recounted each time) arrived safely and on time in our new city. Another couple of station wagons with roof racks took us to our eighteenth-century colonial house in the heart of the city. Bolivia is unusual in separating its constitutional capital, Sucre, from its functional capital, La Paz. When we opened the heavy wooden door to an entrance built for horses and peered into our flower and tree-filled courtyard garden, the trials of travel melted away. This would be a great family home for the first year of what we all hoped would be a more peaceful new millennium.

Early days in Sucre were spent settling the family. It took thirteen trips back and forth to the visa office to get our one-year residency permits. My repeated requests for a list, like my negotiations at the airport, fell on deaf ears. I also prepared for my Chayanta field research. A wonderful departmental archive close to our home became my favourite reading room, a welcomed return to my days as a graduate student in history. I discovered fascinating studies about the peoples of Chayanta; some on century-old paper that looked like it might crumble any minute. Others were far more recent like the Spanish publications of British anthropologist Tristan Platt. His insightful local articles from the late 70s and early 80s had not been available elsewhere.

MORE WRENCHES IN THE WORKS

Less than three weeks after our arrival, the unexpected again occurred, and my friend Jaime Bravo once more came to our rescue. It was Kelsey's first week at school and a few days before her eleventh birthday. I was planning to meet with the Sucre-headquartered NGO that had agreed to host my research – Instituto Politecnico Tomas Katari (IPTK) when I received a call from Kelsey's school. "Could I come and get Kelsey," her principal asked, "she's complaining of bad stomach cramps." Within a few minutes of our return home, Kelsey's complaints intensified. Maybe it wasn't simply an adjustment to new food and water. Since we hadn't had a chance to even think about identifying a family doctor, I ran to our neighbor, Lia, the neighbourhood matriarch I had encountered the day we arrived. Lia had helped me outfit our home with domestic supplies, including surprisingly good sheets and towels from the used-goods market. There was a surgeon on our street with a good reputation, she assured me. We headed to his house and knocked on his door, knowing that we would be disturbing his lunchtime siesta, the custom in Sucre. The housekeeper who greeted us was hesitant, but Lia insisted that she summon her employer. Within minutes, our new doctor was checking Kelsey who, by then, was both in pain and very frightened. Her appendix was about to burst, the doctor reported. We should meet him at the hospital without delay. Jaime, much to my relief, happened to be in town to discuss some work matters with me. (While on sabbatical I was checking in with him about once a month.) Sensing the panic behind the calm I worked hard not to convey in Kelsey's presence, he offered to come along to the hospital. Looking back, we could not have managed without him.

When we reached the hospital, a thousand thoughts furrowed my brow. What was the hospital's track record, and who was this surgeon anyhow? I knew the operation was pretty straightforward. There was, after all, some déjà vu in all of this. I had made a similarly quick decision for myself in 1986. Within a half day of my own painful cramping in Kathmandu, Nepal, I had an emergency appendectomy in a hospital not unlike this one. But Kelsey was my kid, my baby!

The supplies for Kelsey's operation, it turned out, were our responsibility. We were given a prescription sheet with a long list. Since the hospital pharmacy was out of several of the required products, Jaime and I grabbed a cab to take us to the nearest pharmacy. That pharmacy also did not have all the goods we needed. It took trips to two more before we returned with the required materials, and my heart by then was beating like a drummer on speed. I hugged Kelsey tightly before they peeled her out of my arms and onto a cold gurney for her ride into the operating room. She was as brave as one could expect of a child with few words of Spanish in an all-Spanish facility. Having turned over the needed drugs, thread, and disinfectants to the staff in surgery, I permitted myself a deep sigh of relief. All seemed in order.

My calm was short-lived. Within about twenty minutes, someone knocked from a small sliding window in the wall beside the operating theatre. I headed over, the window slid open, and I was given another prescription and told to purchase the material at once! "Jaime!" I shouted. He read the prescription. It was for thread for her sutures – juvenile thread. The drugstore had apparently given us an adult version that was too thick. Imagining that Kelsey had already been sliced open, I flew like a madwoman, Jaime running to keep up with me. Another taxi was hailed, and once again we were forced to do the rounds until we succeeded on our third attempt. We were back in the hospital in record time, the driver having been under strict orders to find the fastest route possible. I knocked on the little window. It slid open and a hand took the thread from my now shaking hands. An hour or two later, Kelsey was wheeled out, waking from the anesthetic like a small lioness. "Don't touch me," she shouted in her half-sleep. But she was fine. The doctor soon appeared with what to me seemed a shriveled, tiny tissue in a small container. "See," he said, "her appendix was clearly ready to burst."

Kelsey returned home from the hospital a few days later. Family life settled into a calmer routine. Well, that's almost true. We did have Robin, Kate, Jeff, and Nick, four of my five stepchildren, stay with us for various periods over the next several months. Between 12 and 22 years of age, they added some adolescent drama, but much rich colour to our family's Bolivian tapestry. With Kelsey, they also helped Pat and me to connect to Sucre families, who in turn enriched our family's sense of belonging in Sucre and helped me to enhance my understanding of the world of the urban mestizo.

I can laugh now (although I did not do so much at the time) at how I became an instant mother to another teen staying with us, Kate's Swiss friend, Katla, when she too awoke with cramps one morning. Pat was sent across the street to bang once more on our neighbourhood-surgeon's door and I took Katla to the same hospital where, within just a few hours, like Kelsey, she had her almost-exploding appendix removed. "What is it with mountains?" I remember musing. This time I managed without Jaime, having learned to scrutinize prescription lists with great care. Thankfully, by that time we also had Marta, our wonderful *emplea-da* – housekeeper – from 9 am until 2 pm, Monday to Friday to help keep order, cook lunch, and, what I was most thankful for, to wash the jeans, t-shirts, towels, and sundry items that, when we were all there at once, seemed to pile up as fast as the last load was washed, folded, ironed (Marta insisted), and put away. There were no automatic washers and dryers in our centuries-old home.

As is generally the case with young people, both Katla and my daughter bounced back quickly. Their stitches healed and their energy soon revived. A happy skip returned in Kelsey's walk to her new school. We finally held her postponed birthday party. It proved a great success, renewing her sense of adventure. The giggles of pre-teen girls competed with the chatter of birds in our courtyard, which was now filled with streamers. It was a cacophony of happy sounds, suddenly shrill when Kelsey's new friends pushed her face into the cake. The unexpected shove, she learned, was a popular tradition in her new country.

I had made a wish for world peace when I entered Bolivia at the start of the new millennium. Just two months into that year, my wish was far more personal – a little family tranquility would do. But those first two months, however chaotic, taught some important lessons. They helped me to learn that my Western penchant for being in control would not serve me well in my temporary homeland. "Breathe, Susie, breathe," I remember repeating more often than not.

FINDING MY COMMUNITIES

With Kelsey back at school, I was again able to make plans with IPTK, heading to their rabbit-warren-like offices in the heart of the local *campesino* or farmers market in the hills just outside the colonial centre. To help me identify the communities that I might choose to work within, IPTK offered to take me to their field stations and several communities in two regional municipalities. On the back of a dirt-bike, mountain-friendly I reassured myself, extension workers, called *técnicos*, would show me the lay of the land. Over a two-week period, especially memorable because of the incredible feeling of freedom an open-air ride through the mountains evokes, they did indeed guide me through village after village, sixteen in total. I selected two for my study, thankful for permission to explore their world. That world, with all its beauty, hardships, strengths, and complexity, is both the subject of, and inspiration for, this book.

THE DEVELOPMENT GAME

When I arrived in Bolivia, I must confess to having been less interested in the particular culture of the people of Chayanta than in questions related to the broader development field that I had been working in over the past decade and a half. I had originally planned to tackle literacy education among Indigenous peoples as my research theme; but what I really wanted was a first-hand opportunity to explore and reflect on some troubling contradictions and paradoxes I was witnessing and experiencing time and again within my international development career.

The big-picture development industry was troubling enough. I had both read the theory behind, and seen example after example of, large-scale development initiatives run amuck – colonialism in sheep's clothing, the critics said. Fortunately, I rationalized, I belonged to the more modest, more authentic part of that bigger picture, having worked in comparatively small organizations, closer to the grass roots. But even there, I had to admit, the incongruities were plentiful. Among the most concerning to me were the "in and out," rather superficial, community monitoring visits I undertook, too often dominated by the shaking of

officials' hands and lengthy speeches. The communities dressed up for
our visits, putting on their best clothes and faces. How could we possibly
grasp the complexity of the change process or even the impact of our
assistance? During my most cynical moments, I asked myself: "Are these
exchanges really based on authentic collaboration? Or, are they completed to fill in the monitoring check-lists our donors require?"

The trick, I knew, was to de-emphasize my role and place more
authority in the hands of competent, trusted, and long-standing local
partners and/or local advisors. I had developed reasonably good relationships with mine, Jaime being an excellent example. But I also knew that
even the identification of trusted local staff or partners could be fraught
with challenge and uncertainty, particularly in politicized local contexts
or when there is insufficient time for a thorough identification process.

A "one-too-many" experience with development planning in a hurry
and self-serving motives was in fact the tipping point into this year of
applied field-based research and reflection. My employer at that time –
Canadian Lutheran World Relief (CLWR) – was offered a multi-million
dollar contract in Africa to undertake a program designed to redress the
serious mistakes of the Canada Wheat Project, a development project
launched in the 1970s ostensibly to help Tanzania build self-sufficiency in
wheat production. The project did boost wheat yields and availability:
one per cent of the urban Tanzanians wanting bread could find it in their
city markets. But there were serious sustainability and justice issues.
Machinery shipped from Canada rusted in the wheat fields; there were
no spare parts available nor people trained to repair the machines. Synthetic chemicals sprayed on fields of wheat monoculture depleted soil
fertility and contaminated local water sources. Most egregious was the
serious displacement and impoverishment of the semi-nomadic Barabaig
community. Pushed from landscapes suited to pastoralist livelihoods
onto marginal lands lacking in resources, the health and nutrition levels
of the Barabaig declined significantly. The project, I argued in an unpublished paper about the subject, was a clear-cut transplant of Canadian
frontier development, predicated on the notion that there were vast,
unoccupied lands waiting to be developed. It was also a "Development
101" case study of tried, and failed, aid.

The dislocation of the Barabaig attracted a lot of bad press at the time.
The Canada Wheat Project's controversial antecedents allowed, therefore,
an opportunity to engage in the month-long project viability assessment
that my organization requested. Another failure was not an option.

The review process was really tough going. But I managed to interview some key and insightful actors, both in the region and en route, including leaders within the Barabaig people at the centre of the program and a leading Barabaig specialist, London-based anthropologist Charles Lane. Lane's insights and the often-conflicting responses to my questions among the Barabaig themselves about their community's needs and aspirations left me increasingly uneasy about the proposed plans. A "deep throat" close to the funder confirmed my growing suspicions that this project might again be off the mark. I returned home recommending a much more cautious approach to proposed assistance and a further six months of on-site assessment and planning. I was appalled at how unaware the designers of this new project seemed to have been of the socio-political minefield they had entered. It was as if the project was more an attempt to clean the slate than get it right. I discovered growing divisions among the aggrieved Barabaig, exacerbated by the idea of significant new development dollars and the promise of several vehicles. And one of the more difficult characters in this minefield – having wanted the project for his Canadian NGO employer – publicly accused me of being a neo-colonialist![3]

My report back to the funder proved to be highly unpopular as well. Our request for a still more substantive on-site planning mission was refused. CLWR wisely took a pass. The project was shelved and I received a very angry letter from one of its designers, an anthropologist, ironically enough.[4] It was my first real experience of the "kill the messenger" phenomenon and I lost a lot of sleep. In hindsight, it was also my first deeper exploration of the consequences of "Trojan Horse" aid.

A number of factors undoubtedly contributed to the flawed program proposal I investigated. One factor I was convinced of, however, was the overriding issue of development objectives and planning processes that give priority to a donor's needs and world view versus local ones. By the year 2000 I was eager to take a much closer look at local contexts and at the nagging question about who really benefits from and in the development enterprise. A Social Sciences and Humanities Research Council (SSHRC) grant allowed that to happen, as did my extremely obliging employer and my equally flexible family.

DISCOVERING CHAYANTA

Thanks to NGO colleagues in La Paz,[5] I was introduced to IPTK and the Chayanta communities I would study in Northern Potosí. When I was informed about the distinguishing characteristics and practices of the farmers I would study, I soon became excited. Northern Potosí was a centre of resistance to colonial and post-colonial domination. Chayanta's peoples maintained an unusually high level of pre-Hispanic ethnic traditions and dress as well as farming and governance systems. Last but in no way least, this was an amazing centre of plant diversity, especially of the country's beloved potato.

Curiously, with the exception of embryonic research focusing on the group's exquisite textiles and cultural traditions, there were no substantive tracts about the province's Jalq'a, an ethnic group with very distinct dress. My research about the Jalq'a experience with outsiders would be original. The history of development intervention in their home territory was also uneven. Less isolated Jalq'a hamlets had a long history of collaboration with development organizations. Other more isolated communities had much more recent engagement, if any at all. Some had literacy training, others not. The Jalq'a of Chayanta would be ideal for comparative research, offering learning that exceeded my expectations. I was soon marveling at my good fortune.

THE BEST LAID PLANS

There was one final wrench in that good fortune that bears mentioning, since it too helped me to gain further insight and perspective, both about the importance of going with the flow and about how we can make very different decisions about the same problem when the context shifts. About midway through my research year, I managed to chip my elbow – twice – within a six-week period. "Murphy's Law in overdrive," I remember thinking.

The first chip to fly off my left elbow occurred during a weekend retreat in a magical getaway outside Sucre, *Bramadero*. Near the end of a quick sandal-clad walk with Kelsey to catch the sun's descent behind a neighbouring peak, I climbed over a locked wire gate leading to the inn. My sandal strap caught on a piece of barbed wire and I dove elbows first onto the rock-hard earth below. I was soon loaded into the back seat of my host's van and driven into Sucre, all passengers holding their breath every time he maneuvered around potholes, boulders, and curves during our two-hour journey.

The doctor who examined me in Sucre was pleasant and rather nonchalant. I was handed a prescription for painkillers and told to wear a sling. "It will heal nicely on its own if you rest and avoid strenuous activity," the doctor said. "Come and see me in about three weeks and we will x-ray it once again." Since travel and fieldwork conditions were anything but restful, I was advised to stay home during the roughly three weeks it would take for the chip to fuse back to the bone. It was my left arm. While I could not type, I could continue to do Sucre-based research and write in my journal. I remained reasonably philosophical about it all – until the second fracture!

The fall happened during a huge storm, the kind mystery movies feature. I awakened to the sound of a flapping shutter in the kitchen. So I slipped out of bed and made my way to the kitchen to shut it. I purposely left the lights off so I wouldn't wake anyone. The entrance of the kitchen in our over two-centuries-old home had marble stone steps worn smooth and shiny with age. In the pitch black, I managed to slip off the top one, and my elbows landed smack on the cold marble. I let out a scream that had my family spring from their beds in the belief that I was being murdered. I knew immediately that the recently fused chip in my left elbow had again broken off. The idea of a second recovery period made me furious. I stopped screaming as soon as the family arrived but the tears flowed freely this time round.

There was no time for self-pity, however. After leaving the doctor's office the next day, I determined to return to the field, broken arm or not. And so I did – same context, different decision – although this time I knew what it was like to cope with such an injury. After three days, I took a dilapidated public bus to Ravelo. The ride proved straightforward except for the occasional bounce that would send a bolt of electricity up and down my left arm.

I was greeted with much sympathy when I walked into my two research villages, admired in fact for my tenacity. Of course, when compared with the villagers' ability to stare adversity down, my experience paled. Pampering yourself is simply not an option in their world. Nor is it for anthropologists or development workers for that matter. Necessity was the mother of my courage, as I suppose it often was for my Jalq'a friends.

THIS BOOK
A decade or so since those days in their highlands, I am back in my *querida* (beloved) Sucre at my favourite hostel, Su Merced, with the intention of turning my doctoral dissertation of a decade ago into a book. I cannot help but smile at the irony in writing a book about

Indigenous peoples' struggle for respect and justice in a home built by a
member of the eighteenth-century ruling elite. Unlike the peeling walls
and worn stone steps of that charming but long-neglected Sucre house
we grew to love, this colonial family home, with its intricately carved
balcony boxes – a Sucre trademark – has been impeccably maintained.
The inside courtyard has two exquisite Bird of Paradise plants, flowering
vines, fuchsia-coloured bougainvillea, a lovely tile mosaic on the wall
behind a small fountain, and several terra cotta pots along the stairs
brimming with bright red and pink geraniums. It is also wonderfully
affordable – kept reasonable thanks in no small measure to Sucre's tiny
airport and its inability to accommodate large tourist charters. Most
importantly, the ambience is welcoming and calming, just the right
atmosphere for me to begin a book that captures the year that began so
eventfully.

I am also itching to put pen to journal, feet into hiking boots, and,
after I complete a short return visit to the Chayanta communities that
hosted me so graciously in 2000, fingers to keyboard. My observations
during this 2011 visit, building on another three brief return trips in
2002, 2003, and 2007, will be captured in the book's epilogue.

I think back now about how I first thought about taking a shortcut
in the writing of this book. My full workload as the Executive Director of usc Canada inspired thoughts that I might get away with simply updating my 350-page dissertation. It was, after all, well received
when completed in 2003. Of interest to the eclectic mix of academics
who read it then – an economist, three anthropologists, and one ecologist – was its framing of the Jalq'a story within the context of their
resilience and complexity thinking, ignored then and arguably still
undervalued today. In updating their story, I hoped to inspire sober
second thought about what, in my mind, are contradictory and self-
serving development assistance trends today – that "will we never
learn from our mistakes?" question that seems to haunt our human
species.[6]

A wise editor, and some sober second thought of my own, has made
me realize that a dissertation is not a book, that this story about Trojan-
horse development assistance should not be another academic account
of modern-day imperialism. A more accessible book would make more
sense, one that tries to capture the complexity of the insider-outsider
relationship. And since I have shaped and been shaped by my experiences in the story, I plan to enter this book in a more central and candid

way. The incongruity and paradoxes in the twin fields I have chosen to pursue make me vulnerable to some of the same contradictions I uncovered within the communities and organizations I explored in the year 2000. I was, and I am, complicit in some of the behaviours; I was, and I am, quick to judge. And, in relation to the people I studied then and engage with now, I was, and I am, "the other," an outsider who, like them, bears a blended identity.

DUELLING IDENTITIES

I went to Northern Potosí, for example, with two sets of lenses, those of a doctoral student in anthropology and those of a seasoned development worker. Each of these professionals has been known to look at each other with disdain. Indeed, when I entered the field of anthropology as a part-time doctoral student, I was hesitant to admit this new personality to Andean field colleagues, let alone the farmers they worked alongside. Anthropologists, they had been quick to explain, had all too often extracted information and rarely gave anything back.

The anthropological studies I was reading, on the other hand, critiqued NGO programming that they considered short-sighted, grounded essentially on superficial understanding of their participants and of the long-term consequences of their interventions. This critique too hit a responsive chord in me. How to reconcile this uncomfortable dichotomy?[7] So, stitched into my account of the troubling aid paradox I discovered within the Indigenous communities I grew to know and respect in the year 2000 will be moments of frank observation as well as personal reflection about my own contradictions and competing motives – "the development worker" who seeks to assist the disadvantaged and "the researcher" who seeks to gain information and insight. These actors are sometimes distinct and sometimes, as in my case, one and the same.

While Westerners like me struggle with dual, indeed duelling identities, Bolivia's Indigenous peoples have long embraced them. Their rituals and traditions, in the past and today, are steeped in the idea of opposing forces and juxtaposition: male versus female; Indigenous versus mestizo; rural versus urban; Quechua, Aymara, Guarani languages versus the Spanish language; local versus national; socialist versus capitalist; the Altiplano landscape versus the Yungas (or jungle); pan-Andean versus Indigenous nationalist; *campesino* versus miner (or proletariat); *coylla* (from the highlands) versus *camba* (from the Amazon basin)[8]; law versus custom; and in the case of the Indigenous group I studied, Jalq'a versus

Llamero. And with shifting contexts and demands can come shifting identities and responses. There is little that is certain in a life that depends intimately on nature's collaboration.

My tale about my 2000 travel to Sucre and our first days settling into a new system, while now amusing stories for family lore, also foreshadowed the ever-shifting and unpredictable ground I would tread throughout the year and the need to accept uncertainty as a given. This is particularly hard going for a Westerner taught to reconcile contradiction. That Zen Buddhist maxim John Lennon popularized about life being what happens to you when you are making other plans captures beautifully the reality of peoples who count on favourable weather to survive; but, it also rang true for me, a Caucasian expat – *gringita* – seeking to peel back the layers of an exceedingly complex insider-outsider, anthropologist–development-worker, Occidental-Indigenous dialectic.

But I am getting ahead of myself. On now to a more comprehensive introduction to the book's contents and themes and most importantly to the Jalq'a of Chayanta, Northern Potosí, who helped me both to appreciate the skill in farming challenging mountain landscapes and to learn from and embrace life's ever-present contradictions.

I

Introduction: Packets of Paradox

The political leaders of the dominant minority have striven to create a development process which slavishly imitates a model taken from other nations ...
Imported rural schooling, political party activity, and agricultural technology
promotion have not produced significant developmental changes in the countryside and the nation. We remain convinced that true development will only
occur when we ourselves become the authors of our own progress and destiny.

Tiahuanaco, Bolivia Manifesto, 15 September 1973[1]

DIVERSITY HOT SPOT

The highlands of western South America are an imposing, at times mer-
ciless, landscape of arched-backed ridges, yawning gullies, sculpted rock
faces, quilted patches of green, purple, red, and gold at harvest, and rib-
bon-thin roads connecting scattered villages of adobe. When the early
morning sun creeps over and down sleepy mountain ridges, their beauty
takes your breath away. But their splendor reaches beyond a command-
ing appearance. Their Indigenous residents can also lay claim to one of
the world's greatest shares of cultivated plants and more particularly to
the centre of origin and diversity for potatoes, the world's fourth most
important food crop and the crop that provides 40–50 per cent of the
total calories consumed by rural highland households.[2] The farms where
my research was located, in Bolivia's most southern department, Potosí,
are considered to be one of the centres of biodiversity for the potato
species in a country that is one of the world's ten most megadiverse. (See
maps in figures 1.1–1.3).[3] In Ravelo, the regional municipality that is
home to the two Quechua-speaking Jalq'a communities that welcomed
my research, agronomist Regis Cepeda analyzed and catalogued as many
as 53 genetically distinct potato varieties and dozens more varieties of
morphologically different types.[4] Ravelo's Jalq'a farmers, however, were

not generally recognized for this primordial diversity but rather for their production of commercial potatoes that help to feed the roughly 200,000 residents of the country's constitutional capital, Sucre, a three-hour potato truck ride from the village of Ravelo. On Sucre streets, Ravelo's rural folk were often referred to as *los paperos* – the potato producers. Ironically, although perhaps not surprisingly, Ravelo's commercial potatoes were of greater benefit to their urban consumers than to their producers. A study of Ravelo producers in the mid-1990s on behalf of the country's national potato research centre, Proyecto de Investigación de Papas (PRO-INPA), argued, in fact, that the surpluses from Ravelo farms serve to maintain the non-productive classes of the city.[5] Like that of their displaced *compañeros* from the silver and tin mines that once drew the wealthy to Potosí, the story of the peoples of this region is an inverted "rags to riches" tale in which the rich of the metropolis feed off a hinterland of producers "in rags."[6]

Nor was this exploitation unique to the twenty-first-century Indigenous farmers of Ravelo's home province of Chayanta. Research on the ethnic *Llameros* from a sister municipality has established that during the eighteenth and nineteenth centuries, a greater Chayanta – consisting of the five provinces that now form Northern Potosí – was the principal supplier of wheat for three of the nation's departments: Potosí, Oruro, and La Paz. Chayanta's Indigenous farmers were in fact among the richest in Bolivia until the termination of protectionist policies at the end of the nineteenth century. Lower priced Chilean and Peruvian wheat imports grabbed important shares of the market. This liberalization of trade, together with the sacrifice of this region's agricultural wealth to the highly extractive mining industry, contributed to the area's rapid return to subsistence.[7] The open veins of Potosí, it is said, capitalized Europe.[8] Yet, in 2000 and still today the department is among the hemisphere's poorest.

In the year 2000, the family farm economy in Ravelo's 104 villages was thus one of subsistence and semi-subsistence agriculture.[9] There were a number of comparatively successful petty commodity producers on primary transportation routes. But for most of Ravelo's Indigenous farm families cash earned from market sales was rarely enough to cover costly agricultural inputs, let alone household supplies, such as the kerosene to fuel makeshift lamps when darkness fell. It was not, therefore, their direct link to the market economy that sustained Ravelo's Jalq'a. Rather, generations of resilience strategies kept these subsistence communities and

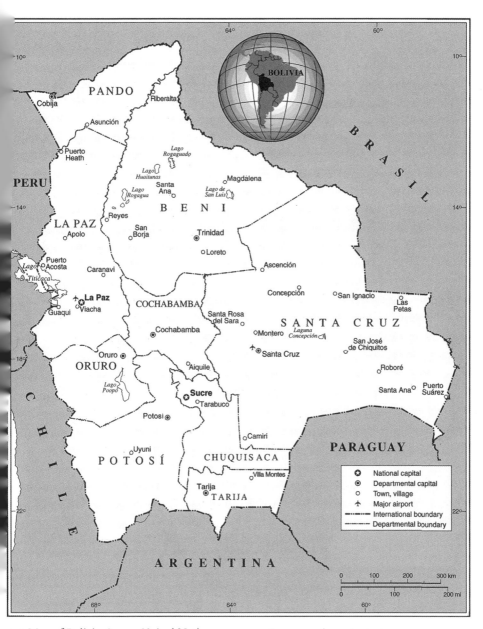

1.1 Map of Bolivia. *Source*: United Nations map no. 3875 rev. 3, August 2004

1.2 Map of Chayanta. *Source*: Instituto Politécnico Tomas Katari

1.3 Map of Ravelo. *Source*: Instituto Politécnico Tomas Katari

their people alive. But the conditions of their semi-subsistence were such that migration to cities for cash remuneration, however temporary and integrated into their resilience strategies, was growing more and more important and frequent.[10]

In addition to food policies and commercial production practices favouring urban consumers, factors offered to explain the decline in rural livelihoods over the second half of the twentieth century included the climatic extremes attributed to global warming, competition from foreign potato producers, the growing popularity of rice and pasta throughout the country, the collapse in the mining sector and thus of mining-community markets, and *minifundismo* – land shortages and soil infertility due to the land's continuous subdivision among male blood relatives. At the heart of this last problem is Bolivia's 1952 Agrarian Reform Act. In one paradoxical stroke of the legislator's pen, this law not only put an end to the quasi-feudal land holdings of colonial rule but also to the territorial usufruct or customary rights within the Indigenous traditional governance system or *ayllu*. Ignoring long-held Indigenous practices, such as the rotation of shared lands and collective land-management strategies, legislators sanctioned individual land titles and entrenched in Bolivia the concept of individual peasant producers.[11]

My research among the Indigenous Jalq'a farmers in Ravelo and the non-governmental organizations at work within their communities suggested that there was yet another deeply ironic contributor to the marginalization and impoverishment of the municipality's Indigenous farmers. The humanitarian development assistance delivered through non-governmental organizations (NGOs) had been quietly but steadily eroding the inherent strengths of these Indigenous *papero* communities. It was well-intentioned, well-funded, and achieving some of the stated goals. Local infrastructure and primary health care services, for example, had improved considerably. Community organizing based on Western models took root as hoped. But the agencies that delivered these programs approached the development process in ways that were ultimately weakening the capacity of these Indigenous farmers to live independent and productive lives on their ancestral lands. Whether coming from the political left or right, these agencies failed to take seriously the very different world views and knowledge systems of their Indigenous "beneficiaries." They were caught within a development industry that focused on the idea that something was missing – a deficit theory of social change. Western science was considered far superior to other knowledge systems and farmers were treated as being all the same –

homogenized into the concept of small-holder producer in need of "modern" ways.

The modern ways offered included the use of and subsequent dependency on packages of external seeds and the synthetic inputs these foreign seeds needed to survive on their landscapes. More insidious perhaps and ultimately more damaging was the use of Western pedagogy and the promotion of linear reasoning. Over the longer term, these approaches threatened to weaken livelihoods that depended on the capacity to deal with ecosystems that were anything but linear.

Nor had the organizations I reviewed reconciled the built-in power imbalances that privileged the Western point of view and approach. In sum, the development assistance paid insufficient attention to centuries-old resilience strategies that had enabled Indigenous people to survive in places where the natural world usually has the upper hand. Particularly problematic was the outsiders' failure to appreciate the conservation of biodiversity and the plant genetic resources at the core of such strategic thinking.

Critics of aid programs that fail to deliver the goods sustainably are plentiful. But the focus of such assessment is generally on the kind of assistance offered. There is, for example, a significant body of research that examines the North-South transfer of inappropriate and expensive technologies. The social, political, and economic structures and ideologies that arrive with the assistance are also subject to many a critic's tongue-lashing.[12] Less understood and discussed in both academic and development circles is the issue of how a development organization's approach to knowledge, imposed within well-intentioned training activities, might itself have an impact on the social change process. How aid is delivered, I would venture, can be far more consequential than what is delivered. In a time when knowledge about environmental complexity is at a premium, the imposition of Western ways of thinking on peoples who understand that complexity best deserves our full and immediate attention.

Through a first-hand treatment of the development interventions of three non-governmental organizations at work among the Jalq'a *paperos* I studied in 2000, this book focuses on the "how" of aid delivery. It challenges the ever-present notion that "capacity-building" programming – particularly related to Western-styled literacy and food production – is essential for farmers on the margins. The NGOs I reviewed during a year of intensive field research would have been more successful had they recognized and supported the skills and active agency[13] of the Indigenous farmers they worked with, turning the deficit – the poor are lacking – argument for development assistance on its head. It was not what small-holder, Indigenous farmers lacked that required their endorsement and support but what they already had – highly threatened but sophisticated knowledge about their ecosystems and strategies to conserve them.

MAKING THE CASE

I defend this argument within thirteen core chapters built around my direct experience with the Jalq'a of Northern Potosí. An additional chapter suggests an alternative and more respectful way forward, drawing on my broader experiences in the field of food security and food sovereignty. The book closes with an Epilogue that takes us back again, with my March 2011 return to the Bolivian highlands after a decade of enormous change and historical significance for the country's Indigenous majority.

Finally, stitched into the chapters of this quilted narrative about the Jalq'a, are field journal entries that offer frank, sometimes sobering, observations about what I saw and how I felt. These accounts are included with two objectives in mind. I hope to offer readers an opportunity to experience in a less academic way the rich fabric of life in the Bolivian highlands. I also want to highlight the complexity of both the Jalq'a world I uncovered and that of the development-worker often faced with contradictory marching orders. I claim a fairly central voice in these field notes. My clear presence in this narrative is a deliberate commentary on the fact that the objective distance between the observer and the observed, between the narrator and the story's central characters, is essentially a very fine one.

2

Beyond Donut-Style Research

It is better to be approximately right than precisely wrong!

John Maynard Keynes[1]

Living full time among your research subjects for a period of a year or two is a common practice for those engaged in ethnographic research. Participant observation, the trade name for this practice, is a welcomed chance to experience first hand and up close the day-to-day character of the host community and its people. The immersion is intended to enhance the authority of the scholarship and does, when conducted thoroughly, enrich its quality. My international development career precluded a two-year stint. Nor was the development worker in me entirely comfortable with the idea of full-time residency in a single community. Do outsiders have the right to fall privy to confidential matters and local secrets, so easily confessed or witnessed when living in a hamlet of only tens of families, I asked myself? The approach and kind of relationship established with the local community determines, of course, the nature of the experience for both parties. My thoughts reflected as much on my own sensibilities about the rights of the outsider and my own sense of privacy. Would I like to be in someone else's fishbowl on a full time basis?

There were other practical considerations. I wanted to research at least two communities and also spend time getting to know the other "subject" of my study – the NGO actor – much better. Finally, my own family was in need of a larger community for employment and school. So I divided myself in four, resigned myself to a ton of back and forth road travel, mostly in the back of a potato truck and hiking, the happiest part of my journeys back and forth. My status, in short, was that of a frequent visitor to the villages of Chimpa Rodeo and Mojón. From the IPTK field station in Ravelo, where I spent much longer stretches of time and on which I also focused my research, I would head to each of the villages, usually for three days at a time and spaced over the full agricultural and annual livelihood cycle. I was particularly pleased about the opportunity to share in the community life of my village hosts over four distinct seasons. As a development worker, my previous field trips had been timed to correspond with the beginning of the harvest. The chance to observe landscape and weather changes throughout the year, as well as participate in festivities closely linked to those changes, was very satisfying.

If my understanding of the culture and community of Chimpa Rodeo and Mojón in the year 2000 was circumscribed somewhat by my divided roles and residences, there was a flip side to that coin that may well have enhanced my experience. Possibly because I was not a constant or imposing presence, there was a wonderful openness to it. The people of both Chimpa Rodeo and Mojón displayed an enormous generosity of spirit.

This openness paved the way for a very enriching and hopefully mutually beneficial research experience. However, I was aware that the methods I chose to help me learn about and from the participants in my research could make or break my experience and also theirs. From the early days of colonial exploration and frontier development to the not so distant past, the West's construction of Indigenous peoples has frequently been the product of research that placed Indigenous peoples on the margins of the process, outsiders looking in. And when the researcher left for home, their communities were often left with knowledge potholes, their stories and insights having been excavated like precious minerals, emptied into the scholar's satchel. Anthropologists have arguably been among the most enthusiastic to engage in knowledge mining. They may well have been willing to risk life and limb on the frozen tundra or within the darkest jungle in an effort to enlighten the Western world about non-Western peoples. But when push came to shove, with some very fine and notable exceptions,[2] many felt entitled to their bounty. They could not, or chose not to, challenge the Cartesian logic of the day. Nor could they resist feeding their findings into policy papers and government programs designed to make these "strange people" act "just like us."[3] Critics, anthropologists among them, have rightfully called such mainstream anthropology the child of imperialism.[4]

Indigenous challenges to Western dominion[5] inspired the development of new ways to understand and engage with peoples on the fringes of Western privilege. Research approaches that consider the "researched" as researchers and address issues of power and control have thankfully surfaced, within anthropology and more broadly. We are at long last shifting from an extractive mode to an interactive one built on the notions of co-responsibility, two-way learning, and intercultural negotiation.[6] This move to more mutually beneficial research, with its more participatory alternatives, has been painfully slow in coming. And there remain postmodern anthropologists who continue to insist that the dialectic in the anthropologist's role – the effort to humanize a system inherently designed to exploit the weak – is not the sin of a by-gone era but alive and well today, especially within my host discipline, development anthropology.[7]

Nevertheless more and more scholars today are attempting to eliminate extractive, or what I call donut-style, research. The researcher cuts out and consumes the best inside bit, leaving a hole in their subjects' knowledge of how their story would be used. Reflection on technique and process is finally seen to be inseparable from the presentation and analysis of research findings.[8] But the right of applied researchers to enter the lives of Indigenous peoples remains contested. Nor is the quest for authentic relationship and genuine reciprocity terribly straightforward.

For graduate students like me in the year 2000, institutional, methodological, timing, and funding concerns were constraining, contributing very often to a "best one can do under the circumstances" approach. But a flawed and "best one can do" approach should not be confused with permission to enter into a stranger's territory armed with only the "best of intentions." It takes much more than good intent to complete responsible and ultimately useful applied anthropological research. Every effort must be made to ground one's research in processes that are ethical, appropriate within the local context, respectful of the people whose lives the research touches, and sound methodologically. Appendix I provides a synthesis of the research methods I implemented in an attempt to practice solid and accountable scholarship. It captures my blending of more conventional qualitative research with methods reflecting my interest in the application of Participatory Action Research (PAR) techniques and principles.[9]

Of the four qualitative field research methods I chose, three could be found with a PAR toolbox: participant observation, informal and semi-structured interviews, and the intensive Participatory Rural Appraisal[10] workshop I held in each community. The fourth, a benchmark household survey, has long been practiced in the applied social sciences and was, in that sense, more conventional in its orientation. To my unexpected delight, it proved especially useful in establishing a rapport with participating households. Appendix 2 offers my critique of the strengths and shortcomings of these methods, providing the interested reader with further insight into the ways that I came to understand the people and issues of importance to this inquiry. In the remainder of this chapter, I would prefer to focus briefly on a few broader issues that speak to the relationships at the heart of any successful research process.

ETHICS

My initial meetings with my organizational and community hosts included a review and discussion of the ethics of my research and the process I would follow. I wanted to ensure that I was respecting local procedures, norms and confidentiality considerations. The confidentiality issue proved an unexpected dilemma, however. Some of my informants, most particularly my Indigenous informants, wanted and deserved direct acknowledgement for their insights and contributions to the analysis shaping this book. This was entirely understandable. For too long, Indigenous peoples' voices have been silenced or lumped into a homogenous "Indigenous" perspective.

There were others, however, whose insights, although equally valuable, were of a more critical and controversial nature. Open acknowledgement of their contributions risked some potentially hostile reaction. I decided, finally, that, when appropriate, I would acknowledge my principal informants in a general way, through the use of their first names and, if applicable, with the respectful salutation *Don* or *Doña*, the local equivalent of Mr and Mrs. Thus, while their assistance is acknowledged, their full names have not been linked to a particular commentary or point of view. This use of first names, however insufficient, reflects my attempt to acknowledge the many and diverse Indigenous voices that help to shape this narrative.

Finally on this matter, some of the NGO extension workers I interviewed quite extensively during my research were nervous about the idea of an open acknowledgement of their points of view. As a result, I have not included their names. They too, however, deserve a lot of credit for having helped me to understand the local, regional, and national contexts within which they operated.

LANGUAGE

My need for Spanish-Quechua translation naturally affected my grasp of the culture as well as my relationship with the people I sought to understand. Developing fluency in Quechua was not feasible in the short time available prior to field research. Participation in elementary Quechua language courses during my early days in Sucre did enable an exchange of basic greetings in Quechua. Residents appeared to have appreciated my effort. I also gained an appreciation of the structure and character of the language.

For interpretation services, I thus depended on IPTK's extension workers with, according to their own reports, about an 85 per cent proficiency level in Quechua. When the *técnicos* were not available, local residents with about 70 per cent fluency in Spanish helped out. This communication fissure clearly affected my relationships with locals unable to communicate in Spanish, particularly the women. Most women in the two villages were unilingual Quechua speakers. The observations and findings in this book must clearly be considered with this deficiency in mind.

I did discover a silver lining in this language cloud, however. During community meetings when Quechua dominated the discussion, or when I found myself alone with women who were unable or too shy to speak Spanish, I was able to pay attention to detail and activity that I would have likely missed when concentrating on the main conversation. Tensions in the faces and bodies of those listening to a speaker, for example, sometimes told a different tale than that on the public record. Women's comings and goings during meetings, young children in tow, became far clearer, as did their location on the edges of decision-making circles. Researchers often need to complement verbal reports with observations of behaviour. As Stanley Barrett writes, "the focus can never be solely on what people say; instead, it is on the relationship between norm, act, attitude and behaviour."[11]

I also discovered a very pleasant camaraderie with women with whom non-verbal communication was my only option. Whether peeling potatoes together, their speed putting mine to shame, dancing arm in arm during a festival, laughing together at chickens fleeing the butcher's knife, or exchanging a smile over a young child's new discovery, there seemed to be a connection that transcended the need for language. I especially remember moments when one of my women friends and I would catch each other's eye and grin while a Spanish speaker, usually a powerful male, would go on and on and on and on. Translation to help us communicate was appreciated when available. But our silent friendship proved to have its merits as well. I was also afforded an unexpected and, in my rather garrulous culture, rare opportunity to ponder first-hand what knowledge transmission and learning without words could be about.

My research journey into the Bolivian communities of Chimpa Rodeo and Mojón began, as I said, in IPTK's Sucre headquarters. IPTK had been working in Chayanta since the early 1970s and within the regional municipality of Ravelo since the early 1980s. Interested in the questions I hoped to explore, IPTK and I negotiated a research protocol that included: the assistance of IPTK field staff; the generous provision of a research base in one of their four field offices; and my commitment to providing a Spanish-language document capturing my principal findings. IPTK's solid reputation in the area enabled a very pleasant and straightforward entry into the region and later helped me to obtain written permission from local authorities.

Heeding IPTK's advice, I first sought verbal permission to explore the possibilities from the head of the farmers' union movement for the district. To my delight, the *autoridad maximo*, Don Angel, offered his support. Once I had identified my two primary research communities, he prepared the way for my formal request for permission from the subdistrict level of the farmers' union. Obtaining subdistrict and community-level permission proved, however, to be a different process for each of my two host communities.

With respect to Chimpa Rodeo, I requested the subdistrict authorities' permission during a meeting of local *dirigentes* or union leaders. The permission process went quite smoothly. After an introduction by the IPTK extension worker, I outlined my process, my commitment to an ethical approach, and to the confidentiality of individual informants. I also committed myself to the presentation of an oral and written report to the participating communities once the research was complete, a promise I was able to keep in May 2001. The *autoridad maximo*, Don Angel, added his endorsement, and a lively discussion ensued in Quechua. It included a thoughtful discussion about the pros and cons of such research. Once in agreement, representatives with signing authority, including Chimpa Rodeo's *dirigente*, reviewed, stamped, and signed the permission form that I had prepared in advance.

The next day, IPTK's extension worker, together with two local leaders, helped me to identify families in Chimpa Rodeo who might be willing to

participate in a benchmark household survey. In an effort to formulate a
representative group, we identified families that would reflect the three
different levels of livelihood security within the hamlet: subsistence; semi-
subsistence; and *excedentaria*. The NGO community commonly used this
latter term to refer to those able to accumulate some capital and invest in
modest infrastructure.[12] The leaders' ranking gave more weight to the
number and kind of animals a family owned than to the annual family
income or the condition of the homestead's infrastructure, an important
indication of the differences I would encounter between Western and
Indigenous understandings and perspectives. I followed the advice of
these leaders.

Each family was approached about the study and informed about the
purpose of the research and the benefits the study might bring to the
community, such as the gathering of information of potential use to crop
diversity and the conservation of their *saber Andina* or Indigenous knowledge. With one exception,[13] all families that were initially approached
agreed to participate, the extension worker providing signed testimony of
their verbal permission to proceed. I chose not to request written permission from the farm families. Given the low levels of reading and writing
skills, I did not consider a request for this level of trust at such an early
stage in the process to be appropriate or ethical.

The local union leader – *dirigente* – in Chimpa Rodeo facilitiated the
community's approval of a participatory rural appraisal workshop. He
issued a written *convocación* or notice for residents to attend the meeting.
With the help of IPTK staff and visual aids, I presented an overview of the
entire research process, noting my personal goals and how I hoped the
research might benefit the community. Through consensus, participants
agreed to participate in the research.

Obtaining the authorization of the people of Mojón required a slightly
different tack. There were no subdistrict meetings scheduled. Several of
the community authorities, including the Mojón *dirigente,* were tending
fields in their valley lands. However, the *autoridad maximo*, Don Angel, did
speak with the acting *dirigente* in Mojón. With the help of IPTK's extension
worker, I obtained verbal permission to proceed with a community meeting to discuss the research. Once the *dirigente* returned from the valley, he
gave me written authorization to continue the research. Despite the
absence of a few leaders, we had solid participation in my introductory
meeting. Participants approved support, with several families lining up to
register for the benchmark survey. This unexpected but welcomed volun-

teering to participate in the household surveys would complicate, I thought, my intention to choose a representative cross-section of families as had been the case in Chimpa Rodeo. I was soon to learn, however, that the overwhelming majority of families in Mojón were largely subsistence farm families, producing little surplus produce for the market.

In both communities, my expressed desire to document and celebrate the culture and skills of these Jalq'a stewards of potato diversity contributed to approval. Mojón residents appeared especially taken with the idea of championing their potato diversity – of conserving and recovering native varieties they were losing at an all too rapid rate. IPTK's solid reputation in both communities no doubt also influenced a positive reception.

In preparation for my research, I also made a courtesy call to the mayor of the municipality, a former IPTK employee and member of the IPTK Board of Directors. This contact, which eventually included an in-depth, semi-structured interview proved helpful to my work, but not central. From the beginning, it was clear that consensus-based approval from Jalq'a authorities directly involved in community governance was the key to an open door.

ARCHITECTURE

Quality architecture, we all know, requires the construction of a foundation with materials that are strong and grounded. In openly ideological research there is a particular need for rigor in order to, as anthropologist Pattie Lather, puts it, "protect our research and theory constructions from our own enthusiasms."[14] Four strategies designed to strengthen the quality of my observations – called validity checks – proved especially helpful to my inquiry. They were: *triangulation* – the use of varied methods, multiple data sources, and the seeking of counter patterns as well as convergences; *construct validity* analysis – the comparing of observations, data and document study with the knowledge or theory one already has (a priori) to determine whether the data fits or changes the logic of the theory that influenced the research; *face validity* analysis – a recycling of the analysis back through a sample of research participants; and *catalytic validity* analysis – *assessing* the degree to which the research process "re-orients, focuses, and energizes participants."[15] This last process is akin to the Brazilian philosopher-educator, Paulo Freire's "conscientization" and his call for empowerment.

When measured against this last criterion, my participatory research process felt less successful, at least during my primary research period from January to December 2000. Being linked to a Northern NGO had its advantages however. On my return to my position as the organization's Latin America Program Director responsible for their Bolivia program, I was able to direct very modest funding to pilot programming for the conservation and enhancement of ancestral potato varieties in Chimpa Rodeo and Mojón, programming that participants in my research were eager to begin. Further discussion about this ensues in the final chapter.

The demands of a university-funded research framework, with its tight timelines and deliverables, can also limit a researcher's ability to place participants at the front and centre of the research, determining the focus and leading the way. To the extent that I could, I applied participatory research principles that offered participants a good opportunity to shape my interpretation and understanding of their world. But I cannot, of course, claim to tell their story as they might tell it, or to tell it on their behalf.[16] There is an important corollary to this point as well. If knowledge is, first, "produced in the process of interaction" and, second, a product of interaction that is "critical, engaged, personal, and social," as I will argue in chapter seven, I was to some extent an architect versus a recorder of reality.[17] The account of the Jalq'a people within this book reflects, therefore, my construction of their story. I listened carefully to the reports and teachings of the Jalq'a participants and then to the local extension workers with whom we both interacted. But my values and world view, as that of scholars and development thinkers whose work I admire, strongly influenced the story I am about to tell.

Finally on the matter of authentic scholarship, the story of the Jalq'a is layered and complex. They are Indigenous peoples in a country where categories of belonging since colonial times have emerged in different ways depending on political and social imperatives. My observation must be considered within this ever-shifting context.[18]

3

Embedded and Invented

In the communities, from childhood on, you learn that the earth is alive, that she is called *Pachamama*, that she nurtures mankind ...

San Martin, 1997[1]

THE JALQ'A FARMERS OF CHIMPA RODEO AND MOJÓN

Tucked within the spiny ridges of the Cordillera of Potosí, a small mountain range within Bolivia's Southern Andes, are Chimpa Rodeo and Mojón, the two Jalq'a settlements that agreed to let me glimpse their family and community character. In return, they asked only that I share coca leaves, food, my photos, and the products of my research – signs of respect and appreciation. Chimpa Rodeo is an ex-hacienda hamlet[2] and home to 33 families. Mojón, with 46 families, is an "original" or *originario* community. Its residents were never subject to the servitude of the large landowner or *hacendado*.[3] A snapshot of their respective demographics can be found in Appendix 4.

On highland *chacras* – their term for their productive fields – farmers in both communities grew rain-fed crops such as potatoes and uniquely Andean tubers like oca, papa lisa, and izaño. These were rotated after the first year with leguminous, nitrogen-fixing fava beans or tarwi, the latter another highly nutritious and uniquely Andean crop.[4] The following year the field would be planted with barley or oats for fodder, and then left to recover its vitality during a one- to three-year fallow period, depending on the amount of land the farm family needed to return to production.[5]

Both communities were also able to integrate corn, wheat, and fruit crops (peaches) into their diets, in the case of Chimpa Rodeo through bartering and market purchases. Mojón's farm families, with their practice of dual homesteading (described below) were able to grow these crops on their valley lands. In Chimpa Rodeo, tomatoes, carrots, and lettuce were sometimes grown in the low-cost greenhouses or purchased from vendors in the village of Ravelo. The freeze-drying of potato and oca to produce a winter staple – *chuño* – was common to both Chimpa Rodeo and Mojón. Neither community had micro-ecosystems that offered sufficient rainfall for a second *miska* harvest. Appendices 5 and 6 list the field crops and cropland fallowing periods in both communities as well as their infrastructure and animals.

In an effort to strengthen their family's livelihood, farmers in both communities dedicated some of their tuber cropland for commercial produce. But the dream of lucrative market sales was elusive for the majority. Most farming was of a subsistence and semi-subsistence character. As suggested in the introduction, successful petty commodity production ended for most food producers in this region when the government put the interests of silver and tin barons over that of their local farmers and when they liberalized trade in the final years of the nineteenth century.[6]

At approximately 20 km and 10 km from Ravelo, the municipal capital and transport hub for Sucre, both Chimpa Rodeo and Mojón had reasonable access to city markets. Like most of their neighbours, however, few of the 79 families of these two settlements had managed to benefit economically from their surplus produce. Chimpa Rodeo had an advantage over Mojón when it came to potential gains. A 45 minute walk takes one from Chimpa Rodeo to the relatively dependable main road, albeit with curves, cliffs, and potholes during the rainy season that leave newcomers either awestruck or with eyes shut tight. Chimpa Rodeo also has a comparatively good secondary service road making motorized travel possible except during the worst of the rainy season. None of the hamlet's residents owned a vehicle. But farmers belonging to credit associations occasionally did pool funds to hire tractor services for a few hours during the planting season.

The trek into Mojón was another matter. Mojón's service road was barely navigable at the best of times[7] and impassable during the rainy season. One heavy thunderstorm could convert the winding, boulder-filled road into a rushing river, as I discovered when water reached my knees during a lonely hike into the community. Motorbike travel was thus the favoured option for extension workers in a hurry. Local residents and regular visitors like me generally tackled the two-hour or so journey on foot. Mojón is clearly the more isolated of the two communities, not so much for residents used to regular treks to valleys but undoubtedly for development agents. In the year 2000, Mojón residents' interaction with external institutions was in fact only four years old. In contrast, Chimpa Rodeo had an approximately twenty-year history of external development assistance.

At almost identical elevations of 3,550 and 3,500 metres respectively,[8] and being just over 10 km apart, climatic and land conditions in these *puna baja* or lower-level highland communities are comparable. Geographers classify the area as semi-arid.[9] Hail, frost, and water shortages are a constant worry. The topography in both communities is uneven, intensely eroded, and heavily deforested. Large gullies are a common feature, since there are few trees and bushes to stop the winds and rains from digging deep. Root-hungry sheep, introduced by Spanish conquistadores, have cleared Indigenous foliage all too efficiently. Soils are lightly acidic (6.8 pH) with organic matter levels poor to moderate.[10] It is important to note, however, that the ecosystem diversity characteristic of the Bolivian Andes is applicable to these communities.[11] Land fertility can vary from hill to plateau, requiring differing fallow periods and a variety of land-use strategies. But a consistent theme which emerged in all my conversations with residents of both communities was how *cansado* or tired all their land had become.

Farmers blamed this growing infertility on a number of factors, including deforestation and land-use intensification to satisfy family consumption needs and to grow surpluses for city markets. *Minifundismo* – the gifting of parcels of lands to male children – was also noted as a key factor in fertility loss. Some farmers, particularly the older women among my informants, pointed an accusing finger at the increasing use of chemical fertilizers and pesticides that rob the soil of valuable nutrients.

In the Andean highlands multi-generational households living in clusters of adobe buildings tend to be the units of ceremonial and economic participation. This is the case in Chimpa Rodeo and Mojón. Their households are not dependent on a wage and monetary economy in the Western sense. Rather, they are semi-autonomous units that, in addition to their farming activities, also depend on labour exchange, dual homesteading, and temporary labour migration to fill consumption and income needs.[12] Land inheritance rules reflect patrilineal or husband-centric structures. My informants repeatedly noted that the male heads of households in Chimpa Rodeo and Mojón pass land onto their sons.

Stemming from strict exogamic rules, meaning marriage outside your kin, virilocal marriage sends a woman from her hamlet birthplace to that of her future spouse.[13] But if a man has no heirs, he may give his daughters a part of the family holding. With land to boast, such daughters become attractive brides for the sons of families with limited land on offer. Widows, I was to discover through my friendship with a Chimpa Rodeo woman, Doña Lucilla, can also own land and a man may choose to marry a woman with land in the valley, generally to re-establish a pattern of vertical control (addressed below) in circumstances where such land has been lost.[14]

Among my research participants, there were also cases of residence with the wife's parents – a practice anthropologists call uxorilocal marriage. Three families within my host communities also reported highland titles in their mother's name. Such strategic marriages ensure access to adequate land, and caution against a strict pigeonholing of this society as patrilineal. The patrilineal biases that exist in these communities, as Andean scholars of Quechua communities elsewhere have argued, may have been influenced by Spanish administrators' insistence on male-headed households.[15] Still, I could find no evidence within my communities of land ownership favouring women nor of the bilaterality – a system that allows men or women to pass land onto their kin – that is often found among the highland Aymara in the Department of La Paz, for example.[16]

While Catholic clerics would have had it otherwise, betrothed young women tended to leave their parents' homes almost two years before the official ceremony. In Chimpa Rodeo and Mojón, trial marriages were the norm.[17] Like the llama-herding, Llamero ethnic group[18] in neighbouring communities, and not so different from the changed norms of the West, Jalq'a marriage did not appear to be approached as a "once and for all" matter. Rather, it seemed to represent a progressive process of cementing a union through a series of informal and formal events.[19] In response to my question about the rationale for the lengthy co-habitation, my Jalq'a research participants noted only the practical need to raise funds to finance a wedding.

HOMESPUN WOOL AND POLYESTER

In their clothing, textiles, and cultural celebrations, the patterns and trends in Chimpa Rodeo and Mojón were uniquely Jalq'a. "Traditional" women wore a long-sleeved black dress called *almilla* that falls just below the knees and has a vivid, multicoloured embroidered band circling the hem. They balanced a *juq'ullu* or cream-coloured bowler-like hat on their heads, designed along the lines of the European Derby of the eighteenth and nineteenth century and trimmed with a removable, multicoloured woven band. *Ojotas* or flat leather sandals with the soles of tire tread were worn year-round, in rain, wind, hail, and temperatures that can drop well below freezing. I was always amazed not to find blackened or missing toes. A black, body-length woven shawl called *llijlla* was thrown over their shoulder, especially on colder days.

Doubled over the back half of their *ch'umpi* waist belt was a hip-wide, two-meter long *axsu*, named after the tunic of their pre-Columbian female ancestors.[20] It offered added protection from the always-chilled earth and served as a padded seat when cooking, attending meetings, or socializing among families and neighbours. What stood out about this enormously sensible garment, however, were the intricate patterns of supernatural animals called *khurus* – wild, indomitable animals impossible to domesticate. Some were easily recognized but zoologically impossible, such as llamas with three humps. Others were more obscure. They were crimson red or bright orange and woven into backgrounds as black as a moonless night or brown like *Pachamama's* virgin soils. There was an almost total absence of mirrored symmetry.

These *pallays* – tableaus of *khuru* figures – revealed a dualistic world view that is fluid and continuous yet dark and without reference points. Like abstract paintings, they communicate a way of experiencing the world, without having to verbalize that experience.[21] The lack of symmetry and precision in the textiles' figures struck me as possibly an effort to either illustrate the complexity in their world or to suggest that tidy definitions of their identity imposed by the powerful were rejected – a form of cultural resistance that other Andeanists have captured so well in their work within the Peruvian Andes.[22] My informants offered a more straightforward explanation for the designs and figures in their traditional *axsu*. The figures in their weavings were revealed to them in dreams, they reported. That is why no two weavings are ever the same.

Traditional males also wore a *juq'ullu* hat and *ojota* sandals, as well as an *almilla*, only in their case an *almilla* was a white shirt. The shirt was sufficiently long-waisted to be tucked into trousers, called *calzón*, the Spanish term for underwear. Since the *calzón* had no real waistband and barely covered the buttocks and pelvic area, a rope pulled tightly around the hips kept the pants in place. It was a look not unlike the jeans on a Canadian teenager today, although the shirt stayed nicely in the pants, I was happy to observe. Both the edge of the *almilla's* sleeves and that of their trousers had a very thin band of colours embroidered on them, embroidery that the men themselves completed to personalize or label their uniform.

Wrapped around their waist was a shorter and thinner *llijlla* shawl. It was usually converted into a carryall for small bundles of produce or other items travelling from market to home or vice versa. Finally, a dark *poncho* of black or brown with almost invisible stripes was pulled over their head and shoulders when the sun set for the night. Some ponchos also contained a faint border of the *pallay* figures similar to those featured in the *axsu*. Both the men and the women slung a tiny woven purse over their neck and shoulder to hold their coca leaves.

Of particular interest in the men's traditional outfit were the black bands or large rectangular patches a third of the way down each shirt-sleeve. These stood in sharp contrast to the predominantly white fabric of the rest of their outfit, a symbol that represented the oppositional forces in the universe. These patches of black on white are a stark reminder, elders explained, of the need to be awake and vigilant at all times.[23]

The majority of Mojón participants reported preferring traditional dress.[24] For almost 75 per cent of the village's residents, however, pressures to adopt more Westernized garb had contributed to a switch to "modern" dress within the previous ten to twenty years. Western clothing for males was almost indistinguishable from that of the mestizo male in urban centres, with a baseball cap or fedora crowning the look. A close inspection revealed shirts and trousers, sometimes jeans, which were generally patched several times over, stitched or fastened with a safety pin, and crusted with dust since water to wash clothes was extremely limited. Most of this modern clothing, although occasionally produced at home among the very few families with sewing machines (usually the gift of a charity), was more often than not purchased from stalls that sold diverted donations from Western shops and church basements. The prices requested, in fact, were frequently higher than those scribbled on the leftover tags of charities from afar. I found a Value Village[25] price tag for CAD $3.00 on an article the shopkeeper wanted US $5.00 for, and no bargaining was permitted in that case.[26] As for their footwear, the vast majority of men I met continued to wear the traditional *ojota* sandals.

For *Jalq'a* women, the shift to "modern" clothing did not mean a transition to the Western dress you would find on their *mestizo* counterparts. They wore, rather, an Indigenous version of Western clothing somewhat reminiscent of colonial styles but uniquely their own. Their outfit included: a *pollera* – a very full, gathered skirt of polyester satin that reached just below the knee and covered polyester or cotton crinolines; a synthetic satin, front-buttoned blouse; a synthetic wool cardigan; and a large synthetic wool shawl or blanket worn as a shawl. A wide-brimmed straw hat with a bright ribbon was the preferred protector against the sun. Like the men, women wore the traditional *ojotas* on their feet. None of the females I encountered in either community, including the smaller girls and teenagers, wore trousers or jeans. Wool tights and leggings under their skirts, on the other hand, were permissible and common during the cold, windy months of June, July, and August.

The elder women I interviewed had little good to say about the flimsy synthetics of this newer outfit from the city. They complained of their poor protection from the weather. One grandmother in the traditional hand-woven dress asked, "How can we [otherwise] protect ourselves from the cold and rain?" Younger women countered that their "modern" clothes were lighter and more comfortable. They were definitely flashier and if there was water available, much easier to wash and dry.

Whereas the men who have switched to modern clothing have done so in its entirety (apart from their sandals), the women have developed a new style which is neither traditional nor modern as understood in urban Bolivia. This uniqueness in women's adapted dress is rather curious, a reflection, Andean scholars have suggested, of women's ongoing construction of their gendered identities. Women's clothing choices more generally, the theory continues, reflect a politics of resistance – of bonding together and belonging – given their presence on the edges of the dominant power structures.[27] I was unable to explore this issue in any depth, but the notion of the Jalq'a women having selected clothing as a means to claim some power is certainly intriguing and possible.

The more complete adoption of Western garb among the males, however, should not necessarily be interpreted as welcomed acculturation. Males of all ages noted that temporary migration for urban employment forced city clothing onto their backs. One aging farmer sighed with sadness over the change, equating the loss of traditional clothing to a loss of the Jalq'a culture. I also heard complaints among the men about how the cold seeped into their bones during the winter season thanks to their poorly insulated clothes from the city.

Once again, however, the new had merged with the traditional. During cool highland evenings and bone-chilling nights, the males of both communities proudly cloaked themselves with the finely crafted, hand-woven sheep-wool *ponchos* generations of wives and sisters had created. The complex *khurus* of the *axsu* were no longer evident in the patterns of these contemporary weavings. Their bright colours from artificial dyes and their symmetrical figures reflected a new generation of taste as well. A decline in the inter-generational transmission of the chaos-creation beliefs explained further below might have also been at play. Still, the artistry in these entirely memory-based creations remained strong. On an *awaykurqu* – a loom of smoothened tree branch poles that leans loosely against an adobe wall – and with a needle of chiselled sheep-bone, young women produced textiles of a quality Westerners would proudly frame for their living room walls.

GENDER COMPLEMENTARITY?

Jalq'a husbands were proud of their wives' ability to weave beauty from the matted wool of local sheep. They openly valued other skills as well, such as their spouses' expertise in animal husbandry. And while virilocal marriage places a young wife at the mercy of her spouse's family and friends in her new hamlet, I did not pick up on any sense of unhappiness about the move to the in-laws. Nor was there a strict gender-role stereo-typing, which is often found among the more affluent *mestizo* residents in Sucre. Farming, for example, was a joint, family activity. There was some task differentiation. The men prepared the furrow or trench, guiding the heavy wooden plough that was pulled by a pair of *yunta* or oxen. Women cooked the midday meal. Because of their fertility, women usually placed the tuber seed in the *surco* or furrow, although I noticed some pragmatic exceptions. But both genders lined up behind the *yunta* to complete the *siembra* or planting.

In the case of potatoes, the sowing process included verification with a pick-axe that the furrow was a sufficiently deep trench, the dropping of the potato tuber, the application of purchased fertilizer, especially in the case of introduced varieties, the addition of sheep manure or *guano* for indigenous and new varieties, and the covering of the furrow.

Both women and men joined forces when the crop was ready to be harvested and sorted. Potatoes were generally divided into five categories according to use: seed, immediate consumption, bartering/gifts, sale, and post-harvest processing into freeze-dried food, like the potato or oca *chuño*[28] needed to get through the long, cold, and dry winter. I managed to observe several families making their potato *chuño* in June, when the temperature fell below freezing at night. They would place a large pile of potatoes in the waters of a nearby river or stream, let it partially freeze in the freezing night-time water, and then stomp on the pile in daylight to squeeze the water out. Once sufficiently emptied, the tuber was then spread out so each piece could dry well in the midday sun.[29]

Heavy infrastructure projects were generally left to the men of the community, as was the delivery to market of surplus produce. Exceptions generally occurred in the case of women-headed households or when the male member of the family was unable to contribute his labour for community work. During the road maintenance activities I observed, for example, there were always a few women present. Their strength and agility with a pickaxe seemed equal to that of any man on the road crew.

Gender-based differentiation applied to the care and management of livestock. Men husbanded the large animals, like cattle, while women, with the assistance of their children, bred and cared for the smaller livestock that included sheep, goats and a few pigs. Women's animal husbandry was much valued. Sheep were especially crucial to the entire community. They provided the manure for crops, the wool for clothing, the bones for implements, and the blood and food for ritual celebration.

Women's role in sowing the seed reflected, as suggested, an honouring of women's fertility and their capacity to nurture. The men, however, expressed mixed feelings about this power to create, as suggested in the following legend about the origins of the potato:

An Inca prince went on a walk with his sister and brought her into the farthest mountains. He left her there and said to his parents that she was the victim of the voracity of a serpent. The parents cried but later forgot about her because the prince had paid the witches and shamans to say that the princess had caused the ruin of the Inca Empire.

In the meantime, the Princess cried tears that were alive and the teardrops fell and grew into beautiful plants and flowers that produced fruit in a short period, in hours, and so the Princess who was by then starving took the fruit, examined it, smelled it, took a bite, and then ate it. She then fell asleep. In her dreams the moon revealed that the best fruit was actually in the earth. When she awakened, she dug up the plant and discovered tubers as large as the head of an Indian. She separated the tubers and saw that they were mealy and good to eat. Thereafter they were her only food during her entire exile.

After ten years, a group of merchant Indians encountered the Princess. They led her to her village after having seen much [of her] labour. The Indian girl brought many potatoes and tubers that were later planted and cultivated. The Inca [King] rejoiced at seeing his daughter and called his son to reprimand him for his conduct; but the Prince continued to insist that the Princess had really been the tragic victim of a snake. The Princess said nothing against her brother. But the Inca was not content with his son's response. So he called the prophets once again. Petitioned for a second time, they declared that God had given them this message. The disappearance of the Princess has saved the Imperial Empire from great calamities and her reappearance was a sign of wealth for the Empire. Evil had been converted to enormous good and forever more we will have continuous examples of this good in the form of new potatoes.

The Inca King was satisfied, gave thanks to the Sun and hosted a great banquet for all the people of the village to celebrate his daughter's discovery. During this feast, everyone came to know the miracle potato and later they shared its seeds with all in attendance. At the request of the Princess, they planted the precious plant, with each plant yielding one hundred more.[30]

Women's fertility was both celebrated and, it would appear, somewhat feared. This fear may have explained, in part at least, women's vulnerability to spousal abuse during festivals if their husbands drank to excess. One male informant said to me with a slightly nervous laugh that wife beating during festivals was a welcomed release. I remember feeling very uncomfortable when this otherwise likeable man confessed this behaviour to me, hoping his comment was inappropriate bravado. But when the eighteen-year-old daughter of another well-respected man I knew confessed that she did not want to marry because men beat their wives, I was forced to acknowledge this uglier side of community life. Is this binge drinking and consequent need to dominate and rage from time to time linked to men's marginalization and sense of powerlessness, I wondered? The hard truth of the matter is that violence against women in the Bolivian highlands is far too common to blame simply on binge drinking and a need to counter feelings of inadequacy.[31] In a 2007 Bolivian study, over one-third of the 137 male respondents surveyed reported using physical force at home, and more than half thought it was unacceptable for their partner to refuse sex for no apparent reason.[32] The degree of male violence suggests that patriarchy in the year 2000 knew no borders or classes. Change on this front is of course possible; but its agents have their work cut out for them.

With respect to corporal punishment of children in Chimpa Rodeo and Mojón, I saw no evidence of its presence. While I occasionally witnessed a mother, father, or sibling swat the hand of a child away from something dangerous, the behaviour seemed genuinely protective, out of concern. Nor was childcare a uniquely female task. The colourful *awayo* or baby blanket strapped infants and toddlers onto the shoulders of men as well as those of women and older siblings. Both parents openly demonstrated tenderness and affection for their young children and shared responsibility for their discipline.

The bulk of other domestic responsibilities fell squarely on women and their older daughters. As heads of the household the men had additional civic responsibilities to tend to. Still, their spouses often bore the heavier workload, as they admitted quite freely. Their wives farmed as hard as they did, but they also had to feed and take care of the family. It would be unfair to characterize women's work as all work and no play (or social time) however. Like the men, women found time to join neighbours for conversation, always sharing food when visits corresponded with mealtimes. Women also seemed equally enthusiastic participants in community festivals when everyday activities and responsibilities were eased somewhat. Many of the NGO extension workers I met subscribed to theories about gender complementarity in the Andes.[33] Communities in the countryside demonstrated comparatively strong gender equity, they argued, especially when compared to mestizo patterns in the city. Despite task differentiation, they further suggested, both genders contributed and participated in the life of the community on an equal basis.

The duality within the Andean world view or *cosmovision* lends weight to this perspective. Jalq'a respondents to my questions about gender used the single Quechua term *khariwarmi* – male-female – to describe their gender relations, the two sides of the same coin. (Neither Jalq'a men nor women, I should add, seemed terribly eager to discuss questions about gender relations). The women I met were certainly not defeated or downtrodden. During festive occasions they claimed important social spaces. Special celebrations, like that of Our Lady of Guadalupe, required both a wife and her husband to serve as the festival's *madrino* (godmother) and *padrino* (godfather). These frequent celebrations were fun; women's laughter was notable.

When important production, purchasing, or parenting decisions had to be made, husbands always consulted their wives. During community meetings that I attended, for example, a man often asked if the final decision could be postponed until he had a chance to consult his spouse. When widowed or abandoned, women had the option of returning to their home community or remaining in their married home. If the latter, in-laws assisted as needed.

Still, women's voice in the public governance of both communities was indirect and quiet. Recent scholarship on the dynamics of gender complementarity in the Andes points to many negative repercussions in rural women's lives.[34] Except when widowed or if there were no brothers, equality of land rights remained elusive for most in Chimpa Rodeo and Mojón. The political leverage of a woman-headed household was marginal.[35] Women were, for example, present at the meetings I attended but were only invited to speak up when I asked to hear their perspectives.

Women's involvement in public office and as union representatives was also limited and recent, with the modest gains the result of national policies calling for greater gender representation in public life. The pool of women with the experience and confidence needed to assume such roles was much smaller of course. Girls were the first to be plucked from school to shepherd domestic animals. Literacy rates certainly reflected this imbalance. Less than half of respondent families in Chimpa Rodeo had members who could read, write, and perform basic arithmetic; only a third of them were women. In Mojón, the gap was still more dramatic. Only 28 per cent of those surveyed had some level of literacy. Of this 28 per cent, 3 per cent were women.[36]

Andean colleagues whom I respect a great deal, females and males, insist that gender discrimination and gender-based violence has grown out of, and been exacerbated by, colonial and mestizo patriarchy. A thorough analysis of the factors that might explain women's inequality is beyond the scope of this book. Nevertheless, the second-class citizenship I observed cast an ugly shadow on the Andean notion of gender complementarity.

COMMUNITY CELEBRATION

If domestic violence revealed a dark side of community life, pageantry, music, and dance revealed its joyous one. Religious festivals, national holidays, and special family events were almost always occasions for community celebration, as seen in the ensuing excerpts from my September 2000 field journal written during one of the most popular festivals of the year, the Festival of the Virgin of Guadalupe. It was a real delight to discover this jubilant three-day gathering of Chimpa Rodeo residents as well as families from the broader region. They embraced my attendance with a spirit of genuine warmth and acceptance. I also experienced some frustration and anger. The deeply paternalistic and chauvinistic Catholic priest conducting the ceremonies got me grinding my teeth. A former Catholic from small town Quebec, I quickly saw how this colonial institution, while modified to suit Indigenous world views, continued to exert considerable power.

OUR LADY OF GUADALUPE: 8 SEPTEMBER 2000

After several failed attempts to reach Cornelio on the village's single *Entel* telephone to inquire about his availability to serve as my interpreter, I am heading solo to Chimpa Rodeo. I will participate in the *Fiesta de La Virgen de Guadalupe* without my regular translator, no intermediary, no one to help me find a place to stay if Don Angel's family is unable to house me. I was half hoping that I might not be able to reach Cornelio. I am anxious to discover the most popular annual festival of the region on my own. I have been told that the event unites not only Chimpa Rodeo's residents in celebration but, in light of their chapel's legendary significance, residents from Jalq'a communities throughout the region. This auspicious occasion is also the preferred date for marriage. Ravelo's Catholic priest will join several Jalq'a couples from the surrounding area in "holy matrimony" during a mass in the chapel on Saturday afternoon, once he has issued each couple a marriage license.

I arrive in the late afternoon to find my regular hosts able to house me. Angel is already at the festivities but eighteen-year-old Lucia is home and willing to serve as my new interpreter during conversations with her mother, Desideria. They seem genuinely pleased to see me and to have me participate in this festive occasion. My small gifts of sardines, pasta, and marbles for the boys and a small tube of hand cream for Lucia appear to be much appreciated. I leave my belongings, a small knapsack and sleeping bag, on the bed that Lucia graciously offers me when I stay overnight. I grab my camera and flashlight and head up the hill to the open-air festivities outside the community's small adobe community centre.

I plan to be the self-appointed photographer of these festivities. From my first day in this village, residents have always demonstrated a great interest in my photos of their community and more particularly of themselves. Perhaps that is because there are no mirrors in the hamlet.

Capturing a photographic record of events is consequently very straight-forward. And having received copies of photographs taken during previous visits, residents trust that I will produce the promised copy.

Off to the side of the circle, I photograph a recently butchered cow being expertly carved into roasts, steaks, and chops. This year's event is an especially important one for Chimpa Rodeo since one of their own, twenty-two year-old Victor, will be married tomorrow to his twenty-year old common-law spouse of the past four years. The food for such occasion should be tasty and plentiful. There are many guests to feed. Several sheep have already been sacrificed. Their cleaned skins and rib cages have been hung to dry in the noonday sun, their intestines put to boil in a large stew pot and their blood smeared on Don Victor's and his fiancé's face as well as the faces of the *Padrino* and *Madrino* for this festival, Don Eduardo and Doña Antonia. The sheep's blood, extracted only from a white-fleeced male, has been painted on their faces to ensure that no disease enters their bodies or homes. The lattice of sinewy tissue on Eduardo and Antonia's hats will augur good fortunes as well.

Beside the kettle of hard boiling innards, there is a huge vat of potatoes and an equally large pot of cornmeal soup, the latter heated by placing extremely hot stones from the cooking fire directly into the soup. Mutton and beef are roasting above the slow-burning wood coals of an *asado* or barbecue pit. Several women have gathered to prepare the food, with each family contributing what it could. There should be enough to go around, although the crowd keeps growing. Every time I look around, there seem to be more outsiders. The few families with small greenhouses of adobe and plastic sheeting have contributed lettuce.

I regret not having brought food to contribute. Cornelio would have undoubtedly advised me to do so, never forgetting to contribute himself. But I do know that my gift of coca leaves will be much appreciated. Indeed, when I do pull out my bag to drop quarter handfuls into cupped hands, there is a rush to get some. Don Caspian tells the anxious recipients to calm down and wait their turn. Chimpa Rodeo's elders should be the first to receive their share, he reminds them.

As dusk turns into a moonlit night, the young devil dancers pull onlookers into the circle to dance. My arm is tugged and I join in, working hard to catch a rhythm that feels rather awkward at first. After several dances, food is served. Much to my dismay, my plate arrives with a healthy helping of sheep's intestines. I eat a small piece that to me tastes like stewed elastic, then manage to pull it from my mouth and onto a dog's salivating tongue without others having taken notice, at least that is what I tell myself. I eat as much as I can of the mound of potatoes and slabs of tough, extra lean meat remaining on my plate. I then take a small plastic bag out of my pocket, explaining that I want to save some food to share with IPTK compañeros, an acceptable explanation for not having finished my meal.

I am also given *chicha* to drink quite frequently throughout the late afternoon and evening. I drink this fermented corn brew from conch-like *tutuma* shells placed in both my hands (in honour of the forthcoming union of the bride and the groom). I sip it gingerly, concerned not so much about possible inebriation since it is not terribly strong, but instead with the particles of dirt floating on the surface. *Pachamama* gets a particularly generous offering from me before each sip until one of the women observes my extravagant splash. She reminds me that I need only give *Pachamama* a drop or two. So I resign myself to a probable short course of antibiotics after my return to Sucre.

Drinking shots of 80- to 100-proof home-brewed alcohol is another matter altogether. I simply can't handle this more potent distillation. I accept the small cup, wet my lips, and again give *Pachamama* a big slurp. Since the shots are considerably smaller, this strategy works reasonably well. But like a hot brick in bare hands, I pass the shot cup onto another before it is once again filled. Given residents' willingness to share what little they have, I haven't the heart to turn down any of this generosity. I have thought of feigning illness or suggesting that my religion forbids meat and alcohol. But in the end I decide that such a simple demonstration of appreciation should not be passed up.

The meal is over and it is time to prepare for the community parade down the hillside to the chapel. The *Madrino* and *Padrino* will lead the parade with a community banner announcing Don Victor's marriage. Each host is taken into a separate room for sprucing up and, I suspect, a bit of sobering up. It has been a long day of celebration already. The hosts are finally ready. They lead the parade, followed by five women holding hands and dancing joyously behind them, occasionally weaving their snake-like chain into a circle. A woman grabs my arm and I am pulled into the chain and danced down a gully, then narrow mountain path, along with the rest of the crowd. While I must stoop to hold the hands of women a good eight inches shorter than me, they laugh at my occasional tripping on a loose rock or rubble. I have my hiking boots on, after all, and they wear only their simple *ojotas*.

Music, as expected, is our constant companion. Chimpa Rodeo's band accompanies our march down the hillside and when we arrive at the chapel, I discover bands from other communities, each taking their turn at serenading the crowd. The music will continue until dawn, I am told.

There are no formal proceedings tonight. Instead, people file quietly into the chapel to light a candle and pray. I take my turn, eager to visit this legendary small chapel and to view the painting of the Virgin and her son. I am somewhat awed when I finally enter. This humble memorial to honour Mary stands in such sharp contrast to the ornate, often garish, monuments I discovered in Sucre's numerous Catholic churches. The altar is flush against its mountain wall. On it are a plain cross of thick tree branches, fastened with leather twine, and the boulder with the painting of the Virgin, made visible by the flickering light of numerous small white candles. The painting is still vivid, its colours likely touched up from time to time, although legend would suggest that it remains as it was when first discovered. I light a candle below the painting and hear a woman whisper words of devotion to *Pachamama*, interspersed with words to the Virgin Mary. After leaving the chapel, I sit with the women on the chapel steps for a while. Lucia is not around to help with translation and the Spanish-speaking men are deep in their own conversations. So we smile a lot once my basic conversational words run out.

After an hour or so, my eyes are stinging and watering, likely from something in the smoke of the several small bonfires keeping participants warm. They sting to a point of considerable discomfort. So I am heading back up to Lucia's room. I am also anxious to jot this rich experience down in my field journal. I meet Desideria on her way down to the chapel. Her children are all settled now and she can finally join the others. Her eyes, arms and few words of Spanish ask me why I have decided to head back well before midnight, when most women will journey home. I gesture that I am tired and bid her good night in Quechua.

The music is still blaring in the distance as I put this journal down, zip my sleeping bag up to my ears and switch off my flashlight. Will I dream of the devil's dance, doves and revelations, *Pachamama*, or Desideria, a tireless Jalq'a mother finally able to relax and have fun?

VICTOR'S WEDDING: 9 SEPTEMBER 2000
Cornelio arrived this morning with regrets that he had not received my messages until earlier that morning. He has been asked to serve as one of

Don Victor's witnesses so he will attend the marriage service that, he tells me, will be the first of three masses. The other two services will be offered in honour of the festival of Guadalupe and to baptize children. A sole priest will lead this trilogy of worship. There will be quite a crowd, I am told.

As it turns out, the priest, one of the Ravelo parish's two clergymen, started his day with a very heavy workload. Since 9 am, from a small table at the back of Chimpa Rodeo's small community centre, he has been issuing marriage licenses to eager young couples, twice as many as anticipated. Since the Festival of the Lady of Guadalupe has fallen on a Saturday, today is an especially auspicious day to wed.

I head to the licensing session. With the encouragement of my local friends, I gently push through a small crowd at the entrance of the building. The classroom-size community centre is completely jammed. I squeeze my towering frame (in that context anyway) to a spot behind the priest to observe the proceedings. Don Victor, Doña Angelica, his bride-to-be and their witnesses are there, close to the front. The groom-in-waiting who is first in the queue is asked if his parents were legally married, although no legal evidence is requested. Next, he is asked to recite the "Our Father" followed by the sign of the cross, as evidence of his Catholic upbringing. The groom and his bride then sign a certificate, with a thumbprint if necessary. The young couple's witnesses also sign or add their thumbprint to the certificate. Their form is then stamped and signed by the priest. The women, many unilingual and unable to read and write, observe with nervous, often frightened eyes.

During several of the "Our Father" recitations, the grooms are cut off before the prayer's completion. Aware of the unusually large number of couples this year, the priest wastes little time. Don Victor completes the requirements. He seems extremely relieved when he holds his certificate firmly in hand.

In contrast to my trek down to the chapel the previous evening, my journey to the chapel in broad daylight is sure-footed. As I approach, I see families and friends throughout the meadow surrounding the chapel, dotting the countryside like families at a big community picnic. As I draw closer to the clusters of kin, I see that in each grouping there is a young about to be bride and groom. The future bride is in a white *cholita* wedding outfit – a shiny white *pollera* that sits just above the ankles, a satin blouse, a polyester white cardigan, and a muslin veil that falls to the edge of her *pollera*. She holds a small bouquet of white carnations. Her *ojotas* have been replaced with new white sandals fitted over feet in white knee socks or stockings. Her young partner looks rather more uncomfortable in his Western business suit and stiff-collared white shirt. He wears a tie but I notice that many other grooms have preferred an open collar in the very hot noonday sun. The men's footgear is varied, including running shoes, black leather shoes, and *ojotas*. Later, in the chapel, I discover that a few couples have chosen to don beautiful, newly woven traditional Jalq'a outfits.

In the daylight I notice that there is a small, very shallow river running through this landscape. Since I am the only Gringa in evidence and do not want to attract too much attention, particularly to my camera, I cross the river over a log bridge and find a quiet perch above the bank with a good view of the increasingly large gathering. On my way, I pass several small merchants selling refreshments and small snacks, including a vendor from Ravelo who recognizes me. She calls me over and we chat for a while. This is one of her best days of the year, she informs me.

As three o'clock approaches, I make my way down to the chapel, having observed Don Victor and his party move in that direction. There are now at least twenty couples waiting to be married, so only they and their witnesses are allowed in the small church. Victor has asked me to photograph the ceremony so I am allowed in, although I feel a little guilty as I glance at the faces of excited relatives lining the chapel's exterior. The doors, they are assured, will be left open for those in hearing distance.

Over an hour has passed and still the priest fails to arrive. One young woman looks as if she is about to faint from the heat, although she will not fall far given the shoulders of others pressed against hers. For a moment, my mind wanders to my days in India where the crowding of people into small spaces was not out of the ordinary. Someone passes a bottle of water to the young woman and she seems to revive a little, although her panicked look remains. The priest and his lay assistants finally arrive. They are an hour-and-a-half late. I subsequently hear that the priest stopped for lunch after signing the last license, likely not wanting to faint from hunger himself.

The ceremony begins with group confession and a lecture to the young couples. It is no longer just the airless crowded room that makes my blood boil. In Spanish and Quechua, the men are not only asked to fulfill their responsibilities as providers, but admonished to work hard and avoid excessive drinking. The women are instructed to be good *ambas de casa* or housewives and reminded how the white they wear symbolizes purity. They must stay pure, he emphasizes and must remember that the union they will enter into is until death draws them apart. Divorce will be out of the question. The men, I notice, have been spared the lecture on fidelity.

A short mass ensues, hurried no doubt by the increasingly obvious need for fresh air. The noise of the bands outside has forced the closure of the doors. It would otherwise drown out the vows. The priest moves to each of the couples lined in two rows near the altar to witness and bless their vows. When it is Victor and Angelica's turn, I squeeze over to a spot at the side of the altar to take photographs. Once the white candle they each carry in their hands is lit, symbolizing the hearth, and a single gold chain symbolizing their lifelong bond is placed over their heads to join them together, they repeat their vows. When it is time to exchange rings, they hand their candles over to their witness. They each take their turn at placing a gold wedding band on their partner's right hand. Coins to represent future wealth, and herbs to represent good health, are also held in trust by the witness, passed back to the bride and groom once the priest declares to all that "what God has brought together, no one shall separate." There is no kiss to cement the union. Simply being the centre of attention seems enough cause to blush.

I take a huge gulp of fresh air when we all spill out of the packed chapel. Squinting through the blinding sunlight, I notice that the numbers have continued to expand. Possibly as many as four hundred people colour the landscape. Several of the wedding parties now appear to have their own small band as well as devil dancers. There are also some boom boxes blasting pop tunes from worn cassettes. While there are two more masses still to go, the celebration has already begun. Flirtatious young men, emboldened with *chicha* and beer, shout at the only Gringa present to take their picture. I avoid their calls and wander over to Victor's wedding party. Cornelio is there. After a congratulatory handshake, I bid Victor's family and friends farewell. They don't need me to help them to celebrate. It will be a long night of partying and possibly excessive drinking that I would prefer to avoid. I also would prefer not be repeatedly called on to be the resident photographer for all these groups.

There are several more requests to join the various parties as I climb back up the mountainside, some from friends who have just arrived. I wave goodbye and shout out my regrets and trek back to Angel and Desideria's home, content to have had the opportunity to witness this very moving segment of the Jalq'a story.

Like cultures the world over, music, dance, special foods and special dress mark special occasions like that of Don Victor's wedding during the Festival of the Virgin of Guadalupe. When I first reached the community field on the first evening of celebrations, for example, eight teenage men performed a devil's dance with beautifully crafted wooden or papier-mâché masks and colourful costumes. They danced in a circle to the sounds of a community band of a drummer; a *charango* player, with his small lute-like instrument; and two able pan-flute performers. Their acknowledgment and honouring of the darker forces of nature and the spirit world would help to protect the brides and grooms from harm.

As in all dynamic societies, with time, longstanding traditions give way to the new. Residents over 30 years of age in both Chimpa Rodeo and Mojón lamented the decline of the more discernible expressions of their traditional Jalq'a culture. They were especially unhappy about the disappearance of the Jalq'a *charango*, differentiated as Jalq'a by its comparatively larger size and because of its more voluminous sound. Traditional Jalq'a songs and dances, they also complained, were simply failing to capture the imagination of their youth. A majority of the 25 families I surveyed said that their children did not know Jalq'a songs and almost half hadn't learned Jalq'a dances. While the new dances and songs of their sons and daughters were folkloric in style, they were mostly fused versions from *barrios* on the edges of the city. Jalq'a youth had transported them home from the high schools and cities that for many symbolized a more exciting future.

Parental concern about the impact of these 'modern' influences was considerable. Within Chimpa Rodeo, 50 per cent of respondent families were concerned their grandchildren would no longer follow Jalq'a ways. In Mojón, 64 per cent predicted a switch to "modern" living within two generations. Like them, I wondered about the future of the youth returning from temporary migration to the city, their large boom-boxes perched on their still narrow shoulders. But the parent in me, and I suppose the development anthropologist as well, made me question the inevitability of rural depopulation.

The popular argument is that dreams of a more adventurous and a brighter future – however elusive for the majority – will inevitably lure rural youth into the cities for good. There is simply not enough to keep them in the countryside. And as will be discussed in the final chapters, the farming methods outsiders have imposed do not bode well for a viable farming future. The returns are not enough to make farming worthwhile and most of my research participants were not optimistic. I am more so.

The parents of the Jalq'a youngsters I met had maintained an incredibly strong sense of being Jalq'a, despite generations of outsiders telling them what to think and how to be. Their "devil's dance" during the Virgin of Guadalupe celebrations were but one concrete example. Children internalize more of their parents' values and ways than they often like to think or than the parents themselves anticipate. These Jalq'a children were schooled in the navigation of competing worlds by masters of the give and take. By adding new traditions and dropping some of the old, and by returning to more resilient farming systems if such systems were allowed and encouraged to flourish, Jalq'a youth could well be ready to stay in the countryside. Since the cities they admire from afar are generally not equipped to provide a more secure livelihood, there will be additional incentive to return to the land. The eager look I saw in the eyes of young urban migrants returning to their home settlements during the planting season betrayed a very strong sense of such priority. And as the next chapter suggests, the strong spiritual dimension in their rural experience revealed a connection to the land not easily obscured by city lights.

4

Deep Connections

The Jalq'a's Indigenous-Catholic spirituality is intimately linked with a homage to nature. Mother nature is called *Pachamama* and is honoured as the earth-goddess responsible for the earth's flora, fauna, health, food, fertility, and the "children of the earth" who respect her.[1] Through libations called *ch'alla*, Pachamama is continually thanked for the gifts she shares with her stewards. A local corn-based brew, *chicha*, is prepared for this purpose, with thimblefuls splashed onto Pachamama's soils every time her human children need to acknowledge or petition her help.

During festivals and saints' days, the ritual is more formal and elaborate. In addition to *chica* libations, there is coca leaf distribution, the offering of a plate of special herbs and chalk figurines of special significance obtained from a *curandero* or faith healer, the smoking of a cigarette to pacify the devil, and the consumption of chasers of 80 proof alcohol brewed in the region. Anointment of these offerings takes place in all four directions.

Pachamama has been given a Catholic base by her people as well. During the two major religious festivals I attended – Our Lady of Guadalupe, described above, and All Souls Eve, featured below – I repeatedly heard prayers that used *Pachamama* and Virgin Mary interchangeably. The legend about how the Virgin of Guadalupe festival gained importance in Chimpa Rodeo highlights this syncretism – the intimate marriage of Indigenous and Catholic belief. An elder from Chimpa Rodeo recounted this story to one of my IPTK colleagues.

This event occurred more than a hundred years ago, around the year 1862. Don Vincente Ticona was admiring a very pretty stone in an area called pasto cancha, the pasture field. Out of curiosity, he picked it up. As soon as he did, his calzuna or pants fell down without anyone having touched them. He tried to pick the rock up again since he wanted to take it home, but each time he attempted to touch the stone, his waist belt loosened even though it had been fastened tightly and his pants fell down again. So he decided to leave the stone in the same place, thinking that it might be a sacred object. Indeed, it wasn't just an ordinary stone, but rather had, on one side, the image of the Virgin of Guadalupe.

Don Vincent Ticona was the arrendero (a local leadership position within the arriendo, the colonial land demarcation system that incorporated local hamlets) and advised the people of the area to move the object to a secure place, in the middle of a craggy peak that was nearby. Afterwards, Juán Ckasickora took it to his house in Ravelo and there the image of the Virgin of Guadalupe disappeared.

One day, those who were shepherding sheep in the pasto cancha, saw in the sky a splendid dove that was flying in the direction of a rock. It approached and sat there, completely still. And so the shepherds approached the rock to see what would happen. But they did not see a dove. It had disappeared. What they saw in this space was once again the image of the Virgin of Guadalupe. It was a miraculous apparition for the shepherds. It is possible that it was present to appease, reflect on, and correct the situation of the Natives who were suffering the abuse and exploitation of landholders who benefited from their free servitude.

Once the people of the Chimpa Rodeo arriendo learned of this miracle, they decided to construct a small chojlla [house] on this spot. They also informed the patrón, landowner Fortuoso Ramos, the mayordomo, or arriendero Mayor, Valintín Mamani, and the administrator Ricardo Muñoz. The patrón didn't believe them or pay much attention to the report.

There was one of those days of black clouds and storms, when you feared nature's power. So they had a meeting with the mayordomo, the administrator and the people of Huayllas and they constructed a chapel on the site where the rock with the image of the Virgin of Guadalupe stood.

At that time, a foreigner, Don Pascual Choquiviri from Condo in the department of Oruro, arrived with his llamas. When he saw the image [of the Virgin] he attempted to capture and visualize it by painting it [on the rock]. He was not successful and fell gravely ill. His son, therefore, had to complete his father's work.

Afterwards, the parish of Ravelo was invited to exorcize and bless [the chapel] and celebrate a mass, where many people had gathered. Later, the Bishop of Potosí also celebrated a mass there. Since then, every September 8th a mass is celebrated and they have a festival with much devotion.[2]

As well as demonstrating the grafting of Catholic symbols onto Indigenous ones, this story appears to have foreshadowed liberation from the *hacendado* landlord. Myths and legends often represent a weaving of long-standing beliefs into one's experience of the new social or political order. In cases of oppression, they can invert, even subvert the oppressor's message through a comparatively safe critique of the dominant order – the insider joke the outsider doesn't quite get.[3] This local legend also demonstrates the error in assuming that physical and political domination also lead to a colonization of the spirit.

This deliberate, albeit often clandestine, cultural defiance of Western authority became still clearer to me during a tour of the exquisite coin museum in the Potosí's capital city – Potosí – and earlier in the day when my family and I toured a worker-run, subsistence mine. This once favoured industry had not only robbed Potosí's Indigenous farm families' of the agricultural bounty their ancestors once enjoyed, and of the sons who could earn additional family income, but also of a connection to land that was profoundly spiritual. Not surprisingly, a good measure of that spirituality found its way into the mineshaft.

POTOSÍ, 17 AUGUST 2000

At almost 4,000 meters, this city is supposed to be one of the highest in the world. We drove here from Sucre yesterday in just over two hours on a well-paved road, thanks no doubt to Potosí's once successful mines and to the city's status as the capital of the department. But how dramatically different this historic city is from its far wealthier cousin over a kilometer down the mountainside. In its sixteenth- and seventeenth-century mining heydays, the city was one of the wealthiest in the world. Now it is Sucre, the intellectual heart of the country thanks to its government agencies and well-established universities, that offers greater comforts.

Potosí has its charms. Its residents are warm and pleasant. And there are colonial buildings that, while unattended, still impress. But this miners' town seems naked, raw, unrelenting in its demands, clearly ignored by the powerful now that the mining industry has essentially collapsed. There are still working mines. But only a couple of comparatively minor operations remain mechanized.

It is so-called cooperative, hand-to-mouth artisanal mining that shapes this city's character today. Many of its miners have no other choice but to continue to eke a living out of a system that seems to be on life support. Miners' lung prevents travel to other elevations or back to the land of food producers. So with headlamps to guide them, down they descend, every day, through a maze of pitch-black tunnels. They use pick axes to chip out bits of the low-grade ore that remains, hoping to collect enough to sell in the already depressed market.

It is an incredibly dreary world down there. An interest in tourist dollars allows those of us who can handle enclosed spaces to climb down with a guide – a former miner, we were relieved to learn. We were given raincoats, rubber boots, hard hats, headlamps, and assurances that we would not be in any real danger. We were also told to purchase dynamite, coca leaves, a tiny flask of whiskey, and cigarettes to offer as gifts of appreciation. The miners needed the coca to curb their appetites and the sticks of dynamite to find the more productive veins. The cigarettes, a handful of the coca leaves, and the flask of whiskey were actually for El Tío (the uncle), the spirit owner of the mountain. He is represented by a devil-faced mannequin sitting in a grotto-like altar on every level of the mineshaft. If honoured properly, he will keep his miners out of harm's way. If not, he shows no mercy, evidenced in the long list of lives he has claimed over the mine's history.[4] We managed to make it down into the third mineshaft, Kelsey clearly the quickest at scurrying down the rope ladders that were anchored only at the top. It was an experience unlike any other. The El Tío we found on level three was the largest in the mine, we were told, and the most menacing. Our guide encouraged us to set down the appropriate libations for this venerated devil-god and then to hand over the remaining offerings we had purchased to nearby miners. We seem to be missing one stick of dynamite. "Perhaps we miscounted," I thought. (On our return aboveground, we discovered it in Kelsey's oversized left boot!)

I had read about El Tío but was grateful for this "face-to-face" opportunity to witness yet another reinterpretation of Christian symbolism. For a moment, my fascination with El Tío made me forget about the absolute drudgery of the work I was witnessing. In my fifteen or so years of work in international development assistance, I have witnessed some pretty depressing working conditions. This need to enter the bowels of a desolate subterranean world on a daily basis might well top the list.

Earlier this afternoon, we had the opportunity to see the "flip side of the coin," literally. Potosí has maintained an impeccably designed museum, La Casa de la Moneda, to chronicle the transformation of the ore into the silver currency that once lined the pockets of the aristocracy of Imperial Spain. The extensive collection of early European coins, like the refurbished machinery used to produce it, was pretty impressive. Seeing the drawers and trunks spilling with coins and actually getting to hold a handful made the idea of Potosí as one of the richest cities in the sixteenth century imaginable. But it was the collection of colonial paintings on the walls of the museum's high-ceilinged rooms that proved to be my most interesting discovery.

As we travelled from wall-sized fresco to fresco of European gentry on horses, in battles, adoring their saints, our guide repeatedly pointed to small anomalies. The Indigenous artists who had produced the paintings, it turns out, had painted carefully disguised images of Andean mythology and beliefs. If you look really carefully at the giant paintings of generals or gentry, you can find tiny laughing devils or many limbed animal figures (like *khurus*) hidden in the background images. While the Hispanic commissioners and audiences of these massive works of art admired the might and majesty of Spanish and Catholic imperialism, their Indigenous subjects cleverly mocked them.

The stitching of the modern onto traditional ways or vice versa, although neither straightforward nor free of tension, should not, as noted in my comments about Jalq'a youth, be interpreted automatically as a sign of unwelcome acculturation. Nor was the abandonment of more traditional ways straightforward or uniform. For instance, while *curanderos* – faith healers – were no longer a presence in Chimpa Rodeo (although they were in Mojón), I found evidence of Chimpa Rodeo residents continuing to use such services. They were quite familiar with Western medical services. A small health post was a mere forty-five minute walk away. The international NGO delivering health programming in the area repeatedly advised against dependency on *curanderos*. Yet, even though travel to an Indigenous healer was often a much longer trek than that to the nearby health post, or to Ravelo's municipal health centre, I discovered continued use of *curandero* services. Indeed, one of the *curandero's* patients was a trained healthcare promoter from Chimpa Rodeo. She sought the services of a *curandero* to deal with severe headaches, dizziness, and blurred vision (that sounded to me like a migraine condition). She had tried the remedies offered through the local health post – quite likely mild painkillers, since staff rarely had stronger, more expensive medicines to offer. They hadn't worked. After just two visits to the curandero, she reported that the headaches and other symptoms had almost entirely disappeared.

Longstanding traditions, rituals, and belief systems are not easily abandoned; to the contrary they can offer a sense of continuity and comfort, especially if the push into another system is forceful. The continuing practice of All Souls Eve and All Saints Day in Mojón, described in this next journal entry, is a striking example of resistance to forces that might lead to disconnection from one's ancestral and spiritual roots. It was also on this occasion that I learned, the hard way, about the deep-seated importance of respect for ritual and cultural norms within Jalq'a society.

ALL SOULS EVE, MOJÓN, 1 NOVEMBER 2000

All Souls Eve and I have finally made it to Mojón. The trek took me at least two hours longer than usual since the shortcut I tried to take led me to another valley, down the wrong ridge into another village. I had to climb still further down to the river to get my bearings and then climb all the way back up a ridge to find the road to Mojón. The brutality of, by then, the midday sun was an especially humbling reminder of my vulnerability in the mountain world of the Jalq'a. The shortcut had seemed so straightforward when I was last guided through it. How eagerly we fool ourselves! These sculptured ridges refuse to let me lower my guard.

My truck ride in from Sucre to the foot of my hiking trail was also no picnic. All Souls Eve marks the beginning of the planting season, with seeding begun immediately after the three days of festivity. It draws Sucre's temporary migrants back to their villages in droves. The *flotas* or buses are packed so tightly there is barely room to exhale. I opted, therefore, for a lift on a potato truck. It was surprisingly empty when I jumped into its wooden carriage. I thought, "humph, that's lucky." Not long after, I realized that I had simply arrived early. The truck was full to the brim when the driver put it into gear for the three-hour trip ahead. By the time we rattled onto the potholed dirt road outside Sucre's city limits, human, animal, and agricultural cargo occupied every inch of the floorboards, except for a tiny patch that riders had cleared in a flash after a toddler lost his breakfast. I settled myself on my knapsack, my back against the carriage wall, my knees jammed tightly against one of the several bags of the popular 18-40-60 fertilizer, compliments of the Japanese government's aid program. The young woman beside me was soon snoring comfortably on my left shoulder. The comparatively new tires on the truck left me somewhat reassured that it could handle the hairpin curves of the mountain switchbacks. I was less comfortable with thoughts of what might happen to the full canisters of cooking gas several riders used as seats. "What if this truck hits a particularly stubborn pothole, an unexpected boulder or heaven forbid, another vehicle?" I said to myself. "Don't go there, Susie!"

Fortunately when the cramps in my legs felt almost unbearable, about half way there, we stopped for a bathroom break. I found what I thought was a discreet spot behind some boulders and proceeded to empty a very full bladder. Nearing completion I looked up to find that on the opposite ridge another lorry filled to the brim had arrived. "Could they see me blush?" I wondered. Back on the truck, I decided to stand for the rest of the journey.

And now as I head to the Mojón cemetery with Elvira and her children to witness the rituals of *Todos Santos*, I find myself in almost complete darkness. The overcast moonless night befits the fast-approaching visitation of the dead. My small flashlight, with a very low battery, barely lights the narrow footpath and I stumble several times on its many small boulders and rocks. I am careful not to drop the large bag of coca leaves I purchased during our stopover in Ravelo, knowing the importance of an offering to dead souls and especially their living offspring. I only hope that I have brought enough.

We arrive at the cemetery, trading the dark for a brightly lit walled cemetery. Inside the stone fencing, this graveyard has been transformed into an amazing candle-lit tent community. One of the many hosts present greets us at the gate and grants us permission to enter. Elvira warns me to enter with my left foot to protect me from the forces of death. "Asi no moremos," she advises. ("This way, we won't die!")

Surrounding each of the tombstones of participating families are cave-shaped tents made of bent branches that are covered with a dust-coloured canvas. The opening is wide and inviting in the front and narrow and stooped at the back. There is enough room in each for about ten people. Ornamentation is saved for the tombstones themselves.

Drab, flat slabs of cement have been turned into giant "wedding cakes" – three-tiered altars decorated with colourful hand-drawn or cutout images of a spirit world and figures, much like those of the creation-chaos cosmos in their traditional weavings. There are crosses in these images, however, acknowledging the Catholic roots of this celebration, betraying again the post-colonial fusion of Catholic and Indigenous imagery.

The candles that offer both light and heat are of all shapes and sizes, the largest, at least a meter tall and 10 centimeters in diameter. It was no doubt purchased from the stalls of candle merchants that line the gates of Sucre's many Catholic churches. Most of these candles are painted with large, gold crosses.

Family members sit on either side of the altar, there to welcome deceased relatives who are "returning" to give spiritual counsel to their offspring. They mourn, reminisce, pray, and give offerings both to a recently deceased grandparent, parent, spouse, brother, sister, or child as well as to their more distant ancestors and of course *Pachamama*. Coca leaves are the most important offering, but *chicha* and alcohol are also sprinkled onto the tombstone and *Pachamama*'s soils. For this occasion alone, *mast'akus*, dolls made of unleavened bread, eyes blackened with wood charcoal, are placed on the altar to feed the hungry spirits. As with all auspicious occasions, cigarettes are smoked to placate the devil. The men in particular consume large amounts of chicha and alcohol throughout this dusk to dawn memorial. Participation is not restricted to one's own tent. Every tent is visited to ensure that all spirits, many of them of near and distant relatives, are shown their due respect.

With its unfolding just prior to planting and its emphasis on the return of the dead, *Todos Santos* is mythologically associated with the power of growth and reproduction.[5] This calling of old and young spirits to return to the family hearth for a brief reunion, strikes me as a useful mechanism to cope with the grief of death that comes all too frequently on tough rural landscapes.

As outsiders, albeit invited ones, my teacher-guide, Elvira, her children, and I decide not to overstay our welcome within this otherwise private, community-based memorial. Despite repeated invitations to spend the night, we leave the increasingly boisterous gathering quietly, making our way down the now almost invisible path home. We agree to return at dusk to witness the close of these ceremonies.

ALL SAINTS DAY, 2 NOVEMBER 2000

I awake at the crack of dawn, as usual not having slept terribly well
thanks to the chorus of mice running wild in my makeshift bedroom in
the family's kitchen. Despite my requests that we get a move on in the
early morning, we leave for the cemetery later than I had hoped. When
we approach the cemetery, I see that it has been stripped of its festive
mantle and a final group of mourners is heading down the path. One of
my friends shouts from a distance for me to join them. I hesitate because
by now the level of intoxication is such that the chatter will be incessant
and I will likely not have a chance to see the cemetery in its pre-festive
state. I decide to run to the cemetery for a quick look before joining him
and the others. I dash ahead, step through the gate, snap a few quick
photographs of the now emptied graveyard, then head back down the
path to the group.

As I approach my friend, I grasp and actually gasp at the error of my
Western way. I want to kick myself. Of course, the cemetery is a sacred
place. I need permission to enter. Damn! The others seem oblivious to
my actions, caught up in their own chatter and thoughts. But I overhear
my friend and his wife discussing my arrogance. I have betrayed their
trust. I apologize profusely, explaining that I had assumed that the permission granted the night before would suffice. But in my split-second
decision to satisfy my curiosity, I become just another *Gringa* researcher,
out to get what I needed. I fear that there will be little that I can say or
do in the limited time left of this research year to rebuild that trust. For
a second time in twenty-four hours, I have lost my bearings and I am
forced to appreciate my vulnerability in the world of another.

My friend and I did speak again today. He was polite. But he seemed
to want to avoid me. In his now cautious eyes, I am reminded of the pre-
cariousness of the insider-outsider relationship and of how easily greed –
in this case my desire to get those damn photos – can trump respect.

During my early days with the Jalq'a farmers of Chimpa Rodeo and Mojón,
they struck me as active agents in their transition to a world of blended
traditions and practices.[6] My first-hand experiences in their festivals rein-
forced this thinking. They made choices and constructed meaning that
made sense to them within a context of cultural and historical realities
that were in a state of flux, not unlike the ecological conditions they had
to monitor so carefully.[7] It is to this specific understanding and interaction with the ecology of their landscapes that this book will soon turn. It

does so via a short chapter about the crucial theoretical construct for the book – resilience. When I headed to the majestic mountains of the Jalq'a in the year 2000, it was through a resilience lens that I hoped to gain insights into their world and time-tested knowledge systems. And it was indeed through this lens that I grew to appreciate the significance and sophistication of those systems for survival on their ever-challenging and unforgiving Andean landscapes.

5

Bouncing Back

This habit of observing natural objects and natural processes in their isolation
... detached ... from the whole vast interconnectedness of things ... [presents
them] ... not as essentially changing, but as fixed constants; not in their life, but
in their death.

Frederich Engels, circa 1875[1]

"All effects we observe in the world of experience," wrote Johann Wolf-
gang von Goethe in the late eighteenth century, "are interrelated in the
most constant manner and merge into one another. From the first to the
last, they form a series of undulations."[2] With these words and within
many of his scientific writings, Goethe, philosopher, scientist, poet, and, I
would add, pioneer ecologist, challenged his fellow citizens to consider
nature and humanity's role within it as dynamic and interconnected, an
ever-changing web of activity. I can just imagine him rolling his eyes with
impatience at his contemporaries who were determined to break nature
down, order, compartmentalize, and sequence nature's component parts.[3]
There have of course been other scientific rebels who subsequently questioned the Cartesian logic of seventeenth-century rationalism.[4] In the
1930s and 1940s general systems theorists, for example, refuted the value
of isolating the particular to explain the whole.[5] They asked their fellow
scientists to consider instead the interrelationships, context, and feedback
mechanisms of natural systems. Understanding, they insisted, comes from
an exploration of how the parts operate together, not from examining
them as separate entities.[6]

Grabbing the baton these system theorists tossed to them, as well as that
of complexity theorists in their wake, are the new rebels of the natural sci-

ences – resilience scientists. These scholars, many of them ecologists, also question the adequacy of models and perspectives based on compartmentalized research and sequential, linear processes. They focus instead on the diversity within, and complexity of, our natural and social resource systems and call for new strategies to manage that complexity. We need qualitative data to complement quantitative data, they propose, and multiple perspectives in the analysis and stewardship of complex ecosystems.[7] But what exactly is resilience?

Resilience, in essence, is the capacity of a system to cope with disturbance, stress, or change without altering its fundamental character or identity in any dramatic way. The concept is built on longstanding study of the capacity of ecological systems to cope or cave with disturbance. There must be built-in options and enough redundancy in the system to better respond to perturbations. The theory has its strongest roots in ecology. C.S. (Buzz) Holling defined resilience in the early 1970s as the ability of a system to adapt to change and disturbance while still remaining within a critical threshold. Ecological change within this definition is not continuous and gradual but rather episodic. An earlier and more traditional definition – engineering resilience – drew on traditions of deductive mathematical theory and engineering. It concentrated on stability near an equilibrium state, with the focus on resistance to disturbance and on the speed of return to equilibrium.[8] With the emergence of the Resilience Alliance at the beginning of the twenty-first century (described below), the two definitions merged. Resilient systems, it is commonly accepted, self-organize, learn, and adapt to stresses.[9]

More recently, psychologists, mental health specialists, and a still wider range of social scientists have entered the field of resilience, paying particular attention to the concept as it relates to people and their capacity to deal with adversity.[10] The intimate connection between ecological and social resilience has also fostered research into the resilience of social systems. The emphasis here is on the notion of how social cohesion and a society's ability to innovate build resilience.

The broadening and popularization of resilience as a leading concept among development and environmental agencies occurred in the early days of this new century. In June 2002, scientists from across the globe – many of them ecologists – gathered in Stockholm to review progress on conservation initiatives launched at the Earth Summit ten years earlier. They issued this statement: "Resilience is important because resilience systems persist, prosper, innovate, and give rise to the systems of the future.

There is no optimal path for systems of people and nature, but there are desirable and undesirable ones. We can use resilience to break down undesirable paths and create or sustain desirable paths." [11]

A consortium of institutions and research groups – the Resilience Alliance – subsequently formed to advance the idea that environmental management and climate change work must be assessed through a resilience lens. Members emphasized three critical features of resilient systems: the ability to maintain a particular pathway or set of conditions, despite disturbances; the capacity for self-organization (as opposed to either a lack of organization or organization forced by external factors); and the capacity for learning and adaptation. [12] Since resilience is concerned with a system's ability to absorb or buffer disturbance without undergoing fundamental changes in its functions or basic characteristics, it is correctly associated with diversity. [13] Inter- and intra-species variety, numerous and varied human opportunities, and a good selection of economic options enhance a system's capacity to "withstand shocks and surprises, and if damaged, to rebuild itself." [14]

Attention to the interaction between ecological and social disturbances is thus especially significant. Disturbances within a system are not only generated through naturally occurring events like forest fires and insect outbreaks, [15] but human-induced ones, like pollution or overfishing. A natural system's responses to resource use and the reciprocal response of people to changes in the natural ecosystems, resilience scientists report, "constitute coupled, dynamic systems that exhibit adaptive behavior." [16]

Social and environmental systems are, of course, very complex and our knowledge of them is always incomplete. We must, as a result, strive to reduce the degree of uncertainty about their dynamics. We need, in short, to look carefully at what is going on, what we have going for us, where the gaps are, and what we can do to manage our risk. The back-up system to be found in an area rich in biodiversity, for example, is at the ready should the unexpected happen. A culture of innovation to handle change that cannot be predicted is also a must. [17] Building resilience is therefore rather straightforward. To maintain it, we need systems thinking and adaptive management. Adaptive governance has emerged, in fact, as a central concept for the management of complex ecological and social environments. [18]

An especially useful idea employed to assess the resilience in natural systems is that of a critical threshold. When resilience is strong, disturbances may modify but not fundamentally change the system's core structure and strength. When resilience is weak, a disturbance can overtake a critical threshold, contributing to what ecologists have termed a "flip," the shift to a state that is less desirable and sometimes irreversible.[19] Social systems also have critical thresholds, with less resilient social systems demonstrating vulnerability to environmental and social change or economic or political upheaval. In the short term, they may be able to continue to generate resources and services, but only as long as the disturbances or stresses do not exceed the systems' capacity to cope. Once at the threshold, popularly called the tipping point, even the smallest of disturbances – the proverbial straw that broke the camel's back – can send a social system over the brink and into a new reality. For many Newfoundland coastal communities, the loss of the cod fishery is an example of a human-induced flip. Not only did their fishing industry collapse, but related businesses also failed, sparking significant outward migration. Even the survival of the codfish itself is in question. Within Atlantic waters, at least, scientists fear that cod numbers might never revive to viable commercial fishing levels.[20]

The catch of one too many cod off the Eastern seaboard is linked, of course, to the institutional systems that governed and guided fishers' activities. Human decision-making plays a key role in the resilience equation. When a community resource like cod becomes a diffuse global commodity, exploited in huge volumes in an effort to gain the competitive advantage – an uncaught fish being a lost opportunity – there is a tendency to ignore declining stocks until they are quite visibly threatened. The community resource becomes an industrial commodity divorced from its place in the natural environment or its role in building a thriving community-based and culturally important enterprise.

The socio-cultural context within which change takes place is thus central to the resilience of institutions and communities. So too are the knowledge systems that influence human interaction with the environment.[21] For an effective assessment of a particular community or region's resilience, local residents, their knowledge and their institutions, must be at the centre of this evaluation process, setting criteria and establishing the protocol. There are, nevertheless, general principles and characteristics of community resilience that could serve as useful guidelines. Borrowing, adapting, and adding on to Simon Levin's insightful "commandments" for the management of complex environmental systems,[22] I developed a list of nine indicators of community resilience to guide my research in the year 2000 and my professional work more generally.

COMMUNITY RESILIENCE

Resilient communities, I would suggest, have the following, often over-lapping, characteristics. First, they act in ways that reduce uncertainty and risk. There is a careful reading and monitoring of internal and external forces that can affect their status and a deliberate spreading of risk. With-in mountain farming systems like those in Bolivia, for example, risk re-duction would involve knowing the diverse ecosystems and their func-tions well and consciously producing on landscapes with diverse growing conditions.

Second, resilient communities are prepared for surprises, exhibiting strong adaptive management strategies. To do so, rigid structures are avoided and change is embraced. Rules and protocols should be adjustable, constantly monitored, and changed on the basis of new infor-mation or new insights. There is a continued probing of alternative man-agement strategies and therefore considerable flexibility and openness to learn. Knowledge is grounded in experience. It is dynamic and evolving.

Heterogeneity is a third fundamental component of a resilient system. Within ecological systems, the maintenance of biological diversity, in all its forms, is key. As we lose species, we lose options. Cultural or generational homogeneity similarly contributes to a narrower knowledge base from which to solve problems. Variability within systems and among systems, including culturally based knowledge systems, broadens our choices.

Sustaining modularity within a system – independent components that are interlinked but can be disconnected when necessary – is a fourth important element in a resilient system. Within ecosystems, modular structures provide a buffer against cascades of disaster. Institutions within communities and social systems likewise have a better chance of survival against internal or external upheaval if they are decentralized and multi-faceted.

A fifth characteristic that is too often missed by those eager to create "efficiencies" in their organizations is the importance of thinking long-term and preserving redundancy. Redundant components in a system are those whose value becomes clear only when other parts are lost – like the back-up copy of a belaboured and beloved manuscript. A lack of redun-dancy in tightly rationalized Western institutions can mean the loss of critical functions when unexpected disturbances require institutional memory and experience. Similarly, the knowledge of seniors and elders within a community can be critical to coping with an unexpected crisis.

To encourage behaviour for the good of the commons and its inhabitants, the distance between decision, activity, and benefit must be shortened and a sense of shared responsibility and ownership of the activity strengthened. The sixth critical ingredient for community resilience is thus tight feedback loops. Consideration of the scale of an activity is therefore critical.[23] Failed or abandoned large "white elephant" programs that were run from above, or from afar, are all too common examples of structure and scale that did not offer local ownership or the opportunity to learn.

Linked to adequate and tight feedback is the building of trust, the seventh key ingredient in a resilient community. Trust is perhaps one of the most difficult characteristics to sustain. Essential for its maintenance is leadership that establishes governance systems at a size that allows for the negotiation of a common agenda. The larger and more centralized the universe of actors, the harder it is to build confidence in the other. Getting to know the key actors through repeated engagement is also important, and may even lead to reciprocal altruism, or at the very least, reciprocal exchange, since reciprocity in a relationship often has a very pragmatic base. In sum, creating a culture of trusted decision-making, and enhancing opportunities to build on each other's knowledge, is crucial to strengthened resilience.

Characteristic eight is the commitment to act for the collective good. Unbridled competition and divisiveness can send a community into an abyss of conflict and destruction. Again, the decline of the cod fishery is instructive.

Finally, any worthwhile assessment of a community's ability to maintain heterogeneity and diversity, to learn to live with and learn from change and disturbance, to carve out meaningful spaces for the building of trust and for practices in favour of the common good and finally, to nurture and act on knowledge that is helpful to the community, must assess the question of power. Who gets to make the decisions and who will benefit? Resilient communities are open, willing to share knowledge and to address control and ownership issues in inclusive ways.

As with all concepts that come into vogue within the field of international development assistance, there are now critics of resilience, largely related to when it is used as a mechanistic instrument for social change. Misuses aside, as a guiding principle for lasting change, the strengthening of resilience is an extremely attractive alternative to the more limiting, often pejorative, concept of poverty reduction. When we think about poverty, we tend to think about what is lacking either within poor communities or within the psyche of their residents. The dearth of healthy soils for food production, for example, leads to conclusions about local capacity to effect change. "These poor farmers cannot even manage their soils," the thinking goes. This conclusion, in turn, contributes to an outsider-driven program to fix the problem or fill the void, often with recipes that either worked for the outsiders or that suit their interests. A resilience approach to soil erosion would look first at what already exists or had existed, not the least of which could be long-standing local practices to enhance the soil that for one reason or another had been abandoned. Once these practices are identified, factors that are undermining them – internal and external – are investigated and addressed. You start, in short, with strengths that can be built on and then trouble-shoot. Even in the direst of circumstances, there is resilience to be found, since the act of survival is itself an example of core strength and staring down adversity.[24]

I headed to my fieldwork with a conceptual understanding of resilience. The Indigenous farmers of Chimpa Rodeo and Mojón taught me most about its application. Of particular interest was their practice of a once broad-based, pan-Andean, governance and food production system – ecological complementarity. This system is intimately linked to their sense of who they are, of their landscape, and of their responsibilities to each other. Because it informs their application of ecological complementarity and the broader concept of resilience, the next chapter begins, with a discussion of the hitherto little-studied history of the Jalq'a and their somewhat puzzling place within that pan-Andean governance system.

6

Ecological Complementarity

REINVENTED

The story of ethnicity of the Jalq'a people of Chimpa Rodeo and Mojón is a rather mysterious and confusing one. The Jalq'a speak Quechua, a language with an estimated eight million speakers spread largely in the Andean regions of South America. They proudly claim descent from the Inca Empire. They are easily identifiable through their unique clothing, instruments, songs, rituals, and weavings. In Bolivia, they are largely smallholder farmers of the valley hilltops and lower highlands. Their presence at these elevations is, however, the first signal of some perplexity. In Peru, the term *jalka* or *jalca* is used to refer to residents of the upper highlands or *puna alta*.[1] The Bolivian term Jalq'a seems not, therefore, to be borrowed from Peru.

Another explanation for their identity as Jalq'a may rest in the meaning of a subset of their name: *alqa* or *allqa*. This term, used in both the Quechua and Aymara languages, describes an optical representation of contrast and disjunction that can be seen in Jalq'a textiles.[2] Jalq'a clothing and textiles reflect an extensive use of opposing colours and figures: black and red, green and red, and blue and orange, with patterns that are geometrically divergent and animal figures that are morphologically impossible. This explanation of their name, although tempting, is speculative since, as noted, there is very little documentation about the Jalq'a people. My archival research in Sucre, for example, uncovered no mention of this particular ethnic group. There are comparatively recent pamphlets about the Jalq'a's exquisite weavings, rituals, and world view, further addressed below. But as the anthropologist I met from a Sucre-based foundation that produced these short texts confirmed, the Jalq'a appear to be absent from the scores of colonial and early republican chronicles that they combed through. In contrast to the substantial tracts capturing the life and times of neighbouring llama-herding groups, one is hard pressed to find specifics about the Jalq'a name, culture, history, and traditions.[3] Since the Jalq'a are one of the major ethnic groups within a two-hour radius of the country's constitutional capital, this seems a rather curious oversight.

The location of the Jalq'a within the *ayllu* system of traditional governance that continues to operate in this region[4] is especially confusing. An *ayllu* is a complex, segmented land management strategy as well as social and governance system that has existed over a broad area in the Andes from pre-Inca times to the present. In the Bolivian *puna* or highlands (low and high), the households of individual hamlets formed segments of more inclusive and larger social groups – minimal to maximal. Each territorial and kinship unit is a part of an even larger one – like nesting dolls or inlaid boxes – culminating in one large entity or tribe that itself has two halves, called moieties. These bifurcated moieties relate to each other as complementary opposites based on unilateral, or independent, descent, as well as on opposition such as below-above, masculine-feminine, older-younger, and so forth.[5] At the core of this *ayllu* system is a very sophisticated and multifaceted regional governance and livelihood strategy called ecological complementarity.[6]

In a 1994 atlas of the *ayllus* of Northern Potosí,[7] researchers do list the Jalq'a. Yet, they are simply listed as members of one of three subgroups of the maximal *ayllu*, Tinkipaya Chhaxru, the two others being the Tinkipayas and Yamparas. A publication two years later suggests a slightly more complex pattern. The Jalq'a are named as a subunit of both the Yampara ethnic group and the Tinkipaya subgroup. Both subunits, it is suggested, ultimately belong to the Moromoro *ayllu* of the Qharaqhara *ayllu*, the lower moiety of its maximum twin, the Charkas ayllu.[8] Making sense of this extremely complex system is mind-boggling. Early on in my research, I thought that it might be best to settle for the verdict of elderly informants in the 1996 *ayllu* guide. They declared with confidence that the Jalq'a have existed since the time of the Incas.[9]

Not long after reading the guide, during a stroll down my home street in Sucre, Calle Potosí, I happened on a museum that shed further, if still incomplete, light on their origins. The museum, conveniently located a half block from my home, was filled with Jalq'a textiles. The organization running the museum was an association of Bolivian anthropologists, briefly mentioned earlier. It was called the Foundation for Anthropological Investigation and Ethno Development, commonly referred to by the Spanish acronym, ASUR. The museum's window display of exquisite handspun and woven wool textiles drew me inside. I was thrilled to discover that this work was the artistry of the Jalq'a of both Chuquisaca and of my research focus, Potosí.

The foundation had determined to revive and revalue the Jalq'a's art form – it had begun to disappear in the late twentieth century – with great success it turned out. Large tapestries were attracting foreign visitors and robust foreign sales. I picked up a booklet about the textiles that included an interesting hypothesis about the origins of the Jalq'a. The idea was that as a unified group with distinct dress, rituals, and so forth, the Jalq'a might well be a reinvented or reconfigured ethnic unit. Indeed, the Jalq'a might well have represented a corporate coming together of various disenchanted *ayllu* units seeking a refreshed identity. Their beginning might have been as recent as the nineteenth century.[10]

While Jalq'a origins may always remain a mystery, their world view and ways of interacting with each other and the outside world do not betray transient or superficial invention. The thought structure so pronounced in their weavings and rituals reveals complex beliefs that differ significantly from those of their Llamero neighbours. The Jalq'a, as noted, adhere to a chaos-creation world view, whereas the Llamero are oriented toward conservation of order. In sharp contrast to the Jalq'a, Llamero patterns on textiles, for example, are very symmetrical and ordered. Still, both groups share the concept of duality that is characteristic of a pan-Andean world view.[11] My own observations of the Jalq'a I interacted with support this conclusion.

Despite some intrinsic structural differences thanks to their differing relationships with external actors, both Chimpa Rodeo and Mojón appeared to embrace the common macro-identity of the Jalq'a. The ex-hacienda residents of Chimpa Rodeo did not reference participation in a particular *ayllu*. The residents of the *originario* or untouched Mojón did. Still, both communities held on to *ayllu* governance practices, like consensus decision-making and rotational leadership, even within imposed union structures. Of course, the ability to deal with differing or opposing orientations at once is hardly unique within the Andean context. And while we may not be able to link the Jalq'a name to contrasts and opposites in any definitive way, their material culture reveals deep interest in disjunction and juxtaposition.[12]

The differences between ex-hacienda and originario communities were connected to their varied histories of interaction with the outside world and development agents. As will be seen in Chimpa Rodeo and Mojón, these were largely related to their land-use practices. More generally, however, I observed Jalq'a household traditions, festival celebrations, and attitudes that revealed a Jalq'a identity that was both unifying and elastic all in one. An incident within a municipal planning workshop that gathered Jalq'a representatives from across Ravelo offered a particularly strong example of the strength of the unity side of the equation.

Representatives from the originario Jalq'a community of Qhara-qhara joined the Ravelo meeting. Departmental bureaucrats from Potosí had drawn them into the neighbouring municipality of Ocuri, a largely Llamero territory. This technocratic decision did not sit well with Qharaqharanians. So, they determined to participate in the meeting of *their* people and sent a full delegation to the Ravelo meeting. Much to the dismay of municipal officials, their Jalq'a kin welcomed them with open arms, insisting on their participation. The authorities were given no choice but to count them in. They participated in all planning exercises. The broader group also pledged to campaign against the government's unilateral redrawing of the political boundaries. Borders be damned, they would not be told where they belonged.

Another characteristic of the Jalq'a people is of relevance to this study and might indeed support the notion of a reinvented Jalq'a lineage. Jalq'a reports about their socio-political structures and claims to ayllu membership were often vague. In originario Jalq'a communities selected residents maintained their traditional titles, like the local mayor – *acalde local*. But in contrast to some of the larger ethnic units in Northern Potosí, like the Macha and Tinkipaya, accountability to large regional *ayllu* authorities was less clearly defined.[13] Strong union and NGO influences undoubtedly served to diminish the authority of this traditional leadership.[14] My NGO colleagues insisted, in effect, that the union structure was the predominant one in Ravelo. However, I discovered long-standing ayllu-based production and governance practices woven into the new structure of their mestizo-dominated union world that made me question such a conclusion. Union rules were regularly broken when they didn't suit the decision to be made. There was a clever combination of traditional practice and new ways of behaving, with the former often winning the day. This flexibility blended with an inclusive world view to create a hybrid governance system. The strong duality of the Jalq'a cosmovision demonstrated a fascinating capacity to entertain co-existing and often-contradictory world views.[15]

When asked about their Jalq'a origins, participants in my study could not solve the puzzle for me. They reported only that their parents, grandparents, and great-grandparents were Jalq'a and that they were very different from the Llameros, particularly in their temperament. The Jalq'a, they insisted, were much less aggressive than their Llamero cousins, who, they noted with somewhat disparaging tones, still practised *t'inku* or ritualised battle. Several also claimed to be quite different from the "civilized" people of the city. They were simply who they were.

Clearly, there is no neat and tidy way to capture a peoples' ethnicity in all its complexity. But this unsolved tale of the conception and gestation of the Jalq'a identity and my readings about Andean identity more broadly have helped me to understand the question of identity in a new way.[16] As Andean ethnographers before me have written, pinpointing precise genealogy, lineage, or kinship boundaries may be of less importance than a focus on the changing nature of identity. As people encounter and manoeuvre through lives that are multifaceted and subject to ever-changing contexts, the dialectic or tension between the imagined and the real shapes experience.[17] In response to different political and social demands, new categories of belonging and membership will emerge. Nor can we forget that the worlds we construct must be seen in terms of the powers and pressure we face.[18] Finally, people will talk about themselves and their reality in different ways depending on where they are and with whom they are speaking. In the case of the Jalq'a, shifting context appears to have influenced reinvention.

"AYLLU … IZED" UNION

In both Chimpa Rodeo and Mojón, the more formalized *ayllu* structures had, as noted, given way to the Western structures of organized labour. In both Chimpa Rodeo and Mojón, it was the local *dirigente del sindicato* or shop steward of the local farmers' union who called the community meetings to order. An agenda was determined, participants' names recorded, minutes taken, and rules of order established. When I sat in on these meetings, however, it was soon clear that traditional governance systems had not been replaced entirely. The rotational leadership structure of the allyu system, for example, had been stubbornly maintained. The *dirigente* position rotated to a new family every year. Consensus decision-making and shared responsibility were also consistently preferred over a voting system in which a narrow majority ruled. These Jalq'a farmers welcomed resources from outsiders to help them to assert their rights vis-à-vis the dominant society. Within the mestizo-ruled world that had historically made them sit on the edges of power, the union structure, with its collective character seemed the best bet. But the wholehearted adoption of a majority rules system with winners and losers did not sit easily with people accustomed to cooperation and consensus for their survival and ultimate prosperity.

Nor did the value of "minutes" – the documented interpretation of the literate few – in any way outweigh the value of an openly negotiated verbal account of events and decisions. First, the minutes were very brief, largely capturing the fact that the meeting had taken place, the names of those in attendance, and sometimes the few points the meeting addressed. Discussion or important decisions were rarely captured on paper. The practice of having oral versus documented evidence offered the flexibility essential for people who placed community harmony ahead of a decision that in time might lose its relevance. Even when it was etched on paper, it was never etched in stone.

Mojón residents, less exposed to the practices of modernity, held on to more overt components of *ayllu* governance. Residents retained a couple of traditional positions including that of a community mayor or *alcalde comunal* and two local healers – *curanderos* – who practised a blend of faith healing and curative medicine. Local shrubs, herbs, and other substances with medicinal value, such as the use of human urine to treat a nagging cough, were in common use. The community mayor was tending his valley lands when I first spent time in Mojón and, for one reason or another, I never met him. I did get to meet the *curanderos*, thanks to the community's schoolteacher, my local host during overnight or multi-day visits.

DUAL HOMESTEADING

The best example of the continued application of the ayllu socio-political and economic system within my research communities was the ongoing practice of ecological complementarity. At the heart of the traditional *ayllu* governance and livelihood system is the simultaneous control by a single ethnic group of several dispersed ecological tiers – lands at differing altitudes – and the farming practices within those fields.[19] This system, initially referred to as a vertical production system featuring *doble domicilio* or dual homesteading, has since earned a more comprehensive label to reflect its more comprehensive character – ecological complementarity. The *ayllu's* internal processes of differentiation and governance are beautifully crafted to facilitate the division and management of these dispersed landholdings. The multiplicity of lands, spaced between *puna* and valley ecosystems, but of sufficiently close proximity, can serve both as an adaptation to high levels of climatic risk and as an effective method of generating wealth.[20] Marriage within the same larger clan – endogamy – is common, useful to the administration and control of lands spread over dispersed ecological zones. Built-in labour exchange mechanisms and the possibility of at least one of the ecological tiers – altitudes – surviving the hard lessons of an unpredictable mountain microclimate[21] contribute to an increased likelihood both of adequate subsistence and of production surpluses.

Ecological complementarity is, therefore, a very strategic approach to community food security, especially since the long-term security of any population is based on the options diversity offers, particularly during periods of weather extremes and maximum scarcity.[22] Attention to the reproduction of growing conditions and soil fertility – the land's productive capacity – must, therefore, trump a narrow focus on productivity and yield in any particular year. As the data in Appendix 4 reveal, in Mojón dual homesteading and migration to valley lands for several months at a time was extensive. In the wake of colonial land grabs, Chimpa Rodeo residents had abandoned this practice. Many male heads of households, however, still travelled to valleys after the planting season to graze their large animals, trading the services their animals can provide for the opportunity to have them graze.

Ecological complementarity is also a system that reconciles efficiency with labour requirements. Fields at higher altitude are repositories of clean potato seed [tubers] that can supply the lower intermontane valleys. This vertical organization permits a sequential timing of production tasks through a series of consecutive, although overlapping, agricultural cycles. Households can spread the demands on labour more evenly over the year while, at the same time, providing families with diverse and nutritionally balanced food from different ecological zones.[23] This was clearly the case in Mojón.

An especially impressive component of ecological complementarity is the ecologically friendly land management practice called *manta*. Within hamlets that practise it, including Mojón, a large number of fields are subject to communal decision-making. A plot of land, for example, might belong to a particular household within the community. But the decisions about which crops and which variety, to sow from year to year, about the crop rotation process, and about the fallow period for this manta field is communal.[24] This group decision-making structure ensured adherence to crop diversity, crop rotation, and fallow cycles that benefit both the community economy and the commons. Like marketing boards, inherent in this community decision-making process are market control mechanisms conducive to better returns on surplus production.

There may also be a justice ethic at work within this system. Mantas distribute risk among the family members of a hamlet, ensuring that all will receive at least a minimum level of production to satisfy their basic needs.[25] Through mantas, the community assumes responsibility for the welfare of the "old, the disabled, and the 'poor.'"[26] It has also been suggested that the manta system serves as a mechanism to increase a household's leverage when disputes arise over lands bordering a neighbouring ayllu. Community management reduces individual vulnerability to land usurpation. In sum, the system maintains an important internal control of vital resources.[27]

Another substantive feature of ecological complementarity is product exchange or bartering. Called *trueque*, it is an expression of Andean reciprocity between the *puna* and the valley. Anchored in a cosmovision that recognizes the give and take within both the natural and supernatural world, *trueque* is at the same time a practical response to the need for seeds or food that are unavailable at home and yet required for a balanced family diet. Diversity flourishes within this exchange mechanism.

The introduction of money into the livelihood system has reduced barter. But in 2000, and from what I observed during subsequent visits, it remains a critical ingredient in the subsistence and semi-subsistence strategies of farm families in Northern Potosí, including Jalq'a communities like Chimpa Rodeo and Mojón. Hand in hand with this product exchange is labour exchange. Three of the most common forms I observed in my research communities were: *ayni*, whereby a farm family will offer services, products, tools, or animals in direct exchange for another farm family's services, products, tools, or animals; *minka*, the name for group work parties that perform a service for a particular household with the hosts providing food and beverages as well as in-kind payment (produce) for their day or days of labour; and *faena*, the practice of having several households or the entire community pitch in to complete community service projects. I regularly found Mojón residents, for example, working together to repair the road into their community.

Scholars of the *trueque* system write that such transactions are often linked to a quest for social prestige and acceptance.[28] The families I grew to know well did not betray such motivation. They appeared to be more pragmatic about the exchange than anything else. However, my stay with them was too short-lived to assess this matter well. Whatever the inspiration, in contrast to the rules of competition in a Western market economy, these reciprocity processes are, with rare exceptions, of benefit to all involved parties.

The need for cash for products that cannot be harvested from the land such as metal tools, school books, clothing, or medicines, requires another strategy that is not always well understood by outsiders: temporary migration for paid labour. Most families I came to know in my host communities and beyond sent one or two of their young adult members to the city to work as day labourers or domestics for weeks at a time. Government and NGO extension agents tended to assess such migration as a sign of failure. The statistics are up, they would say with a discouraged sigh.

Families I talked to in Chimpa Rodeo and Mojón did not report this temporary departure in a negative light. Short-term labour migration was of long-standing and averaged a total of 29 days and 25 days among my respondent families in Chimpa Rodeo and Mojón. In colonial and early republican times Indigenous labourers were regularly plucked from their Potosí *parcelas* or fields for temporary work in tin and silver mines.[29] In 2000, Chimpa Rodeo and Mojón's youth were fortunately not forced into backbreaking labour inside their Potosí hillsides. But a journey to neighbouring Sucre, and in some cases Cochabamba, to support the family economy was anticipated. For first timers, it was an unnerving but expected rite of passage.

Two final features of this land management and livelihood system deserve to be highlighted. First, community leadership positions are rotational. In Chimpa Rodeo and Mojón they lasted a year and alternated among the male heads of households. Responsibility for governance was thus non-hierarchical and shared. No single family bore a long-term sacrifice of its strongest male producer; and no single family was afforded the opportunity to dominate the community's direction and affairs. Loyda Sanchez, a well-respected Bolivian educator whom I met in Santa Cruz,

explained to me that this communal sense of rotational leadership reflected an Andean preference for knowledge sharing and shared responsibility. She gained this insight the hard way, she explained. An activist working
the Bolivian front lines in the mid-1970s, she had attempted time and
again to organize Andean campesinos into syndicated cadres along "rational lines" that favoured the election of the "strongest" leaders. Until she
finally realized that her organizational logic just didn't fit with the
campesinos' sense of community, she failed miserably each time.[30]

Last, but in no way least, ecological complementarity has a very profound spiritual and intuitive dimension. Among Chimpa Rodeo and
Mojón residents there was a consistently strong consideration of the
broader cosmos evident in their land-use and production practices. Planting and harvest activities always began with a *ch'alla* blessing. A *ch'alla* is
likewise performed on new animals, tools, and agricultural inputs. Babies
are protected through the *ch'alla* long before parents bring them to the
Catholic priest for baptism. Most farmers I met also noted their consideration of the lunar cycle when deciding to plant or harvest their crops. To
ensure that one's steer will be *gordo* or fat, it should be castrated when the
moon is full. A careful monitoring of the flowers of the peach tree in the
valley will help one to predict the season ahead. During the Festival of the
Virgin de Guadalupe some people checked to see if it would be a good year
for production by looking to see if the *muña* flowers were blooming toward the sun. If their petals drooped like tears, or if there were few
blooms, it would be a bad year.[31] Few research participants could articulate a clear explanation for these beliefs, except to note that this was the
way of their grandparents. But the cosmovision they reported clearly
reflected the circular, holistic, and connected knowledge systems of
Indigenous peoples worldwide.[32]

Of course, the diversity of thought and approach common to all human
societies was present as well, as was the desire to be practical. One senior
respondent told me, for example, that he had experimented with planting
when the moon was full. He observed no noticeable difference and so
continued to plant when it was most convenient. Freed from the need to
reconcile competing ideas and processes into a single logic and way, these
Jalq'a farmers, like generations before them, were able to live with more
than one logic at a time.

Ecological complementarity, multifaceted, complex, and with an
embedded spirituality, represents both a pragmatic strategy to maintain
environmental resilience and a means of protecting the highlanders' inter-

nal cultural and symbolic transcript. It is a system that, when left to flourish, has offered its Indigenous practitioners a chance to both protect their environment and livelihoods and to connect with a broader cosmos on their own terms. Attempts to erode this sovereignty have been plentiful and largely successful. Until, and even after, INRA – the land reform legislation of 1996 that permitted territorial claims – colonial and post-colonial regimes have repeatedly undermined the system or sought to destroy the territorial rights at its core.[33] The fact that, in places like Northern Potosí, principal components have managed to survive five hundred years of colonial and republican domination is a remarkable achievement.[34]

With its risk management and collective decision-making structures; seed, product, and labour exchange; temporary labour migration that helps people to stay on their land; and rotational leadership at the community level, it is tempting to paint ecological complementarity with a utopian brush. Those who have studied the system more closely will quickly counter that it is not conflict-free or completely egalitarian.[35] Inter-*ayllu* conflict over land occurs, sometimes with violent and tragic consequences, as appeared to be the case along Potosí's border with the Department of Oruro in 2000 (although colonial and post-colonial land demarcation may well have fuelled this feuding). When land is scarce, the youngest sons can be turfed from their highland homesteads onto more marginal lands.[36] Women, although regularly consulted, still remain largely outside the leadership structures of public governance. And while exchange mechanisms within the system reduce the possibility of individual families going hungry, inequity between and within participating hamlets is present. In short, as with all systems, there are flaws in the design which, in addition to outside factors, weaken it.

Ecological complementarity is, however, a system that has allowed habitation beyond hand-to-mouth subsistence. The robust wheat economy of the region before tin and silver mining became the nation's priority is strong evidence of such vigour. The affective identification with, and intimate knowledge of the environment – embedded as it is in cultural and spiritual practices that are much stronger than any objective justification for environmental conservation – suggest that that this system is one of deep ecology.[37] Of particular importance to this study is the fact that ecological complementarity has, at its core, a broad cross-section of resilience principles, notably the stewardship of one of the greatest shares of cultivated plants and intra-specific crop diversity on this planet. If valued and supported, ecological complementarity – a resilience strategy par excel-

lence – might well ensure successful adaptation to the increasingly unpredictable and extreme climate events that will undoubtedly visit their highlands in this new century.

The most defining differences between the two communities that I discovered related to their respective application of ecological complementarity, arguably at the core of community resilience on highland landscapes. Without exception, my Mojón informants practised *doble domicilio*
or dual homesteading and had valley lands in production. Indeed, with
migration to the valley lands for periods of an average of 5.2 months, my
respondents practised doble domicilio generally with the entire family in
tow. Only a third of my respondents in Chimpa Rodeo owned valley
lands. Respondents there spent, on average, less than two months in valley regions in order to pasture their animals and barter for valley products. When they were not needed, they lent their animals, particularly cattle, to valley farmers in need of their manure and the services of a *yunta*.
In exchange, the host farmer agreed to monitor and pasture the animals.
Greater preoccupation with school attendance in this ex-hacienda community also motivated mothers with school-age children to spend the
majority of their time in Chimpa Rodeo.

Both communities practised *trueque, ayni,* and *minka* on a regular basis.
Both farming communities also used the *yunta* and a wooden plough to
till their lands, although as noted in the opening pages of this chapter, if
cash was available, a significant number of Chimpa Rodeo's farmers also
pooled their resources to rent one to three hours of tractor services to prepare the land for planting. Both communities also engaged in rotational
cropping and expressed a strong belief in the value of a healthy fallow
period for nutrient regeneration. Land-use pressures, particularly in Chimpa Rodeo were a significant limiting factor. In contrast to Chimpa Rodeo,
Mojón farmers practised the *manta* land management system.

Within the manta system, harvested crops are not necessarily collective
ones. It is the decision-making that is shared. The community determines
production strategies, crop rotation, and fallowing options. Mojón's
manta fields are indeed a source of considerable pride. During my first
visit to Mojón, my local guide, Don Justo, pointed to and rattled off the
names of sixteen different *mantas* on the surrounding hillsides, much like
a prolific father racing through the names of his offspring. All had
descriptive names making them easily identifiable by local residents. In
Chimpa Rodeo, farmers regularly consulted extended family members
about farming decisions. Structurally, however, individual families made

land-use decisions. Elsewhere in Potosí a few large *hacendados* or land-lords had implemented the *manta* system, wisely recognizing its social and environmental benefits. This was not the case in Chimpa Rodeo.

My intention in raising the issue of the differing degrees of ecological complementarity practised in Chimpa Rodeo and Mojón is not to offer definitive judgement about their respective resilience. Such assessment, if at all feasible given the complexity of such an analysis, would require a considerably longer sojourn within each community and the active participation of a broader cross-section of residents. My purpose here is rather to raise the question about the criteria that development interveners use to assess poverty and determine progress. "The poor in the Andean world," wrote the first and most prolific chronicler of ecological complementarity, John Murra, "were those who grew up without the necessary kinsmen to support their claim for the resources of the ethnic group."[38] An adequate land base on which one could cultivate foods and husband animals was of chief importance. With their valley and highland fields, and a *manta* system that considered, among other things, the water table and soil erosion concerns, the people of Mojón had a proactive adaptive-management strategy to maintain an adequate land base. These fundamentals keep people on the land over the long haul.

However threatened and eroded, the ecological complementarity system I found in Chayanta was maintaining these fundamentals. While government and NGO partners were encouraging more and more commercial potato monoculture, most farmers refused to abandon their plant genetic diversity. Farm families in both Chimpa Rodeo and Mojón held on to anywhere from a handful to dozens of Indigenous varieties, both for consumption and because they knew it made good sense. By broadening the scales at which their communities relied on ecosystem functions, farmers, especially those in Mojón, substantially reduced risk. Niche-specific cropping patterns included companion planting to avoid pests and soil management strategies that considered the interconnectedness of nature's resources. When land was not scarce fallow periods could last up to 10 years,[39] although in the case of my host villages, the periods were one to two years for Chimpa Rodeo and a full three years or more in Mojón. In the eyes of outsiders concerned with efficiency, such fallowing was impractical and "redundant." The farmers I knew considered such fallowing to be critical to the restoration of the soil's microbiology, even when land availability was tight. The growing of food on multiple sites at different altitudes also provided buffers against the domino effects of natural disaster. Their collaborative hamlet-based governance structures helped them to react and reorganize quickly under the ever-changing circumstances of mountain ecosystems, the very definition of adaptive management.

Collective land-use decision-making, as was the case in Mojón, also enhanced environmental and social cohesion. And the grafting of ayllu consensus processes onto the union structures, together with the annual rotation of local leadership among hamlet families in both communities, was building trust, balancing power and responsibility, and ensuring that knowledge was shared and dynamic. Figure 6.1 features a resilience lens that I have developed to demonstrate the very strong convergence between ecological complementarity and resilience.[40]

The outer ring of this lens represents the central principles of resilience while the inner ring captures the chief components of ecological complementarity. Principles in the outer ring can be shifted one or several notches clockwise or counter-clockwise to reveal a new convergence with the components of ecological complementarity. For example, if the "action for the common good" principle is shifted one position clockwise, it also corresponds with the ecological complementarity component "consensus and rotational leadership," given the public good achieved in not vesting too much power or knowledge in the hands of one leader. If shifted over two positions, action for the common good likewise fits with "multi-level ecosystem management," in light of the enhanced opportunity for food and environmental security. Similarly, if one shifts the resilience principle "tight feedback loops" one position counter-clockwise, there is a new convergence with "modular" or decentralized governance. Decentralized local decision-making units facilitate enhanced communication as well as a sense of responsibility and ownership. In the relationship between ecological complementarity and resilience, there is a very positive convergence.

On first glance, newcomers to Chimpa Rodeo and Mojón might easily dismiss their farming systems as not viable. Spanish *conquistadores*, mestizo republicans, and the more recent pull of a market-driven development enterprise trumping values of competition and comparative advantage seriously undermined the full application of ecological complementarity. Still, despite enormous pressures to

Outer ring: resilience
Inner ring: ecological complementarity

6.1 Resilience lens

adopt agricultural modernity, farm families of both Chimpa Rodeo and
Mojón hung on to ecological complementarity's strongest principles and
practical features. Their resilience thinking, undervalued and eroded, continued to pay careful attention to the "reproduction" side of the food
equation – the need for landscapes that will produce food well into the
future.

Some scholars, I should point out, dismiss any championing of Indigenous communion with nature as wishful thinking, a naive nostalgia for an
exotic, simpler way of life. There are anthropologists who argue against
the conservationist orientation of Indigenous peoples. They suggest, for
example, that the mass extinction of North American megafauna during
the Pleistocene era was due to reckless over-hunting, not climate change.

Other researchers point out that the ancestors of today's traditional peoples in New Zealand, Madagascar, and Australia were responsible for the extinction of many species of wildlife on these islands and archipelagos.[41] The conservationist ethic is not unique to Indigenous peoples, still others add.[42]

DANCING WITH THE WOLVES

The advancement of an essentialist, homogenized characterization of Indigenous peoples as ecologically noble clearly is not useful or correct. As two Native American scientists, Raymond Pierotti and Daniel Wildcatt's observe:

> Those wanting to embrace the comfortable notion and romantic image of the Rousseauian "noble savage" will be disappointed. Living with nature has little to do with the often voiced "love of nature," "closeness to nature" or desire to "commune with nature" one hears today. Living with nature is very different from "conservation" of nature. Those who wish to "conserve" nature still feel that they are in control of nature, and that nature should be conserved only insofar as it benefits humans, either economically or spiritually. It is crucial to realize that nature exists on its own terms, and that non-humans have their own responses for existence, independent of human interpretation ... Those who desire to dance with the wolves must first learn to live with them.[43]

Still, there is convincing logic in the notion that people who depend on nature for their survival in very tangible and immediate ways pay much closer attention to the elements that foster its sustainability. They are forced to respect and admire its power and force. Reading complex ecosystems well requires fine-tuned awareness of the interconnections and dynamism of those systems.

The importance of the relationships and the interconnectedness of the things we think about and come to understand is captured in a theory about knowledge called connectionism. With the exception of cognitive anthropologists, however, development practioners and thinkers rarely mention this theory about the way human beings learn, hold, and process knowledge. Since it is very compatible with resilience thinking and had a strong influence on my both my appreciation of the Indigenous views and practices I observed in Chimpa Rodeo and Mojón in 2000 and on the development assistance they received, a concise overview is presented next. Connectionist ideas about how we learn belie all-too-common notions that the Indigenous world view is somehow less sophisticated and dated. To the contrary, in this age of rapid ecological change and increasing complexity, we dismiss Indigenous knowledge systems at our peril.

7

An Interconnected Web

Andean society conceives of the cosmos as a totality, that everything is connected and no entity is perceived as resting on the margins of other things.

Ralph Grillo, 1985

Like resilience theorists, proponents of connectionism emerged in the latter half of the twentieth century at a time when a growing number of natural and social scientists were questioning the value and validity of reductionist approaches. Scholars from fields such as psychology, philosophy, the cognitive sciences, ecology, and anthropology were engaging in research that cast light on complex patterns of interconnection between diverse components within and between systems. Each of the properties of the components of a system, they argued, be it an organism, ecosystem, or society, is not sufficient to allow one to predict future behaviour. Rather, complex living systems evolve through continuous self-organization along unpredictable, creative paths. Knowing, connectionist theorists suggested, lies not so much in our individual minds, but emerges in relationship and through participation.[1]

The treatment of connectionism in this book will hardly do the theory full justice. Connectionism is currently employed within the cognitive sciences to study mutational complexity and artificial neural networks – artificial intelligence, in short.[2] As with most theories in psychology and cognition, it has its share of critics, a discussion of whom is beyond the scope of this book. The literature I reviewed in more detail comes from a branch of my own field, cognitive anthropology. The particular interpretation that struck a responsive chord was the nicely straightforward and convincing account of British anthropologist Maurice Bloch.[3]

PATTERNS AND BEST EXEMPLARS

Children, cognitiive scientists once assumed, learn classificatory concepts as minimal and necessary definitions for learning what things are. In the early 1990s, Bloch took issue with this assumption, as did a group of like-minded cognitive anthropologists in the United States.[4] Citing the work of cognitive psychologists,[5] Bloch postulated that concepts are formed through reference back to rather vague and provisional "prototypes" that anchor loosely formed "families" of specific instances. We learn the concept of a house, for example, not by listing essential features (roof, door, wall, etc.) that have to be checked off before deciding whether or not the whole thing is a house. Rather, we consider something a house by comparing it to a loosely associated group of house-like features, no one of which is essential, but which are linked by a general idea of what a typical house is. It follows, therefore, that the mental form of classifying concepts, essential building blocks of culture, involves loose and implicit practical cum theoretical patterned networks of knowledge, based on the experiences of physical instances or "best exemplars."[6]

The significance of looking at classificatory concepts in this fashion is that they correspond with the idea of chunked networks of loose procedures and understandings – scripts and schemata – which enable us to deal with standard and recurring situations that are culturally created.[7] This idea that there are small networks of typical understanding and practices concerning the world calls into question the old checklist of necessary and sufficient conditions which linked concept formation with language. Concepts, therefore, can and do exist independently of language, as evidenced by a child knowing the concept of house before she can say the word.[8] Bloch further proposes the existence of a dialectic or tension between language and mental concepts that partly transforms non-linguistic knowledge as it becomes linguistic.[9] Much knowledge, it follows, is fundamentally non-linguistic. "Concepts," he explains, "involve implicit networks of meanings, which are formed through experience of and practice in the external world. And under certain circumstances, this non-linguistic knowledge can be rendered into language, thus taking the form of explicit discourse, but changing its character in the process."[10]

Another crucial piece of Bloch's analysis of language and learning is his emphasis on the importance of non-linguistic knowledge in the development of expertise. Drawing on anthropological accounts of Polynesian peoples, ethnography of Liberian tailors, studies on automobile drivers, and research on master chess players, he proposes a strong link between observation, hands-on practice, and skill development.[11] The process of mastery involves the construction of a cognitive apparatus dedicated to coping with complex tasks. An apprenticeship approach is thus key to knowledge acquisition. The performance of complex practical tasks, in fact, requires that it be non-linguistic.[12] Automobile drivers, for example, need to transform their teacher's verbal propositions into non-linguistic, integrated procedures before the task can be effected rapidly, efficiently, and automatically. Expert chess players do not differ from novices in their knowledge of the rules of chess or in performing such motor tasks as moving the pieces. What seems to distinguish the expert, Bloch notes, is not so much the ability to handle complex strategic logico-mathematical rules, but rather the possession, in memory, of an amazingly comprehensive and organized store of total or partial chessboard configurations. This stored knowledge allows the expert to recognize a situation in an instant so as to know what should be done next.[13]

Such findings on expertise suggest that humans go about the whole process of thought in quite a different way than had been previously assumed. We access knowledge, either from memory or as it is conceptualized from perception of the external world, not as a serial process of analysis along a single line, but rather through a number of processing units that work in parallel and feed in information simultaneously. The information received from these multiple parallel processes is analyzed simultaneously through already existing networks connecting the processors. "Otherwise," Bloch muses, "given the conduction velocities and synaptic delays in neurons, it is a physical impossibility for the number of steps required by a logical sentential model of the mind to be carried out in the time in which even the simplest mental tasks are ordinarily performed." [14]

Connectionism, as noted, is controversial.[15] Some linguistic anthropologists are uncomfortable with the idea of separating non-language and language. Speech production, they argue, is the exemplar par excellence of "embodied expert knowledge."[16] This critique, however, does not put to rest the doubt that Bloch, and the scholarship he reviewed, cast on the centrality of verbal articulation and sequential processing for the learning process itself and hence, on the requirement of reading and writing for advanced problem-solving and abstract, *scientific* reasoning. Indeed, even Bloch's linguist critics hint at a somewhat similar point, arguing, "Culture is shaped in everyday practice below the threshold of awareness."[17]

There is one additional point about connectionism that deserves mention. We should not assume that what people say or do not say is necessarily a reflection of what they know. Different types of knowledge are organized in different ways, each with its own specific relation to language and action.[18] The most profound type of knowledge is not spoken at all but rather implicit, since it is because one is unable to speak of it that it can be used with speed and suppleness. If a race car driver, for example, were to articulate his moves he would lose the race. Attempts to speak about this knowledge would, by definition, change its nature and the outcome.

This interesting contention lends itself to growing arguments against the so-called scientization of Indigenous people's knowledge and to the idea that once this knowledge is verbalized or transcribed onto paper the knowledge is transformed. Efforts to make Indigenous knowledge useful to development programming by documenting it risk generalizing particular practices and in so doing sanitizing or changing them.[19]

Within this growing critique of conventional understanding about Indigenous knowledge systems, some research goes so far as to challenge even the notion of freestanding Indigenous knowledge. Scholars of farming systems argue that Indigenous knowledge systems are a set of improvisational capacities called forth by the needs of the moment. Reminiscent of practice theory, agricultural practices among Indigenous farmers are considered performances rather than predetermined designs – "sequential adjustments to unpredictable conditions."[20]

The need for rapid assessment and sequential adjustment to conditions of the moment is, in my view, quite correct. But the idea of improvisation alone, outside an accumulated body of knowledge, misses the mark. What I observed in the highlands of Chimpa Rodeo and Mojón is calculation about the present based on long-standing experience and careful observation of ever-changing landscapes. Farmers in Chimpa Rodeo and Mojón were thinking about the future while reflecting on strategies in the past. But there is no expectation that past practices will necessarily be sufficient to handle new conditions or stresses. Strategies may not easily be verbalized; this may give us the impression of improvisation. We should not underestimate, however, the deep-seated understanding that expert farmers have of the complexity of the ecosystems they husband[21] – nor the fact that their lives, literally, depend on it!

Cognition theories such as connectionism are complex subjects requiring their own books.[22] My objective is hardly to offer a comprehensive defence of this theory or to suggest that it is the only way to look at human knowledge and behaviour. But connectionism, as Bloch and his cognitive anthropology colleagues have framed it, comes closest to explaining the resilience practices and approaches to knowledge I have witnessed again and again within Indigenous communities around the world, including Chimpa Rodeo and Mojón.

In sum, connectionist theory, like resilience theory, represents a shift away from the persistent drive to break complex matters into simpler, concrete parts, toward a messier but essential analysis of their interaction and the bigger picture. The following overview of research into the character and practices of Indigenous knowledge systems outside my direct field research – profiles of peoples from varying landscapes in Canada, then the Andes – supports the importance of this concept for thinking about engagement with Indigenous peoples. It also reveals how the complexity thinking that gave birth to a system like the ecological complementarity that I found in the Bolivian highlands is generally present within Indigenous communities more broadly.

INDIGENOUS WAYS TO KNOW AND LEARN

Everything an Indian does is in a circle, and that is because the power of the World always works in circles, and everything tries to be round.

Black Elk[23]

Watch and listen and do it right!

Aboriginal teacher from Kahnawake, Quebec[24]

Just before heading to Bolivia in 2000, I was flipping through a popular development journal when an article about Bao, a four-row *mancala* game, caught my attention. It was a short, but fascinating, piece about the Bao players from Zanzibar. Bao is played primarily in East Africa and in some pockets of Sri Lanka and China. It uses a board with four rows of eight holes each, and 64 seeds. The objective of the game is to empty the opponent's front row.[25] Its complexity reflects two aspects of the game: its tiered rules, which make it necessary to apply several rules at the same time to any one move, and which create many complex rules in situations where two rules apply simultaneously; and the high turnover of seeds and therefore the high number of changes on the board with each move that is played. This is known as mutational complexity, and it increases the difficulty of calculating even one's own move.[26]

Profiles of Bao masters demonstrate that education, literature study, and social successes are not essential for the acquisition of this expertise. Indeed, until recent Internet interest in the game, and with the exception of the article I found, there had been no written material explaining this game. The people who excel include those who neither read nor write as well as highly schooled individuals. The learning tools these individuals use seem particularly appropriate for the calculation of rapidly changing information. Skilled players do not memorize a situation on the board; rather, they concentrate on the changes of information.

Although connectionist theory was not cited in the piece, a convincing case was made for the role of experiential, rapid, schemata-based learning in the mastery of mutational complexity – for neurons operating in overdrive. Players draw on knowledge experienced and in constant flux. This type of knowledge system is, in fact, a common theme in the work of scholars who study Indigenous peoples. It is certainly the case with Alaskan Native hunters.

Alaskan Native hunters seek to understand the irregularities in the world around them by first recognizing that many unseen patterns of order exist under the surface. Native elders predict weather based on observations of subtle signs that presage subsequent conditions. The wind, for example, has irregularities of constantly varying velocity, humidity, temperature, and direction due to topography and other factors. There are non-linear dimensions to clouds, irregularities of cloud formations, anomalous cloud luminosity, and different forms of precipitation at different elevations. Behind these variables are patterns such as prevailing winds or predictable cycles of weather phenomena that can be discerned through long observation.[27] A seasoned and experienced hunter has learned to decipher and adapt to the constantly changing patterns of weather and seasonal cycles.[28]

Another account about Indigenous peoples' memory-based, flexible, non-linear, and schemata-based knowledge came from a more unusual source, a book about work among the Aboriginal clients of a lawyer within the Canadian criminal justice system.[29] The author, Rupert Ross, challenges the ethnocentrism of conventional scholarship, which tends to describe Aboriginal thinking as simple, unscientific, concrete, and trapped in the present. Proposed instead is an intriguing connection between Einstein's theory of relativity and a great many teachings of aboriginal peoples. In both visions of the universe, all existence is seen as energy – or spirit – that manifests itself through matter by organizing and reorganizing that matter in ever changing (but patterned) ways.[30] The Chicksaw-Cherokee scholar Sakej Youngblood Henderson, former director of the Native Law Centre at the University of Saskatchewan, has this to say about the Indigenous mind:

Indigenous people view reality as eternal, but in a continuous state of transformation ... It is consistent with the scientific view that all matter can be seen as energy, shaping itself into particular patterns. The Mi'kmaq language affirms this view of the universe, building verb phrases with hundreds of prefixes and suffixes to choose from, to express the panorama. The use of verbs rather than nouny subjects and objects is important; it means that there are very few fixed and rigid objects in the Mi'kmaq worldview. What they see is the great flux, eternal transformation, and an interconnected order of time, space and events.[31]

A particularly telling example of this fluidity is found in how the Mi'kmaq language deals with trees. They are called by the sounds that are made in the branches, in the autumn, during a special period just before dusk – "known and talked about in terms of how they interact with certain aspects of their surroundings [and] in terms of how the individual observer perceives them." It is a very interactive process, with room for individual construction.[32]

Research into the landscape ecology of Canada's Algonquin people reveals a dialectical approach to the science of their landscapes akin to that of that of Alaskan Native peoples and the East Coast Mi'kmaq.[33] Knowledge, we are told, is progressively revealed to individuals through their guided experience on the land. Truth is never absolute, but rather directly connected to knowledge of the land; changes in truth statements, therefore, are linked to changes in the land.[34]

Like Mi'kmaq, the Anishinaabe language of the Algonquin is focused on the relationship between things. Place names, for example, do not just mark places but bring places together in relation to each other, providing a mental map of the land. *Azaatiozaagaigan*, for instance, means a lake where trembling aspens grow while *Ogishkibwaakaaning* is the place where wild potatoes grow. These are the reference points on which the creation of spatial patterning of the landscape is built.[35]

Perception of temporal dynamics among the Algonquin is also linked to an awareness of changes that occur in the landscape and is marked within the language in different ways. There are six Anishinaabe seasons, for example, with each season's name describing a change in the landscape. *Tagwaagin* begins when the leaves turn colour and fall from the trees. *Tagwaagin* turns into *Oshkibiboon* when all the leaves have fallen and the first snows are falling, and so forth. Europeans name their seasons as well, of course. The difference here is that the Anishinaabe words emphasize the act of change, not a fixed date.

To the extreme north of the Algonquin lands, the Inuit of North Baffin Island also demonstrate the importance of observation, relationships, apprenticeship learning, and non-verbalized knowledge.[36] The Inuit there have a word for their concept of knowledge transmission – *isumaqsayuq*. *Isumaqsayuq* captures the idea of knowledge being passed along through observation and imitation of activities embedded in daily family and community life.[37] Not unlike master chess players or Bao masters, Inuit learners typically develop concepts and skills by repeating tasks in many different situations, such as hunting under varying conditions of weather and animal movement and with various types of equipment. Traditionally there are few explicit verbal formulations of the rules for success. Rather, the Inuit recount what they have experienced through stories, which present concepts and principles implicitly. Formulation of the big ideas is left to the minds of individual participants.

Language, in short, while capturing or reflecting a people's knowledge and understanding is less important than the practice of that knowledge. When asked about the importance of the Inuktitut language to the maintenance of Inuit identity and the ways of that identity, research participants in a study of the Inuit of the Canadian eastern Arctic noted that Native language was not essential. Fourteen of the fifteen respondents stated that any person whose parents were Inuit, and/or who was himself or herself living the Inuit way, should be considered an Inuk, even without any knowledge of Inuktitut. A few respondents gave the example of the Mackenzie Inuvialuit, who remain fully Inuit even if they have now lost their language. They also explained that *maqainniq* – going on the land for hunting, fishing, and trapping – is the activity most essential to the preservation of their Aboriginal identity and way of life.[38] Southerners unfamiliar with this type of contextualized knowledge development and preservation are often convinced that their Northern students don't know a particular topic or concept when they cannot verbalize the knowledge. They assume that verbal abstraction is a necessary mediating step in high-level understanding.[39]

Collaborative learning with limited direct instruction – less verbal elaboration and thinking out loud – is the Inuit student's preferred approach. Arlene Stairs, an educator who spent years working with the Inuit of North Baffin, shares a story in her work on this subject that really made her pause. A young Inuit woman from North Baffin complained to her

Caucasian professor that she over-explained things. Her tendency to "over-explain," the pupil said, was just like "over-sleeping."[40] Too many words, like too much sleep, leave a person in a haze – less alert and ready to grasp the complexity of the bigger picture.

The importance of apprenticeship and non-sequential, non-linear learning are consistently highlighted in the writings on language and cultural content in North American Native education more generally. Native children learn skills not by having adults tell them what to do in recipe or instruction-manual fashion, but through experience with adults. Learning activities, therefore, are more effective if Native students participate in real-life tasks and challenges, whatever the skill set or knowledge desired.[41] Not unlike Bao players, they keep a number of related ideas in mind, without assigning them an order or hierarchy. They tend to approach an idea or a topic from many different directions.[42] Native scholars Raymond Pierotti and Daniel Wildcat captured this distinction when they said: "Western Europeans look backward and forward in time to obtain their place in history while Indigenous peoples look around them."[43]

Monographs about the knowledge and world views of Andean Indigenous peoples have also been fundamental to my appreciation of the interactive, non-linear character of their learning systems. Studies of Andean cosmovision[44] repeatedly tell a tale of the Andean perception of the world as a "living being, its totality not only including natural elements such as plants, animals and humans, but also the spirits, ancestors and future generations."[45] Nature does not belong to humans but humans to nature. Humans must, therefore, negotiate their space with all other beings, animate and inanimate. The interconnectedness of all matter influences the treatment of all matter with bargaining based on respect and knowledge of one's own vulnerability.[46] (My All Souls Eve hike into Mojón and my experience in the tent community certainly brought that message home.)

The Quechua word *pacha*, for example, captures a concept akin to the Occidental notion of the whole conformed by time and space. It has three spheres of life that flow together and interact: material life, social life, and spiritual life. They are in a constant and dynamic interaction with each other, with the evolution of life seen as a spiral. The future is seen as a repetition and expansion of cycles and rhythms that draw on the past for guidance.[47] Here we again see universal themes describing Indigenous knowledge – fluid and non-linear, relational versus separate or individualized, the notion of energy as a critical force, and the importance of observational skills and keen spatial perception. With landscapes humanized as beings with agency, interactions with them are more personalized. Relations rather than resources are managed, contributing, in turn, to more multi-faceted and varied interactions within one's territory. A practical consequence of this world view is a reduction of risk.[48]

To conclude, Indigenous approaches to science seem to be less on the characteristics of things than on the relationships between them. Since experience is what nourishes an understanding of ever-changing relationships, experience, not language, nor the documented expression of that language, appears crucial for discovery and the flourishing of Indigenous scientific knowledge. Language follows experience. With studies such as these increasingly available, it is surely inadequate to attempt to understand ecological complexity, let alone a sophisticated system like ecological complementarity, through scientific activity organized along traditional disciplinary lines.[49] These findings force us to question the Occidental approaches to development assistance among Indigenous communities that feature sequential and compartmentalized interaction and logical planning frameworks – logframes – focused on precise indicators and time-bound results.[50] At the very least, as Paul Sillitoe suggests, "it is necessary to abandon assumptions that we can record and document Indigenous knowledge and pass it 'up' to interested parties as technological packages are passed 'down' to beneficiaries."[51] Yet, as I have discovered time and again throughout my career and more particularly through more intensive research in Chimpa Rodeo and Mojón, these instrumental frameworks and packaged strategies – such as the "green revolution" approach to crop production to be discussed next – are deeply embedded in development assistance programming, repeatedly passed down to "beneficiaries" as effective recipes for change. The next three chapters chronicle, in fact, how in failing to understand the connectionist knowledge systems among the Indigenous farmers they engaged with, development assistance interventions repeatedly undermined sustainable practices and local resilience.

8

Breaking the Balance

In the end farmers are made identical to the image ascribed to them in modern agricultural science: invisible men.

Jan van der Ploeg, 1993[1]

"Mi papa me ha enseñado, mas que los técnicos!"
(My father taught me more than the extension workers!)

Chimpa Rodeo farmer on potato diversity, July 2000

FOREIGN POTATOES

"We [the aid institutions] broke the equilibrium that existed before!" So began my conversation with a former manager of one of the country's first national potato institutes, the National Potato Seed Project (PROSEMPA). A well-known agronomist with a residence in Ravelo, he studied the history of Bolivia's 1982–83 El Niño drought emergency response programs during his five-year tenure with PROSEMPA in the early 1990s. He was extremely sympathetic to the desperation of the times. Communities forced to eat their seed[2] – their future harvests – had pushed policy-makers into a panic. But there was no doubt in his mind that the decision to implement a blanket distribution of high yielding, foreign potatoes throughout the Bolivian highlands threw an otherwise balanced system completely out of whack. The emergency response ignored local successes and initiated a dependency on synthetic chemicals and prescribed approaches that would, if left unabated, undermine sustainable production on highland soils.

El Niño, however, was not the initial catalyst for the entry of external development agencies into the municipality of Ravelo in the early 1980s. They had arrived shortly before. It was the Bolivian government's desire to promote "Green Revolution" food production, originating in Mexico in the late 1940s and spread like wildfire in the Indian Punjab in the 1960s, that brought the *ingenieros* and *técnicos* to Ravelo.[3] They were agronomists trained in urban universities, taught to value modernity and to dismiss the connectionist logic of their Indigenous ancestry. Yield productivity was the Holy Grail, and they went to Ravelo's hamlets tasked with replacing "antiquated" farming practices with modern, technologically savvy systems. Chimpa Rodeo's farmers spoke of having interacted with external development agents at about that time. Their recollections of dates and factors influencing their arrival were not precise. However, most who remembered these early relationships recalled state-supported agricultural extension agents as the earliest development actors to visit their homesteads. An accessible community like Chimpa Rodeo was high on the list for assistance. One of the first institutions to work within the municipality of Ravelo, and Chimpa Rodeo shortly afterwards, was the now-defunct, government-sponsored, Bolivian Technical Institute for Agriculture and Animal Husbandry (*Instituto Boliviano Tecnico de Agropecuaria* – IBTA). In 1980, IBTA set up a program to test and promote *improved* potato varieties and the synthetic inputs that would enhance their health, size, and yield.[4] There was a gradual but steady introduction and training in the use of these new varieties and technologies. When *El Niño* wreaked havoc on the countryside in 1982, however, the push was intense. Agronomists became emergency workers charged with ensuring future potato harvests in the face of heavy crop losses. Green Revolution approaches seemed the best and only option. With funding from the Inter-America Development Bank, unscreened, introduced potato varieties, initially from Argentina, flooded aid distribution networks and local seed markets, even though farmers in the municipality of Ravelo had actually managed to conserve 30 per cent of their own seed for the next year's planting season.[5] Crisis management and national concerns fed short-term thinking and across the board measures that overrode local considerations and contexts. Plant diseases previously unknown to the region arrived with the donated hybrid varieties. Since potato seeds are vegetative, with their tubers asexually propagated, viruses and other diseases accumulated and contaminated new crop generations.[6]

To treat these diseases, pesticides were required. Chemical fertilizers were also recommended for introduced varieties unaccustomed to the weathered soils and still harsher climate of highland farms. Both required cash which, in turn, created a need for higher production volumes.

Chemically induced yields and the larger more uniform varieties put
the less prolific, albeit more resistant, native potato varieties to shame, or
so it seemed to the eager young extension workers. They certainly outperformed the local varieties during their first two years in the ground. So,
farmers raised on the principles of reciprocity accepted the gifts of introduced tubers, promoted as superior and commercially viable.[7] More and
more turned to one or two of the introduced varieties along with the recommended package of synthetic inputs, unaware of the damage they
caused to soil fertility.

With Dutch and Swiss help, new agencies emerged to help manage and
shape this new potato monoculture. In 1983, in cooperation with IBTA, a
national seed distributor formed, called la Unidad de Producción de Papa
or SEPA (The Potato Production Agency). The introduction of new high
yielding tubers and techniques also required external training and ongoing
advisory services. So in 1989, IBTA, again with European assistance, launched
PROSEMPA – *Proyecto de Semillas de Papa* (the Potato Seed Project) – and its
research twin, PROINPA – Proyecto de Investigación de la Papa (the Potato
Research Project). These two quasi-governmental agencies[8] superseded
SEPA, emerging as the central producers and distributors of the country's
potato seed. In 1994, the government merged these services, closing PROS-
EMPA and shifting the bulk of its work to PROINPA. Through seed cleaning
services, PROINPA maintained a connection with Ravelo *paperos* in the year
2000. By then, they had discontinued their training program in the area.[9]

While El Niño did not prompt the arrival of non-governmental organizations (NGOs) in Ravelo, the NGOs that arrived in its wake did wholeheart-
edly adopt the "Green Revolution" approaches the disaster had inspired.
This was the case for the NGO with the longest and strongest overall presence
in Chimpa Rodeo and Mojón, Instituto Politecnico Tomas Katari (IPTK).
Given IPTK's leading role in the development programming within these
communities, the next two chapters chronicle its intervention strategies.
The two other important NGO actors at work among Ravelo's Jalq'a farmers,
the American-headquartered Food for the Hungry International (FHI); and
the multilateral United Nations Children's Fund (UNICEF) each have their
own chapter.[10]

BUILDING CAPACITY?

IPTK was named after the seventeenth-century Indigenous freedom fight-
er from the community of Macha, a six-hour road trip from Ravelo. The

organization arrived in the municipality of Ravelo in 1982 with a forestry program featuring the planting of the fast-growing but water-thirsty eucalyptus tree. Many forestry programs in the 1980s featured this import, as they did imported pines.[11] Ravelo's Jalq'a appear to have appreciated the forestry program, but the assistance was finite. They remained more curious than keen about this new actor in their communities. IPTK emerged as a really significant development actor in this zone only at the end of the decade. They had by then earned a solid reputation for their health services in neighbouring Ocuri, the organization's provincial headquarters about three hours from the village of Ravelo.

Activists from the Catholic Left founded IPTK in 1976, the most prominent being a mestizo sociologist from Ocuri, Frans Barrios. Barrios – at one time exiled to Chile for his political views – and his "comrades" were determined to assist the long-neglected Quechua farmers of the area to take greater control of their lives. The municipality at the time did not receive a single peso from the national government. Indeed, prior to a radical municipalization plan and accompanying legislation in 1994 (the People's Participation Law), outside the most densely populated urban centres, municipalities seemed not to exist in the eyes of national legislators. A huge vacuum in public services and political representation existed.[12] One of the first things I noticed when first arriving in Ocuri was the village's 2000 millennium hillside sign made of letters formed by rocks. IPTK and Our People 1976–2000 – IPTK y Nuestro Pueblo 1976–2000 – the sign proudly declared.

From their base in the village of Ocuri, IPTK first tackled the abysmal child and maternal mortality in the region. Drawing a small amount of assistance from Europe, the fledgling IPTK began with a one-room hospital in the founder's residence. In a little over two decades, Ocuri staff developed one of the best-equipped regional hospitals in the country. Infant mortality rates that in 1976 had averaged 205 per thousand, averaged 110 per thousand in 1998, an impressive 46 per cent decline.[13] With additional support from European patrons, the organization also launched a health care facility for Sucre's ever burgeoning peri-urban population – people residing on the periphery of the colonial centre. This hospital offered affordable urgent care for campesino migrants, not the least of whom were their compañeros from Chayanta, including Ravelo. In time, IPTK added to their Sucre programming a training institute designed to help migrants and their children adjust to urban society and a national radio station that targeted both peri-urban and rural audiences.[14]

An innovative national training program for campesino youth with leadership potential, *Centro de Profesionalización Rural* (CENPRUR) also emerged as a major IPTK initiative in the late 1990s, grabbing international accolades in the process. In 1996, the UNDP rated this program to be one of the six most successful training programs of its nature in the country.[15] Villages from all over the country were asked to select their best and brightest youth to send to the Ocuri training centre, perched on a mountain ridge overlooking the small village.

Once admitted to the occupational college, students participated in a three-year, government-accredited training program to become intermediate-level technicians or *medio-técnicos* in one of four fields: agriculture, nursing, civil engineering, and public administration. CENPRUR program graduates, I soon learned, were very popular with development institutions in the region. I was repeatedly introduced to medio-técnico graduates who had joined the ranks of municipal government staff, including Ravelo's municipality, and the offices of Potosí's departmental government. Graduates were also scooped-up by the international development community on a frequent basis. International agencies like UNICEF, the World Food Program, and the United Nations Populations Fund (UNFPA) regularly hired them. I also found one working with CARE, USA in Potosí and another with the Mennonite Economic Development Associates (MEDA), a bi-national North American NGO that focused on micro-credit and small business development. Sucre's largest public university also sent practicum students and interns to CENPRUR. IPTK itself hired its share of their medio-técnicos. IPTK earned a very solid reputation as a trainer of qualified extension workers, extending its influence well beyond the organization's institutional borders.

IPTK's extension programs reached into all four of the regional municipalities within its Chayanta program: Ocuri, Colquechaca, Pocoata, and Ravelo. They initially covered primary and curative health care, literacy and gender equity education, and agricultural production training. The government's increasing assumption of health-care programming in the 1990s and the arrival of UNICEF's literacy program for women in the region influenced a gradual retreat from direct programming in two sectors and an increased emphasis on agricultural production. The strengthening of the farmers' union movement also grew increasingly important,[16] alongside the organization's growing political ambitions, manifested in their establishment of their own socialist political party in 1985, MBL – Free Bolivia Movement.

Specific initiatives undertaken in Chimpa Rodeo included reforestation through community tree nurseries, the genetic improvement and health care of livestock, fodder production, the design and provision of appropriate technologies such as grain silos and low-cost greenhouses and irrigation systems, and community road improvements. There was also substantive area-based farmer training on improved seed, animal husbandry, the benefits and use of chemical fertilizers, pesticides and insecticides, and the merits of a strong local union structure or *sindicato*.[17]

Off the beaten track, Mojón's relationship with IPTK, and any other outside agents for that matter, was recent. IPTK staff headed to Mojón for the first time in 1996 to implement a potable water program, co-funded with PROSAVAR, a government organization specializing in water services. Exposure to Mojón's needs, coupled with residents' eagerness for more assistance, inspired the establishment of a longer-term relationship. As had been the case in Chimpa Rodeo, a forestry program, featuring community tree nurseries, kicked off this longer-term assistance. Ultimately, in both hamlets, the approach shifted to family-managed nurseries because individual families assumed greater responsibility for the new patch of forest. This initial IPTK program with Mojón also included a training component for local agro-forestry promoters.

Like their PROINPA and PROSEMPA colleagues before them, program documents and my conversations with extension staff revealed that in the early years at least, IPTK's extension staff – university-trained agronomists as well as some of the medio-técnicos from CENPRUR – considered unsophisticated production practices and low yields to be a primary explanation for the poverty among the farm families in their target communities. IPTK's openly socialist ideology had contributed to an awareness of broader geo-political and economic forces marginalizing these farmers. The need to organize campesinos to effect political change shaped an emergent political identity that set IPTK apart from a majority of NGOs in the department.[18] When it came to farming, however, it was clear that the scientific conventions and technical solutions of the day guided these university trained agronomists, and more particularly their organization's managers. Western approaches were applied to multifaceted and complex local situations. Like development assistance the world over, there was a tacit deficit orientation to their assistance.[19] The focus was on Indigenous farmers' perceived lack of skills and they were there to teach them. In a report that captured the findings of a planning workshop among field staff, local deficiencies listed included: a farmer's poor negotiation [of prices] due to low levels of education; *minifundismo* – continuous land subdivision; the limited application of technology; and the low levels of forage production for animal feed.[20]

To IPTK's credit, they consistently hired local staff. A good number of the Ravelo program staff members were from Chayanta families. Several others were just a generation away, urban sons (there were few daughters) of rural migrants. They did not always appear entirely comfortable with the training and the messages they were asked to take to their rural compañeros. Some, in fact, modified their approaches. Still, at the decision-making level of the organization, little serious attention was given to Indigenous governance structures and alternative knowledge systems, even though the studies of anthropologists like Tristan Platt were readily available on IPTK bookshelves.[21] Such attention to Indigenous farming and homesteading practices might have complicated their mission to organize a campesino proletariat and thus needed to be avoided.

Some components of the Indigenous farming systems were very much appreciated and encouraged, crop rotation and fallowing systems being two especially welcomed strategies. Product and labour exchange mechanisms were also recognized as important to the local economy, although, if programming documents offer any indication, on a fairly superficial level. But the more fundamental system of the dual homesteading that their program communities followed to varying degrees was considered, for instance, more of a nuisance than something worth promoting. Staff members were respectful of the farmer's production responsibilities and availability when scheduling training events. Still, they expressed frustration with the repeated departure of program participants to valley lands. The idea of programming within both highland and dispersed valley communities does not appear to have been given much thought. The complex logistics and expense of dual-track programming may well have quashed that option. Staff members worked incredible hours, and their family lives were regularly disrupted. Additional travel into the valley would have been an additional burden to avoid. And, as suggested, continued *doble domicilio* would make it hard to organize farmers politically. With influential institutions – from the Sucre-based Faculty of Agricultural Engineering in San Francisco Javier University to the powerful World Bank – also backing the benefits of Occidental education and technologies, Western perspectives and practices ruled the day.

Area-wide and in-situ workshops, for example, focused on increasing yields. Farmers were encouraged to stay put, intensify production, and to adopt new agricultural production systems. The logic was that if farmers were able to farm better – to enhance the quality and quantity of their crops for the market – they could earn the funds needed to purchase the goods their families so desperately lacked. They would in effect be able to consume their way out of poverty, a message whose irony these critics of capitalism seem not to have considered.

Improved productivity for income generation required a shift to higher-yielding potato varieties. Compared to the rather humble, pockmarked, and curvy local varieties, these foreign interlopers were handsome and comparatively unblemished. They grew quickly, were more uniform, and were considerably easier to peel. They were very attractive to urban consumers in a hurry and more suited to the machines used to turn potatoes into popular potato chips or French fries.

To survive on the hillsides and valleys of parched highlands, however, these introduced varieties needed a chemical fix – vigorous doses of pesticides and chemical fertilizers. Farmers were told that the funds earned thanks to higher yields would be enough to pay back the loans needed for their chemical cocktails. They were *not* advised about the leaching that happens to soils when doused with synthetic fertilizers or that their tubers would need a costly chemical bath to survive from year to year. Nor were they told that the high water content of the less mealy, more uniform potatoes decreased their nutritional value or that they would take extra time and fuel to cook. Diversity, they knew from their grandparents and parents, had, on its own, been a critical strategy to deal with the extreme mountain weather events. How would these new tubers perform when the weather turned mean? For the first couple of years, the introduced cousins outperformed the local tubers. Potato monoculture, featuring two, then three types, took hold, especially on farms closest to transportation routes.

Most families, preferring the flavour and density of their native potatoes, held on to at least a handful of their favourite traditional varieties. The Jalq'a families of Chimpa Rodeo and Mojón were no exception. A few, inspired by their parents' proud husbandry of ancestral varieties, also committed to the conservation of far more. Most families also refused to make a complete switch to purchased fertilizers, although the amounts of sheep manure used decreased significantly in the early years of this new system. Still, farmers were planting more and more of their fields with the introduced tubers, abandoning or neglecting a significant percentage of the varieties that their lands and hands once nurtured.

One of IPTK's extension workers with family in the municipal capital wistfully recounted this anecdote about his own mother's response to the potato revolution she was witnessing. On seeing the rapid growth and substantial yield increase of the introduced potato crop her clever son had planted when he had returned home with his university degree in hand, she abandoned the approximately twenty varieties in her native collection, sowing her son's single variety. This story is a useful reminder of the broader impact this new agriculture – indeed any development intervention for that matter— had not only within participating communities but on communities outside the direct reach of an NGO or development institution. During the first years of program implementation, neighbours observed the high yields of NGO program participants and sought out the new varieties. The promotion of new ways of farming extended, in short, well beyond communities directly partnering with IPTK or with other development agencies with a similar program. Mojón's Indigenous farm families, for example, did not engage with IPTK until 1996. Yet, they too abandoned many traditional varieties to make room for the exciting new interlopers.[22]

Increasing yield and productivity is a central objective in any farming system. Ravelo farmers, like those the world over, would be the first to identify enhanced productivity as a primary concern and goal. IPTK's approach to enhancing yield, however, rested on a narrow set of criteria and undermined longstanding systems. The cost outweighed the benefits. Potato monoculture and the consequent dependency on synthetic chemicals brought a farming system into the region that was not only contributing to dramatic soil erosion and infertility, but also disrupted traditional patterns of exchange. On-farm experimentation declined considerably, as did organic production practices. These shifts, in turn, weakened the genetic vigour of farmers' Indigenous varieties.[23] When productivity based on yield is the singular focus of intervention, farmers get into trouble.

Working with the conditions nature throws farmers way, in contrast, requires attention to a broad range of production considerations and challenges, especially within the context of highly diverse mountain ecosystems. Yield objectives never trump the need for crop stability and plasticity, particularly the capacity to adapt to varied and changing environments. To survive on exceedingly challenging landscapes, a wide range of performance criteria is required.[24]

IPTK, like others in the region, mistook low productivity for weak skills, ignoring the long-standing assault on local farming systems, not the least of which was the priority given to the extractive metals industry. Nor did they give sufficient thought to the precarious nature of the city market and how commodifying the local economy might produce a mass of small producers in competition with each other, or to the consequent drop in unit prices once yields and product volume improved.[25] The impact on the reciprocal exchange mechanisms at the heart of ecological complementarity also seems not to have been considered. Field staff I interviewed confessed, in fact, to not having paid much attention to the market at all in the early days. Their job, they believed, was to be technicians, charged with improving production and yields.

Farmers able to access credit for this more expensive production system entered a vicious cycle of needing more volume to make up for lower unit prices to be able to pay back loans for agrochemicals essential to increase volume. The challenge shifted from having enough surplus production to obtain a modest level of disposable income to one of trying to cover debts and make ends meet. And since the additional land needed for expanded production volumes was scarce, fallow periods were shortened. Overused fields and drug-addicted crops made the soils *muy cansado* or very tired. Farmers frequently referred to the land as being *enfermo* – sick – or *muy quimicado* – burnt.[26] The soil's reduced fertility, in turn, affected the viability of local varieties in need of healthy soils to thrive.

A number of field workers expressed their concern with the expanding potato monoculture. One veteran IPTK extension worker, himself from a rural community in Chayanta, explained that he was incredibly worried about the loss of potato diversity.[27] A CENPRUR graduate from the region told me that, "these professionals don't know about this diversity." "What I have learned about diversity," he said, "I learned through discussion with other *compañeros* (fellow farmers)."[28] Other extension staff in Ravelo were less forthcoming. But when the subject of biodiversity loss came up I could see apprehension in their furrowed brows. Out of loyalty to the greater cause or perhaps concern for their jobs, they kept these opinions to themselves.

Farming practices aside, by the year 2000, development assistance, globally and locally, had begun to change. Most staff members I met were quick to criticize the *asistencialismo* or charity orientation of the late 1980s and early to mid-1990s. Too many handouts and not enough local ownership of the development process had created uncomfortable dependencies, they confessed. There were other important international and national influences as well. Donor evaluations called for enhanced com-

munity ownership of the change process and a re-thinking of reductionist, or simplified, development strategies. The federal government's 1996
Popular Participation Law (Ley de Participation Popular) was also decen-
tralizing municipal resources and decision-making, transferring 20 per
cent of its budget to the country's 311 municipalities. This shift required
local planning and budgetary oversight.[29] To assist municipal authorities
to use their newly acquired resources in ways that would benefit their citizens, IPTK restructured its program approach to include more comprehensive and integrated programming and direct assistance to municipal
authorities.[30]

Communities, like Chimpa Rodeo and eventually Mojón, were invited
to engage directly in community planning and implementation. Consultation events became par for the course, as did the training of community promoters to motivate and monitor the application of the techniques
they learned.[31] IPTK became a major player in the municipality's strategic
planning, serving as the facilitator for five-year and annual planning
exercises as well as the for municipal census-taking. Critics have since
suggested that intermediary NGOs like IPTK neutralized the growing critique of the country's Indigenous peoples, paradoxically playing into the
hands of the national government.[32] Given the subsequent rise of a unified Indigenous party in the Movement Towards Socialism (MAS), their
interventions seem not to have undermined the change process substantively. They may well have supported it. IPTK's efforts were certainly well
intended.

There was a good dose of irony, however, in the actual practice of participatory municipal planning. The need for community representation in
planning exercises proved a particular challenge. Rather than choose village representatives with literacy and numeracy skills, participating villages selected leaders with the most experience and authority, whether
they were literate or not. The development planners' sets of criteria and
measurement for effective change, such as data capturing yield per hectare
for example, were also at odds with a people accustomed to reading their
landscapes and their successes through a much different lens. In the end,
as the ensuing journal entry reveals, the Western thinkers were forced to
do the data collection and planning themselves.

My journal entry also exposes an experience during the municipal planning event in Ravelo that, although regretted at the time, enhanced my
understanding of the challenges facing IPTK's field staff as well as development workers more broadly. When a celebratory drink in honour of

our work together turned into a night of heavy drinking, I was forced to reflect more deeply on an extension worker's bifurcated life. Many of my colleagues were deeply torn between work and family responsibilities. They spent a lot more time in the field than at home. It was hard to fully belong to either world and it could get very lonely.

MUNICIPAL PLANNING

14 AUGUST 2000, 6 PM
I am delighted that IPTK has asked me to assist with my NGO Program Director hat on with the new five-year participatory municipal planning process (one of the exercises that I have reviewed earlier). The local authorities have engaged IPTK to facilitate the event. I feel I have graduated to a new status somehow, no longer a Canadian gringa trying to find her way, but a member of the team. It will likely be a very demanding two days. Farmers from every corner of the municipality were trained to collect the data to feed into this process. We will all gather at the municipal grounds – *Alcladia* tomorrow for the presentation of findings, and to help identify priorities both for participating villages and for the broader municipality. I hear my colleagues calling me for an orientation meeting. We will likely discuss tomorrow's plans then head to one of the two "pensiones" cum restaurants for some dinner.

15 AUGUST 2011, 8 PM
I am so exhausted, full of guilt, and still a little hung over. I would rather hide under my sleeping bag than write in this journal. But here I am writing, trying to assess the experience! What a day – the worst and the best given how incredibly interesting the dynamics were. First, about last night. Wanting to be the ever-grateful gringa (so much for my confidence at just being one of the gang), after our "plan to plan" meeting and dinner, when we got back to the field-station, I presented a gift of a bottle of Canadian rye to our team. There were more than a few of us but there would be enough, I thought, for us all to make a couple of toasts for a successful endeavour over the next couple of days. My gift, it turned out, inspired the purchase of other alcohol and partying that lasted, for the most seasoned partyers, until an hour before our resident rooster issued his brutal wakeup call. After a 3 am retreat to my bed, I managed to crawl out of my sleeping bag at about 7:30 am. I braved an ice-cold shower (our solar panel doesn't warm the water up until about

2 pm) so I would be a little more alert for the 9 am start of our
meeting.

With one exception, we all managed to turn up and muster the best
professional energy we needed to get through the day. The one exception, unfortunately, was a less experienced consumer of alcohol whose
drinking provoked a more violent reaction than the rest of us.

Having worked on Latin American programming for almost ten years
now, I know that binge drinking – defined here as consumption until
there is not a drop of alcohol to be had anywhere – is not limited to the
farming communities the extension workers engage with. The drinking
is a welcomed release from a compartmentalized life with tons of
responsibility and, when it comes down to it, limited opportunity to
ever really feel at home. Rural extension workers spend 20 to 23 days in
the field away from their families every month, have 3 long days of
report writing in the office when they return home, and then less than a
week of "free" time catching up on all the family events and problems
that occur in their absence. Their dual residence comes with transient
identities.

I think about my IPTK lawyer friend's comments about a month ago.
"I have two completely separate lives," she said to me one evening over
dinner, "one in the city with my family and friends. The latter is very
contained and far too short. I wear city clothes. You wouldn't recognize
me. My life in the countryside includes a completely different set of
friends. There, I am never really accepted as a local and I don't even really share many of the same values." She paused, and then added, "I no
longer travel back and forth with a suitcase. I keep my wardrobes and
personalities distinct, in separate closets, in distinct residences. I am two
people and sometime I feel like I don't really belong in one identity or
the other."

I think too about other NGO colleagues who have families in Sucre
and a girlfriend, sometimes with children, in the countryside. These are
not openly acknowledged relationships; but they are obvious to everyone. I wonder of course about the impact on and expectations of the village women that they bring into their lives. Is this just a case of Latino
machismo? I don't think that it is quite that simple. I see lonely men in
need of companionship and intimacy and young women hoping for a
way out.

I can barely keep my eyes open. More tomorrow night...

I am back in my room and back from day two. Day two was much better. We managed to sleep off our hangovers and the municipal officials appeared pleased with our efforts today. Community representative after community representative presented their hamlet's wish list in order of their priorities. A community sports field – or *cancha de futbol* – for their youth topped the list of several communities. My IPTK colleagues responded with a plea for the prioritizing of more urgent needs, like potable water, agricultural inputs, or a health post. But the farmers' reasoning also made good sense. Their children needed to be able to play. Work alone would not keep their children happy and on the land.

While our tired crew's performance improved, we discovered a major wrinkle in the baseline data collection approach. Following the national guidelines for participatory development planning, IPTK and municipal officials had made every effort to gather a broad cross-section of representatives from across the municipality to ensure as participatory a process as possible. For the data collection, communities had been asked to build a team that consisted of their union leader, a female representative, and someone specifically delegated as the community researcher, able to read and write well. Most community teams, it turned out, had two representatives and rarely a female. My review of the list of 150 registered participants also revealed that 25 per cent of those present in this data retrieval workshop had registered with their thumbprint. The signature of many others was shaky at best.

When the completed *boletas* or questionnaires with demographic and production data were quickly reviewed, we knew we were in trouble. I was asked, along with my teammates, to animate smaller working groups for those teams where it was really obvious that they had had serious difficulties reading and understanding the instructions. The overwhelming majority of the questionnaires were incomplete. Component percentages cited often added up to more than 100 per cent. In one case that I personally observed, the researcher had placed *si* – yes – in boxes that required numerical information about potato distribution and yield. It was soon clear that participating hamlets had not selected farmer-researchers based primarily on reading and calculation skills, but based rather on their status and knowledge of their farming system. Even those selected who had a grade-five level of formal schooling had not used their primary school literacy for years. Nor did their way of looking at the world fit the process. They were accustomed to describing their landholdings and landscapes based on their geological characteristics and location, not on metric measurements. It was more common to define your homestead by boundaries such as the mountain stream on the one side and the open pasture on the other. The Western forms that they were being asked to fill in simply didn't make much sense.

In desperate need of data to complete their part of the census – due in provincial offices so it could be rolled up to departmental and then national level statistics – the municipality agreed to IPTK's offer to have its workers complete the job. The catch, of course, is that the number of staff members able to get the job done are far fewer. Given time pressures and distances, their best judgment – guestimates really – will have to do.

IPTK's increasingly participatory approach to engagement with local farmers corresponded with a reduction of the really intensive, chemically dependent monoculture of the early days. International criticism of the way these monocultures were destroying biological diversity had its impact, as did first-hand discoveries of the degree to which synthetic chemicals were killing soil fertility. Indigenous farmers were encouraged, therefore, to reduce agrochemical treatment of their potatoes and to rely more on sheep manure as they had in the past. Initial applications of seven bags or 644 kilograms of fertilizer per hectare were lowered to a recommended maximum of five bags or 460 kilograms per hectare.[33] Crop diversification away from potatoes was also promoted, since it had become increasingly clear that commercial potato production was not proving to be viable for the majority.[34] Enhanced wheat production, including intraspecific diversification was encouraged, given its affinity for Ravelo soils, as was the planting of species once indigenous to the area, such as the leguminous pearl lupin called tarwi, and native tree species.

More and more, IPTK acknowledged the value of indigenous plant varieties and the importance of inter- and intraspecific crop diversity and intercropping. This incipient recognition of the importance of biodiversity did not extend, however, to an embrace of its importance to potato production. Program designers in Sucre offices did not challenge potato monoculture in any significant way. For the paperos of Ravelo, the vicious cycle and tight grip of production for a competitive market was not easy to break.

DIVERSITY FAIRS

There were rebels on staff who found a way to promote the value of the potato plant's genetic diversity, at least among the farmers who had enough land. Added to the events within the local *feria* or agricultural fair was a competition for the greatest variety of potatoes. Within the two fairs I attended, one in Ravelo and one in Qharaqhara, the winners displayed 39 and 76 varieties, respectively. The Jalq'a farm families in the contest, twelve in Ravelo and ten in Qharaqhara, were extremely enthusiastic about this contest. They expressed a determination to produce more varieties every year by collecting additional varieties from neighbouring communities, during agriculture fairs, or by bartering with *comuñeros* in the valley.

Prizes awarded in this competition also attracted participants. They highlighted, however, a further contradiction that the *técnicos* promoting this event either missed or perhaps chose to ignore. In the Ravelo *Feria*, prizes included a shovel, a 92-kg bag of introduced, non-indigenous, seed potatoes (tubers), and agrochemicals with a large yellow applicator for spraying, the latter without the safety gloves or eyewear these farmers could ill afford. The IPTK-sponsored Qharaqhara fair that I attended the next month did not contain fertilizers and pesticides in the prize list thanks, I like to think, to our conversations after the Ravelo fair. If I had an influence, however, it was not quite what I had hoped for. The prizes continued to include bags of introduced seed potatos and the chemicals' sprayer, although not the chemical.

The nature of the chemicals on sale at a merchant booth within the Ravelo fair also merits comment. Right next to IPTK's information booth was a large display promoting Novartis products.[35] Their display included a large sign promoting the company's Ridomil, a systemic fungicide for use on selected crops to control diseases caused by members of the phycomycete family of fungi.[36] Syngenta's website with product information noted that the chemical was highly toxic. Yet, there were no pamphlets, drawings, or posters on the safety precautions required when spraying this chemical. The website further urged users to wear a long-sleeved shirt, long pants, shoes and socks, chemical resistant gloves made of waterproof material such as polyethylene or polyvinyl chloride, and protective eyewear. It also called on farmers to wait at least 48 hours before re-entering the sprayed area.[37] During my exchanges with Ravelo farmers, the use of Ridomil was not reported, possibly because it had just arrived in the area. But this dangerous fungicide was being promoted in a region with high levels of illiteracy and low awareness of the consequences of unprotected chemical applications. The cost of protective gear was prohibitive. Nor did most people own the recommended shoes and socks, let alone have fences on their properties to keep children and animals out.

Tamaron, a Bayer product distributed through Chile, was the soluble insecticide of choice for potatoes in Chimpa Rodeo and Mojón. Bayer's website noted that it was extremely dangerous – "*sumamente peligroso!*"[38] "It is especially harmful for humans when it comes into direct contact with their skin or eyes, if inhaled, or if used regularly over a long period," Bayer's scientists warned. "It is also," they added, "harmful for the environment, animals and fish."[39] Again, I did not observe protective gear among the farmers using this product. Nor was I able to find any public education materials warning of the hazards of its application and the need for careful storage. As for the warnings directly on product labels, again, few users had the literacy skills needed to decipher them.

Most troubling to me was the continued purchase among 44 per cent of the farm families in my study of a banned pesticide called Folidol. When it came to toxicity, it was off the scale and thus banned internationally. But it was very cheap and, contrary to the official record, readily available in Bolivia thanks to its manufacture by Bayer in Brazil.[40] NGO workers stressed that they regularly warned farmers about the dangers of this product. I witnessed these warnings myself. But their concern seemed to stop short of an aggressive educational campaign to stop its purchase or, better still, organized legal action to prohibit its sales. I heard one particularly sad story about how a young girl from Mojón poured some Folidol into her uncle's drink as a joke, thinking that it would simply make the drink bitter. Within minutes, he keeled over and died. Shortly after hearing that terribly sad story, I reviewed Bayer's website on Folidol. It opened with "DANGEROUS POISON" and "KEEP OUT OF REACH OF CHILDREN."[41]

The grainy fertilizer applied on potato tubers – a Japanese make that farmers referred to as "18-40-60" reflecting the percentages of nitrogen, phosphorus, and potassium, was not toxic like the insecticides and pesticides in use in the region. However, farmers deposited it into their furrows with bare hands and in their *ojotas* or open sandals. When the men, women, or children applying the fertilizers stopped for lunch, the hands they used as eating utensils did not get rinsed. Water was rarely available. So, at best, hands were wiped on an apron or pants already dusted with particles of the fertilizer.

Use of artificial fertilizers in the year 2000 was reduced, as noted, but still generous. I was told repeatedly that the amounts of pesticides and insecticides used during each planting season were, in contrast, comparatively modest. Their modest use explained, although in my view did not excuse, the low level of attention to safety issues. Fortunately, the farmers themselves were beginning to have their suspicions about the impact of even modest levels of application. When I discussed the use of agrochemicals with a community leader from Chimpa Rodeo, he remarked, "The women of my wife's generation are not as strong and healthy as the women of my mother's generation. I think that the introduction of agrochemicals into our fields has something to do with it." [42]

During this period of institutional restructuring, IPTK helped to organize producer credit associations. Based on the principles of group collateral, it was hoped that these community credit groups would minimize individual risk and facilitate access to credit for costly inputs. Yet another irony overshadowed this program component. The lending institution that IPTK partnered with, the Asociación Nacional Ecuménica de Desarrollo (ANED) tied its loans for the farmers in this region exclusively to the purchase of the synthetic agricultural inputs. They needed the yields to be high enough for the surplus production that would provide farmers with the sales income for a loan repayment. [43] Credit, in short, was specifically targeted for the purchase of a chemical fix. Both ANED and IPTK staff I spoke with about this requirement were uncomfortable with this incongruity. But directives from the top had to be respected. Rocking the boat, they worried, could put their jobs at risk. And jobs were very hard to come by.

I wrote this journal reflection after my interview with the ANED *técnico* in Ravelo. When we parted, I immediately thought about a fellow doctoral student's research experience with the Grameen Bank, where the field workers' "public transcript" of success was at odds with their "hidden transcript." [44] This conversation about the contradictory nature of the support also provoked further reflection about the contradictions in my own attempts to promote sustainable change. ·

RAVELO, 8 AUGUST 2000

I met with ANED's program officer today. He is from a farm family and understands clearly the contradiction in providing credit for purchases that undermine the sustainability of food production. Our discussion reminded me of Amin Rahman's insightful, albeit extremely critical, book about the Grameen Bank and that organization's award-winning microcredit program. I read Amin's manuscript before heading to Bolivia, just as it was heading to the publisher. I had an advanced copy because Amin and I were in graduate school together.

The "public transcript" of bank workers, Amin wrote, championed the ethical and socially just nature of the program. Among themselves, however, workers confessed that the program was deeply flawed. Their jobs depended on a normative behaviour that suited their superiors, so their "hidden transcript" was tucked away.[45] They knew the women were not benefiting as suggested. If anything, the program was masking patriarchy's deep and continued entrenchment.

Like their Grameen counterparts, the IPTK and ANED employees have families and need jobs and decent salaries, especially within a national context of serious employment insecurity. The "hidden transcripts" of Ravelo técnicos do not travel much beyond conversations with friends over a few beers. Having shared social time with these friends, as well as extended conversations while hiking into villages, I know better than to judge and lay the blame for these inconsistencies at their feet. The issue of compromised values is much bigger than their particular choices. The tensions field workers experience between their beliefs and the behaviours foisted on them are really a part of a much more fundamental dilemma or dialectic, both within the international development field and within academia.

I also understand this dilemma and contradiction at a gut level. The technology that allows me to fly into this country is hardly a product of our harmonious relationship with nature. The over-exploitation of fossil fuel and the monoculture agriculture that I rail against not only dominates our world economy but also warms my house and feeds me oranges in the deep of winter. I am a development worker cum anthropologist whose income is dependent on the flaws in the bigger system. A hidden transcript indeed! Development agents in Ravelo are told and expected to help with the building of a "productive municipality" – *município productivo*. They know that this is shorthand for the strengthening of commercial agriculture based on high yields and purportedly efficient returns on investment. They also know that the micro-credit lending program they are asked to implement is intimately linked to this commercial system. But without a more supportive policy and organizational framework, they find themselves in an almost untenable position. They are "damned if they do and damned if they don't."

While moving toward more sustainable practice, when it came to the municipality's most important and remunerative food crop – potatoes – IPTK's programming during this new phase of work continued with the approaches that preceded their arrival. With the Sucre market so close by and the demand for potatoes still high, extension workers and farmers were not ready to wean themselves from a logic that stressed the importance of higher yielding, and thus chemically dependent, varieties. The primary objective in IPTK's 1996–99 plan for Ravelo, although noting the importance of sustainable production, continued to emphasize the primacy of yield criteria: "to increase the agricultural yields of farm production units among the subsistence-farmer strata of Ravelo's *puna baja*, conserving and enhancing at the same time the natural resources of these farms."[46] Sustainability was desired but in a competitive world of commercial agriculture, short-term interests overshadowed the longevity side of the equation.

Another more potent element influenced IPTK decision-makers. They needed and desired a united farming community ready to coalesce under a nation-wide campaign for social justice. As the next chapter reveals, there was little room for complex ethnic and cultural reconciliation work within their strategy to organize peasants against capital.

9

Farmer Proletariat

CONCIENCIA CRITICA

True to their socialist roots, IPTK trainers and extension workers promot-ed a critical consciousness (*conciencia critica*) among participants. Staff consistently informed farmers about their rights as farmers and citizens, as well as about the importance of union solidarity to confront corrupt and incompetent local, regional, and national governments. IPTK's field workers, some of whom, as mentioned, were from Chayanta and had trained in CENPRUR, were also invited to become active within the politi-cal arena. They were encouraged to run for municipal office and to seek out and train young Indigenous leaders with similar aspirations and potential. This political work attracted its share of critics. Not the least of these were NGOs who considered political campaigning to be in conflict with a mission of service. Salaried NGO staff members on municipal coun-cils, they further warned, would represent a conflict of interest. In some target regions, farmers themselves did their share of complaining, as evi-denced in a damning letter from a group of angry citizens that surfaced during my time in the region.

Historically, however, IPTK's most troublesome critic was a Bolivian gov-ernment anxious to maintain control over a left-wing group bent on orga-nizing peasant farmers. Early on in the organization's history, police forces raided the Ocuri hospital and its offices. Staff members were roughed up and held for a day, threatened, and told in no uncertain terms that they would be watched very closely.[1] IPTK obviously outlived the intimidation of that particular regime. But concerns about the group's longevity, including worries that donors might not want to risk support for an organization on the government's blacklist, understandably took the sting out of their political critique. I was repeatedly told how the messages in IPTK's weekly paper, *Prensa Libre* (Free Press) had been toned down significantly since the early days of its publication. The year 2000 editions that I received were moderate in tone, more like a popular community digest rather than the radical voice of the peasant farmer. The inclusion of a provocatively dressed young woman on the front cover to boost sales would not have been present in the early days.

Interest in electoral victory within municipal, departmental, and national elections not only quieted IPTK rhetoric, it appears to have shifted the organization's ideological position. The organization's more moderate strategy paid dividends. In the 1995 municipal elections, Its political arm, the Bolivian Liberation Movement (*Movimiento Boliviano de Liberación* – MBL) succeeded in gaining the highest number of Indigenous campesino councillors, a total of 90 in all.[2]

By the end of 2000, its share of victories also included electoral success for staff or ex-staff. IPTK's former Executive Director, for example, became the mayor of Sucre. CENPRUR graduates and former IPTK employees were elected mayors in two of the four regional municipalities in Chayanta: Ravelo and Ocuri. During the *Movimiento Nacional Revolucionario* (MNR) administration prior to Hugo Banzer's final administration, IPTK's founder and board president, Frans Barrios, was elected to the national congress. Staff members also claimed that the Popular Participation Act of 1994 was MBL's brainchild.

In the June 2002 election, in an attempt to gain still more power, MBL allied itself with the MNR. This move backfired. Reaction by supporters ranged from puzzled to enraged. A major split ensued that heralded the party's eventual demise, facilitating, in part, the MAS sweep of available seats in Chayanta. A few candidates succeeded outside the province, the most significant being the election of IPTK's founder, Frans Barrios, to the Senate.

Of importance to this discussion about IPTK's political identity is not so much the numbers they sent to government over their party's short history but what I perceive to be a critical factor in the organization's reluctance to acknowledge substantively the Indigenous character and world view of the Indigenous people they engaged with. As suggested, IPTK's need for a uniform and unified movement of peasant farmers to back its political ambitions – that included an end to their oppression of course – explains, in my view, their preference for the homogenized identity of a "farmer" proletariat. In a context of often corrupt, neo-liberal government beholden to international financial institutions, IPTK's leaders appear to have decided that Indigenous politics were too costly and too messy. The political momentum needed for social change required participation under a single, unified banner.

The concept of a monolithic farming culture swallowed up the notion of diversity and Indigenous distinctiveness. Solidarity for IPTK meant solidarity with their *hermanos campesinos*, a pragmatic but nevertheless assimilationist orientation. They consequently dismissed the ayllu as regressive and neglected long-standing ecological complementarity in need of strengthening, not disdain. For political reasons, IPTK's leaders seemed willing to ignore the work of anthropologists like Tristan Platt and even their own researchers in Sucre, including an excellent study produced in 1999 just before my arrival entitled: "The Market as Complement: Exchange in the Province of Chayanta, Northern Potosí." An excerpt from this frank critique of the development assistance of the time is worth repeating here: "The limited knowledge among the institutions about the subsistence strategies of the families in the communities within the province of Chayanta ... results in generalized proposals that don't consider subsistence strategies and their connection with the market as part of a logic of self-sufficiency, consumption diversity, and sustainable production."[3]

IPTK was not alone in its neglect of the resilience strategies of the people they set out to assist. Development organizations more broadly, although aware of the practice of ecological complementarity in Northern Potosí, dismissed it as largely a practice from pre-Hispanic times. This attitude fed indifference to an abundance of scholarship on its practice and critical role in the local farming economy. When anthropologist, Silvia Rivera, queried development workers in the region about the ayllu governance system at the heart of ecological complementarity, she repeatedly heard:

> that the *ayllu* and its authorities were corrupt and manipulated by the State; that the *ayllu* and its authorities don't know anything about projects to modernize their economy; that the *ayllu* and its authorities don't understand the political and economic dynamics of contemporary Bolivia; that the *ayllu* and its authorities are not democratic; that the *ayllu* and its authorities are only interested in festival parties and *chicha*; that the *ayllu* and its authorities are incapable of forming an

alliance with the mining federations; and finally, that the *ayllu* and its authorities are folkloric relics of a dead civilization.[4]

Such complaining, Rivera went on to say, was based, in part, in ignorance and, in part, in the paternalism and racism that defines the urban political and Creole class in Andean countries.[5] A homogenized concept of farmer was clearly not unique to IPTK, nor was it recent. The language and policy of the 1952–53 Reforma Agraria (Agrarian Reform) fostered such thinking. Designed to spearhead the development of a strong and modern nation, the legislation privileged the *mestizo's* emergence as the dominant actor – the fused inheritor of the *Indio* and the Spanish legacies."[6] To pave the way for small-holder land distribution favourable to their growing power and control, writers of this agrarian reform legislation deliberately ignored Indigenous calls for territorial title, preferring and thus promoting the concept of campesino versus Indio.[7] IPTK's approach to campesinos is thus consistent with the historical treatment of Indigenous peoples throughout the country. Having worked in the most isolated of communities with traditions and land-management and governance systems found in few other Bolivian departments, IPTK can certainly not plead ignorance of the Indigenous systems that once kept these communities vibrant.

The paternalism of a Western development worker was undoubtedly also at play here. Racism as a motivating factor, on the other hand, seems too quick and harsh an explanation for IPTK's positioning, at least among the majority of the staff I came to know both in Ravelo and Sucre. Committed, and hard-working, many with significant amounts of Indigenous blood flowing through their veins, staff members spend long hours alongside Indigenous program participants, learning as well as instructing. They worked in the most isolated of communities. With often-blistered hands themselves, they would plant crops and trees alongside their Jalq'a *compañeros*. They spent long nights in planning and training meetings to avoid having to ask participants to spare yet another daytime away from their farming. I saw one extension worker bite the testicles off a ram during an on-farm workshop to demonstrate a comparatively painless way to castrate animals in the absence of expensive sedatives and sterilized tools. They also returned at night to staff quarters that were not that much better than those in the adobe villages they visited, pit latrine and all. Electricity had only arrived in Ravelo a couple of years before I lived among them, and there were certainly no heaters to warm their hands and feet on the endlessly cold winter evenings. I did encounter one field staff member with a clearly racist attitude. In the rest I saw respect and concern for the Indigenous farmers they were genuinely hoping to assist.

From what I was able to gather, executive staff had also all lived or worked in similar conditions in the countryside for extended periods at a time. One veteran executive did complain that the collective ideology of Indigenous peoples was static, curtailing the questioning of one's conditions and situation. He seemed to be justifying the organization's campaign to mobilize a more *forward-thinking farmer* and in that moment at least betrayed a sense of superiority. But in general the organization's reluctance to consider the Indigenous character of their program communities in depth appeared to me to be a strategic choice rather than a deep-seated sense of superiority. Their political ambitions and socialist goals accounted for a purposeful blind eye to the resilience in their midst. A complex blend of political strategizing, ideology, and shared experience with the Indigenous peoples they supported had shaped their organizational identity and development approaches, as I learned more clearly during a May Day celebration in their Chayanta headquarters. Again, as the ensuing journal entry suggests, my personal learning from this experience was considerable. These development actors were not the standard Western developers imposing their way. Their motives were based on a profound desire to build a more socially just world. I discovered deeply committed and caring staff facing social change work within a context of competing visions and cultural norms.

IPTK REGIONAL HEADQUARTERS, OCURI, 2 MAY 2000
After my experience yesterday, May Day for me will never quite feel like just any other day, as it generally does in Canada. My experience began with a tour of the CENPRUR operations that included a short visit to the small library. In keeping with IPTK's very modest infrastructure, the room was simple. A large wooden table with chairs sat in the middle and the whitewashed walls were lined with bookshelves filled with books. I scanned the shelves and in no time caught sight of the library's most impressive collection. It was a full set of Lenin's writings. They were bound in at least twenty volumes, resembling an encyclopaedia set or a series of dissertations. We needed to leave for the May Day – well May Day night – parade so I only managed to leaf through one volume quickly. "Wow, I thought, these guys really do have socialist roots." I wonder if I'll have a chance for a more thorough review at some time. I certainly hope so.

The central square where we were to start the parade was hilly, not your typical town plaza. Nor was there much flatland to walk around. Ocuri is on a mountainside with the flatter bits above housing the training centre. Our march was thus a constant up and down and around. Thanks to the kerosene torches we held high over our heads, the village fast became a mass of flickering light in the pitch-black sky. Our feet kept rhythm with the local band. The entire community seemed to be in the march.

After the speeches, rather fiery in their own right, we headed to the CEN-PRUR residence for a drink. A rather reflective discussion took place among my friends. They told me about how this event made them deeply nostalgic. It brought back memories of the early days when there had been such a strong community spirit. They lamented its loss. Everyone felt equal in those days and everyone always pitched in. From manager down to staff on the first rung, from washing dishes to cleaning toilets, they all shared in the chores and in the joys of working communally. The pay was bad. That was a fact. But the camaraderie and sense of family was incredibly strong. They also reminisced about long debates about the path to a more just world, well into the morning hours. The expansion and "professionalization" of the organization and the need for specialized staff to manage donor requirements had changed their character. That happens all the time, they knew. They remained politically ambitious, they added. But there was a sense that when it came to IPTK's deep social justice values, they had lost their way.

This sense of loss was certainly not present in the IPTK lawyer I met this morning at breakfast. His passion was fierce, as was his candour. In response to a comment I made about the valuing of Indigenous knowledge systems, he shouted, "Bolivia's inability to move beyond its status as a living museum of exotic peoples was keeping the country and its people from the unity needed to challenge the injustice of capital."[8] I have subsequently discovered that he is the lawyer staffing an IPTK program in a neighbouring municipality heavily conflicted over the ayllu versus union governance model. There has been some nasty interaction that has no doubt complicated his work life.

My lawyer acquaintance's very open suggestion that Indigenous peoples' systems and movements were dividing the socialist movement is not echoed by any of the other staff I have met to date. Perhaps they are more discreet. More conflicted would be my guess. Still, this lawyer inspired a deeper level of reflection about IPTK's institutional quandary

– how does an organization committed to a unified class struggle incorporate diverse ethnic groups and world views?

In the 1996–99 program phase and into the new phase begun shortly after I arrived in 2000, "culture" did emerge as a more significant operational concept. Programming included the sponsorship of cultural events, featuring traditional costumes, dance, songs, and food. Materials recognizing cultural traditions were also produced, such a beautiful almanac wall calendar charting historical events and local festivals of importance to the lives of Chayanta's Indigenous peoples throughout the year. Native plant varieties and subspecies diversity, as mentioned, were also beginning to be promoted in the agricultural fairs the organization sponsored. This attention to culture, while a very important step forward, still fell short of a robust appreciation and integration of alternative world views and knowledge systems. The etic of culture – the external, material manifestations of identity – were honoured.[9] The emic or cognitive components of culture, the alternative cosmovision and perspectives on knowledge and the nature of the universe, were purposely left obscure, except, as noted, within some very solid research documents that, like the study on Indigenous market and exchange mechanisms, collected dust on crowded bookshelves.

Without a whole-hearted acknowledgement of the differences between Western and Indigenous peoples' learning styles and knowledge systems, or of the political biases shaping these perspectives, Occidental approaches *to capacity building* are bound to rule the day. Then, as anthropologist Jane Collins so aptly put it about research she observed in other Andean regions, "science not only mirrors the society from which it emerges, but recreates those mirrored images in other societies to which it turns its attention."[10] Despite genuine respect for the skills and stamina of the farmers with whom they interacted, IPTK's agronomists went to the field either with Western plant-scientist tools or as activists focussed on the workingman. They were intent on "a tooling of man to fit in," as the iconoclastic development thinker, Ivan Illich, has suggested of much development intervention.[11] The community-based planning exercises that IPTK implemented in Chimpa Rodeo and Mojón certainly attested to this importation of the Occidental way and point of view.

As part of an agency's *Diagnostico Rural Particpativo* (DRP) – the popular planning system by then used across the country – extension workers headed to Chimpa Rodeo and Mojón with flip chart paper, markers and the latest tool kit of rural and rapid appraisal (RRA) methodology.[12] They hoped to offer participants a stronger voice in the design of their community's development program and thus enhance the effectiveness of their own program. During a three-day workshop, participants learned to draw informative maps of their community, to chart the rhythm of their agricultural season, to document migration patterns, to sketch purchasing flows, and to outline the timing of local festivals. Memory-based information was, for the first time, captured on paper. The information solicited was very useful, particularly to proposal writers in Sucre. However, the products were descriptive and extractive rather than analytical and empowering, addressing immediate needs rather than the community's strategic interests. Participants proposed improved infrastructure and basic farming techniques as solutions to their problems. Staff members bemoaned the community's apparent unwillingness to move beyond a discussion of basic needs.[13] But documentation of this event, coupled with comments made to me thereafter, suggested that they had not considered (or perhaps were unaware of) methods that would encourage analysis beyond practical matters. Diagrams, charts and tables are meant to be used as discussion starters, not an end in themselves. Nor were there exercises designed to analyze external challenges and obstacles, not the least of which was an outside push toward a market with highly unfair terms of trade. And not until I conducted my own PRA workshop within these communities two years later, did either a verbal or written report on these workshops make their way back to the community.[14]

Methodologies used with people accustomed to an oral transmission of knowledge were likewise biased toward Western perspective, planning objectives and linear thinking. People who do not read Western script do not necessarily relate to a left to right orientation. Yet, data gathering with diagrams and matrices ran sequentially from left to right. The workshops also required reading, writing and a solid measure of the Spanish language skills that favoured a tiny minority of literate participants. They were often IPTK-trained union leaders more familiar with Western logic and process.

To IPTK's credit, Quechua was the predominant language of instruction and discussion (not always the case within the NGO community), with Spanish the language that flowed from pens and markers. Writing and reading tasks for even the literate participants, however, were not completed with ease. Técnicos in the community were counted on to draw up and interpret project documents.

The extension workers facilitating this process spoke enthusiastically about the more inclusive process of the DRP planning system. If the results were in practice extractive, their intent was certainly not. As university-educated scientists trained to be technicians, not change agents, they were also not very familiar with Indigenous learning styles. Nor did donor-driven program expectations, timelines, and forecast programming results make attention to interconnected, Indigenous learning systems very realistic. I want to spend a little time discussing this last issue, since such donor expectations are illustrative of a bigger problem. They have certainly been a source of frustration for me as a development worker.

Financial contributions from international organizations, governments, and NGOs alike, generally require the use of Occidental planning systems that are frequently diametrically different from the Indigenous ways. Proposals and reports, for example, are built around a linear logical framework analysis (LFA) or its updated results-based management (RBM) methodology. To obtain the money to proceed, there is a need, from the start, to prepare a framework that identifies inputs (dollars and resources), activities, short-term outputs and the indicators of those outputs, medium-term outcomes with their indicators, and finally long-term impacts that can be measured over time. This information is meticulously plotted on pages of boxes, tables, and charts. These methods are with rare exceptions sacrosanct, a "paint by number" requirement essential for a donor's assessment of the merits of the program. In theory, the idea is a good one. Rather than receive a list of activities that it is hoped will influence change, the donor hopes to get a better sense about how the key development actors plan to achieve their objectives. Also, the information should be gathered through participatory methodologies with targeted beneficiaries playing a key role in data collection.

In practice, however, such a process is best suited to concrete infra-structure programs with clear and easily measurable targets. Even then, it can require time and experience that local participants rarely have. For Indigenous communities that see change as dynamic and in a constant state of flux, the approach can be particularly problematic. And as the Ravelo municipal planning exercise captured in my journal entry so clearly demonstrated, more often than not, it is the outsider – the intermediary – who completes the exercise.

The approach can also be very costly. Less experienced NGOs, both local and international, are often forced to hire an $800 a day external consultant to assist with these complex planning exercises or to *polish* the presentation of the information. One step removed from the project, this well-intentioned coach often has difficulty understanding the local dynamic enough to move the exercise beyond a mechanistic exercise, although I have seen gifted individuals do much better. Development anthropologists Gardiner and Lewis go a step further in their assessment to suggest that this project orientation is really about engineering the path the donor seeks: "The idea that economic and social change can be framed within projects is central to the top-down, controlling urge of development activity. When questions are asked within the central conceptual framework of a project, it is all too easy to submit to the idea of "social engineering" and to forget that most "complications" involve real people in real-life situations around which straightforward decision-making boundaries cannot be drawn."[15]

My review of IPTK's project documentation suggested that IPTK's very competent project management staff in Sucre had mastered the LFA approach rather well. Submissions and reports followed donor guidelines very carefully. Evaluators sent to assess the implementation of participatory methodologies were for the most part positive. Shortly after the completion of the community DRPs (Participatory Rural Appraisals) in Chimpa Rodeo and Mojón, a donor-sponsored evaluation praised the Ravelo team in particular for its effective DRP work, concluding:

> While there are limitations within the project ... we consider that there are a group of successful elements that can and should be systematized and then shared. [These include] the training methodology for farmers and the role that the trained agricultural promoters play [in their communities]; the participatory methodology used in the design of DRPs through which the farming population are able to analyze their socio-economic situation, prioritise their needs and build community plans; the strengthening of the community's ability to become interlocutors in order to insert their community plan into the municipal POA [annual plan].

Considered within a Western development framework, IPTK's Ravelo team took to heart the participatory training workshops organizations like the ones the United Nations Food and Agricultural organization (FAO) and their European patrons had sponsored. On the surface, their training workshop looked good. Through interactive exercises participants charted their needs. The community promoters they trained

seemed, in turn, well equipped to use the Western formulas they had
learned. Each in their way was satisfying the requirements of their
patrons. But none of these actors, it appeared to me, seemed terribly eager
to invite participants to ask more profound questions, such as the primary reasons for their marginalization. Why, for example, were their soils *que-
mada* – burnt? Nor did they question the *participatory* exercises so keenly
implemented. Were the methodologies used to fill in the matrices and
charts on flip-chart papered walls really useful to Indigenous participants
with a very different world view and minimal skills in the written language?" Did this chance to participate really make up for the enormous
cultural and power imbalances among the parties involved? A report of a
national workshop on the environment and sustainable development in
Cochabamba in 1994, sponsored by one of IPTK's major sponsors, suggested that while there was a willingness to acknowledge the complexity
of the challenge, the change formula promoted was rather standard and
rote.

DEVELOPMENT RECIPES

In the European funder's opening remarks to the plenary, its representative
began with a question about why, after so many years of human and financial investment, conditions in many rural communities remained as desperate, or perhaps more desperate, than they had been before all the investment. Paraphrasing another development administrator, the speaker asked:
"if we had put all the development dollars of cooperation in a bank in the
USA and distributed the interest to the beneficiaries of our policies and programs, would that not have been better?"[16] This question was intended to
be rhetorical and yet it was most profound. The speaker went on, to
hypothesize that at least part of the problem lay in the fact that the NGO
community had not grasped sufficiently well the complexity of the development challenge. They required a more systematic approach. Nor were
they working in a sufficiently concerted, strategic way, instead confusing
their beneficiaries with their divergent strategies. He closed with a recommendation for an improved, more integrated and cooperative approach,
one with a gender focus and based on farmer participation.[17]

Most participants in the room would have been able to recite this oft-
repeated development recipe by heart: cooperative, integrated, systematic,
gender-sensitive with adequate farmer participation. If the workshop
report I read offered a fair overview of the proceedings and discussions

thereafter, the analysis of the complexity and challenges they all faced merely skimmed the surface. There was some acknowledgement of the importance of Indigenous knowledge to the campesino economy as well as a general recommendation to incorporate cultural and biodiversity considerations into strategies and work plans. A more in-depth exploration did not occur.

My point in highlighting this event and report is to suggest that IPTK's reluctance to ask the harder strategic questions was not unique. The organization's personnel operated as members of a broader development community reluctant to entertain the possibility that for just and sustainable work among Indigenous campesinos, it might not simply be a matter of improving the poor performance of tried and tired aid delivery. Nor would consulting more with participants to ensure a better reading of their needs and desires do the trick. A fundamental rethinking of the interaction was in order.

The broader development industry that IPTK operated within did not appear ready to negotiate an agenda that might radically change the rules of the game as well as the power structures that defined them. They appeared unprepared to investigate whether flawed intercultural understanding and skills on their part might explain investments that were not achieving the expected results. Interestingly, the aforementioned external evaluation report completed for the sponsoring organization three years after the Cochabamba workshop referred exclusively to campesinos and noted with confidence that within Chayanta, "the *natural* organizations of these communities are the farmers' union." IPTK was dependent for its financial resources on external organizations that appeared to accept the dominant development discourse favouring the Western strategies of the day, however much it was couched in participatory language.

Near the end of my research year in 2000, IPTK had launched the new lands rights education program for rural campesinos referenced earlier. It was designed to raise awareness about rights related to Bolivia's 1996 land reform act, the national Law of the Agrarian Reform Service. This newest version of INRA had amendments that clarified land claim processes, allowing for territorial claims. It also recognized the legality of ethnic land-use practices and customs that reflected Indigenous governance and decision-making mechanisms.[18] IPTK had obtained some modest resources to train "barefoot lawyers" – local promoters – to carry the information to their communities.

IPTK's workshops were very popular, with standing room only for the latecomers. Participants spent bone-chilling nights in crowded, dimly lit rooms to learn about such rights. As my journal entry based on participation in one of these workshops reveals, however, I was greatly disappointed with the process and products of these IPTK-facilitated workshops. The transmission of the information was again largely descriptive. The sessions lacked opportunities to analyze the information or strategize about next steps. Discussion of controversial issues relating to alternative land holding or systems of governance were entirely absent. I also struggled with the obvious paradox in the idea of the text literacy needed among people with enormous ecological and landscape literacy.

SAUCE MAYO, 15 NOVEMBER 2000
We are sandwiched into the small school here. There is little room to move, or breath for that matter. It is getting dark but IPTK has managed to hook a generator up to provide some light. The session is very popular. A large group of people are hovering outside the open door and windows. Land-rights are such an incredibly important issue.

Two of IPTK's lawyers explain the latest information on the Land Reform Act (INRA) and how it might affect them. They are doing their best to be dynamic and get their messages across. This audience, they know, needs to be able to pass on their learning to their neighbours. It is not going so well however. Participants are looking frustrated, in some cases completely lost. While the animators generally communicate in Quechua, there is a lot of Spanish legalese in the mix. And posted on the room's walls are sheet upon sheet of flip chart paper with Spanish explanations, accessible only to a tiny minority of literate Spanish-speaking participants in the room. "How can I possibly report this information to my family and neighbours?" they must be thinking. "Am I expected to memorize this complex stuff?"

Maybe later they will send emissaries of sorts to copy the posted material. That is what happened in a farmers' meeting I witnessed recently. At about 8 o'clock in the morning after the session, I found two teenage girls making detailed notes from the flip-chart papers still dangling on the walls. When I asked about their purpose, they explained that they had been sent by their community to transcribe the information from the night before. None of their community's representatives could read or write script.

This presentation on land rights is also painfully unidirectional. Participants have been told to ask questions; but the animators seem so anxious to communicate all they know, that they are offering little opportunity for participants to speak up. The presentations are also detailed to a point of obscurity for the untrained observer. Nor do the presenters offer substantive suggestions regarding strategies that might make this INRA legislation work in favour of Ravelo's Indigenous campesinos. The messy politics related to territorial, ayllu-based claims and Indigenous governance options are not on the agenda.

Surely this could be done differently, I say to myself. I also can't help thinking about how things might be different if the audience *were* literate. I debate the literacy issue back and forth in my head and, for a moment, I am drawn into the dominant thinking – the broader development context *requires* literacy to be at the top of the development priority list. Then I think about alternatives. There are creative, interactive ways to communicate such matters effectively without the use of reams of text. It is not the NGOs fault, I argue back to myself. There are so few resources for this kind of work. Still, the approach I am witnessing just isn't good enough.

My internal debate continues and my frustration grows. Cynicism tugs at my sleeve. I feel a mixture of anger with the injustice and greed that marginalizes people in the first place and a sense that it is just too big and too messy to do much about it. Somehow, had these trainers been government officials, I would roll my eyes and assume we NGOs could do better. "We can, can't we?" But it is so very hard to get these very complex matters right. About this conclusion, both the anthropologist and the development worker in me agree.

When Indigenous identity is obscured, so too are the skills and knowledge linked to that identity.[19] Within Ravelo, and more particularly Chimpa Rodeo and Mojón, resilience strategies like ecological complementarity and biodiversity conservation were downplayed in favour of an industrial-oriented model designed for large-scale food production that would never suit their landscapes.[20] IPTK committed to work in Chayanta for the long haul. They chose to assist within the most marginalized areas, not an easy feat within a context of weak provincial and national government presence. They resisted tremendous pressures to adopt the dominant neoliberal economic agenda and determined to help campesinos find their voice in a world that an elite mestizo minority dominated. They understandably turned to a political path that required a united movement with a common agenda and perspective. But solutions and a struggle for power predicated on their Western terms and options were simply not working. They had not reaped the benefits envisioned.

In the year 2000, estimates and reporting errors notwithstanding, the average family among my Chimpa Rodeo respondents earned approximately $265 CAD from their backbreaking labour, sad testimony to their terribly weak bargaining power in the marketplace. Mojón families in the survey had a negative income, losing $35 CAD in the process, largely because 45 per cent of those surveyed decided that the rock bottom prices on offer for potatoes that year were an insult. They refused to bring them to market. "We would rather give them away," these frustrated farmers said. Unable to barter enough produce or labour to meet all their needs, families in both communities once again turned to temporary labour migration to meet their family's requirements. Their young men and some young women were forced to head to the city to be, as one IPTK extension worker from another Ravelo community remarked, "maltreated and to work like slaves."[21]

Farmers with the means to leverage loans from the ANED/IPTK credit scheme used for their agrochemical purchases actually fell into debt in 2000, since the previous year had not have been much better. A 1999 evaluation report on IPTK activities in the broader municipality listed the average income of farm families then at $206 US, the bottom 16 per cent earning $25 US and the top 8 per cent earning $500 US.[22]

The Participatory Rural Appraisal (PRA) workshops I conducted in both Chimpa Rodeo and Mojón that had participants assess conditions before and after external development actors arrived in their communities revealed that soil conditions and potato diversity had deteriorated dramatically since external institutions like IPTK first set foot in their settlements. Four of the six smaller groups I divided participants into also reported that commercial production had weakened significantly. In a complementary PRA exercise on the "History of Potato Production" in Chimpa Rodeo and Mojón, participating groups also reported a substantial rise in the use of synthetic agro-chemicals since El Niño relief agents sent potatoes with pests into their fields.

TIRED SOIL AND TIRED SEED

Factors influencing the decline of soil fertility and biodiversity are, of course, many and complex. It would be unfair to point only an accusing finger at the development community and more particularly at IPTK for that matter. It should also be pointed out that participants in the "Before and After" exercise from both Chimpa Rodeo and Mojón reported improved health and education services, forestation, and animal health and infrastructure conditions. Nevertheless, the strategies IPTK applied to reach their primary goal – enhanced agricultural production for sustainable livelihoods – had not reaped the anticipated outcomes. Nor did their investment stop the most repeated and troublesome problem facing these farm families, soil infertility and landscape deterioration.

For subsistence and semi-subsistence farm families, "tired," "sick," or "burnt" soils can indeed sound the death knell to their livelihoods. *Tierras vírginas,* virgin fields that have never been chemically treated are the ideal according to several Indigenous farmers I spoke with. For although these Indigenous farmers have resisted a complete switch to *new* and *improved* varieties, preferring to consume their more tasty and *arinosa* or mealy ancestral varieties, they have abandoned a considerable amount within just two generations. This abandonment was a response to the push all around them to grow the introduced varieties. But the decline in native varieties also reflected deteriorated genetic stock and the fact that a lot of the Indigenous varieties no longer grew well on blanched, overused, and heavily treated soils. The shift in the soil's microbiology meant that there simply weren't the nutrients for their local landraces.[23] In response to my questions about the reasons behind their abandoned traditional varieties, farm family after farm family in both communities reported that their soils were no longer fertile enough to grow the varieties they preferred and indeed dearly missed.

These trends were worrisome indeed. Chimpa Rodeo farmers in my survey, of an average 35 years of age, reported a 56 per cent loss of the subspecies *tuberosum andeum* since they first helped their grandparents and parents cultivate their family's food crops. Although Mojón farm families interviewed each had on average about two varieties of *tuberosum andeum* more and respondents were an average of 11 years older, their 57 per cent decline was equally troublesome. Participants also reported that their introduced tubers were degenerating far more rapidly, forcing them to purchase new seeds on a much more frequent basis. More and more of Chimpa Rodeo and *Mojón's* Indigenous farmers were forced to join the growing number of potato farmers throughout the Andean region in a chorus of *"ya no tiene fuerza"* (they have lost their vitality).[24]

The farmers I engaged with also lamented the loss of knowledge about alternatives to chemical treatments for disease control. They had witnessed their grandparents using alternative pest-control strategies, such as companion cropping, as well as lengthier fallow periods. In each community, farmers also noted the name of a farmer or farmers who had maintained their potato diversity and continued to have the skills needed to do so. But, they lamented, many of the techniques that their own families had once used to keep the family land healthy and robust for production had been abandoned or forgotten. A CENPRUR graduate from another community within the municipality had this explanation about the loss of this knowledge: "There was organic control in my grandfather's day ... certain plants were used, for example, but it became easier to use the *fito sanitarios* (chemical treatment)."[25]

Mojón's farm families, as noted, were not the recipients of nearly as much NGO assistance. However, as experienced migrants to valley lands, they had witnessed production yields in NGO-sponsored fields that in the initial years seemed very attractive and followed suit. They were, nevertheless, the ones who expressed the most regret over their abandoned varieties. They were also the farmers who expressed the most enthusiasm for programming that might help them to return to earlier levels of biodiversity within their much beloved potato fields.

The farmers' reflection about this loss of knowledge draws to mind a comment made early on in my field research. Miguel Holle, a well-known potato breeder, made this strong plea when I met him in his office at the International Potato Centre (CIP) in Lima. "Worry less about the actual loss of varieties and more about the loss of knowledge needed to maintain them."[26] Again, the critical issue here is the reproduction of the conditions that facilitate both that production and ultimately the survival of the farming economy.[27] Reproduction in farming – attention to the soil microbiology and the gestation and nurturing of conditions to ensure future production – is a piece of the food production puzzle that is so very often forgotten when the key focus is on yield and short-term gains through commercial sales.

IPTK's program, although failing to engage in a process to build long-term sustainability and community resilience, was, during my final days in the region, beginning to show some promising signs of change. Staff members were increasingly and openly critical of the scientific arrogance of the early years. Most of the Ravelo staff I interacted with appeared very interested in training that might help them to move the organisation closer to a more balanced, intercultural strategy. Within the 1999–2002 program strategy document, there is acknowledgement, albeit all too brief, of the need to respect cultural diversity.

There were also new research efforts to examine alternatives to potato monoculture, with staff expressing considerable enthusiasm for programming to preserve the biodiversity of the area through the recuperation of traditional potato varieties and soil restoration strategies. The 1998 CENPRUR curriculum for agricultural technicians included content on Andean technologies, Andean cosmovision and several other topics in support of ecological agriculture – a system that blends the best of traditional knowledge with useful principles in modern agricultural sciences – the subject of the last section in this book. My conversations with a new generation of leaders within the organization also suggested that there was a growing openness to reconciling political ambitions with Indigenous identity questions. Two veteran managers also expressed interest in alternative visions of governance and development strategies.

Within the IPTK culture new trends were always welcomed. The adoption of more promising approaches seemed likely. I was rooting, of course, for a change in the fundamentals – a willingness to drop the idea of something being missing or wrong and to work instead with the resilience that was already present. There were individual staff members who seemed to be pushing for such substantive change. By the time I headed for home, however, political party ambitions and continued pressures to deliver donor-driven results within a Western development framework with strict, imposed timelines remained significant challenges. "Deficit development" remained the dominant concept.

Deficit development thinking was even more predominant within the second NGO of significance to the residents in the region and to the farmers within Chimpa Rodeo, Food for the Hungry International (FHI). "F-eh-A-che," as they were commonly referred to, was very direct about their intent to fill the void. They openly sought to convert Indigenous campesinos into faithful, God-fearing Western farmers, without apologies or excuses. Since the organization was not present in Mojón in 2000, this field based review in the next chapter focuses on their work in Chimpa Rodeo – programming that started with the provision of flush toilets and drinking taps for every interested household and eventually included support for health care and food producer associations.

1 0

Hungry in Body and Spirit

DEVELOPMENT AND SPIRITUAL DEFICITS?

In 1998, Food for the Hungry International (FHI) made its way to Chimpa Rodeo determined to address both the community's development deficits and its spiritual ones. Founded by American conservatives of the Christian right, the organization that arrived was substantive in size and grip. Since the organization first entered Bolivia two decades earlier to launch a child sponsorship program, it had built up a core staff of over 200 people to oversee programming affecting over one hundred thousand direct *beneficiaries* located within the highlands of the country's most food insecure provinces.[1] During my research term, it was one of the four organizations that the United States Agency for International Development (USAID) had designated as its principal aid delivery partners.[2] With its healthy budget, doors were opened, not the least of which were those of cash-strapped municipalities at the bottom of the UNDP's Human Development Index. According to the Ravelo municipality's annual report for 2000, FHI contributed roughly 46 per cent of the income Ravelo received from external, non-governmental sources.[3]

The organization began work in Bolivia during the *El Niño* disaster in 1983, when its staff set up an emergency food relief program. In cooperation with UNICEF in two provinces of Northern Potosí, the organization also dabbled in literacy programming.[4] Particularly welcomed in the Chayanta region was their support of a chagas disease reduction program in thirty-eight communities. They built pest-resistant housing and fumigated other buildings that might have carried the insect vector responsible for this sometimes-fatal disease.[5]

By 2000, the agency claimed to have completely moved away from relief to longer-term development, with a special emphasis on agricultural productivity, child nutrition, and maternal and reproductive health. These were the programs they focused on in Chimpa Rodeo. However, as late as 2002, as this next journal entry reveals, I saw FHI food relief packages in the school that Chimpa Rodeo's children attended. This was during a return visit to the area. A break in my schedule allowed for a short walk to the school and a meeting with the school principal. It turned out to be a very informative conversation. I had had no idea, for example, that FHI was continuing to supply school lunch programs with a powdered drink from outside the region. The principal was clearly not a fan of this approach, complaining that local farmers, if supported, could do the provisioning. His clear distrust of NGO intermediaries was also very instructive.

PATA RODEO, 25 MAY 2002

It is almost noon so the sun is high and finally taking the chill out of the day. I pull off my sweater and let the rays warm me up. As I walk along the road and toward the school, I notice the principal in the schoolyard. I have long wanted to meet the man running the school Chimpa Rodeo's kids attend. It just hadn't worked out in 2000. And there, coincidentally, he is standing close by. I approach, say my name, and he says that he remembers my attempts to meet him. He was ill for a while that year. He invites me into the school. On goes my sweater again. The narrow windows in these thick-walled adobe buildings keep them very cool, too cool for my liking.

The school is like most I have seen this year and in past visits to Bolivia. The classrooms are small, crowded with basic wooden tables and long benches. Each has a worn blackboard at the front and a combination of educational cutouts hanging from the ceiling and posters on the walls. Pata Rodeo is on the road into Ravelo, so there is electricity. Two light bulbs dangle from the ceilings at either end. The infrastructure improvements promised in La Reforma Educativa have not yet reached this school. The upgrades will happen soon, people have been told.

The principal, on the other hand, is not of a past vintage. He is middle-aged but seems to have fresh ideas and dreams. He tells me about how he welcomes the promised changes in the reform program. He just worries that the resources needed to make them work won't be forthcoming. And his teachers, he says, are not well equipped for the changes ahead. I detect discouragement, although not yet resignation. He is doing his best to remain positive and professional.

The children are about to have lunch. Staff members are settling them in their seats. I notice a packet, some powdered drink of sorts. I ask Señor Director what they are. This is a nutritional drink mix that "FH" is providing along with the World Food Program. With an obvious note of sarcasm in his voice, he adds: "Before the NGOs we had to do it all ourselves. Now everything is free."[6]

His comments hit home. I share his frustration. The children he serves need the additional nutrients. There is no doubt. But there are other options. We begin to discuss the local food crops that could be feeding these children and could be expanded if the aid investment was to go directly to the food producers themselves. Indigenous potato varieties and crops like oca and tarwi are full of micronutrients and anti-oxidants. The local potatoes, in fact, have one of the highest protein levels within the major food crops. And *tarwi galletas* or cookies are easily available in city markets. Almost every farm family in their region could have the right combination of food and would happily bring that diversity back into production if these crops and varieties were valued more. Some training money would, of course, also be needed to revitalize skills lost when synthetic chemicals replaced the need to keep the farmers' knowledge current.

It just seemed so obvious to us as we chatted this warm March afternoon. Yet, apparently it was not so obvious to the decision-makers set on a packaged approach to health. *El Director's* handshake is warm as I offer mine to say goodbye. But his smile remains wry. How much longer will he stay, I wonder.

FHI did not minister only to the hungry, including through continued food aid it would appear. The organization was also eager to feed the "hungry in spirit." It was, in fact, openly evangelical in its approach, offering assistance that staff defined as holistic, explained on their 2000 web site as "meeting needs with holistic ministry."[7] A slogan on the wall of their field station wall in Pata Rodeo, Chimpa Rodeo's neighbour, was still more precise: "Proclaim to all who suffer from physical and spiritual hunger." Also posted on the wall was a mission statement with the words, "God calls us and we will be there until there is an end to physical and spiritual hunger world-wide."

The organization's core principles listed below the slogan were to value "the supreme reign of Jesus Christ, love that builds a complete person, integrity, transparency, and justice." "Unity and diversity" were also advanced, but this unifying vision was one that included a powerful call to promote the supreme reign of Jesus Christ. One my principal FHI informants, in fact, described this as a "Christian cosmovision."

The installation of flush toilets and potable water taps for individual households were, as noted, the first FHI projects to be implemented in Chimpa Rodeo. These were provided to families able to contribute a small amount toward their construction. About half of the flush toilets seemed to be still in use whenever I visited the community. Another quarter were not functioning and the last quarter were used for storage. An often-expressed concern among NGO colleagues I discussed this project with was the amount of water such a flush system demanded of the area's semi-arid landscape.

CHRISTIAN COSMOVISION?

Training workshops that espoused a Christian cosmovision that might put an end to what a Bolivian FHI staff informant called "the animist fatalism of the Quechua farmer" accompanied the flush toilets and potable water project.[8] About this fatalism, he further explained: "People in this region are very conformist. They don't really aspire to have more. They are also animists who always consider themselves punished. They can't see the future, only today. They seed so they can eat, not more. Why should they study? For what? If boys learn to read and write, it is to get a job. They don't aspire to be professionals. We have to change this."[9]

The notion that Indigenous fatalism was the major obstacle to forward-looking thinking – to a vision beyond concern for basic needs – seems to have been more than merely the opinion of the staff person I interviewed. Under a subsection of FHI's "Institutional Identity" document, entitled "Community Vision," the broader institution appeared to endorse this perspective. "The community and its peoples should advance towards the potential God has given them to progress beyond the satisfaction of their basic needs."[10] In response to a question about the broader socio-economic and political roots of the extreme poverty of the area, my principal informant explained that FHI did not address issues that might be construed as interference in the internal affairs of the nation. Besides, he argued, "the real causes of the extreme poverty in this area were fivefold: man's sins; his lack of knowledge and awareness; Satan's grip; a lack of resources; and an absence of assistance." He also added that FHI had serious concerns about the "pagan cult" of *Pachamama* inherited from the Inca period. The agency was more comfortable, he insisted, with "the more powerful" Inca concept of *Pachakama*, which they interpreted as "God is sovereign."[11] When asked about the extent to which the organization had integrated an intercultural approach into its program, he responded that interculturalism was not an operational concept FHI employed. He did, however, admit to FHI's need to conduct more research on the cultural identity of their participants to understand them better.[12]

When it came down to agricultural production systems, this informant, an agronomist by training, expressed admiration for long-held Indigenous crop production strategies like crop rotation and fallowing, as did a group of FHI agricultural extension workers I met by chance and briefly in Pata Rodeo. In every other way, however, their approach to farming was in keeping with the industrial agricultural model that dominated this region. Their focus, according to my informant, "was on marketable crops for profit." "Andean products (i.e., Indigenous varieties)," he declared without hesitation, "have no market."[13]

FHI's central office team also included an environmental specialist – an American – to advise on reforestation and environmental impact issues. I sought her out one day when I heard that she was in the region. After my brief explanation of my research, however, she quickly said, "We don't do biodiversity programming, so are you sure that you want to talk to me?"[14] I was later to discover that FHI's local field staff members in the municipality of Ravelo were not at all oblivious to the importance of diversity. They had, possibly following IPTK's lead, organized an agricultural fair in Pata Rodeo that included a diversity competition for farmers with the highest number of potato varieties. As with IPTK and NGOs more broadly, head office staff clearly did not always rule the day. Nor, I discovered, did all FHI's employees share the agency's official ideology and Christian orthodoxy. My key informant's thoughts were well in sync with those of his bosses in the country, or at least reported to be so. But to reduce this organization to a completely homogeneous entity would be to fall prey to the reductionism this study seeks to challenge.

Despite staff resistance and this particular initiative to enhance potato diversity, commercial considerations were paramount within FHI's approach to crop production. Introduced varieties and agrochemicals were offered through a low-interest credit scheme, not unlike the ANED/ IPTK system described in my previous chapter, but with the addition of a rotating seed-loan fund. There was a twist, however, in the approach. Producers FHI gathered into groups were not set up as independent producer associations, as was the case with the ANED/IPTK model. Rather, they were organized as FHI producer "clubs." In addition to the offer of credit to purchase synthetic agro-chemicals, they received counseling and instruction in Christian beliefs, ethics, and morals. Participation in the club, in fact, required agreement to practise such values, beginning with a pledge not to consume alcoholic drinks.

The field staff I encountered expressed a strong desire to strengthen the independence of these producers' groups, turning them into associations. This transition seemed especially urgent at the time, since the organization was due to leave the region in 2004. FHI, I was told, usually spent a maximum of six years in any given region. The staff members were therefore anxious to initiate a process that would ensure that these groups could operate on their own. But the strategy expressed was rather nebulous and, in light of what appeared to me to be an exceedingly paternalistic approach agency-wide, would have required a considerable shift in approach. Moreover, with funding patrons, like the United States Agency for International Development (USAID) sponsoring messages like the one cited below, external pushes to abandon paternalistic policy and practice would be long in coming. I found this passage in a 1998 USAID and Peace Corps co-funded pamphlet given to farmers in another region of Bolivia. People who were already masters of reciprocal working arrangements and descendants of the Indigenous designers of *ayllu* governance and ecological complementarity were offered this advice: "Why Organize? Often working with other people can make our lives easier and more productive. For example, if you have to carry a big, heavy box alone, it is very difficult, but if you have a helper it is easier. You only have to carry half the weight. Working together can make your life in your fields easier and can help to make life in our community easier. If we work together we can help to achieve more in our community."[15]

Of all the passages I gathered during my research for this book, this one topped my list of the most patronizing. Not only did its authors seem oblivious to the collaboration inherent in *ayllu* governance, they also appear to have confused weak reading skills with stupidity.

The pamphlet containing this passage was not, I should stress, written by FHI. Although FHI was one of USAID's chief implementing agencies in the country, I do not assume that FHI field staff would have endorsed it. But the term naïve did come to mind when I witnessed attempts to turn the members of their production clubs into good Christian citizens. Club members, as noted, were asked to refrain from any drinking in their festivities, whether FHI staff were present or not. Time and again I witnessed club members feign faithful sobriety in the presence of senior FHI staff. But once FHI was gone from their village, they did as they pleased. On more than one occasion I had farmers ask me to warn them if an FHI extension worker was around. I was also not terribly surprised to discover FHI field staff of local descent willing to help themselves to a beer or two when the boss was not around.

My several attempts to interview the FHI field station manager at the agency's regional headquarters in neighbouring Pata Rodeo, and to participate in one of their agricultural training workshops, proved to be in vain. I spoke briefly with the manager during an unexpected encounter in their field station residence. He seemed interested and asked me to call him when he would have more time for a more complete discussion. But after several calls and two missed appointments on his part, I had to accept defeat on that front. The approach and subjects covered in the FHI agricultural training workshop, like the field manager's take on things, would remain a mystery.

As the next journal entry reveals, I did manage to catch an FHI session on reproductive health for a group of Chimpa Rodeo women. One of FHI's Bolivian nurses conducted it, together with an American volunteer.[16] While it would be wrong to draw too many conclusions from this one participant observation of a FHI workshop, the tense atmosphere and clear discomfort of the FHI staff confirmed my sense that the conflicting value base between FHI and the residents of Chimpa Rodeo was contributing to a far more transactional relationship than an engaged and authentic one.

CHIMPA RODEO, 2000 (PRECISE DATE NOT RECORDED)
I am sitting in Chimpa Rodeo's tiny community hall – more the size of a small classroom – with six Chimpa women and the two FHI trainers hosting the workshop. The nurse seems very comfortable in her surroundings. The American volunteer is less so, not surprisingly since she speaks very little Quechua. If I am not mistaken, she is reasonably new to Bolivia. Participants greet me warmly. I know most of them quite well. I haven't managed to participate in any other FHI workshops, so I am pleased and very grateful to be able to witness their approach in this one today.

The workshop is a part of a series planned to raise awareness about reproductive health issues. There are about six of us in the room. Our session, to run for about an hour and a half, begins with short introductions, names mostly. Our facilitators proceed with a short presentation on feminine hygiene. Repeated late arrivals are interrupting the flow of the discussion. Our trainers greet the latecomers sarcastically with "*buenas noches*," although nightfall is hours away.

The final participant count is ten women and one man, the man standing in for his wife, who could not attend. (I have seen women attend meetings on behalf of an absent husband, so it is interesting to note that this practice also works the other way around.)

Since neither the American nor I speak enough Quechua to follow the dialogue well, the nurse translates frequently.[17] When Quechua is spoken, I am able to concentrate on body language and the mood. While somewhat shy at first, the women participants have opened up and, to my surprise given the topic, seem relaxed. They appeared to welcome an opportunity to discuss health and reproductive matters and are surprisingly candid. The facilitators, on the other hand, appear increasingly uncomfortable, tense, and impatient with participants, who are not responding as they had probably hoped. The positive mood and tone has changed. One participant has bluntly asserted that girl babies are not nearly as valuable or as welcomed as boys. FHI's trainers are visibly upset. They contest her declaration but they don't seem to know what to say next. The discussion ends rather abruptly in fact, as does the session. Homework is announced. The group is to design a socio-drama on reproductive health. I stay behind to chat with the trainers. They comment on the need for considerable patience. It will take some time yet to make an impact.

These young trainers strike me as well-intentioned young women struggling hard to reconcile the dramatically different perspectives they hold from those of the people they hope to serve. I wonder whether their faith motivates a determination to be patient with what they seem to consider local "ignorance." But they are careful not to say anything that direct. Nor has there been any religious commentary. I suspect that connection with these women will take some time. For one, there is a notable absence of food, beverages, and most importantly coca leaves for sharing. This is not a good start for women accustomed to these symbols of respect and reciprocity.

ASISTENCIALISMO?

Although unwilling to offer coca leaves to their host communities, FHI
was willing to contribute comparatively expensive material assistance, and
the flush toilets and household water taps and sinks they originally
arrived with were considered by many to be excessive given the low water
levels and other, more urgent needs. For members of their agricultural
associations, they also provided delivery services for goods such as fertilizers, although a big delay during the year I conducted my research had
association members very worried. Being forced to put off planting
beyond the optimum time makes farmers very nervous. This type of direct
assistance contributed to suggestions among NGO workers in the region
(and indeed in other parts of the country) that a type of religious gerry-
mandering was at hand. FHI, in other words, was soliciting converts
through generous handouts. They also expressed resentment that FHI's
asistencialismo or charity orientation had contributed to rumblings of discontent among farmers when their own organizations didn't offer such a
generous helping hand. IPTK was one of those. In the four short years since
IPTK had discarded its own *asistencialismo*, FHI had revived it in spades.

FHI's approach to agricultural production, although far more paternalistic than that of IPTK, nevertheless had much in common with its most
significant counterpart in the region. FHI peddled the "green revolution"
model that characterized the entire region well. As suggested, their development assistance was tied to an ideology that was unapologetic in its
devaluation of Indigenous world views. The knowledge at the core of
resilient Indigenous agriculture was, in the case of FHI, of little interest
and largely dismissed.

As the Chimpa Rodeo women participants during the session on reproductive health illustrated, and as with the rule against alcohol, the people
of Chimpa Rodeo did not simply embrace what their latest wealthy patron
preached. Their Indigenous hybrid of Andean spirituality and Catholi-
cism, so clearly demonstrated during festivals like that of Our Lady of
Guadalupe, seemed impervious to the more literal, evangelical Christianity of their foreign donor. Proud highlanders of the Andean cordilleras, they
were able to juggle the less desirable components of the support, like tem-
perance, in order to access the benefits. For their part, FHI, misjudged the
shrewdness of the people with whom they were dealing. While practising
tied aid, commonly referred to as "rice Christianity," their impact on the
spirituality of the "heathens" they attempted to shepherd appears to have

been marginal. The impact of their agricultural assistance, like that of IPTK's described above, was another matter, however.

If there were serious deficits to uncover within the Jalq'a region in 2000, they appeared to be strongest in the thinking of organizations hoping to lend them a hand. This assessment is not to suggest that the Jalq'a were passive victims of misguided assistance or to romanticize the Jalq'a world. They, too, made choices that weakened their resilience. But in a context of powerful and often heavy-handed governmental and non-governmental assistance, their particular responsibility for the mistakes made is almost impossible to isolate.

My intent in delivering this critique is not simply to wag a reproachful finger at the outsider. Nor do I intend to fall prey to a sustainable development discourse that too often relies on polemic and oppositional categories.[18] My purpose is to identify serious shortcomings that can be acted on, and by way of conclusion to suggest alternatives. As James Joyce wisely insisted, "mistakes are the portal of discovery."

The final development assistance organization within my research lens — the United Nations Children's Fund (UNICEF) – made far more valiant attempts to value and build on the Indigenous knowledge systems so evident in their program communities. In practice, however, the deficit development thinking so prominent in the broader development industry was not so easily set aside. This was especially the case with their literacy work, a program delivered through local promoters to the residents of Chimpa Rodeo over a two-year period. Since literacy training exemplifies, like no other development program, a deficit starting point, we leave the world of the Jalq'a briefly to explore how the sacred cow of international development assistance – literacy – both reflects and has helped to embed the notion that within "disadvantaged" communities there is something lacking or broken, possibly even an inability to conceptualize a better future.

I I

"Dipstick" Development

We told them [the Iroquois] that we know all things through written
documents. These savages asked "Before you came to the lands where we live,
did you rightly know that we were here?" We were obliged to say no. "Then you
don't know all things through books, and they didn't tell you everything."

Louis Hennepin, 1626–1701[1]

OUT OF THE DARKNESS

Since Louis Hennepin's seventeenth-century adventures in the New
World, thinking about the primacy of Western literacy has not shifted dramatically. Even a quick scan of the work written about literacy and literacy education will elicit quote after quote with implicit, sometimes explicit, assumptions about the deficiencies or "backwardness" of peoples who
cannot read and write text. "Reading and writing," said the World Conference of Ministers of Education on the Eradication of Literacy in 1965,
"should not only lead to elementary general knowledge but to training for
work, increased productivity, a greater participation in civic life and a better understanding of the surrounding world, and should ultimately open
the way to basic human knowledge."[2] A World Bank Regional and Sec-
toral Study in 1994 noted that " another advantage of education, particularly for Indigenous peoples, is realized in the farming sector ... schooling
produce[s] cognitive skills, which make it easier for farmers to seek, find
and manage information."[3] In 2010 members of the editorial board for a
series on literacy, representing universities from around the world, wrote:
"While language defines humans, literacy defines civilization."[4]

Hennepin's admission implies that some have had second thoughts
about such superiority. And there are more and more scholars who critique the equation between literacy and knowledge. But the belief that

reading and writing are a cornerstone for sustainable development seems as entrenched today as ever. Leading into International Literacy Year and the International Literacy Decade in 1990, the United Nations Educational, Scientific and Cultural Organization (UNESCO) – founded in 1945 to foster and spread worldwide literacy[5] – defined a literate person to be one who, among other skills, would be able "to use reading, writing and calculation for his own and the community's development."[6] The goal proposed to launch the decade was "the elimination of illiteracy by the year 2000." Decision-makers settled on massive reduction rather than its elimination, understanding the impracticality of complete eradication. But as with popular vaccination programs of the era, governments were called on to pledge significant resources to fight this widespread "disease."[7] A briefing in preparation for the 2000 International Literacy Year included this testimonial about an Ethiopian participant: "At 27, Birk enrolled in a literacy centre and after 6 months of conscientious and courageous attention, she began, she said, to be aware of many things. 'It is like being reborn, like a blind person recovering his or her sight.'"[8]

A 2008 UNESCO primer on literacy, designed for planners and policy makers, keeps up this theme of literacy as a prerequisite not only for development success but also for being smart. The booklet, as one would expect, cites literacy as the key to achieving "improved nutrition and health, increased productivity and poverty reduction, enhanced political participation, conscientization of the poor, empowerment of women, [and] sensitization to environmental issues." It goes one step further, however, suggesting, "literacy is necessary to facilitate any further learning."[9] UNESCO's media release for its 2010 International Literacy Day again called literacy "an essential foundation for development," linking it to personal rewards and broader human development. "Literacy is not just about educating," their media release insists, "it is a unique and powerful tool to eradicate poverty and a strong means for social and human progress … an effective way to enlighten a society and arm it to face challenges of life in a stronger and efficient way.[10]

Education specialists are not the only ones citing illiteracy as the "main obstacle to development."[11] In 1997 the United Nations Development Program's (UNDP) study on sustainable development also advanced literacy as the path to much needed knowledge and labour productivity: "Better-educated and trained people have a stronger appreciation for the environmental resources and greater ability to protect and regenerate them … Primary and secondary education creates access to opportunity and can increase labour productivity by increasing people's willingness and capacity to learn." [12] The UNDP's annual global index on human development, the HDI, includes literacy levels, combined with school enrolment rates, as two of the three key assessment variables. [13]

The World Bank – of late the primary multilateral funding agent for international literacy programs[14] – has long married literacy and education with enhanced environmental management. "Schooling," a 1990s report on Indigenous peoples and poverty argued, "produces cognitive skills which make it easier for farmers to seek, find and manage information."[15] The Tzetzals of Mexico, some of whom are able to recognize more than 1,200 species of plants but are unable to read and write text, would undoubtedly find this declaration rather curious.[16] Multilateral and government institutions stand in good company in their promotion of reading, writing, and technical training as essential components for meaningful development. Most non-governmental organizations (NGOs) and civil society organizations charged with the task of assisting marginalized communities to grow self-reliant have long considered literacy training and capacity building to be critical to a community's struggle for power, justice, and equality. Indeed, literacy classes are often run as the entry point to other development interventions.[17] The benefits are thought to be numerous, with literate, trained members of these communities considered to be at a clear advantage in defining their path to full and meaningful citizenship.[18]

In my Bolivia-based research in 2000, literacy was frequently touted as the foundation of the learning process.[19] Such views appear to have persisted. A 2008 report about Bolivia's national campaign to eradicate illiteracy – spearheaded and claimed a success by the country's president, Evo Morales – exemplified such thinking. "Freddy Mollo, 43," BBC News reported, "said that not knowing how to read and write was like having a disability, it was like being blind." Daria Calpa, 62, of Potosí, was cited as having not even felt like a "real person" before becoming literate.[20] Participants in government, multilateral, and NGO training programs, it seems, have learned to equate the inability to read and write text with ignorance. In report after report and story after story the "great tragedy of illiteracy" is assumed. Gaining sight and being reborn are common metaphors.[21]

A number of critics, as mentioned, have stepped forward to challenge this resolute faith in Western literacy.[22] In 1994, for example, Heribert Hinzen of the Institute for International Cooperation of the German Adult Education Association, lashed out at this unquestioning complacency about the benefits of literacy programming: "Do we, as adult and literacy educators, involved in planning, coordination and research, take a critical look at our work or do we prefer repeating old slogans and reinforcing myths and wishful thinking?"[23] Hinzen went on to suggest that to "see literacy as a prerequisite and panacea for all related problems is a dangerous misunderstanding."[24] He cited several cases from Asia and Africa where literacy did not dramatically alter the situation of poor and disadvantaged people. One Indian example was especially telling.

An international NGO sponsored a new literacy program to help participants take greater control of their lives. There were particular concerns about unscrupulous moneylenders and corrupt landowners, the need to improve agricultural practices, and the need to help women to raise their status. When an evaluator returned some years after the program's completion, little initial progress had been sustained. Moneylending practices had not changed significantly. Only 3 per cent of those questioned noted any improvement in farming income and only 4 per cent of the women reported an increase in status.[25]

It could well be argued that these programs had simply been poorly implemented, that they were not sufficiently comprehensive, community participation was weak from the start, or there had not been enough follow-up. Such explanations are common. However, the challenges for communities like those in India, Bolivia, or elsewhere, I would argue, were and are much more fundamental. Illiteracy, while consistently cited as a cause of underdevelopment, is never the source of injustice or even, necessarily, a deficiency. A group of female participants in a more recent study in El Salvador reported what I consider to be a far more helpful analysis and place to start. They were not suffering primarily through their lack of reading and writing skills, they argued. Rather, the sites of their struggle were those of poverty, scarcity, and hegemony.[26]

But as the citations earlier suggest, the majority of development thinkers continue to ignore what American historian Henry Graff has called the "myth associated with social and economic progress, political democracy, social and educational mobility and the development of cognitive skills."[27]

There is also a more pragmatic interest in the championing of literacy among governments, multilateral institutions, and NGOs. It is so much easier to communicate with people who can read, write, and use the Occidental logic that literacy training brings with it. Agencies engaged in community development consistently draw literate minorities into leadership positions because these skills facilitate an ability to get the job done much faster and, arguably, more efficiently. I have often seen a community's natural but illiterate leaders overlooked. The same literate individuals participate in the bulk of the courses offered by the various development agencies. Many, although not all, emerge as an elite of comparatively affluent promoters with closer ties, at times, to their benefactors than to their communities. Development agencies unwittingly transform the leadership roles and practices of participating communities, with varying and unpredictable consequences.

MEASURING LITERACY

Literacy as a concept is not a simple one, of course. It has historically represented and continues to represent different things to people.[28] The literature on this subject is vast, and theories are hotly contested, sometimes contradictory, and always thought-provoking. Researcher bias and donor influence in countries like Bolivia must be factored into any analysis of the literacy situation and of proposed strategies.[29] And when we think about literacy policy more broadly, we should not forget that it is case-based, interpretive, highly contextual, and, by definition, political.[30]

Still, however much the political dynamics of literacy are appreciated in the discourse about literacy, its technical aspects – the abstract set of reading and writing skills or abilities that exist independently of their context – continue to dominate approaches to its instruction and dissemination.[31] As the next chapter reveals, this was definitely the situation in Bolivia in 2000. To cite just one example, the deep-seated challenges facing adult women participants in literacy programming were poorly considered. Classes took place at night after long days of caring for family and fields. Most instructors were young men with very limited understanding of women's particular needs and interests. The women "graduates" that I interviewed in Chimpa Rodeo managed to learn to sign their names but not much else. Nor was the follow-up support needed to ensure the continuation of literacy skills present. The model reflected what another well-known critic on the literacy question, Stephen Reder, called the "dipstick model." "Literacy," he explained, "is thought of as something people carry around in their heads from setting to setting, from task to task ... [an] individual's head can be opened up, a linear instrument inserted (the dipstick), and a measurement taken of the individual's literacy level." If there is not enough literacy inside, it is assumed that more can be added through formal instruction.[32]

When literacy is defined as the mastery of reading, writing, and arithmetic, it may appear to be value-neutral and objective. Yet it is, in fact, often rooted in development theory that is instrumental – separating knowledge from an individual's actions, experience, and social context. Individuals and societies are labeled as inadequate when they do not contain enough of the valued product.[33] Much like the mainstream Western thinking about knowledge production and effective development assistance that this book has challenged,[34] dipstick literacy rationalizes social and economic inequity, as well as class stratification, as inevitable and objective outcomes of the sorting process of the education and social systems.[35] There is a deliberate diminishing of the one – the illiterate – to strengthen the other – the literate. For scholars like Henry Giroux, our Western deification of literacy is really about our utilitarian and imperial objectives. "Literacy becomes the pedagogy of chauvinism dressed up in the lingo of Great Books."[36] After studying the impact of Australian literacy policy for Aborigines and Torres Strait Islanders, Allan Luke concluded, "universal print literacy has been a widely documented precursor for the expansion, distribution, and consolidation of capital, though obviously not in equitable ways."[37]

To be fair, most multilateral institutions and NGOs in this new century have moved beyond strictly utilitarian definitions of literacy to recognize the wider ideological constructs shaping the educational enterprise. UNESCO, for example, champions literacy as a basic human right and emphasizes programming that integrates cultural content and critical thinking into the curriculum.[38] Literacy training in one's mother tongue and the importance of cultural context and culturally relevant curriculum are, at long last, also promoted.

There are, as well, other less tangible benefits of literacy training that might be reason enough to invest. For women who are otherwise isolated in their households, the opportunity to meet and discuss issues on a regular basis and to learn about one's rights can be a critical first step to organizing. But do peoples on the margins necessarily require literacy training to enjoy fulfilling lives? For women farmers, able to read their landscapes like we read a favourite novel, should Occidental literacy training always be the highest priority on a long list of their needs? Within multilateral, government, and non-governmental institutions the predominant answer continues to be yes. "How can anyone argue against the critical role literacy plays in the transformation of an impoverished person's destiny?" the thinking goes.

A seminal piece on the subject in the late 1960s, "The Consequences of Literacy," had precisely this kind of message and influence. The combined brainchild of a well-respected social anthropologist, Jack Goody, and literary critic Ian Watt, the article took the academic and development world by storm. From all accounts, it seems to have persuaded generations of readers about the intimate connection between conceptual, abstract thinking and the ability to read and write. There was a more contentious dimension to the analysis, as well, that is of still greater relevance to this book. To advance their arguments, Goody and Watt, focused on illiterate *Indigenous* peoples. They thereby not only influenced the discourse about literacy education more broadly but more specifically the debate about how Indigenous peoples think or "can't think" in the absence of a tradition of reading and writing text.

THE GREAT DIVIDE

The world is complex, dynamic, and multidimensional; the paper is static, flat.
How are we to represent the rich visual world of experience and
measurement on mere flatland?[39]

Edward Tufte

Tracing the impact of Occidental literacy on knowledge transmission and critical thinking from its earliest Greek origins to its late twentieth-century manifestations, "The Consequences of Literacy" suggested that, while it is important to move beyond simplistic and ethnocentric characterization of oral societies as *primitive* and literate societies as *civilized*, clear distinctions between oral and literate societies could be made. Within oral societies, Goody and Watt posited, what an individual remembers is of great importance in his experience of the main social relationships, with the "whole content of social tradition ... held in memory."[40] "There is," they wrote, "an unobtrusive adaptation of past traditions to present needs."[41] Consequently, oral cultures have "little perception of the past except in terms of the present."[42] The cultural repertoire of literate societies, in contrast, "has been given permanent form. They are thus impelled to a much more conscious, comparative, and critical attitude to the accepted world. Writing provides an alternative source for the transmission of cultural orientations [and thus] favours awareness of inconsistency."[43] "The annals of a literate society," these scholars asserted, "cannot but enforce a more *objective* recognition of the distinction of what was and what is."[44]

Goody and Watt allowed for skepticism in non-literate societies. But such skepticism, they suggested, took a personal, non-cumulative form. It did not lead to deliberate rejection and re-interpretation of social dogma so much as to a semi-automatic readjustment of belief.[45] Literate societies, on the other hand, "cannot discard, absorb, or transmute the past ... [I]nstead their members are faced with permanently recorded versions of the past and its beliefs; and because the past is thus set apart from the present, historical enquiry becomes possible. This in turn encourages skepticism; and skepticism, not only about the legendary past, but also about received ideas about the universe as a whole."[46] History replaces myth and there is opportunity for political and intellectual universalism.[47] The abundance of information within literate societies had its drawbacks, according to Goody and Watt. "No structural amnesia prevents the [literate] individual from participating fully in the total cultural tradition to anything like the extent possible in non-literate societies."[48] They were also careful to note that writing was an addition, not an alternative, to oral transmission and noted the importance of rejecting any dichotomy based on the assumption of radical difference between the mental attributes of literate and non-literate peoples.[49] But this attempt to acknowledge that the illiterate are not inferior intellectually rings rather hollow in a thesis that otherwise treats non-literate society as homeostatic, homogeneous, simpler, trapped in the present, and unable to see the particulars that are critical to rational thinking. The political dimension of discourse and text, the writer's production and management of interpretation, and the fact that text often embodies myth are simply ignored. Goody and Watt consider literacy as central to abstract and deductive reasoning processes. A literate population, they claim, enables society to move beyond "its legendary past" to a more sophisticated, objective, critical, and dynamic perspective on life and the world.

Almost three decades later, Goody cautioned against overstressing the homogeneity of non-literate societies. He nevertheless continued to maintain that there was a broad distinction to be made between culture in "simpler" and "complex" societies that related to their means of communication. "Oral societies," he wrote, "are spared what Benjamin Franklin called 'the restless interventions of the printer.'" "They are also spared," he went on to say, "the disturbing and creative presence of the writer. And the absence of writing clearly has some relation to their homogeneity, since at the very least new forms of knowledge, new symbols, and new meanings are created in this medium that affects the culture in far-reaching ways."[50]

Within the past two decades, several scholars of literacy, culture, and knowledge and Indigenous peoples have challenged the writings of Goody, Watt, and other likeminded scholars responsible for what had been called "great divide" theory.[51] Particularly under fire are: the view of Indigenous cultures as one-dimensional and homogeneous; the strict division between oral and literate modes of languages, with literacy contributing to *higher order, rational* thinking; the failure to recognize the central role of power relations and ideological positioning in literacy practices; and last, but in no way least, the emphasis on language and literacy in the transmission of knowledge.[52] In fact, the whole concept of a single literacy based on reading and writing skills has been called into question. Socio-linguistic and anthropological critics now speak of a "plurality of literacies" and promote literacy programming that considers social, political, and economic context.

Rather than see culture as a noun, inert and objectified, I agree with scholars who suggest that culture should be considered as though it were a verb, the active construction of meaning.[53] The use of culture as a noun makes it seem static with fixed boundaries. This may help to explain why Indigenous peoples are too often thought of as "traditional" with "old ways" rather than dynamic actors adapting to ever changing landscapes and contexts. In a similar vein, as Borofsky suggests, knowledge should be considered to be a continuum, with learning following from, rather than preceding, interaction with others.[54] It is not the case that people interact successfully because they share a certain understanding. Rather, they share understanding because they have learned how to interact successfully.[55] Seen in this way, motion becomes inherent in culture and knowledge.[56]

Of still greater significance to this book's thesis, however, is the rebuttal of Goody and Watt's emphasis on language and literacy as requirements for critical thinking. Ethnographic account after ethnographic account make it evident that members of societies with few or no text-based literacy skills can achieve the metalinguistic awareness and perform the complex cognitive processes Goody, Ong, and others would attribute to literate societies.[57] The many "illiterate" small-holder farmers I met in Chimpa Rodeo, Mojón, elsewhere in the Andes, and around the world and the still greater numbers of studies I have read about them demonstrate how "illiterate" Indigenous farmers often employ their own taxonomy, select, breed, field test, and name their varieties.[58] Their understanding of soil and land use involves an assessment of soil properties that goes well beyond the land's inherent fertility.[59] Their practices focus on relational characteristics such as the interaction between crops, animals, and trees and how to achieve synergies that can assist with pest control, crop yield, and ultimately a renewal of soil fertility.[60]

These farmers also pay considerable attention to factors and principles operating within the local context, as opposed to fixed, universal structures and laws. Such detailed observation contributes to Indigenous peoples' recognition of and rapid response to interconnected and ever-changing patterns. Often referred to as *art de localité*,[61] the practice involves a continuous interpretation and evaluation of the ongoing process of production so as to enable intervention at any given point.[62] The interaction between "mental " and "manual" labour and the attention to process within Indigenous farming systems might help to explain what resilience scientists consider to be Indigenous peoples' superior capacity to manage complex ecosystems.[63] This discussion about complexity, of course, brings us back to our discussion in a previous chapter on the ways Indigenous peoples know, learn, and communicate, and to connectionist theory.

Like the cognitive scientists and anthropologists who rejected conventional learning theory with its emphasis on classificatory concepts, researchers into Indigenous education have chipped away at the foundations of literacy orthodoxy.[64] Almost without fail, these critics pay homage to the inspired, albeit at times also contradictory, writings of Brazilian educator and rebel-philosopher, Paulo Freire. His exasperation with the literacy models that taught participants their place within oppressive political and socio-economic structures contributed to the publication in 1970 of a liberation pedagogy that struck a deeply responsive chord with disenfranchised groups and progressive educators around the world. Given his powerful influence on the development of a more critical and political literacy, a brief review of Freire's key messages follows. Here too, however, there is irony and contradiction, further evidence, in fact, of just how deeply embedded our exaltation of reading and writing text is.

LITERACY AS PRAXIS

Drawing on the ideas of social theorists like Antonio Gramsci, Freire advanced a methodology to teach literacy, which offered the marginalized active agency in the social change process. Gramsci considered literacy to be a "double-edged sword" that could be wielded both for self- and social empowerment but also for the perpetuation of repression and domination.[65] Freire's goal was to advance the former over the latter. Mechanistic

conceptions of adult literacy and a "banking concept" of education, with students the unquestioning receptacles of the teacher's view of the world, Freire
argued, domesticated the have-nots, to the benefit of the haves. He championed instead a literacy that was both pedagogical and political, based on
praxis: reflection, dialectical exchange, class-consciousness, and ultimately
democratic transformation for those struggling for a better future. In his
words, "acquiring literacy does not involve memorizing sentences, words, or
syllables – lifeless objects unconnected to an existential universe – but rather
an attitude of creation and re-creation, a self-transformation producing a
stance of intervention in one's context."[66] Central to this argument was
Freire's view of knowledge production as a creative and relational act, where
meaning is constructed through interaction. His writings were reminiscent
of, and possibly influenced by, the ideas of Lev Vygotsky, the Russian educational psychologist who pioneered the theory of social constructivism.[67] In
Pedagogy of the Oppressed Freire wrote: "Knowledge emerges only through
intervention and re-invention, through the restless, impatient, continuing,
hopeful inquiry men pursue in the world, with the world and with each
other." [68]

David Lusted's synthesis of Freire's notion of knowledge as interactive
is especially well done and thus cited now in full:

> Knowledge is not produced in the intentions of those who believe
> they hold it, whether in pen or in the voice. It is produced in the
> process of interaction, between the writer and reader at the moment
> of reading, and between teacher and learner at the moment of class-
> room engagement. Knowledge is not the matter that is offered so
> much as the matter that is understood. To think of fields of bodies of
> knowledge as if they are the property of academics and teachers is
> wrong. It denies an equality in the relations at moments of interaction
> and falsely privileges one side of the exchange, and what that side
> "knows," over the other ... It's not just that it denies the value of what
> learners know, which it does, but it misrecognizes the conditions nec-
> essary for the kind of learning – critical, engaged, personal, social –
> called for by the knowledge itself.[69]

Pedagogy as praxis is thus purposeful, contextual, transformative, and
socially just, an encouraging option for the silenced and oppressed. Freire's
manifesto was a welcome and needed attack on status quo educational
models that dismissed and further marginalized peoples outside the socio-
economic and political mainstream. Progressive educators, social activists,

development workers, trade unionists, and other community-based movements eagerly embraced and adapted this method of helping disenfranchised peoples assert their identities and right to take charge of their lives. Freire's participatory methodology and relevance-based curriculum germinated and flowered in literacy programs around the world. For Freire, to read the word was to read the world.[70] But therein lies what I consider to be a significant flaw in his analysis.

Freire places considerable emphasis on language and the written word as a means to develop critical consciousness, somewhat contradicting his message about knowledge being produced through interaction. He pays little attention to oral or non-linguistic, experiential knowledge transmission that fits so well with his ideas about knowledge as a relational act. Might capturing knowledge on paper arrest its development? In considering reading and writing as *the* stepping-stones to historical sensibility and a prerequisite for critical, analytical thinking, there is an uncomfortable hint of the "great divide" school of thought. In his introduction to *Education for Critical Consciousness* (1973), Freire comments: "The dimensionality of time is one of the fundamental discoveries in the history of human culture. In illiterate cultures, the 'weight' of apparently limitless time hindered people from reaching that consciousness of temporality, and thereby achieving a sense of their historical nature."[71]

In *Pedagogy of the Oppressed* he further states, "almost never do they [the oppressed] realize that they too know things they have learned in their relation with the world and with other men"[72] and "individuals who were submerged in reality, merely 'feeling' their needs, emerge [when literate] from reality and perceive the causes of their needs."[73]

Freire offered marginalized communities, including Indigenous peoples, a guide to a more relevant, critical, and participatory pedagogy and, in so doing, more effective community-change processes. Thanks to his vision, literacy education emerged as a fundamental right within a more progressive educational framework. He asked literacy students to explore the reason for their oppression and warned against the assimilationist, conformist motives of much Western-based education. His insistence on the importance of the written word in a world obsessed with the written language of power is understandable and was politically astute for his support base, Western, urbanized populations in Brazil and beyond. But he paid insufficient attention to alternative modes of knowledge production and transmission in rural and Indigenous societies, or to the issue of how knowledge can change or lose its original meaning when transcribed into text. Freire offered "illiterate" peoples a way to clear the cobwebs of confusion and victimization, unlocking the gate to meaningful development. This assumption brings us back to an ideology that champions literacy as the key ingredient for critical thinking, and thus full circle to Goody and Watts' "Consequences of Literacy."[74]

Challenging the idea of literacy education means challenging something deep in the Western psyche. Successful careers, after all, rest in no small measure on the craft of reading and writing. Mine is no exception, the irony of ironies if I am to be its critic. Shouldn't others have the opportunities I have had? I also think about the dangers that farmers who can't read their pesticide labels face, and more particularly of an incident I captured in my journal when a farmer, dressed in traditional Jalq'a clothing, rushed up to me for advice regarding the sale of his bull.

RAVELO VILLAGE, 8 JULY 2000
The Ravelo skies are a brilliant blue as I navigate the makeshift cobblestone lane to the IPTK field station. I move to a shaded strip of sidewalk to avoid the fire of the midday, mountain sun. My eyes shift from the peeling walls of an adobe house in my immediate gaze to the office. Standing at the gate is a Jalq'a farmer, his distinctive white bowler-like hat in his callused right hand and a torn scrap of wrinkled paper in his left. He looks nervous and anxious, a little impatient. When he sees me, he is obviously pleased, though to me he is a complete stranger.

He immediately shows me his piece of paper. On it I read a few scribbled numbers. These are the prices he has been quoted for the two cattle he butchered that morning. But he wants to know if they are fair and tells me the price per kilo he should get. "Could I please do the calculation?" He tells me their weight and hands me the stub of a lead pencil. I multiply the data at least three times, feeling a sense of responsibility that draws his anxious look into my eyes. I hand him back the paper and tell him the price he should ask for. He shakes my hand in thanks and turns to leave. I shake my head in wonder and turn to thoughts of the complexity of the literacy question!

For people seeking first-class citizenship within our post-industrial and new information age, it is hard to argue anything but a case in favour of literacy training. For states wanting to compete in a globalized, now digitized world, the advantages of advanced literacy levels are obvious. For farmers needing to read the labels of dangerous chemicals, literacy, for at least someone on the farm, is a both a necessity and basic right.[75] While black and white on the page, the reading and writing of text is hardly that. There is, therefore, nuance in my critique of its deified status.

It is when illiteracy is treated as a disease and equated with ignorance and stupidity that there is a real problem. When we claim that civilization itself rests on this narrow set of skills and fail to recognize other forms of literacy, such as the capacity to read exceedingly complex landscapes, Western literacy objectives are misplaced. Reading or writing alone are never agents of social change.[76] The broader socio-economic and political context must be addressed in a substantive way, if literacy education is to be a choice and a basic human right.[77] And as stressed earlier, careful discernment about the need for literacy education is essential. Have we looked at the knowledge already present in a society before we pass through the farm gate with our gift of pencils and workbooks? After a never-ending day of work in her fields and within her homestead, should a woman with incredible ecosystem literacy be asked to learn to read text under the light of a kerosene lamp in the late evening so that she might acquire the basics?

The most nagging question of all for me, although not easily answered, is this: could the very linear, compartmentalized way that basic literacy is taught work against such a farmer's inclination to look at the world as an interconnected and complex web rather than a straightforward and predictable road map? As we will see from the final field-based case study that looks at UNICEF's literary programming, even among organizations with the best of intentions, this important question is not considered.

12

Old Habits Die Hard

In societies without writing, one of the first places where they portray the collective memory is the body ... precisely, the Andean weavings contain more information than if they were a second skin ... [They] offer social information [and] ... represent a conceptual and symbolic universe that is surprising in its richness.

Tristan Platt, 1976[1]

CHILDREN'S MOTHERS

The United Nations Children's Fund (UNICEF) was created by the United Nations General Assembly in 1946 to meet the needs of displaced children from the Second World War. The agency has since emerged as a leading advocate of child welfare and children's rights around the world. In 1965, UNICEF received the Nobel Peace Prize in recognition for its efforts to make the world a safer place for children. UNICEF began working in Bolivia early on, arriving in 1950 hoping to: "safeguard childhood, promote child development, assure a child's legal protection and participation in society within the context of their rights, and extend such protection to women as well."[2] Building on lessons learned in various countries, UNICEF subsequently spearheaded the International Convention on the Rights of the Child, an instrument that outlines how signatory countries are to protect the rights of their children. Bolivia ratified its adherence to the convention in May 1990. In September of that year, UNICEF followed the convention up with an international summit on childhood, after which 150 world leaders adopted the "World Declaration on the Survival, Protection and Development of Children" and plan of action over the next decade. On 14 December 1990, the Bolivian government also committed to this plan.[3] UNICEF's Bolivia program, both in 2000 and today, is grounded in the commitments set out in the declaration.

The Bolivia program in 2000 had two major subsets: the promotion of policy favouring women and children's rights and women's participation in public domains; and activities in support of municipal and family development. Specific objectives of these twin programs included, but were not limited to, a reduction in mortality of children under five from sixty-five to forty-five per thousand, a 50 per cent cut in the level of absolute illiteracy, and significant improvements in women's participation in public life.[4]

UNICEF also set up regional programming. The one of importance to this chapter was called el Programa Andino de Servicios Basicos contra la Pobreza (PROANDES), loosely translated as "The Andean Basic Services Program in the Fight against Poverty." Within Bolivia, it focused on twenty-four municipalities in Northern Potosí and Southern Cochabamba, the two areas with the most extreme poverty in the country. Co-delivered with the federal Ministry of Education and local municipalities, the program also had twin components: intercultural[5] and bilingual education for primary school teachers and village-level school committees; and a women's bilingual literacy program meant not only to enhance reading, writing, and computation skills in Quechua and Spanish but also, echoing the familiar words of other United Nations organizations, "to promote human development." In year two of this latter program, the educational material specifically addressed agricultural production themes.[6]

The first program, Educación Intercultural y Bilingue, which I will touch on only briefly now, was part of a multinational effort to help Bolivia implement its very progressive but enormously challenging educational reform laws. The Ley de la Reforma Educativa (Education Reform Law) was passed in 1992 as part of an ambitious package of legislative reform. In theory, this package was designed to address the longstanding marginalization of the country's rural and thus Indigenous population. I had the chance to participate in a government-run, UNICEF-sponsored training session on the new Reforma Educativa for teachers and presidents of the local school committees. The meeting enabled me to interview personnel within the Ministry of Education, school committee presidents, as well as staff on the front lines – principals and teachers. (At a later date, UNICEF staff in its La Paz headquarters also responded graciously to my queries.) All supported the impressive objectives of the Reforma Educativa. But there were also frustration and disappointment.

It takes herculean effort to turn a public education system that had overlooked the country's Indigenous character into one that champions ethnicity, difference, and rights.[7] The reforms sought were not only ambitious but downright revolutionary. Article 1.5 of the act provided, for example, that Bolivian education was to be structured on a fundamental base that is "intercultural and bilingual because it presupposes the country's socio-cultural heterogeneity in an atmosphere of respect among all Bolivians, men and women."[8] Also posted on the classroom wall of the teachers' workshop I attended was the slogan, "Celebrate difference, embrace equal rights" and another statement that said, "Today's teacher should be one who questions in a way that forces children to reflect. Create a climate of debate that respects diversity!"[9] In a country that had historically promoted acculturation over interculturalism, this message was truly groundbreaking.

Teachers within the long-ignored public education system did not rush to embrace this new thinking, however. Their Quechua (or Aymara) language skills were generally limited to oral mastery. Few could read and write the native tongue they were to teach their students to read and write. Lesson planning for the new curriculum also required hours of additional work for which no extra pay was allotted. Already pitifully paid, teachers in city after city rebelled. There were repeated street protests – *manifestaciones*— and day- to week-long strikes with demands for a more phased-in approach, more teacher training, and salary increases in light of a much heavier workload. A priority in UNICEF's 1998–2002 PROANDES program – Intercultural Bilingual Education (IBE) – was a response to this understandable reaction. UNICEF hoped to kick-start the reform through teacher training on the why and how of a bilingual and intercultural education program.

The agency produced and published three booklets in support of their intercultural programming objectives. The first two, *Cultura 1* and *Lengua 2*, were produced in 1993 as support materials for the training of local trainer-coordinators.[10] Revised and updated from earlier texts produced in Chile, they were straightforward anthropology and linguistics primers designed to enhance understanding of Bolivia's Indigenous cultures as well as an appreciation of the rules of language of Andean peoples. The information was comprehensive and comprehensible, with a research, evaluation, and examination guide appended for use with students. The text called *Cultura 1* contained an extensive discussion of Andean traditions and rituals, as well as a description of the essential components of ecological complementarity.

I was unable to determine the distribution levels of these texts. But the IPTK staff person who passed them on to me, a CENPRUR graduate who was at one time responsible for IPTK's literacy programs in Chayanta, explained that they were given to her in a UNICEF workshop for literacy coordinators. "I was hardly able to put them down," she enthused. "They were so rich in information."[11]

A third UNICEF sponsored text, *Iguales Aunque Differentes* (Equal Yet Different) produced in 2000 by anthropologist Xavier Albó, was designed with a different audience in mind. Its message about the fundamental importance of the intercultural dialogue at the heart of Bolivia's educational reform program was directed at development officials and policy makers. Bolivia's vice-minister for preschool, primary, and secondary education prefaced the book with this endorsement: "[The book] without doubt, supports the effort to translate into state policy and social practice the acknowledgement and revaluing of the different cultures and peoples that form our society."[12]

Iguales Aunque Differentes also includes this revealing passage about the intercultural ideal at the heart of Bolivia's Educational Reform Program. "Each participant in this intercultural dialogue will undoubtedly be enriched by the contributions of the other, and ... their respective cultures can also adopt elements from the others. But the roots of each identity will be maintained, especially through one or another of those elements that we have labelled the symbolic components of culture."[13] UNICEF highlighted the maintenance of one's original identity as key to the success of educational reform. Interculturalism was thus a significant challenge to acculturation and was inherently linked with the notion of resilience.

Meeting such an ideal is exceedingly challenging, of course, particularly when there is a complex mix of political, economic and social factors to reconcile. Within the UNICEF's women's literacy program that I was able to review up close, the intercultural programming fell short of the ideal.

YUYAY JAP'INA

The bilingual literacy training program UNICEF implemented in the municipality of Ravelo and in turn in Chimpa Rodeo and Mojón was called *Yuyay Jap'ina*, a Quechua expression meaning to take or to seize the knowledge.[14] It arrived in Ravelo in 1998, and had originated in 1992 as a Quechua-based program in another part of Northern Potosí. At that time, it was a joint initiative between UNICEF and Food for the Hungry International (FHI).[15] Gathering women together through already existing *Clubes de Madres* or Mothers' Clubs, the original program had five objectives: (1) To fight illiteracy, paying special attention to Quechua and Aymara women farmers; (2) To contribute to the development of the Indigenous culture and to reaffirm cultural identity within the context of women's rights; (3) To elaborate, produce, and distribute literacy workshop materials in Quechua and Aymara; (4) To turn over the management and distribution of training materials to the program supervisors; (5) To develop training seminars, courses, and workshops for literacy workers.[16]

A comprehensive review of all the major adult literacy programs throughout Bolivia conducted in 1994 by staff from the non-profit research organization, *Centro de Estudios Sociales* (CENDES) praised this *Yuyay Jap'ina* program for its didactic pedagogy, for its training of young leaders, and for content that motivated participants to hold their union leadership accountable. Evaluators were also pleased to observe materials prepared to teach basic arithmetic.[17] But they also listed a host of problems with the implementation of *Yuyay Jap'ina*.

First in the list of the program's shortcomings were the poor mastery of teaching techniques and the lack of clarity on the part of the literacy promoters, who were generally in their twenties, about the program's goals and objectives.[18] Other weaknesses noted included an insufficient distribution of learning materials and a failure to take into consideration the diversity of students' literacy levels. These ranged from absolute illiteracy to a Grade Five level of reading, rusty after years of neglect. Participants complained of poorly motivated literacy promoters. They often showed up late or not at all. Classes were frequently scheduled during peak periods of farming activity, contributing to irregular or interrupted attendance. A lack of appropriate physical infrastructure, like desks, chairs, and light to read by, was also problematic. The greatest concerns cited were the program's failure to coordinate its training program with municipal authorities and the resentment that participants felt over the stipend literacy promoters received.

Stipends for literacy promoters, it turned out, were higher than the average municipal wage for unskilled labour. Program participants were not at all happy that their requests for a share of these stipends fell on deaf ears. Nor were they pleased to learn that the food rations that FHI had once distributed to the Mothers' Clubs were not a part of this program.[19] Since there were no immediate and tangible rewards for participation, participants lost interest. The average dropout rate was 54 per cent. Those who continued to participate demonstrated reading and reading comprehension skills well below average.[20]

The literacy training that UNICEF staff launched in Ravelo communities in 1998, this time without FHI's participation, appears to have taken into consideration the CENDES critique. The municipality, for example, was offered a key role in the literary programs' implementation. It would assume responsibility for the program coordinators and the training of the literacy promoters. The municipality also provided classroom space, as well as accommodation and food during training workshops generally lasting four consecutive days. Community-based literacy classes were scheduled when most participants could attend. While infrastructure and equipment remained less than ideal in communities where there was no school or only a one-room school that was small and dark, all participating communities were provided with a kerosene lamp and a ration of kerosene to facilitate evening classes.

The content and distribution of educational materials also appeared to have improved. UNICEF sent its own program staff to explain the organization's goals and the anticipated results of the program. Indeed, the training session I attended offered a very thorough outline, in accessible language, of the literacy program's objectives.[21]

The "new and improved" program had the following four very laudable objectives: (1) To reduce illiteracy by 50 per cent, especially among women over 15 years of age; (2) To promote women's participation as active citizens; (3) To develop skills that facilitate comprehensive reading and writing *as basic tools for human development;* and (4) To develop an educational process that in its second phase would include content oriented toward food production.[22]

Training sessions for literacy teachers, as I witnessed during my participation in three days of a four-day training session in July 2000, reflected pedagogy that was both interactive and entertaining. Quechua-speaking trainers stressed the importance of dialogue and a two-way learning process, whereby, it was stressed, teachers could also learn from students. Role-plays were assigned and critiqued both by the facilitators and other participants, particularly on the verbal and non-verbal messages projected to students. Community maps were drawn, lending themselves to a whole language learning approach to learning to read and write since the labels asked for on the map would have meaning.[23] When attention was waning, a student was asked to pull out his *charango* from his bundle and lead the group in a Jalq'a song.

Community ownership of the literacy program was also encouraged through involvement in selecting the literacy promoter for the targeted area. Stipends were offered, given the considerable time requested of promoters (64 to 76 hours a month). The rate was one that the municipality had sanctioned. In Ravelo, this was 120 Bolivianos or approximately $40 CAD a month.[24]

Most importantly, participants were given material to read and learn that addressed their everyday lives and strategic interests. Basic booklets covered subjects such as maternal health, infant development, sanitation, and rural life. Gender rights and the Popular Participation Act were also included, with a healthy dose of nationalist rhetoric supporting the content on citizenship, a feature that is common to all Bolivian schools.[25] In year one, classes would focus on the participants' mother tongue. In year two, spoken Spanish and Spanish reading and writing skills would be introduced as well as content related to crop cultivation, animal husbandry, complementary economic activities, micro-enterprise, and micro-credit. If CENDES had evaluated this revised curriculum and approach, UNICEF would undoubtedly have earned top marks for having learned from its initial mistakes.

SIGNATURES ONLY

Regrettably, when I focused my lens more carefully on the application and outcomes of Yuyay *Jap'ina*, I found that this improved program continued to fall short of its literacy objectives as well as its intercultural and equity goals. It was not my intent, nor within my capacity, to measure the technical success of the program. But reports and my observations within Chimpa Rodeo and Mojón, as well as during the municipal training and planning event I attended, revealed that with a few notable exceptions, participants had made very minimal progress after two years.[26] One of the municipality's coordinators – IPTK-trained and a native of the municipality – claimed that the UNICEF program had contributed to a 30 per cent decrease in illiteracy in the targeted region since its 1998 launch.[27] What I consistently observed in Chimpa Rodeo and Mojón, however, were graduates from the *absoluto* group – those who had never attended school – who now had the ability to sign their names to documents they still could not read. They expressed appreciation for having learned this new skill. But a signature without the capacity to read can be a dangerous tool, weakening rather than strengthening control of one's life. The documents these non-readers signed their names to could be explained to them by others who might not always have their best interests in mind. And villagers regularly used their thumbprint to denote their approval of documents they could not read. In contrast to a thumbprint, however, a signature generally signals a more informed consent, which was not the case with these functionally illiterate signatories. Signed registers of participants in public meetings and during public referenda could likewise be misleading. The official record would suggest misleadingly high literacy levels. In short, program graduates able only to boast a signature could invite individual abuse as well as State misrepresentation of the true literacy picture.

Participants with some primary school education appeared to have fared better. Lessons jogged their memory, helping them to dust off skills long in storage. Their progress may account for the reported increases in literacy. But from what I saw in both my participatory rural appraisal workshops and in the municipal planning session, these skills remained shaky at best. The reading comprehension and writing skills that I observed were generally well below high school levels. Many of those assigned to fill in the questionnaires from the municipal planning session had significant difficulty with the form. And 25 per cent of the community-selected leaders sent to the workshop were unable to sign their names. Leadership, not literacy, skills seem to have been the priority when selecting participants in the planning process.

In response to my observations, UNICEF's regional program coordinator acknowledged that the poor results I had witnessed were not particularly unusual. He attributed them to a lack of adequate follow-up. Two years, he further suggested, were simply not enough for lasting results. Little could be done, he lamented, since UNICEF intended to leave the country at the end of the 1998–2002 program phase.[28]

Weak follow-up and continuity problems, although important, did not, in my view, offer the most significant explanation for the weak results. The Spanish reading and writing skills of the literacy promoters themselves were weak, and their Quechua literacy skills almost non-existent, as illustrated in the ensuing journal excerpt. Participatory process was championed but as my next journal entry suggests, in this case, the principle trumped the practical, with very poor results.

TRAINING FOR LITERACY TRAINERS, RAVELO VILLAGE, AUGUST 2011
I have finally managed to participate in one of UNICEF's training for
trainers' workshops. There are thirty-six of us, excluding the training
team. I recognize a few faces from Pata Rodeo, and there is Leandro
from Chimpa Rodeo, but no Mojón participants. We gather in a circle to
introduce ourselves. The key coordinator speaks Aymara, not Quechua,
so he has an assistant to help with translation. Seems odd to have sent
someone who is not fluent in Quechua. Perhaps the Quechua speakers
of his level are all booked.

The session is starting with a test to assess the capacity of participants to
write Quechua. From informal conversations, I have gathered that there are
few who can either read or write Quechua. Yet the curriculum that they are
expected to teach focuses on reading and writing Quechua during the first
year of the program. Participants are clearly well aware of the importance
of the Quechua literacy requirement. During this first testing session, I
observe several copying the answers from the few who have indeed mastered the written form of their native tongue. The most advanced Quechua
writers I discover are participants who learned to read a Quechua version
of the Catholic Bible. For those who have not received such Bible training,
participation in a four-day pre–"training for literacy promotion" session on
Quechua reading and writing appears not to have been sufficient.

Spanish reading and writing skills are not consistently strong either.
When I enquire about school experiences, I am repeatedly told of a
grade five completion in the local school. When I ask about other
opportunities to practice reading and writing during the eight to twenty
years since graduation, there have been none. The only books I have ever
come across within the up to twenty communities I have visited this
year were very basic grade-school workbooks, dust covered, torn, with
missing pages. Ravelo's merchants do not sell newspapers, let alone
books. Reading, even among the literate within these semi-subsistence
farm communities, is a luxury few can afford. So, with the exception of
literacy promoters who also serve as the minute takers in local union
meetings, reading and writing for my friends in this session is largely
limited to the UNICEF literacy curriculum.

Many of the participants I have spoken with during this training
workshop repeatedly expressed an interest in more training to improve
their own reading and writing skills. That possibility doesn't seem to be
a part of the program. And the broader culture of text literacy needed to
practice and maintain their skills is simply non-existent. Most want the

job. The stipend is needed. But the odds of a satisfactory experience seemed stacked against them.

If the *Yuyay Jap'ina* program was having difficulty reaching its technical objectives, its socio-cultural ones were even more out of reach. While it explicitly targeted women as trainers and participants, only three of the thirty-five literacy promoters in the Ravelo workshop were women.[29] The extremely high rate of illiteracy among women of these communities offered a very small pool of literate women to draw from. Communities were also reluctant to send unchaperoned young women to workshops for four days at a time. When I discussed this matter with a UNICEF literacy program director in La Paz, she too, like her regional coordinator, expressed concern about these flaws. She remained convinced, however, that the community's selection of local promoters was the best route, despite the problems this system created. More experienced outsiders would not, in her view, have been a better option. Having local people who know the local scene teach local participants was one of the principal tenants of their intercultural strategy.[30]

Principle overruled pragmatism. But principle built on an inadequate assessment of, or commitment to, the longer-term investment needed to assist people lacks conviction. And men teaching mostly married women about content that, in the first year at least, is intended to cover women's rights and concerns, including domestic abuse, is certainly not in keeping with the goal of promoting women's rights and status. UNICEF offered significant human resources and financial support; but through substandard application of the theory, the investment was counter-productive and a lost opportunity.

Yuyay Jap'ina also did not adequately consider the practice of dual homesteading among families in communities like Chimpa Rodeo and Mojón. Promoters generally scheduled their classes in the *puna* or highlands, which made consistent participation a challenge for those with responsibilities in the valleys. This oversight was symptomatic of a more substantive absence of intercultural content. As with the IPTK programming aimed at celebrating Indigenous culture, training workshops and basic reading materials focused on material – etic – manifestations of culture, like the *awayo*, the wonderfully colourful blankets women weave to carry their babies.[31]

Promoters also came up with themes they thought participants would respond well to. But the concepts were extremely simple ones. Superficial and shallow dialogue ensued, a reflection, in my view, of an overdue emphasis on the technical aspects of reading and writing. In contrast to the orientation pamphlets offered to trainers, the sessions did not include any critical discussion about the Jalq'a world or world views. Nor did the value of Indigenous practices, such as ecological complementarity and labour exchange make it into the workbooks teachers used; or information about how the world of the mestizo outsider affected Indigenous culture and options.

The content related to agricultural production, both within the workshop for promoters and within the materials they passed on to their students, was especially conventional. One module actually promoted pesticide and insecticide use. Ecological agricultural techniques and topics such as biodiversity conservation, on the other hand, did not make into student handbooks. Talk of Freirian "praxis" and the importance of didactic and dialogical education could be heard in literary teacher training workshops. But strategic, analytical discussion within the literacy classes themselves was absent. Did organizers think their students incapable of such reflection? The *Yuyay Jap'ina* I discovered in my research region missed the opportunity to encourage critical thinking among young community leaders and participants and to validate Indigenous knowledge and respect for Pachamama. One of the trainer/coordinators facilitating the workshop I attended offered this revealing interpretation of UNICEF's program: "to end illiteracy and teach them (students) *new* knowledge about rural life and agricultural production." After reading UNICEF's early primers on interculturalism, I had been eager to witness their authentic application. Instead, I was left with the sense that UNICEF's literacy program was essentially another dipstick development approach. It attempted to fill a perceived void with the status quo knowledge needed for participation in the world of Western capital, on Western terms.

BLESSING IN DISGUISE?

There was a final irony in the literacy training experience of the *Jalq'a* participants in my study. If we consider connectionism and its challenge to the centrality of language and literacy in the development of knowledge, *Yuyay Japina's* deficiencies might actually represent a blessing in disguise for its unsuccessful graduates. To recap, connectionism argues against a sequential, linear framework for knowledge formation and transmission.[32] We access knowledge – either from memory or as it is conceptualized from perception of the external world – not as a serial process of analysis along a single line but rather through a number of processing units that work in parallel and feed in information simultaneously. Concept formation involves implicit networks of meaning that are formed through experience of, and practice in, the external world. Like the skilled Bao player, the Andean farmer, by continuously monitoring the responses of their numerous plant varieties to ecosystem and production conditions that can change from hillside to hillside, from hillside to valley and from morning to afternoon, has successfully mastered impressive landscape literacy. Training participants to read and write from left to right, letter to letter, word to word, line to line, paragraph to paragraph, and page to page privileges textual literacy over the capacity to manage diversity under rapidly changing circumstances. This new way of problem solving seems ill suited to the management of dynamic and complex systems. The imposition of agricultural approaches that are ignoring the connectionist thinking at the heart of previously resilient food production is bad enough. Pushing so-called illiterate people into a knowledge framework that could further weaken their capacity to manage the complexity at the heart of ecological and social resilience might well seal the deal. Gramsci's double-edged literacy sword takes on a third dimension, introducing the possibility of a fatal blow.

13

The Monocropping of People, Plants, and Knowledge

Development, as in Third World Development, is a debauched word, a whore of a word. Its users can't look you in the eye. Among biologists, the word means progress, the realization of an innate potential. The word is good, incontestable, a cause for celebration. In the mouths of politicians, economists and development experts like me, it claims the same approval, but means nothing. There are no genes governing the shape of human society. No one can say, as a gardener can of a flower, that it has become what it should be. It is an empty word that can be filled by any user to conceal any hidden intention, a Trojan horse of a word.

Leonard Frank, 1986[1]

BAPTISM BY FIRE

Not long after I finished my first professional overseas development assignment, a three-week monitoring trip to Indonesia in late 1985, I read the article containing the passage cited above. Called "The Development Game," the article told the story of a multinational team of "experts" hired to plan a multimillion-dollar program in the northwest frontier of Pakistan. A Canadian economist, Leonard Frank, had penned the tale and led the team. He painted a bleak picture of his team's experience in the region and of the development industry more broadly.

In the picturesque high mountain villages the team was sent to assess, Frank wrote, "the peasants' fair complexions, rosy cheeks and straight noses made it hard to take their poverty seriously." He went on to describe a cast of well-paid development experts with idiosyncrasies and competing interests that ultimately worked against the local population. In particular, I remember his description of the American statistician obsessed with his endless calculations and the way the team pushed the "naïve" Dutch anthropologist aside. She kept insisting that they pay greater attention to the cultural dynamics they were witnessing. Remuneration for the assignment depended on the group pretending not to notice the area's thriving opium business. Better not mess with the real "development" in the region. Frank, it turned out, was the author's pseudonym.[2] Even critics need a paycheque.

The article had quite an affect on me. I had jumped into my program officer position both feet first, having had no academic training in the international development field. I also had the sum total of about five months' experience in the developing world, one in Colombia visiting my then-boyfriend's family and four months in India as a Canada World Youth group leader. My employer at the time, and again after a fourteen-year hiatus, USC Canada, must have seen some potential in me. It worked that way in those days. Whatever their reasoning, my first field trip to Indonesia was a baptism by fire. I remember fourteen- to sixteen-hour workdays, getting soaked to the bone in heavy downpours while helping to push our truck through rivers of mud, and huge headaches when trying to handle the older, very demanding wives of state governors. Their marriages to the governors made them the automatic heads of the state charities we were funding at the time. Neophyte as I was, I found these women and their charities to be painfully condescending to the locals and, needless to say, to me. I also remember my exhausted fits of laughter at the end of some of these long days, as well as moments of feeling completely overwhelmed. Like an onion, Indonesia revealed itself to me one thin layer at a time. From those first days in the field, it hadn't taken long to grasp the complexity of my job. The contradictions Frank pointed out really hit home – and a little of his cynicism even seeped in.

This book has also questioned the complacent and tired definition of development that Frank took to task in his article so many years ago. The "dipstick" model of Western development "poor are lacking" theories, the mere lip-service it usually pays to the legitimacy of alternative knowledge and belief systems, and its commodification of food and nature: all these issues have too often left many on the margins feeling used or abused, dependent on the outsider.[3] Within this development equation, it is the marginalized *unfortunates* – the negated poor – who are considered responsible for the tight mesh of poverty that envelops them.

To differing degrees, this kind of thinking influenced all three non-governmental agencies at work within Chimpa Rodeo and Mojón in 2000.

The "capacity building" programs these partners were implementing, although well intentioned, largely reflected the NGOs' knowledge systems and development recipes, in addition to their own preoccupations with power and political positioning. To implement its strategy for the building of a more just world, IPTK homogenized the Indigenous identity of its program participants into that of a working class producer in urgent need both of greater purchasing power and Western structures of protest and political leverage. The second major non-governmental actor, UNICEF, failed in its more substantive attempt at intercultural praxis by spreading its program and resources too thin. The training, monitoring, and follow-up needed to deliver on its intercultural objectives were simply not in evidence. Convinced of its mission to feed the hungry in body and spirit, FHI attached its still more paternalistic development package to an evangelical brand of Christian belief.

In practice, all three agencies were applying a stagnant interpretation of cultural revitalization in their field programs, focusing more on its etic – surface – rather than its emic – inherent – characteristics. They were caught in the ethnocentric mindset characteristic of the broader development community. They consequently paid insufficient attention to the deeply rooted skills and knowledge systems of the people they were hoping to assist. Rather than build onto the systems already present, like ecological complementarity, they began with the assumption that something was missing and proceeded to try to fill that "void" with knowledge that they sincerely considered to be the best available. Despite very different ideological perspectives, all three NGOs also had the effect of drawing the Jalq'a communities they supported into market economies that worked against both the community justice ethic within ecological complementarity and its diversity conservation dimension. Together with the monocropping of potato plants, there appears to have been a "monocropping" of their Indigenous beneficiaries and the knowledge they possessed. The biodiversity maintained in these communities was in spite of outsider intervention, not because of it.

GREENFEED

The blind or at least half-closed eye IPTK, FHI, and UNICEF all turned to the ecologically compatible food production practices that remained in these communities was, as suggested throughout this book, hardly unique to these agencies. Since its beginnings in the late 1940s, Green Revolution monoculture requiring introduced technologies was and remains in vogue worldwide. The most common international response to a food crisis today, for example, highlights a deeply embedded belief in the power of new technologies to solve our problems.[4] The worry is that we simply cannot feed cities and our growing global population without the West's more "efficient" larger-scale, and increasingly high-tech, production systems. There is an acknowledged trade-off. The environment and thus long-term sustainability are not well served. But, it is argued, the capacity of scientists today to engineer varieties that are both more climate-friendly and climate-resilient has grown by leaps and bounds.[5]

This reasoning can be contested on several counts. First, in the past 30 years enough food was produced to feed everyone in the world had it been more evenly distributed. Most analysts agree that at present (although perhaps not when the planet's thermostat is two or more degrees higher), hunger is not a matter of agricultural limits but a problem of masses of people not having access to food or the means to produce it.[6] The issue is essentially an economic and political one. Second, through various low-tech, peri-urban and urban gardening initiatives, cities are in significant measure feeding themselves. It is estimated that between 15 and 20 per cent of our planet's population is fed through peri-urban and urban food production.[7] Third, comparisons between modernized operations and those of small-holder farmers are often based on an adverse assessment of small-holder systems that, for a host of complex reasons, no longer practise biodiverse polyculture – mixed – farming systems. They have, in fact, lost much of the knowledge they need to do so effectively.

Related to this last issue of knowledge loss, is a fourth counter-argument. Investment in research on small-holder production and the economics of diversity-based ecological agriculture vastly pales in comparison to that spent on conventional or high-tech approaches. It costs an average of $136 million to develop just one genetically modified crop variety.[8] The six largest seed, biotech, and agrochemical companies, who control 58 per cent of the global market – Monsanto, DuPont, Syngenta, Bayer, Dow, and BASF – spend an average of 70 per cent of their crop research and development budgets on agricultural biotechnology.[9] In 2012, Monsanto invested more than $980 million researching new "tools" for farmers. According to their website, the company concentrates the vast majority of its R&D efforts on new biotech traits, elite germplasm, breeding, new variety and hybrid development, and genomics research.[10]

The favouring of high-tech agriculture undoubtedly reflects interest in the potential economic returns. But as researchers into this very lopsided agenda suggest, the explanation likely also lies in long-held assumptions and views about innovation. Genetically engineered seeds are seen as "breakthrough" scientific discoveries – fundamental innovations. Agro-ecological innovations, in contrast, are considered incremental, more plodding, despite their success. The development of wheat-poplar agro-forestry systems that can produce as much "grain + wood" output on 1 hectrare as 1.3 hectare of separate monocultures does not seem as exciting. Nor does the restoration of traditional Inca terracing systems in Peru that increase productivity by as much as 150 per cent.[11]

For the most part, the growing research on the benefits of biodiversity-based, ecological farming also fails to find its way into mainstream policy circles. While we have witnessed a growth in the past decade in the number of studies on the economics of agro-biodiversity, the integration of such economic analysis into the policy process is rare.[12]

As long as high-tech agriculture gets the lion's share of the funding and public policy attention, we cannot say that farmer-led, small-holder systems will by definition underperform the competition. Nor have the hugely expensive "climate-resilient" seeds produced to date proven to be the promised miracle seeds. Benefits are often short-term, with nature continuing to have the last word. There are, for example, more and more super-weeds that are not responding to agro-industry's "crop protection" system.[13] Glyphosate-resistant weeds began popping up in fields around a decade ago. In 2003, there was a large area in southeast Indiana where over 80 per cent of soybean fields had a glyphosate-resistant strain of mare's tale, a weed also known as Canada fleabane.[14]

Were policy makers to look more carefully at the expanding body of research on small-holder ecological and biodiverse agriculture, they would discover comparatively greater efficiency within small-holder farms that are diverse and multifunctional. Study after study demonstrates that the harvestable products per unit area of polycultures developed by small-holders is higher than under a single crop with the same level of management. Yield advantages can range from 20 per cent to 60 per cent because polycultures reduce losses due to weeds (by occupying space that weeds might otherwise occupy), insects, and diseases (because of companion cropping and the presence of multiple species). They also make more efficient use of the available water, light, and nutrient resources.[15] Most importantly, there is sufficient fertility left in the soil for future production.

A further flaw in the high-tech, large-scale argument is the idea that industrial-scale agriculture is actually growing balanced diets that sustain most people on this planet. More and more large farms are growing animal feed, fuel, or ornamental plants. Small-holder farmers who occupy over 60 per cent of arable land worldwide[16] are the ones actually feeding the majority of people.[17] Of the food we consume, 85 per cent is purchased in close circuit markets within domestic boundaries.[18] If we consider that only 6 per cent of the worlds' most consumed food crop, rice, is traded on international markets,[19] there is clearly a lot of local, small-holder rice on the family table worldwide. It may not all be organic or biodiverse, as my Ravelo case study revealed. But with huge spikes in the price of fertilizers (up 270% in 2008 when the food crisis was at an historical high),[20] low-input use is for many the only alternative.[21] If the political will to rebuild knowledge-intensive, polyculture systems were present, transitioning into fully organic and biodiverse operations would be very feasible.[22]

Yet the mounting evidence in support of ecologically sound and farmer-directed systems has not reached, or convinced, a critical threshold of decision-makers. On offer still are Western-styled training and packages of laboratory seeds with the chemicals they need to survive on unfamiliar landscapes. Participants in a 2008 intergovernmental meeting in Rome, called to address the burgeoning food crisis and the billion or so hungry people on our planet, asked governments to significantly increase their funding to impoverished regions for the purchase of "improved" seeds and fertilizers. "The lack of improved inputs is the single most important factor in the continued poor yields in smallholder farming," the members of the Ad Hoc Advisory Group to the Madrid Conference on Food Security wrote in their 2009 report.[23]

The Madrid pledge to boost yields through improved seed and input distribution echoes that of another highly influential initiative designed to stop hunger in its tracks, in this case in Africa. Launched in 2006, the Alliance for a New Green Revolution for Africa (AGRA) is the child of a union between the Bill and Melinda Gates Foundation – the world's largest philanthropic organization[24] – and the Rockefeller Foundation, chief supporter of the first Green Revolution. The Gates Foundation offered an initial contribution of $100 million while the Rockefeller Foundation pledged an additional $50 million to upscale its existing seed programming on the continent. Both foundations expressed interest in supporting a 20-year program and suggested that the sums involved could expand dramatically over this period.[25] In a February 2012 speech to the global agriculture community, Bill Gates pledged another $200 million in grants. With such clout and purpose, AGRA has been able to draw influential personalities to its ranks, including the former Secretary General of the United Nations, Kofi Annan, the first chair of the board of directors.

Africa, it is lamented, missed out on the first Green Revolution. This claim is the subject of some debate. Still, there is agreement that the Green Revolution's reach in Africa was uneven and not nearly as extensive as in Asia and Latin America. AGRA promises that this time around it will be, with messaging about the need for introduced seeds and synthetic inputs that is loud and clear. "Nothing is more urgent than ensuring that farmers have access to the inputs they need to increase farm productivity," AGRA's first president, Namanga Ngongo, insisted in an address I personally attended in 2010. These inputs could in principle be local and organic. Using small-holder farmers in Ghana as an example, Ngongo went on to clarify, however, that the farmers must significantly increase their use of improved seeds and other "modern" inputs to increase their yields and incomes.

Gates himself made the program's focus on new seeds very clear in 2012. In an address to the main international food agencies, he noted, "We are re-investing in projects [like the ones that have] ... supported the release of 34 *new* varieties of drought tolerant maize ... and ... trained more than 10,000 agro-dealers – vendors of seeds and inputs – to equip and train farmers."[26] He went much further in his support of technology-based agriculture, in fact, suggesting that the future of agriculture lies in digitized approaches. "In a world where climate change and plant diseases are threatening small farmers who are already planting low-yielding varieties," he continued, "these new techniques can be the difference between suffering and self-sufficiency." The use of computers to map the plant genome and printers that can build new varieties atom by atom is unquestionably fascinating. But forgotten in such strategizing is the fact that peasant farmers have shown the most innovation over time. Over the past 40 years, Green Revolution plant breeders have released 8,000 new crop varieties, many of them ornamentals. By contrast, the collections in gene banks around the world indicate that since the 1960s peasants have contributed more than 1.9 million plant varieties.[27] And as will be seen in the next chapter, with a first level of assistance from scientists with the initial seed crossing – that scientists refer to as the F1 cross – farmers are succeeding in breeding varieties to suit changing growing conditions right there in their fields – climate ready seeds built on traditional varieties without the need for expensive equipment or the use of costly chemicals.

AGRA's program is a generous one and seeks to strengthen livelihoods among long-ignored small-holder producers. Some very skilled and well-trained staff are on hand to implement their ambitious agenda. Staffing choices, however, have alienated, rather than won the support of the larger small-holder farming organizations needed to make such a far-reaching program work. Early on, the engagement of two senior executives from the biotechnology division of Monsanto, the world's most powerful agro-industry firm, drew the ire of major small-holder farmer organizations, including La Via Campesina and the West African coalition, COPAGEN. Since these broadly representative and important farmers' organizations had already been left out of the AGRA program design phase, the appointments were not a good signal for potential collaboration.

AGRA staff promise to correct the technical errors of the first Green Revolution, such as the overuse of synthetic inputs. Members also vow to pay closer attention to local farming systems and their cultural dynamics, to enhance biodiversity, and to deal with rural infrastructure needs like roads and local seed distribution. But the seeds they are promoting, even from within the continent, are often introduced hybrids that need a package of synthetic inputs to succeed. Given their growing popularity among scientists and executives within agro-industry, it seems likely that genetically modified seed or GMOs will soon find their way into this agricultural assistance program.

Whether GMOs enter the picture or not, AGRA programming, although dressed in new and more progressive language, reveals assumptions that closely resemble those that brought us the first Green Revolution a half-century ago. Scientists who champion the use of the diverse local seeds and natural resources already in farmers' fields and on their landscapes, have this warning. The further introduction of inappropriate exogenous technologies could once again create harmful dependencies, credit vulnerability, and possibly wipe out the genetic diversity of Africa's most vital crops.[28]

AGRA is nonetheless very popular and influential among a wide range of governments.[29] During a meeting I attended in late 2010 that included high-level government bureaucrats, I heard talk of an intergovernmental meeting that had been recently held to discuss the world food crisis. The meeting involved elected officials, their top civil servants, and one private citizen, Bill Gates. Doors open when one of the wealthiest men in the world arrives.

Would that I could have been a fly on the windowsill of that meeting room. Might there have been discussion about socio-economic and political inequities that explain growing hunger and the uphill battle for a viable farming livelihood? Were global trade regulations and the widespread dumping of foodstuffs from large-scale industrial Western food producers debated? Did someone tell Gates that Ghanaian farmers in need of our modern inputs cannot sell their fresh chickens because it is cheaper to buy a bag of subsidized frozen chicken parts from the United States?[30] What does he think about foreign governments scooping up land from hungry nations in an effort to feed their own populations? Or the governments and corporations buying large tracts of fertile land to produce alternative energy sources, like fuel to feed cars. And what about the commodity speculators who purchase and hoard land simply as an investment until the price is right?[31] Since 2006, this diverse set of foreign investors has, in fact, purchased or rented between 15 and 20 million hectares of farmland, the equivalent of the total arable surface of France.[32]

The Indigenous peoples and small-holder farmers that I came to know well both in Bolivia and in many other countries in the global South, would likely not want to throw the philanthropist's child of good intent out with the dirty bathwater. They could use a helping hand; they would want the relationship, however, to be negotiated on terms that welcome broadly representative small-holder farmers' input and place them, not the Western benefactor, in charge. But is such a dynamic even possible? When I think about how both international and national trade negotiations like those within the World Trade Organization (WTO) regularly, if not deliberately, trump those related to other global commitments, such as the International Convention on Biological Diversity, for instance, I, like Leonard Frank, become a cynic. And here again there is further contradiction and paradox.

BIOPIRACY

The knowledge of isolated Indigenous peoples has, it is now commonly acknowledged, fuelled multi-billion dollar trade in genetics supply industries, ranging from food and cosmetics to chemicals, paper products, energy, and pharmaceuticals.[33] Recent and precise figures on their global value and use are hard to come by, buried as they are in reams of reports and proprietary documents. As bioprospecting issues become more publicized, the data are becoming harder to find. Nor has a comprehensive framework to collect such data been developed.[34] Still there are some revealing estimates from the latter half of the twentieth century when data were more accessible. The estimated market value of plant-based medicines sold in OECD countries in 1985, for example, was $43 billion and growing.[35] Evidence of the decline in the diversity of medical plants prompted pharmaceutical industry analysts at that time to warn that the loss of a medicinal plant in the rainforest could cost drug firms sales in the millions, and up to hundreds of millions.[36] And it is not, of course, just a matter of keeping these plants alive. Knowledge of their existence and uses is also vital, as this uncharacteristically blunt comment from researchers with Shaman Pharmaceuticals – once a leading proponent of the ethnobotanical approach to drug discovery – made especially clear: "To preserve the rainforest without preservation of Shamanic knowledge of the plants in the forest would be to cut ourselves off from cures for present and future diseases."[37] As for the extent of the use, by the late 1990s, there were reports that 119 commonly used pharmaceutical products were plant-derived, and some 74 per cent of these were discovered by examining the use of these plants in traditional medicine.[38] In its 2000 report on the need to protect Indigenous knowledge, innovations, and practices, the United Nations Conference on Trade and Development (UNCTAD) pointed to the tremendous role traditional knowledge played in the leading plant-based medicines.[39]

The estimated value of farmers' crop varieties to industry has been equally impressive. Evenson's 1996 study on the use and value of farmers' rice varieties for breeding figured that the global value added to rice yields through the use of farmers' landraces was approximately US $400 million per year.[40] The Rural Advancement Foundation International, now called the ETC Group, estimated around that same time that germ plasm collected in developing countries – in the fields of local farmers, many of whom are Indigenous – was worth at least $5 billion per annum to crop production in developed countries.[41] This massive contribution to developed nations has led researchers of Indigenous knowledge systems to suggest, in fact, that it is Northern governments who should be thanking Indigenous peoples for the enormous foreign aid they have provided.[42] Rural sociologist, Jack Kloppenburg, put it this way, "Indigenous people have in effect engaged in a massive program of foreign aid to the urban populations of the industrial North. Genetic and cultural information has been produced and reproduced over the millennium by peasants and Indigenous peoples. Yet ... the fruits of this work are given no value despite their recognized

utility." Cases such as these have caused leading defenders of the intellectual integrity and rights of Indigenous peoples to call bioprospecting, "biopiracy" – an outright theft of Indigenous knowledge.[43]

I have also had my own encounter with such behaviour. During a visit
to Bolivia's Lake Titicaca in the spring of 1998, my husband and I learned
about Colorado State University's (CSU) efforts to patent a variety of
quinoa called Apelawa, named after the village on Lake Titicaca where CSU
scientists first picked up seed samples. With the support of North American NGOs, including the ETC Group, Canadian Lutheran World Relief, and
Lutheran World Relief, representatives of Bolivia's National Association of
Quinoa Producers (Asociación Nacional de Productores de Quinoa –
ANAPQUI) headed to the United Nations to denounce the patent claim. A
press conference, staged in front of its New York headquarters ensued. The
patent, it turned out, covered a method of hybridizing quinoa that would
also subsume in the claim forty-three other traditional Andean quinoa
varieties, including one, ironically enough, called Oxfam. Embarrassed,
CSU decided to abandon its patent claim. According to Alejandro Bonifa-
cio, a highly respected Bolivian quinoa researcher, had the patent been
enforced, "Andean exports to the growing quinoa markets in North America and Europe would have been threatened. Even local production might
have been affected."

In raising this issue, I want to point to a twinned irony: unlike the dis-
missive development official, the researchers in these industries seem to
very much appreciate the wealth of knowledge of the Indigenous people
that stand before them. But the eagerness of these prospectors to return
home with their "discoveries" sewed in secret pockets has bred resistance
among their increasingly informed Indigenous tutors. More and more are
refusing them entry. These industries could well be shooting themselves
in the foot, especially given species extinction rates. Over the past few hundred years, extinction rates have accelerated by as much as 1,000 times the
rates that were typical over our planet's history.[44] More than 75 per cent
of crop diversity was lost between 1900 and 2000.[45] The net annual loss of
forests – storehouses of medicinal plants – is equally alarming. More land
was devoted to cropland between 1950 and 1980 than in the 150 years
between 1700 and 1850.[46] Between 2000 and 2010 forest loss was equivalent to an area about the size of Costa Rica.

Industry would be wise to tread more thoughtfully within this context
and within the forests they wander. For Indigenous peoples such loss is far

reaching. In her contribution to the late Daryll Posey's thoughtful compendium on biodiversity's cultural and spiritual values, Ruth Lilongula, a Guruvat from the Solomon Islands, wrote: "Biodiversity means our identity and culture survives, and it is also the very core of our existence and life itself. There is no parameter of biodiversity that is divorced from our identity, heritage and pride. There is no separation between our people and biodiversity. We are all part and parcel of one system."[47]

Resistance and resilience in the face of powerful pressures to abandon diversity and flip into a new, "modern" identity are important themes in this book. When I left the Chayanta's Jalq'a *amautas* – teachers – to return to Canada, these proud descendants of the Inca Nation had not succumbed to the "development game" cited in the chapter's opening paragraph. The story of the people of this region was not a straightforward retelling of colonial domination and subjugation. Like many of their neighbours in Northern Potosí, the Jalq'a were stubbornly holding onto traditional ecological knowledge systems, their continued, albeit modified, application of ecological complementarity serving as an excellent example. Their refusal to abandon this system suggests a keen awareness of its importance to the survival both of their ecological systems and their socio-cultural identity.

The Jalq'a farmers I studied and learned from during the course of a year in Bolivia's southern highlands did not, of course, keep the outside world at bay. Nor did they appear to want to. The tale of the Jalq'a I grew to admire is a complex one of cultural decline, cultural change, cultural resistance, and cultural resilience all in one, not surprising, perhaps, given their ability to entertain dual, indeed, multiple realities.[48] The women, men, and children I met were for the most part active agents in the change process, a people in transition faced with, but not avoiding, choices to participate in or resist the trappings of modernity.[49] They were a flexible people of generous spirit, but they did not suffer fools on their own turf gladly.

Engagement with the development community and the Western world on less familiar turf appears, however, to have shaken that confidence. Within this new development arena, the terms of exchange were confusing. Equality was trumpeted, yet the terms still privileged the well-resourced outsiders. Historically, the Westerners who dared to tread on their soils entered as landlords with guns and orders, not options. Their objectives were straightforward. Indigenous resistance was hidden but the need for it was very clear. The economic, political, and cultural offerings of the new actors offering a "helping hand" were not, in contrast, as obvious or well understood. Mistakes that weakened local control over the future were made and regretted by many. Time and again I heard farmers express regret with their decision to buy into a commercial agricultural system that not only failed to reap the anticipated benefits but also robbed their children of the native potato legacy their grandparents had left them. And when it came to the critical intercultural education required for the negotiation of better terms of exchange with developers from the dominant society – information and negotiation skills to exercise the authority they needed to manage this interaction well – their NGO companions let them down.

There were, without a doubt, some positive benefits from the NGO intervention. Staff members with all three agencies can justifiably point to the improved health care and community infrastructure in these communities as solid outcomes. Movement toward greater crop diversification was also occurring. The recuperation and diffusion of the nitrogen-fixing and nutrient-rich *tarwi* legume was an especially welcomed addition to a farm family's fields. In my conversations and workshops with residents, these contributions were highlighted and appreciated. Participants also expressed considerable enthusiasm for reforestation initiatives, thanks primarily to IPTK's assistance. Before my departure, IPTK was showing some positive signs of wanting to change. But in late 2000, the overall picture was not an encouraging one. Evidence of impoverished subsistence and semi-subsistence, including life expectancy rates five years below a national average,[50] suggests that Western prescriptions for a better life were not yielding anticipated results. And the new indebtedness among members of credit associations, the result of returns that were insufficient to repay loans for introduced seeds, fertilizers, and synthetic chemicals, was adding another level of stress. The farmers from Chimpa Rodeo – a community with a twenty-year history of development assistance – had incurred this indebtedness. Mojón farmers, with their comparatively short history of aid and absence of credit associations, were debt free.

As for the nutritional value of the perfectly shaped and uniform tubers that Bolivian farmers were encouraged to grow for urban consumers, the story of the Canadian potato is telling. A 2002 study reported that within the past fifty years or so, the average Canadian spud, "by far the most consumed food in Canada," had lost 100 per cent of its vitamin A, 57 per cent of its vitamin C and iron, and 28 per cent of its calcium.[51]

EXPIRED PRESCRIPTIONS

The harsh results of unsuccessful programming, however disturbing at the time, were not nearly as worrisome as the trends that would undoubtedly impact on the longer-term resilience of these communities. Rather than strengthening the knowledge needed to build resilience, NGOs were contributing to its decline. They were doing so in three important ways. First and most obvious were the encouraged dependencies on the products of Western knowledge systems. To cite but one example, synthetic inputs replaced time-tested approaches such as pest-control through companion planting. Laboratory seeds and inputs lessen the need for constant observation and experimentation, weakening the adaptation skills at the heart of sustainable crop production.

Second, and still more problematic, was the decreased opportunity to practice, and consequently maintain, traditional knowledge systems due to a serious decline in the fecundity of the land. Increasingly degraded soils limit a land's capacity to respond to a cultivator's careful stewardship. Several of my research informants reported that even though they wanted to recover the robustness of their traditional potato varieties, they were afraid that their soils might not be healthy enough to allow them to do so. On this issue, the IPTK agronomists working with these farmers agreed.

The third contributor to their weakened resilience was far more complex. It is a factor that was and is poorly considered not only within these particular agencies but also within the larger development community. It relates not so much to the messages and practices development workers carried and encouraged, but to the logic and methods they used to deliver those messages. The literacy, community planning, and agricultural extension training programs these NGOs offered were built on language-based, and often literacy-based, modular curricula. Even when experiential and in situ, the process was a step-by-step, unit-to-unit, linear approach their Western trainers used to solve problems. For Indigenous peoples dependent on knowledge systems that are anything but linear, sequential, compartmentalized, or documented, this instrumental framework, if absorbed over time, might well prove harmful to their original knowledge base.

Several of the scholars I read when conducting secondary research questioned the validity of Occidental learning theories that place linear, language-based logic at the centre of knowledge production and transmission, particularly for Indigenous peoples managing complex ecosystems. Some, like Bloch, went still further, proposing that for humankind in general "the performance of complex practical tasks ... *requires* that it be non-linguistic." Resilience scientists pointed to the failure of Western educational packages to appreciate and respond to the complexity of natural resource systems.[52] Yet these packages of Western logic, including those offered within a more participatory framework, are regularly delivered to Indigenous peoples without hesitation, as the repeated calls to introduce "modern" ways reveal.

NGOs were not, of course, the only development actors in Bolivia responsible for the environmental decline and livelihood failures. A complex combination of factors influenced this erosion. Not the least of these factors was a history of government policy favouring resource extraction over environmental conservation and small-holder farming and the interests of the mestizo in urban centres over the interests of Indigenous peasantry on the periphery. But the Western rationalism delivered through NGOs was sweeping, reaching into the humblest adobe classroom of a highland village. The Indigenous participants in my study demonstrated a considerable resistance to the logic of the outsider. However, if unchecked and delivered to a next generation of farmers with access to a longer school experience, Western logic will likely rule the day. What then of the capacity to deal with natural resource systems that are layered, unpredictable, and full of surprises?[53]

I could not attempt a definitive assessment of community resilience within Chimpa Rodeo and Mojón. But when I reflect on the more extensive application of ecological complementarity practices in Mojón, some interesting questions come to mind. Less dependent on external intervention and with more fertile soils available, might this "less developed" community prove to be more resilient over the long haul? In the face of climate change or when another El Niño drought scorches Chayantan hillsides again, which community will be best able to cope?

The failure to champion alternative knowledge systems and "place the last first," to paraphrase Robert Chambers' apt mantra,[54] should not automatically be interpreted as intentional or malevolent cultural and intellectual imperialism. For the most part, the NGO actors in Chimpa Rodeo and Mojón appeared committed and hopeful. They worked in challenging conditions within an unstable and sometimes menacing political context. In the case of a local organization like IPTK, they could not easily pull out. IPTK's own institutional survival was never secure, with funding at best only assured for three years at a time. I met many field workers who had developed respectful relationships, at time close friendships, with program participants, often working well beyond the call of duty when additional effort was called for. It would be a serious mistake to treat these NGOs as a monolith of homogenous perspective and approach. Or to forget the demands and complexity of the services they performed. And as my All Souls Eve journal entry confirms, despite our best intentions, mistakes can be fast and furious.

The communities I studied also made many favourable comments about some of their NGO *compañeros*. Participants in leadership training activities expressed appreciation for the organizational strengthening workshops they had taken part in. But the strengthened organizations they were encouraged to steer were again based on Western systems that would ultimately push participants toward Western acculturation. Given the considerable barriers to full-fledged citizenship in a mestizo-run country, the best the men and women of Chimpa Rodeo and Mojón could hope for in 2000 was second-class citizenship. I was hard-pressed, for example, to find Indigenous representatives within the senior decision-making bodies of the NGOs I encountered.

There was some evidence of limited power sharing with the municipal governance structures, through committee work, participation on local councils, and within the community consultation processes. Members of the Farmers' Union were also mobilized to exercise their rights as candidates and citizens in a Western political framework. Yet, once more, the terms of participation and the rules of the game were defined by outsiders unable, or unwilling, to read the cultural and intellectual currents of people schooled in alternative ways of knowing. The intercultural literacy skills and practices of the national, international, and multilateral development assistance actors fell short of the mark.

INSIDE OUT

In closing this chapter and the story of my experience among the Jalq'a, I want to pick up on the Andean duality theme in this book and steal a little from kindred-spirited Chinese thinkers. If my portrait of this Trojan horse aid is mostly ying – dark and negative – there is, thankfully, also some yang – bright and inspirational – to report. Across our fragile planet, there is a growing and increasingly powerful call to turn the dominant dynamic in the development "game" inside out. As a starting point, the outsider "experts" wanting to help are entering the relationship as humbled students, first seeking to learn from insiders. The insiders, in turn, are supported in asserting their right to their own experience, expertise, and world view. Then the negotiations can begin on a more just footing.

It is actors within the emergent food movement – Indigenous peoples and small-holder farmers, like-minded activists, inspired agronomists and academics, and informed consumers – who are showing the greatest leadership and demonstrating a more just and democratic approach to development. After years and years of struggle, experimentation, and back-breaking work in the trenches, they are succeeding in attracting more and more people to their cause.

There is, not surprisingly, a forceful push back from philanthropists, corporations, and governments bent on more of the same – the promotion of the spread and adoption of "modern seeds" and packaged inputs to enhance productivity. It is not yet time to celebrate. But this new food movement is expanding and increasingly broad-based, in part, because the West's own production and resilience is so obviously threatened. Before turning to concrete expressions of this exciting shift in thinking and approach, including a description of the program I know best – USC Canada's Seeds of Survival program – let me end this chapter with a far more hopeful passage than the opening one. It comes from Chiapas, Mexico, from Zapatista leaders who in 2000 issued a declaration about development with dignity intended to inspire their own movement.

> dignity is a bridge.
> It needs two sides that, being different, distinct and distant become
>   one in the bridge
> without ceasing to be different and distinct, but ceasing already to be
>   distant.
> When the bridge of dignity is being made,
> the us that we are speaks and the other that we are not speaks.
> On the bridge that is dignity there is the one and the other.
> And the one is not more or better than the other, nor is the other
>   more or better than the one.
> Dignity demands that we are ourselves.
> But dignity is not just being ourselves.
> For there to be dignity the other is necessary.
> Because we are ourselves always in relation to the other.

And the other is other in relation to us. ...
Dignity, then, is recognition and respect.
Recognition of what we are and respect for what we are, yes,
but also recognition of what the other is and respect for that which is
    the other ...
So dignity is the tomorrow.
But the tomorrow cannot be if it is not for all, for those who we are
    and for those who are other.

So dignity should be the world, a world where many worlds fit.
Dignity, then, is not yet.
So dignity is yet to be.
Dignity, then, is struggling so that dignity eventually be the world.
A world where all the worlds fit.
So dignity is and is something that needs to be created.
It is a path to travel.
Dignity is the tomorrow.

14

Development with Dignity

Food sovereignty is a verb!

Colleen Ross, Ontario Farmer, and Vice President,
National Farmers Union of Canada, 2011[1]

Where people are plentiful and land is scarce, the distinctive adaptation of smallholder households practicing intensive agriculture will appear, just as it has for centuries in a variety of human societies. Farm families train and mobilize, labour, manage their limited resources of land and livestock, claim and inherit rights of property, and produce both for their own consumption and for exchange. They have learned to understand, nurture, and renew the soil and water that sustains them, and the means that they have are devised as worthy of our respect and emulation. The question of whether the practical and coherent smallholder system has a future is not in doubt. It may be more vital and necessary to *our* future than we realize.

Robert McC. Netting[2]

SEEDS OF SURVIVAL

In the highlands of one of the world's biodiversity hotspots, centre of origin for many key cereals and of the exquisite coffee bean that get most of us through the day, a drought in the mid-1980s, much like the one that devastated potato production in the Andes, struck with a vengeance. Consecutive years of low or no rainfall, within a context of a protracted civil war, caused a famine that killed hundreds of thousands of people and left at least a million more destitute. The cruel irony in this tragedy was that grains in one part of the country were kept from the other.

Most of us over 40 years of age vividly remember the daily television broadcasts of hollow-eyed Ethiopian farmers.[3] Their children were so emaciated they were barely able to keep their heads up. We were moved to tears and to massive fundraising campaigns, including the first mega celebrity concerts. Our support was well intentioned and in many cases helpful. There were abuses and outrageous incidents, like shipments of chocolate bars sent to people who could hardly keep a handful of porridge down. But, on balance, our assistance bore witness to our kinder, gentler selves. Pictures of benevolent outsiders soon replaced images of desperation in newspapers and broadcasts around the world.

What did not make the headlines, as it rarely does, were the efforts of Ethiopians themselves to turn things around. It is the quiet but essential local action that is always at the heart of really substantive and lasting change. To introduce this section's review of the alternative to Trojan-horse aid, I would like to take us back to that country, one whose highlands when I saw them for the first time in 2005 made me deeply nostalgic for landscapes of their Bolivian counterparts.

During Ethiopia's mid-1980s famine, Westerners grew to consider the country as the world's "basket-case" when it came to feeding its own people. To the contrary, with its long-standing and continued wealth of plant genetic resources and knowledgeable farmers, Ethiopia has been, and could again be, Africa's breadbasket. But we must first look carefully at what her farmers have to offer. That is precisely what a visionary scientist from the country's national gene bank – the Plant Genetic Resources Center (PGRC) – in Addis Ababa did one bright morning in 1988.

Located on a small hillside within the nation's capital, the PGRC, now called the Institute of Biodiversity Conservation and Research (IBCR), is a crop research facility which, for its size and budget, in the mid-1980s commanded (and still does today) respect from scientists around the world. As the rains began to return to the country, and recognizing that farmers had been forced to eat both their future meals and their plant genetic heritage, Melaku Worede, the institute's Director at the time, headed to the countryside with an idea. Could he and his institute help farmers to recover that heritage – the "landraces" or farmers' varieties that had kept them on their lands for generations? The gene bank had its landraces carefully stored in sealed packages on temperature-controlled shelves.[4] The farmers, he supposed, still had the knowledge to grow them out and bring them back into their farming systems and livelihoods.

Dr Melaku, as he is fondly called, knew he had an important idea. But when he and his staff began to work alongside the peasant farmers, they were soon extremely humbled. They discovered that some, despite a des-

perate hunger, had the foresight and fortitude to keep some of their most
precious seeds, burying them deep in their soils, as is the local tradition.
They were waiting for a day when they could thrive again. Most also
demonstrated a knowledge about farming systems that, while explained
in colloquial terms, was surprisingly sophisticated, rivaling that of the
institute's staff.[5] "I became a student all over again," Dr Melaku told me
shortly after we first met in 1989. It was time to put aside assumptions –
indeed arrogance – about whose knowledge was superior and build a collaboration that blended the best of laboratory and farmers' science. This
collaboration evolved into an international agricultural biodiversity program – Seeds of Survival – attracting support from my employer at that
time (and again after a fourteen-year gap), the Unitarian Service Committee of Canada, now called USC Canada. The main features of SOS were the
rebuilding of local seed security and the placing of farmers' skills and
knowledge at the centre of the struggle to end hunger.[6]

In the early days of the program the attention was largely focused on
applied on-farm or in-situ research based on farmers' varietal selection techniques (PVS) and the expansion of intra-specific crop diversity – the number
of varieties within each species. The gene bank's scientists helped farmers to
select and cross for higher yield. The farmers showed these specialists the
much wider range of selection and performance criteria they used to meet
a far broader set of needs. They based their selections on soil types, rainfall
expectations, the length of the growing season, potential frost, drought and
wind tolerance, cooking considerations, taste, and so forth, focusing not
only on the hardiness of the particular variety but the notion of plasticity –
the ability to grow well over changing environments. Their interest in intra-
specific diversity – varieties within the same crop – also meant that the farmers did not favour the development of a superior single line, as tended to be
the case within conventional breeding programs.

The results of this collaboration among farmers and scientists were
encouraging. Fields of sorghum that had been reduced to a couple or a
few varieties at the peak of the famine produced, in time, several varieties
and more.[7] A farmer I met in 2007 had revived his varieties from three
shortly after the famine to forty-three. Durum wheat, on the verge of
extinction in its Ethiopian place of origin, was recuperated. Families were
able to eat their own produce, bring surpluses to market, select seeds for
planting that suited their diverse performance criteria, and save enough to
place a few in the community gene and seed bank that the program
helped to build. The positive outcomes caught the interest of others,

inspiring the development of an international training program that during the course of the program's more than twenty years has drawn participants from around the world.[8]

With time, the sos program, in Ethiopia and elsewhere, has expanded to be a more comprehensive one. In some countries, this includes participatory plant breeding (PPB) to enhance a variety's climate resilience. In all, ecological agricultural practices – agro-ecology – are promoted that pay attention to the entire farming system and the relationship between each of its components. The habitat above ground and the microbiology of the soil underneath are assessed.[9] In addition to PVS and PPB practices and crop diversification, farmers: expand household seed saving; institute and manage community seed and gene banks as insurance for really tough times; sell and exchange seeds within seed fairs and through traditional means; reclaim land and deforested hillsides through the planting of native trees and vegetation; manage watersheds in ways that conserve water for all who need it; integrate animal husbandry and natural composting into the farming system;[10] process products to add value to them; organize marketing cooperatives or associations; and, within the confines of their particular political context, engage in policy work to enhance local control of food production. Varietal and crop productivity continue to be addressed through collaboration among farmers and scientists. But there is now an equal emphasis on farmer-to-farmer field-based exchanges and training, thanks in part to important lessons learned from the *campesino-a-campesino* movement that took root in Central America in the 1990s.[11]

Partnership within the sos program has its own distinctive characteristics, challenges, and lessons learned. A full description of each unique program is clearly beyond the scope of this book. I present this abridged profile to stress one key point. When programming starts with an acknowledgement of farmers' skills and considers the entire farming system, including external challenges, it will succeed. Here is one example from the sos program in Honduras. After Hurricane Mitch stole farmers' harvests and seeds, farmer-research teams (CIALS) managed within a five-year period (1989–2004) to reduce the number of hunger days from 5.6 weeks to 1.3 weeks.[12] Should another disaster like Mitch strike, there is every reason to believe that their agricultural system will prove more resilient. Surveys conducted in 360 post-Mitch communities in Nicaragua, Honduras, and Guatemala showed that diversified plots had 20 to 40 per cent more topsoil, greater soil moisture, and less erosion, and they experienced lower economic losses than the plots of neighbours engaged in conventional agriculture.[13]

The sos program is now not unique of course. In thousands of communities around the world, similar programs feature biodiversity-based ecological agriculture.[14] They have all consistently demonstrated that it takes small-holder – many Indigenous – farming communities to feed the world in healthy and sustainable ways (up to 70% of us if we include pastoralists, fishers, and harvesters of wild foods).[15] And it is the word "community" that needs to be emphasized here. The growing movement of farmers and organizations looking to replicate the best practices of Indigenous farmers schooled in complexity thinking are reclaiming the culture in agriculture. Their resilience and success rests on harmonious relationships with both nature and each other.

Civil society organizations, including the largest peasant organization in the world with a membership of up to 200 million food providers,[16] La Via Campesina, are also paying close attention to the political and policy context needed to make localized, regional, and community-based food production systems work well. Informing and mobilizing farmers when their practices are threatened is, in fact, proving to be one of the most important acts of solidarity between insiders and outsiders, between Northern and Southern actors.[17] The policy arguments are straightforward. Insurmountable environmental challenges or a lack of local capacity are not the primary factors undermining the livelihoods of Indigenous and small-holder farmers. Unfair trade rules and policies that favour a tight minority of powerful corporations and lead to environmental degradation far better explain their disadvantage.[18]

Campaigns to change attitudes and redirect development investments to more resilient agriculture will require sustained commitment and a healthy dose of pig-headedness. There is, thankfully, no shortage of such determination. Equally important is the evidence-based support for farmer-led ecological agriculture in a growing body of peer-reviewed studies, the most recent being the United Nations' Conference on Trade and Development 2013 report with this revealing title: *Wake up before it is too late: Make agriculture truly sustainable now for food security in a changing climate.* A synthesis statement about the report on the agency's website successfully drives home the need for profound change:

Developing and developed countries alike need a paradigm shift in agricultural development: from a "green revolution" to a "truly ecological intensification" approach. This implies a rapid and significant shift from conventional, monoculture-based and high external-input-dependent industrial production towards mosaics of sustainable, regenerative production systems that also considerably improve the productivity of small-scale farmers. We need to see a move from a linear to a holistic approach in agricultural management, which recognizes that a farmer is not only a producer of agricultural goods, but also a manager of an agro-ecological system that provides quite a number of public goods and services.[19]

The UNCTAD study builds on the findings of its path-breaking older cousin (2009) with a less dramatic and clumsy title: The International Agricultural Assessment for Science, Knowledge and Technology for Development. The product of 400 experts – farmers, scientists, academics, private sector and NGO representatives, and international agencies – and funding from major donors like the World Bank and the United Nation's Food and Agriculture Organization (FAO), the "Ag Report" warns that continued reliance on technological fixes – including transgenic crops – would not reduce persistent hunger and poverty but rather risks exacerbating environmental problems and social inequity. Like the UNCTAD report, it endorses systems thinking, including the need to attend to the multi-functionality of food production systems and to far more ecologically sound, biodiverse farming practices, particularly in the face of increasingly unpredictable and extreme weather patterns.[20]

There are other important new institutional allies. The United Nation's Special Rapporteur on the Right to Food, Olivier de Schutter, is a courageous defender of biodiversity-based ecological agriculture that values farmers as the "co-producers of the knowledge they use."[21] Staff members within various multilateral institutions have over the past couple of decades also helped their organizations to embrace more and more ecologically sound farming. So have some of the larger non-governmental organizations.[22] Pressures from nervous governments, due, in good part, to corporate pressures, have forced some back-pedaling and contradictory programming. But there remain advocates within these organizations who continue to fight hard for biodiversity-based ecological agriculture.

International conventions, treaties, and negotiating bodies are also supportive of the importance of food production derived from Indigenous knowledge and local farming systems. The International Convention on Biological Diversity (CBD) and the International Treaty on the Plant Genetic Resources for Food and Agriculture, with their respective 192 and 127 signatories, acknowledge the critical role Indigenous peoples and small-holder farmers play in the conservation of our plant genetic resources and in food security more broadly. The Food and Agriculture Organization (FAO)–sponsored Committee on World Food Security (CFS), revitalized in 2008 in response to the global food price crisis, is also increasingly acknowledging the essential contribution of small-holder farmers in sustainably building broad-based food security. The CFS has, in fact, allowed the establishment of a vital, pioneering, civil society mechanism – the CSM – with a direct voice at the negotiating table. Finally, and perhaps most importantly, there is the vibrant, peasant-led movement, led by La Via Campesina, committed and equipped to mainstream this approach through the broader concept of food sovereignty.

FOOD SOVEREIGNTY

La Via Campesina coined the term "food sovereignty," discussing it at its Second International Conference in Mexico in 1996 and later at the 1996 World Food Summit to capture a strategy to address the social, cultural, and environmental damage resulting from a privatized food security system.[23]

The concept incorporates the idea of food security, defined as access to healthy and culturally appropriate food for all. It goes much further than the right to food, however, to include the idea of the right to *produce* quality food and the right to exercise greater local and regionalized control of the production system, particularly of the seeds at the heart of that system.[24] There is also recognition that in the large-scale industrial food system, small-holder farmers are generally treated as an underclass. The movement must, therefore, continually assess, inform, organize, and confront the technologies and trade regimes that food giants have designed to maintain their domination.[25]

The food sovereignty movement is, in short, a coming together of peasant farmers, Indigenous peoples, landless peoples, fishers, pastoralists, food gatherers, women's organizations, trade unions, food activists, NGOs, consumers, and academics from all over the planet to refashion and democratize the food system. Food is no longer a commodity on sale to the highest bidder but rather an integral part of community life – tactile, nutritious, delicious, and symbolic. More than any other basic need, food, freshly grown and tastily prepared, has the power to draw people together. The vision is both practical and idealistic.

Within the food sovereignty concept, production techniques ideally build on the traditions of Indigenous peoples, using what nature has to offer. Actions on the ground are never that straightforward, of course, nor that pure, removed from broader regimes of capital and governance. There is struggle and there are debates.[26] While genetically modified crops are uniformly rejected, for example, the need for entirely organic farming practices or certified organic production is contested. Small-scale local farmers cannot always afford the time and resources it takes for full-fledged organic certification. The common ground to be found within this debate seems to be a willingness to agree that a period of transition is in order.[27] A growing number of farmers worldwide are also investigating peer-reviewed certification and open source systems that are less costly yet do not compromise on standards.

There is also the question, of course, of the degree and scale of sovereignty that is appropriate. Or, if a localized food system should really be limited to a hundred mile diet. If food sovereignty is defined as 100 per cent self-sufficiency, what impact, for example, might such rigidity have on consumers in areas with far more restricted growing conditions, particularly when original lifestyles and food production systems have been altered to a point of no-return? And how would 100 per cent self-sufficiency affect landless peasants, farm workers, or small-holder producers, let alone the national economies of more marginalized states, which need export markets with fair terms of trade. Can Canadian consumers and Ethiopian coffee producers not both benefit from justly traded, organic coffee? Finally, a question in need of continuous reflection is the extent to which the movement acknowledges the more marginalized within its own house and engages in the gender and class analysis that will keep it true to its justice values. With its casting of such a broad and inclusive net, the food sovereignty movement is messy, as such movements often are.

Nor is food sovereignty about a purist retreat from interaction with actors outside one's regional boundaries or geopolitical borders. Most food sovereignty advocates are not calling for an all or nothing strategy. While the current international trading system needs radical transformation, the transition to more regionalized systems will take some time. The core question is that of who benefits and who is in control. Inter-regional, cross-national, and indeed international trade can fit within a healthy and vibrant localized food system if the frontline actors and their informed consumers are permitted to negotiate the terms of trade. The struggle is for markets of a scale that permit greater local control of what food is produced and of the stewardship practices that will benefit its future production. The food system must be sufficiently flexible and inclusive if it is to be resilient.

The food sovereignty movement is very much just that – an inclusive and emerging movement – not a pre-defined structure. It consists of other movements and groups that are not themselves always tightly defined or, for that matter, conflict free. I have been at meetings where a Via Campesina representative from one country was highly critical of the behaviours and approach of another. It would be a great mistake to consider this movement as a singular, unified, all-encompassing agrarian entity.[28] To even assume that all food producers and consumers would or should have to join this global movement would also impose a kind a tyranny of participation that scholars of other social movements have critiqued.[29]

Even the term "sovereignty" sits uncomfortably with some. Sovereign is a word that is often equated with the idea of a supreme state authority. The notion of independence implicit in the concept, especially with respect to nation states, can also evoke the idea of isolationism that runs counter to the idea of how interconnected our world has become. Those concerned about the term and definition generally defer, as they should, to La Via Campesina farmers who, during the 1996 World Food Summit, thought long and hard about how to name this movement. Farmers are the ones, after all, who have long needed more autonomy to control their production systems. It is the applied definition and use of the term that ultimately counts.

In March 2009, La Via Campesina met in Nyéléni, Mali to do just that – define its applied components more precisely. Six key pillars or components of the concept were identified. The first pillar focused on the idea that food is for people and should not be treated as a commodity. The second called for the valuing of food providers, from farmers, to fishers, pastoralists, hunter-gatherers, and urban gardeners. The third localized the food system, asking consumers to shop closer to home, thereby shortening the route between their food provider and their dinner plates. A fourth pillar promoted local control of the food system, recognizing, however, that local territories can cross geo-political boundaries. The next pillar celebrated local wisdom and encouraged the passing on of this local wisdom to future generations. The final pillar asked us all to work with nature, improving our capacity to adapt and be resilient in the face of climate change.[30]

As the Zapatista poem on dignity suggests, movements with momentum embrace a gathering of distinct actors united in a common cause. Food Sovereignty is a movement in the making, gathering women and men from different classes, regions, races, and ethnic backgrounds, and from both rural and urban landscapes, from the global South and the global North. It is this act of creating change and of traversing boundaries – from countryside to cityscape and from South to North – that makes the movement especially exciting and hopeful. Community-shared agriculture farmers (CSAs), ecological seed producers, farmers' market sellers and customers, community, school-yard, back-yard, front-yard, rooftop, and guerrilla[31] gardeners, school cafeteria chefs, community food centres, slow food club members, organic restaurateurs, organic and local food retailers, university and hospital administrators, government bureaucrats, and networks like Food Secure Canada, join people who live off the land in the production and celebration of food – from seed to spoon and field to fork. There is religious-like fervor among some advocates, so committed are they to building momentum and broadening the reach. Within this multilayered and diverse food community, resilience is bound to deepen. Development with dignity, especially among Indigenous peoples who have taught us how to farm with nature, will start with the proliferation of this wonderfully collaborative food system.

Paradox, Resistance, and Resilience

Come because your liberation is bound up with mine.

Emele Duitulonaga[1]

RAVELO MUNICIPALITY, 18 MARCH 2011

The shades of red! That's what steals my attention as we turn a curve and I see Yurubamba, the first roadside community that comes into view in the municipality of Ravelo. In fields bursting with produce, there are also wonderful greens, some white, purple, and a little gold. But it is the red of adobe houses and terra cotta roofs, of the rows of quinoa royal that surround potato fields, sown to keep the animals out, of the wind-carved faces in the mountain backdrop, and most importantly of the well-worked soils, that dominate the view. So striking! How the red draws me back. And yet when I look to my notes of a decade ago, red plays a rather minor role in my descriptions of the Ravelo landscape. How could I have missed such a vivid colour? Was I so preoccupied with the vegetation and crops that I missed the stuff they grow in? Maybe the deeply weathered soils attract me now because in the interim, I have come to learn so much more about the incredible diversity of their microorganisms that offer life to the seeds they husband. Maybe the soil should claim the label of the first link in the food chain.

Ramiro Arancibia Araoz, IPTK's current executive director, has generously loaned me his vehicle and driver, Fabien, for the day. Fabien picked me up at the *Su Merced* at six on the dot this morning, early enough for an arrival that will allow for a visit to each of my host communities before the sun sets at around 7 pm. We talk mostly politics on the drive up. A longtime IPTK employee, Fabien has plenty to say about the changes in his country.

Ramiro also phoned Ricardo, his Ravelo-based *técnico* now responsible for the agricultural biodiversity pilot project we began together shortly after my return to work with Canadian Lutheran World Relief in January 2001.[2] Ricardo notified Chimpa Rodeo's farmers about my arrival yesterday. He has not yet managed to get in touch with my friends in Mojón. If we make it there, it will be a surprise visit. Since the rains this year have not completely let up, and the driving is a bit precarious, better a surprise than to have friends possibly wait in vain.

Yurubamba, a village spread over the more fertile valley bottom and thus centre of commercial potato production[3] looks exactly as it had a decade ago and the three times I have passed it since. The village of Ravelo, on the other hand, has the new high school with a bright blue tiled roof, built a few years after my departure. It still shocks me a little when it comes into view. I am mostly happy to see it. The building is a sign that the *Reforma Educativa* has moved forward. Local teens wanting to go to high school will not have to be boarded at a *colegio* outside their district. But its presence somehow jars my sense of the village I came to know well just over a decade ago. And there are those nagging feelings about the kind of knowledge being taught to the next generation of farmers. Have agro-ecology and sustainable food production made it into the curriculum?

The municipal offices on the edge of the town square seem no different, with no obvious paint jobs, although Fabien tells me that the community's communication services are better now. The single Entel telephone, shut into a small locked cabin beside the mayor's office, is no longer the sole and often out of order connection with family and friends in the city. I think back to that night I spent worrying about Kelsey and Pat after I noticed the treadless tires of the bus they were taking back to Sucre, just as it pulled away. I had a moment of wanting to shout: "STOP THE BUS!" That would be over-reacting, my logic countered. The bus was out of hearing distance by the time my internal debate subsided. Off they went, then, through twisting mountain roads with big black bald tires. Once I figured they would be home, I rushed to the phone office. "Sorry, it's out of order tonight. Come back tomorrow." What a sleepless night that was! Of course when I phoned the next day, Kelsey answered, "Oh, hi, Mom, that was a fun trip." Cell phones now work, some of the time anyway.

The town square, a mini central plaza with its fenced-in vegetation, is also exactly the same, down to the height of the trimmed bushes. There continue to be a couple of vendors on each side of the quadrangle selling their wares, and two that also compete for the region's coca leaf customers. I am reminded of how careful I had to be with my purchases, spreading my business around, showing no single preference. I wish I had time to step out of the truck and meet some old Ravelo friends.

We arrive at the field station. Ricardo greets me with a welcoming grin. He and I have travelled back to my host communities twice over the past ten years and I have stayed over in the field station a couple of nights while he was present. So we know each other well enough. Tico (Alberto), my dynamic, then twenty-something IPTK assistant for Mojón, left IPTK not long after my departure. So did my Chimpa Rodeo guide, Cornelio, my senior by a good fifteen years in age and in experience, among the most astute on cross-cultural matters that I have ever met. Cornelio was *padrino* or godfather to many of Chimpa Rodeo's young.

There's a new crew now, young like Tico and just as eager. Ricardo has a new female counterpart, Josefa. They work as a gender-balanced team in their target communities, part of the gender equality strategy integrated into the agro-biodiversity pilot project Canadian Lutheran World Relief now supports. The women farmers are far more comfortable with a female *técnico*. The turnover of women field-staff had been steady, however, much to my disappointment. There has been a new female extension worker each time I have returned. They leave to follow a new spouse, to take a job that is closer to home, or to have a baby. Since there is a much smaller pool of trained female agronomists to draw from, insistence on gender parity is a tall order.

We don't linger at the field station, although I am curious to look around. There should be time for a short visit en route back to Sucre, Fabien reassures me. We will head to Chimpa Rodeo first. The truck can easily navigate the road there. The trip to Mojón, Ricardo tells me, is a bit dubious. The rains this year have lasted longer than anticipated. If it rains today, we will definitely be out of luck. It is a bit overcast as we hit the road again.

MEETING OLD FRIENDS

In the end, the sun cooperates. It is bright and hot when we reach Chimpa Rodeo, about 45 minutes later. The dark blue *gora* or baseball cap that I purchased for this purpose has been left behind in my Sucre hostel. I borrow a fedora-style hat, newly crafted by participants in IPTK's program. As I step out of the truck and look over the village, I am hit with a wave of emotion, not unlike the one I experienced when I first set eyes on this incredibly picturesque settlement over a decade ago. I remember thinking, "wow, this is where I could get to do my research!" Most of the villages I visited during my initial scan of the region were lovely. But Chimpa Rodeo, with its tiered settlement and mix of steep terrain and flowing meadows evoked a breath of wonder.

We climb to the small adobe community centre. On the way I run into Don Angel and Doña Desideria's youngest son. His name escapes me, but he stops to offer a shy hello. He is no longer a curious eight year old, but rather, a strapping young man. "How did that happen so fast?" I wonder. And there, not far behind, is his mother, Desideria, her huge smile and tight hug almost bringing me to tears. Soon Leandro, Domingo, and other familiar faces arrive. Several of their names escape me as well, although I do my best to pretend otherwise. Leandro's comes quickest to mind. His name is the Spanish version of my father's, but that's not why I remember him so well. He was among the most obliging and helpful during my research days. "A leader who will blossom," I had thought back then. He has in fact become the *Maximo Dirigente* or head union leader of the sub-central Rodeo Huayllas.

Rodeo Huayllas is a grouping of five hamlets, including Chimpa's counterpart, Ura Rodeo. I am not surprised to learn that the Ura and Chimpa hamlets of the Rodeos have officially separated; standing now as the independent communities they had always seemed to be in practice. I am more surprised to see that there is an electrical cable running through the community. No longer will those wanting to meet on a moonless night have to crowd around a small kerosene lamp.

Lucia, I am happy to discover, is also present. Since her husband's death about fifteen years ago, she has been the sole breadwinner for her four children. She seems delighted to see me. The feeling is mutual. The first thing she asks is, "where is your daughter?" "It's so far," I reply, "and expensive, so it just hasn't worked out." I can see that I am losing my credibility on that one.

Leandro's grin is equally welcoming and we too hug. Doña Antonia, another good friend, is in the valley he tells me. Don Victor and his wife are also away. I am chided for providing little warning about my visit. They could have gathered more *compañeros* and prepared a more elaborate meal. We sit and chat for a short while, but it is the harvest season and there is much work to be done. I don't want to steal too much of their time. They are also anxious to show me their Indigenous potato fields – *papas nativas* – all grown with local *guano* – sheep manure – and the organic compost and natural pesticides they have learned to prepare.

"*Todo organico,*" they proudly announce. Ricardo adds that IPTK has dropped the chemicals of the past. The food production they now support in these communities, as in the entire region, is entirely organic.

Native varieties are also now far more widespread in Chimpa Rodeo and are here to stay, my friends report. Don Jose alone, also away today, has over 60 varieties now. Don Domingo, probably the most entrepreneurial farmer I have met during my entire time in the region, has twenty-seven. That's about the same number I remember him having when we first knew each other I say to him, teasing a little. He agrees, explaining that he continues to divide his time between Chimpa Rodeo and Sucre, where he and his wife also run a small business. And, I am pleased to find out, he has also become a farmer-promoter for IPTK, travelling from community to community to assist with training, trouble-shooting, and other farming needs.

The pilot project, I also learn, has expanded from Chimpa Rodeo and Mojón to ten communities. Among these ten communities, Ricardo says, there is now a total of 140 varieties of potatoes, 20 varieties of oca, 10 of the still less known *papa lisa*, and 6 varieties of *izaño*, another root crop that looks and tastes a lot like oca. "This level of diversity could spread to other parts of the municipality," he adds, "if only we had the resources to expand the project." My constant rant about how little it would take to spread such important work leaps into my thoughts, although I keep it to myself.

As we cross over into Doña Augustina's native potato field, we find a nasty pest, a tuberworm that eats at the flesh of the potato. I am reminded about how prone potatoes are to pests and disease. Organic production is hard work and knowledge intensive! Don Leandro and Domingo pledge to notify her and help her to remove the pest from her crop, perhaps with an organic pesticide spray or possibly one plant at a time.

En route to the next potato field, the subject of seed banking comes up. "How does it work in other areas," they ask me. I explain that for tubers like potatoes, seed banks are right there in their fields of diversity, their plant genetic diversity conserved by growing many varieties out each year. But community storage spaces or banks for the collection and saving of grain and bean seeds are very feasible. I will pass on to Ricardo more information about the seed banks my current employer supports, I tell them. "Much obliged (or the Spanish equivalent)," they reply.

PROUD WOMEN

For the women present, it is not the fields of diversity that seem the source of greatest pride. Rather, it is their textiles. Collaboration between IPTK and ASUR seems to have borne fruit. Inside the community centre are looms and displays of textiles that recapture the traditional surrealism of dream-induced patterns. There are also finished artisanal products, which the women hope to sell in Sucre markets. The women report that only a few of them have had regular sales to date. But they are trying to improve the quality of their work and they are hopeful. Their enthusiasm is touching. This revival of textile literacy seems to be bringing new meaning into their lives, drawing the women together.

"In order to make it to Mojón," I say, "we have to leave now." "Isn't there time to share some food?" they reply. A pot of potatoes is always put to boil when a guest arrives. To decline at this stage would be rude, so we spend another twenty minutes eating. I have brought a small plastic bag along for the potatoes I can't manage and there are no hurt feelings. It is time for final goodbyes. We do the rounds of the Andean handshake-hug-slap on the back, with the women offering kisses on each cheek, much like the cheek–to-cheek kiss I grew up with in Quebec. I thank them for their generosity again and vow to return. They trust that these are not empty words. I have managed to keep this promise before and intend to again, although I can't really know for certain. Back into the truck I climb, after snapping a few group photographs. Copies of those will also be returned. They trust me on that one too. "By the way," I call out from the truck window, "do UNICEF and Food for the Hungry International still operate in your community?" "They are gone," Leandro shouts back.

The road into Mojón is as I had expected. With its deep gullies and boulders, it is a terrain that only a good four-wheel-drive and a still better driver can navigate. Fortunately we have both this afternoon. Although the skies remain clear, it is not easy going. I offer to hike after two almost, but not quite, breakdowns. "No need," our driver confidently asserts, correctly. We arrive just before the sun begins its descent behind the Western ridges. I see the UNICEF-sponsored latrines that were built after my departure. Like Ravelo's high school, they shock me a little, sitting as they do like blots of white oil paint on a mosaic that is otherwise wonderfully earthy and harmonious with its natural landscape. "The white makes them visible at night," I am told. "Hmmn," I think, reluctantly admitting that for a village still without electricity, the strategy is a clever one.

Whether the latrines are well used is another question. During my last return visit, my requests to use a family's latrine were greeted with, "maybe try someone else's for now." Do farmers still prefer their potato fields to the introduced latrines?[4] I dare not ask my friends that question, but I suspect that things have not changed much on that front.

A SURPRISE VISIT

My arrival is not anticipated, but my luck is good today. Don Mario, Pedro, Marcelino, Juan, and Gregorio are all there, as is Doña Cirilia and Prima and other women I recognize. Don Justo, who first guided me into the village and had recited all the names of the *manta* fields, is now tending to his valley lands. Sadly, I also learn that Don Euserbio, the *Jalq'a* friend I disappointed most in 2000, died of a brain aneurism last year, at just 37 years of age. How sad! He had young children and was such a thoughtful leader. I had felt that we had reconnected a little during my return visits. His reaction to my cross-cultural faux-pas, I came to appreciate, was an admirable claim to agency – to not wanting to feel manipulated.

Although I am not expected, my hosts are obliging and gracious. They take time from their busy day to talk and show me their fields, much like my friends in Chimpa. They also insist that I look at their new improved stoves, which need far less fuel and have chimneys to clear the smoke out of their low ceilinged kitchen areas. As in Chimpa Rodeo, the women ask me to view their textiles, especially Doña Cirilia, the women's group president here in Mojón. They too express great joy in their craft.

I am impressed. There seems to be still finer textile work here in Mojón and maybe even more commercial potential. A few of the pieces are real works of art. The men, I see, have also revived a weaving tradition long abandoned. I am shown some of their work. Both genders show pride in each other's creations. And how expressive and boisterous these women now are, no longer the terrified speakers asked to report to the tall *gringita* during community meetings a decade ago. There is always the chance, of course, that they might be telling me what they think I want to hear. I have been trained to think such thoughts, after all. But I remember how these same women would be flushed and gasping for breath when asked to report or to share their perspectives. There is absolutely no hesitation now. To the contrary, they interrupt each other and in their enthusiasm, talk over each other. It is clear that there is genuine and positive change.

We stop at Don Gregorio's house en route to the fields. We are a smaller group now so the conversation is more intimate. Gregorio spontaneously tells me that while they were once losing their native potatoes, they are now saving them. And their nutrition has improved, as has the health of their animals, thanks to animal husbandry training and the availability of veterinary medicines. He also comments on the women's weaving program. "Although men participate, women take the lead," he tells me. "The key issue there," Don Gregorio insists, "is the need for a quality product, so they can be sold in the city." Some women are already selling their textiles in city markets. "That is helping their families," he adds.

Don Marcelino has joined in on the conversation. He notes the benefits of the association that they have formed around their native potato varieties. As with the textiles, there is hope that their more nutritious and tasty native varieties will soon be attractive to city consumers. I tell them about the rising popularity of the small and colourful "gourmet" potatoes sold in Canadian cities, likely the tuber progeny of their Andean ancestors.

Don Domingo, who has accompanied me from Chimpa Rodeo, speaks next. As a leader in their joint association, he has a lot to say in fact. He delivers a short speech starting with how proud Mojón *compañeros*, together with their compadres of Chimpa Rodeo, should feel to have been one of the two communities that launched a project that is now active in ten communities. He talks about the potential to influence the entire municipality and even beyond. The ultimate goal of the association, he further suggests, is to take over the role of the extension workers and the NGOs. They will run their own program. He also mentions our discussion in Chimpa Rodeo about seed banking, an approach that might well be of use to them.

The potatoes are being peeled just as we start to head out. We explain that we must drive out of the high mountains and back to Sucre before it gets really dark. We are truly sorry to have to leave. Aware that the voyage ahead can be precarious at night, my friends forgive our early departure. There is a round of goodbyes, and then it is back to the truck for another hour or so of bucking-bronco travel on a road that looks more like an eroded riverbed than a roadway. There isn't much time for further conversation when we arrive in Ravelo, just a quick hello to an administrator in Ricardo's office. I express my congratulations for some really impressive work.

LAST DASH THROUGH THE FIELD STATION

Before returning to the truck, I rush around the field station quickly. The sun is just high enough to see it well. The rooms and building remain as they were, although I do notice that they have added two flush toilets beside the two latrines we all alternated between in 2000. There continue to be no curtains or doors. The women, still a minority, clearly have not won that battle. Privacy still depends on loud singing.

Not far from the privy, in the centre of the courtyard, I see sewing machines set up for training workshops. And there, in front of a sewing machine, is my good friend, Don Angel, my always-generous home-stay host from Chimpa Rodeo. He tells me that he has joined the IPTK team as an extension worker. He offers a more reserved, shy greeting than his wife Desideria, in keeping with the man I knew a decade ago. Life is better, he says simply, when we shake hands.

As I leave the courtyard structure, I notice that the greenhouse and demonstration plots have been revived and have crops ready to harvest. They had been abandoned when I was living at the station. There seems to be a new vibrancy in the field station.

BOLIVIA TODAY

In the truck from Mojón to Ravelo, Ricardo and I have time to talk about the country's radically changed political context. Who would have thought a decade ago that citizens in the tight grip of neo-liberal governance would in the first decade of the new millennium elect and then re-elect Juan Evo Morales, Bolivia's first Aymara president and the first Indigenous president of the eighty elected since independence?[5] Successive attempts at economic and political reform in Bolivia had always reproduced and strengthened the colonial pattern of urban-mestizo domination over the rural Indigenous peasantry.[6] For the first time since the arrival of imperial forces and the subsequent establishment of a republican nation state, an Indigenous social movement, MAS – Movement Towards Socialism – won the right to a system in which the rural people, largely Indigenous peasant farmers, have a say in the day-to-day business of governing. Most importantly, there is a shift in the way the Indigenous peasantry now views itself. This largely Indigenous government is also attempting to repair the fractured relationship between nature and culture. Mother Nature, a Bolivian law will soon insist, also has rights, ever-present signs of contradiction notwithstanding.[7] Food sovereignty is also a national government priority now, inserted into the nation's constitution in 2009.[8]

At the local level, there has been some very positive attention to environmental conservation. For instance, the communities of the Llallagua municipality in North Potosí have declared their local government the "Bio-Cultural Municipality for the Conservation of the Native Potatoes," while the municipality of Colomi in Cochabamba now calls itself the "Agro-Ecological Biodiversity Municipality."[9] Ricardo tells me that in Ravelo, the mayor's office has created a unit to deal specifically with the environment. They are proactively insisting on, and helping with, the implementation of environmental impact assessments. IPTK's agro-biodiversity work and new commitment to promote organic production have also been received very positively. There is also a new interest in environmental education for children. IPTK is hoping to assist with such programming. Ricardo is aware of the rumblings of discontent with the current government. "And what about the complaint I heard about *campesinos* being forced to attend village and municipal meetings on the threat of a fine?" I ask. "The farmers I know are OK with that," he replies. "Things aren't perfect, but on balance, they are better."

The academic reviews I have in front of me now are mixed, with some highly critical. Harshest among them are scholars from the Left. While cultivating the image of democratic revolution and pro-Indigenous governance, the Morales government, they insist, has in practice manipulated the social movements to create an Andean-Amazonia capitalism. It is an approach that essentially requires continued strategic alliance with global capital, especially the multinational hydro-carbon corporations and state agro-businesses. Such alliances may well be defended as temporary and pragmatic. Still they continue to privilege wealth, as evidenced in the fact that wages have taken a regressive pattern.[10]

More patient reviewers argue that the Morales government represents a very complex blend of ideology and strategy. They acknowledge the highly contradictory results, as when pushing for hydrocarbon exploitation and considering fracking on the one hand and advancing legislation on the rights for "Mother Earth" on the other; or the promotion of food sovereignty while continuing to turn a blind eye to genetically modified soya crops that are strengthening corporate coffers. But the government's Indigenous nationalism, these more supportive observers suggest, is moving the country toward some of the key goals laid out in the original "cultural democratic" agenda. Rural representatives, for example, are at long last offered important participation in the writing of the country's new constitution. The government's nationalization of its primary industries is an important step toward economic development of direct benefit to Bolivians.

Reports from my friends and contacts are also very mixed. My brief return visits since the first election have not allowed for much more than a gathering of impressions. But my respondents have been a diverse group. I have spoken to city friends around their kitchen tables, chatted with taxi drivers, NGO drivers, and shoeshine men, discussed the situation with Bolivian and expatriate NGO and multilateral agency colleagues and heard from Bolivian and expatriate government officials. All agree that governing, rather than opposing, is extremely challenging. I remember a lecture I attended in the late 1980s in which a leading member of South Africa's African National Congress (ANC) made this very astute observation: "We were weaned on a unified confrontation of the oppressive system. No one taught us the intricacies of managing a complex web of competing versus unified interests."

My Bolivian friends who are focused on the realpolitik of governance, although initially supportive, are joining the growing queue of critics concerned that concrete benefits are simply too slow to arrive. There are also murmurs that highland peoples are being favoured over the peoples of the Amazon basin. The government's intention to build a 300-kilometer highway that would pass through Isiboro-Secure Indigenous Territory and National Park (Tipnis) – an 11,900 square kilometers preserve which boasts exceptional levels of rainforest biodiversity – is being interpreted as blatant disregard for the rights of lowland peoples now that they are no longer needed as allies. The decision, Morales's officials counter, is a purely economic one, with the road essential for the country's development.[11] Whatever the rationale, long-standing tension between transmigrants from the highlands and the lowland Indigenous neighbours appears to have found expression in this recent grievance.

More sympathetic friends focus on the ideological and moral imperatives of Bolivia's new plurinational state. Mistakes are inevitable. But deep-seated transformation – a revolution in the truest sense – requires time and a focus on the longer term. Moreover, they argue, Morales and his party inherited a huge debt load as well as industrial cartels, like the one controlling the country's sugar supply, that are themselves incredibly destabilizing. The globalized power of these magnates makes them almost impossible to control. And why, they ask, can't the complaining be focused on the excessively wealthy, the reason for Bolivia having one of the biggest gaps between the rich and poor in the world. Bolivia still has a high level of income inequality with 10 per cent of the population (mostly white) accessing over 40 per cent of the total income.[12] Under Morales' government, they further point out, absolute poverty has decreased.

Still, continued corruption, both in the trenches and within higher public service and political circles, has both the cynics and the idealists very worried. They do admit that the corruptions of past administrations were worse. Incarcerations without due process, again not new, are another common complaint. And the police, it is generally agreed, simply cannot be trusted. Not much has changed on that front either. The absence of any real opposition to keep the current government in check is new and especially troubling. A growing number among the middle and working urban classes I talked to have their noses seriously out of joint over this final issue, including some very good friends in Sucre. Not surprisingly, in the lands of the Eastern *hacendados* or large landowners, Morales is accused of *caudillismo* or dictatorship. For this country's first Indigenous president, there is a good measure of being damned if he does and damned if he doesn't.[13]

The few *Jalq'a* friends I carefully asked for comment about their Indigenous leadership were hesitant to reply, understandable when for so long their critical opinions were either discounted or the source of possible reprisal. Those willing to comment seemed to be hedging their bets, happy to have their voices taken more seriously but anxious too about seeing concrete and positive results. The political context, like the tiered and varied landscapes they and their fellow Bolivians inhabit, is exceedingly complex.

HOPE

I cannot help but feel, however, that for all the flaws and contradictions, the strengthened and valued identity that this new administration has offered the majority of its rural and Indigenous citizens is a fundamental transformation. I read recently about how a nation must be symbolized before it can be loved, imagined before it can be conceived.[14] Years of oppression breed self-doubt, a reluctance even to consider new possibility. How often have I heard capable Indigenous farmers, particularly women farmers, say "no sabe mucho" (I don't know much), implying that they aren't very smart. However difficult the craft and art of governing will prove for the leaders within Bolivia's Indigenous majority, they have created an ideal – a plurinational country and constitution – that offers long overdue possibility of a more inclusive and just future. There is clear vision to hold on to and there is no turning back.

In 2000, the Indigenous producers I observed in the Chayanta highlands were negotiating contradictions and changing contexts amazingly well, given the broader state of marginalization. They will no doubt continue do so in this second decade of the new millennium, more so if their active agency is understood and truly supported, as should be the case under the current political regime. But theirs is a nation that has never stood still and has regularly attempted to reinvent itself, mostly against its majority's wishes and now for the better. Indigenous mobilization has shifted a seemingly intractable system.

As for our planet's shifting contexts and unstable ground, it is to these rural masters of the unpredictable, and their Indigenous counterparts worldwide, that we may need to turn to teach us a thing or two about how to manage. Not the least of this guidance would be to help us to deal with an angry *Pachamama*, taken for granted and abused all these long years.

With respect to my personal contradictions and shifting contexts, I too have come some way. I have opted to continue the development actor role, and I hope have been "cross-pollinated" with wiser traits, thanks to applied research among those I want to assist. But I remain within, indeed now lead within, a development field that continues to send staff on relatively short orientation and monitoring visits and that, dare I say it, can do as much harm as good.

I will continue to believe deeply in the goodness of most human beings, knowing that this belief will continue to be shaken to the core each time I hear tragic reports about our human capacity to abuse each other and our ever-fragile planet. I accept that my behaviours and leadership are, at times, full of contradictions. I wear these contradictions more and more on my sleeve, prepared to be called on them and to accept this basic truth about our imperfect and conflicting natures. You can't spend a year among Bolivia's Jalq'a without at least that bit of understanding rubbing off on you.

APPENDICES

Overview of Field Research and Methods
January to December 2000

Research Protocol:
Established with my supporting NGO, Instituto Politecnico Tomas Katari (IPTK), February 2000.

Environmental Scan:
With the help of IPTK, I visited 16 communities within the municipalities of Ocuri and Ravelo in Chayanta, Northern Potosí. Informal interviews were held with over 125 local residents, NGO staff members, and local government officials.

Sucre[1]	Ravelo	Chimpa Rodeo (CR)/ Mojón (M)
Meetings with IPTK program management and research staff to discuss my research program and to learn about IPTK's understanding of the issues to be addressed.	*Meetings* with IPTK field staff to discuss protocol, the research process, and to seek their permission.	*Meetings* with community leaders – organized through the farmers' union structure – to explain research protocol and to request their participation and signed permission to proceed.
Semi-structured interviews with staff from: Bolivian NGOs and multilateral agencies (i.e. UNICEF/ UNFPA/WFP); the Bolivian Ministry of Education; the Consejo Educativo de la Nacion Quechua (CENAQ); the Sucre-based foundation Antropólogos del Sur (ASUR); and the Bolivian Potato Research Program (PROINPA) and the International Potato Centre (CIP).	*Semi-structured interviews* with: NGO fieldworkers; municipal and departmental government staff; Bolivia Ministry of Education field-staff; farm union leaders; village promoters; the mayor and municipal councilors.	*Semi-structured interviews* with: local residents; NGO fieldworkers; public health workers; farm union leaders; village promoters; school teachers and administrators.

Sucre	Ravelo	Chimpa Rodeo (CR)/ Mojón (M)
Participant observation of IPTK and UNFPA's peri-urban literacy programs.	*Participant observation* of: NGO field station; Ravelo elementary school (grade one); day-to-day village life; the nation's national holiday festivities; municipal planning workshops; agricultural fairs; professional develop ment workshop for local teachers; training for literacy promoters.	*Participant Observation* of: farmers' union meetings in CR and M; harvesting and planting of potatoes in CR and M; Festival of the Virgin of Guadalupe and community marriages in CR; host-family lifestyle in CR; "minka" (group) construction of a small house CR; teacher's family life in M; elementary school in M; All Soul's Eve and All Saints day festivities in M; other day to day activities in CR and M.
		Participatory Rural Appraisal (PRA) workshop (2 days). These workshops began with an overview of my research aims and approach. Once permission to proceed was granted, we proceeded with the PRA exercises described below.
Primary and secondary document research In Bolivia's National Archives and National Library as well as IPTK HQ offices.	*Primary and secondary document research* in IPTK's Ravelo field office.	*Household benchmark surveys/interviews* (2 hours) with the heads of households (generally the male and female) of 25 families plus two Jalq'a government extension workers from neighbouring hamlets. Surveys conducted with the extension workers influenced my understanding of the broader picture but were not integrated into the data presented on CR or M.
		Survey of potato varieties through a photographic inventory (described below) and through the collection of samples.

Analysis of Primary Research Methods

BENCHMARK HOUSEHOLD SURVEYS

I conducted a household survey, designed with the assistance of the IPTK extension workers responsible for Chimpa Rodeo and Mojón, among fourteen farm families in Chimpa Rodeo and eleven in Mojón, representing 32 per cent of the seventy-nine families residing in these two communities. I was initially rather skeptical about the reliability of the data from this survey. Nor was I convinced of its appropriateness as a tool to establish rapport with members of the community. These concerns reflected the all too frequent errors reported in survey-based data as well as my own impatience with the researchers who land on my doorstep. I must admit, however, that I had underestimated the value of this tool in obtaining an introductory understanding of basic demographic, production, and cultural information. It was a pleasant surprise that the household surveys also offered a welcomed opportunity to establish a relationship with several of the participating farm families. The interview proved to be a two-hour icebreaker that, in some cases, paved a path to a more substantive relationship.

Early on in the implementation process, a pilot phase of sorts, I discovered that the information requested was far too detailed, particularly given the need for Quechua-Spanish translation. When interest appeared to be fading, questions were therefore dropped. Demographic and production findings reported on within this document are thus based on questions consistently posed and answered. For more propositional questioning, I opted for a conversational approach, turning the latter part of the exchange into a semi-structured interview. I also decided to leave the section on participants' production and conservation of potato varieties to a second session, using a system described below. All in all, participants were far more patient and forthcoming than I had anticipated. For that I will be eternally grateful.

One particularly common weakness with surveys, of course, is the temptation to interpret reported data as fact. Within Indigenous communities that are not conversant with or terribly interested in the compartmentalizing of their lives into manageable bites of quantitative data, caution is doubly warranted. While the requirements of participation in a Western market economy have influenced some delineation and quantification of production data among farmers hoping to sell surplus produce, much of this information is memory-based. Documented information, let alone homestead balance sheets, was rarely available. Questions regarding hectares in production, fertilizer quantities, input costs and crop production levels were thus often greeted with a nervous laugh. Answers tended to be approximations. When cross-checked with those of other respondents and with census and development planning data collected by organizations like IPTK, the municipality, or the *Programa de Autodesarrollo Campesino* (PAC) – a European Union sponsored self-development program for farmers that was discontinued in 1999 – the information provided was generally consistent with data for the region, well within an acceptable range. Still here, it is important to remember that the survey data these institutions collected were also based on the approximations and estimates of people with little formal schooling and a preference to consider the bigger picture than to quantify the individual parts. The findings noted in this book should be considered, therefore, as information that helps to frame a general picture rather than a precise account of conditions, trends, and patterns.

The trustworthiness of farmers' reports on potato plant diversity, of central interest to this book, was still more problematic. The reliability of data was complicated by two issues: the use of different Quechua names for the same variety, even within the same region; and the fact that changes in plant morphology can influence a perception of varietal distinctiveness when the plant's genetic structure has not, in fact, changed. Miguel Holle, plant scientist with the International Potato Centre (CIP) in Lima, warned me about this when I visited him in June that year. He explained that laboratory studies to examine the genetic content of in-situ potato variety collections have consistently demonstrated that approximately half of the reported varieties were actually genetically identical to another reported variety. Morphological changes were usually the result of a tuber's deterioration or its development under different growing conditions.

Since the collection and verification of the genetic content of the varieties actually grown in the fields of Chimpa Rodeo and Mojón farm families was beyond my study's scope and budget, Holle's caution about inflated numbers should be carefully considered when reviewing my presentation of farmer's reports on the varieties they produced or remembered seeing their parents or grandparents producing. But even if I were to cut the reported numbers of varieties produced or abandoned by 50 per cent, as will be seen, there would still be a significant decline in varieties produced in my findings. Moreover, the technique I chose to retrieve this information about potato diversity was designed to reduce the possibility of inflated reports. A concise outline of this process follows.

I was not collecting samples from each participant for verification in a lab, and there were no documented data on varieties before 1996, so I therefore decided to have participants review a photographic inventory of genetically distinct varieties in the area, thereby establishing a common universe for assessment purposes. The inventory was the work of Regis Cepeda, a young agronomist from Potosí, based on his 1995 collection, analysis, and cataloguing of varieties from the two most common subspecies in the Bolivian highlands: *solanum tuberosum* and *solanum tuberosum andigenum*.[1] Under the auspices of the Faculty of Agricultural Sciences and Forestry within Sucre's Universidad Mayor Real y Pontifica de San Francisco Xavier de Chuquisaca, and with the assistance of his brother, an agronomist with PROSEMPA, Cepeda collected, dissected, and analyzed the genetic makeup of potatoes from eighteen communities in the Ravelo watershed. He identified thirty-four distinct varieties of the two subspecies central to his study, twenty-nine from the subspecies *andigenum*, native to the Andean region, and five varieties of the *tuberosum* interloper from outside the Andean region. He also found an additional nineteen other genetically distinct varieties; but since these were not from the *andigenum* or *tuberosum* subspecies, they were not included in the inventory.

To ensure that Cepeda's photographs were of sufficiently high quality for solid identification, I showed the catalogue to a potato specialist working in PROINPA's Sucre office. He found them to be of a consistently good standard. Presenting the farmers with actual specimens would have been ideal, of course. Since that was not possible, I was pleased to learn that these photographs would serve the purpose.

I had also attempted to collect a sampling of farmers' varieties. Cepeda had generously offered to conduct genetic testing of their varieties, having access to the appropriate laboratory equipment. However, I was unable to collect specimens during the optimum season for collection and there were scheduling conflicts that precluded assistance from Cepeda. I decided, therefore, to abandon this approach.

All participants in my household survey were asked to examine a photographic entry of each variety within Cepeda's catalogue, which they had never seen before. Each entry included a photo of the complete potato, noting its external characteristics, and a photo of a sliced half of the potato that displayed the internal morphology. The participants were first asked whether they recognized the variety, then whether they still produced the variety, and third, if they did not produce it, whether their parents or grandparents had. The average age of respondents in Chimpa Rodeo was thirty-five years. In Mojón it was forty-six. In both communities, farmers reported a decline in diversity based on a common universe of thirty-four varieties. This limited parameter meant that the presence or losses of other subspecies were not accounted for. However, the common denominator of verified varieties that every participant reviewed in the catalogue allowed me to capture a trend within the two most common subspecies that was not significantly affected by name confusion or by the issue of morphological change. Participants, in fact, did call some of the same varieties by different names.

A final point of relevance to the reliability of potato variety reporting in this study relates to a rapid, but as it turns out, informative memory game on potato varieties conducted in Mojón during the PRA workshop I conducted there. Participants reported a decline in the number of potato varieties produced or abandoned within the community over two generations that was very close to the average loss among Mojón participants in my household survey (50% versus 57%). The game was a simple one that divided participants into two teams, one working inside the schoolroom and the other outside. In a competition lasting fifteen minutes, each team was asked to list the names of potato varieties still produced in the community (not necessarily on their own farm) and those abandoned within the past two generations. Group One listed ten names of varieties still in production and ten varieties abandoned. Group Two identified the names of eleven varieties still in production as well as another ten abandoned. There was significant overlap between the two groups in the names recorded on the list of potatoes in production (60%) and those abandoned

(60%). There were of course varieties listed that were not in Cepeda's inventory, which this community had not yet seen. Nor were all those who participated in my benchmark survey present for this exercise. Finally, this memory game was purposely kept short, meant to energize the group through an activity they might, indeed did, enjoy. To claim this method as verification of the survey information would be overdoing an interesting convergence. Of importance here, however, is the comparative consistency in the percentage of decline reported through both exercises, leading me nicely into a discussion of the PRA-*friendly* techniques used for this study.

PARTICIPANT OBSERVATION AND INFORMAL AND SEMI-STRUCTURED INTERVIEWS

Participant observation methodology has a long history of employment within anthropological scholarship for good reason. As Barrett suggests, the opportunity to wander around a village, talk to residents, spend time in their homes, and join in community work projects when appropriate, represents the field worker's most basic technique to generate both ethnographic data and the empathy needed to build trust that lies at the heart of solid research.[2] Observations are at times systematic, in my case, including such assessments as: the structure and style of the non-governmental organizations working within my primary research communities; the tasks and division of labour during the planting of potato tubers; or the rituals practiced during important spiritual festivals, like the Festival of Our Lady of Guadalupe and All Souls Eve. At others, interaction is more casual, including conversation around the hearth during a meal of potatoes and *yajwah* – a tasty salsa of ground chili peppers – or the discussion of national politics with an NGO colleague over a beer in one of the two Ravelo village *pensiones* or restaurants. Participant observation generated a tremendous amount of information, with one of my biggest challenges proving to be that of detailing my observations in my journal, particularly in my primary research communities when almost complete darkness fell at 6:00 pm and the subzero temperatures at 3,500 meters precluded comfortable reflection. My flashlight proved to be a poor substitute for a reading lamp and my sleeping bag a still poorer alternative to central heating.

Participant observation, on its own, has its limitations, of course. Outsiders, particularly those relying on translation, can easily misinterpret what they hear and see. Time constraints can limit the effectiveness of this tool as well. Conditions in one year or during one season can influence a misleading account of trends or patterns if previous or subsequent years and seasons are not witnessed or taken into account. Although I did not have the benefit of multi-year experience in these communities, I was able at least to witness community life during all four seasons. And thanks in no small measure to IPTK, I also had the good fortune to have been able to identify a solid group of regular informants with whom I was able to discuss my observations, including IPTK colleagues, particularly my IPTK research assistants Don Cornelio and Alberto, and several local key informants. In Chimpa Rodeo, eighteen-year-old Lucia, Spanish-speaking daughter of the *autoridad maximo*, Don Angel, Don Angel himself, whose family hosted my extended visits, Leandro, a young literacy promoter, Don Ciprian, and Don José, community leaders who always found time to answer my questions, and Doña Lucilla, a young widow with four children, were enormously helpful with my efforts to understand the fabric of residents' lives. In Mojón, these guides included the local schoolteacher, Doña Elvira, who let me stay in her home during my longer stays and assisted with translation, an IPTK community promoter, Don Justo, the late Don Euserbio, a promising community leader, and his mother Doña Donata, and Don Norberto and Doña Silvia, a middle-aged couple who always seemed to be home and willing to converse when I was in their community. In Ravelo, two municipal literacy coordinators, Prudencio and Manuel, two municipal extension workers, Justiniano and Irineo, a municipal councillor, Doña Cristina – the first female to win a seat – and a former employee with PROSEMPA, Don Elroy, helped to keep me on the right track. Having my "base-camp" within the field offices of IPTK in Ravelo also offered a welcome opportunity to learn both about IPTK's operations and about the development community in the area.

My close links with IPTK no doubt affected my reception within the municipality and communities and of course influenced my perception of events. Among some critics of IPTK, there was a clear hesitation and reserve in our interaction. Others appeared to accept me on my own terms. On balance, the support and interest of the majority in my research offset the clear reservations of a minority. And my insider's view of IPTK did not preclude a critique of what I perceived to be their shortcomings, a critique made easier by IPTK's repeated invitation to openly express my observations, positive or otherwise.

Informal and semi-structured interviews were also critical to the emergence of what I consider to be a credible and fair account of the character and experience of these communities and the region that housed them. A list of predetermined questions guided but did not limit interviews with informants ranging from a local shopkeeper in Ravelo to farmers preparing *chuño*. As a singular tool, interviews with a heterogeneous mix of people can create a confusing, possibly misleading picture for a newcomer. When coupled with other methods, however, they can contribute to a clearer picture. Semi-structured interviews with Chimpa Rodeo residents, for example, made me aware of some of the residents' continued use of the services of a traditional healer or *curandero*, a practice that did not come out in the survey, despite a question on treatment sought for medical ailments.

There is an additional point about semi-structured interviewing that I would like to stress here. Hoping to respect PRA principles, I approached the interview process with an intention to ignore positivistic textbook pronouncements about the need for detachment and "never providing the interviewee with any formal indication of … [one's] beliefs and values."[3] Although I attempted to avoid leading questions, Ann Oakley's advice about the benefits of a non-hierarchical approach and some investment of one's personal identity for a mutually informative, less extractive exchange seemed infinitely more sensible than a pretence at scientific distance. I consequently chose a conversational approach to my interviews, aware that the flow of the conversation would not always head in the direction I had planned. Participants were aware that I had a list of issues or questions that I wanted to cover, which I did review from time to time. But I allowed the interview to take unexpected turns. Oakley's comments on this matter synthesize my perspective rather well: "The mythology of 'hygienic' research with its accompanying mystification of the researcher and the researched as objective instruments of data production [should] be replaced by the recognition that personal involvement is more than dangerous bias – it is the condition under which people come to know each other and to admit others into their lives."[4]

There is always, of course, the danger of respondents telling the researcher what they think the researcher wants to hear. My informants did not strike me as particularly eager to provide the "correct" answers, but this hazard underscores the importance of methodological triangulation as well as the need for a sufficiently representative sampling of respondents. My extensive experience with semi-structured interviewing also helped me to assess the sincerity and reliability of the informant.

PARTICIPATORY RURAL APPRAISAL (PRA) WORKSHOPS

Within my research context, particularly my part-time and time-bound presence in each community, and given the limited time farmers could spare, I was able to implement only one intensive PRA workshop within each community. Participants' positive response to the workshop exceeded my expectations. Under more ideal circumstances, this workshop would have been the first of several. But then again, that would have demanded more time of participants with little extra to spare.

In Chimpa Rodeo, after a false start earlier in the month when the midwinter winds nearly blew the rock-secured tin roof off the community meeting place, the workshop lasted a full day and a long evening, the night-time session lit by the dim flame of a small propane lamp. In Mojón, residents were able to spare a full two days, and we were not obliged to work after sunset. My objectives for these workshops were four-fold. I wanted to understand the broader community dynamic better through exercises requiring collective process and decision-making that facilitated the participation of residents outside leadership circles. I hoped to demonstrate to residents and my IPTK assistants that it was possible to facilitate community assessment and planning work in ways that were inclusive and enjoyable for those unaccustomed to reading and writing. I also wanted to offer Indigenous participants an opportunity to reflect on their situation, conditions, and options in ways that were more evaluative than descriptive. Finally, I was hoping to get a better sense of participants' perception of their community's conditions before and after intervention by outsiders, particularly conditions related to the conservation of the genetic diversity of their most cherished crop, potatoes. The majority of exercises were adapted from an excellent PRA guide prepared by NGO workers in the extreme north of Potosí, Silvestre Ojeda and Iñigo Retolaza.[5] Brief explanations about my introduction to the workshop, the technical choices I made, the evaluation tool used, and the issue of consistent attendance are in order.

By way of introduction to my research and to explain the journey and preparations I made to arrive in their community, I used three visuals. First, I presented a roughly sketched map of Canada that identified my ancestors' migration from Europe to Canada and my own pattern of migration since I turned sixteen, including temporary residence in five Canadian provinces and three countries outside of Canada. While the distances I had covered were likely unfathomable, and my map of Canada about as familiar as a map of the moon, my story of migration and my decision to travel a long distance to get to know them better seems to have hit a responsive chord with people who also had a long history of migratory behavior, albeit within much smaller boundaries. I also distributed a small album with photographs taken over four seasons in each of the five provinces I had lived in, as well as pictures of my immediate family, then residing with me in Sucre. These photos were the source of much interest and it took some time before the album was returned.

Next, to explain my research in language that was accessible to people less comfortable or unfamiliar with Western development concepts, I drew an illustration of a tree with deep roots. These deep roots, I explained, represented their *saber Andina*, a knowledge base that had nurtured a diversity of crops including potato varieties we have all benefited from, including, I added, Canadian families. The clouds in the illustration represented training that could either help this diversity to grow or drown it. It was my hope, I explained, that my research and our workshop together would help to tell a story about how outsiders have helped or could help them to conserve the tree representing their *saber Andina*, more particularly the native potato varieties this knowledge conserved. I took the significant number of heads nodding during and once the translation was completed to mean that my explanation was essentially understood. Of course, they were also asked whether my explanation had been clear.

Finally, in an attempt to illustrate the flow of the research and my perception of our overlapping roles as well as the research's potential benefits to all concerned, I drew a Venn diagram with overlapping circles. There were fewer heads nodding at the end of this presentation, possibly because my diagram was less clear or because speculation about potential benefits was premature. A more interactive exercise designed to explore our respective interests and potential gains would, of course, have been much better. But this short-cut approach due to time considerations made clear, at least, my desire to respect the need for reciprocity in the relationship.

Reciprocity in a relationship can also be established through attention to process, not only to product. One of the strengths of PRA techniques, when properly applied, is that they facilitate exchange that is accessible, inclusive, and respectful of the local context, offering opportunities for participation for even the most reticent onlooker. The materials used can be very basic, indeed sought from within the community itself. Seeds, stones, and a flat piece of land, for example, make excellent alternatives to pen and paper for those unable to read and write. Climatic conditions, however, can and did throw a wrench in the works. When my communities were able to meet for a workshop with me, the winter winds were at their fiercest, defying my intent to use Mother Nature's implements. So, flip chart paper and markers had to serve as the next best thing.

Again inspired by Ojeda and Retolaza's excellent collection of PRA techniques (1999), the evaluation rating system used for most exercises in the workshop, as well as for the group's evaluation of the PRA exercises themselves, was built on participants' identification with potato farming. Scoring options ranged from one potato to indicate a poor value to five potatoes indicating a very good value. Participants in both Chimpa Rodeo and Mojón appeared to like this system, demonstrating considerable comfort with its use. Potatoes were also used to evaluate the workshop and each of its exercises. In Chimpa Rodeo, since we had worked well into the night, participants were too tired for a detailed evaluation session and opted instead to rate the entire workshop. Participants expressed disappointment with the fact that we were not able to complete all the exercises planned. They proceeded, nevertheless, to give the workshop four out of five potatoes. There was time and energy in Mojón for a more thorough evaluation. The "Before and After" workshop and the "Potato Varieties Game" were both evaluated at five potatoes while the "Crop Assessment Matrix" and "History of the Potato" were given four. Participants' overall rating of the workshop was five. Having had their workshop after the workshop in Chimpa Rodeo, residents no doubt benefited from the lessons we had learned there.

A final word on attendance seems wise. The number and identity of participants in each session did not remain constant, a fairly commonplace pattern that I later observed in the municipal planning sessions and local meetings I attended. Thankfully, there was a solid core of regular participants, albeit largely men. But a break for food or to stretch usually meant the loss of one or two participants for a short time and the arrival of others. Departing participants often returned from the activity that called them away, but not always during the same exercise. The consistent participation of women was particularly problematic, with their attendance fluctuating tremendously. The family and farm animals simply had to be attended to. These comings and goings clearly offered implementation challenges. But one soon learns to relax and go with the flow. I was somewhat comforted by the fact that the more transient participants appeared quite comfortable with the notion that others might speak on their behalf, not surprising given the strong communal sense of rotating leadership responsibility I was to discover.[6]

Interculturalism

The acculturation-prevention work among the Arhuaco of the Rio Negro of Venezuela, led by linguistic anthropologists Mosonyi and González, is credited as having launched the concept of interculturalism in Latin America in the early 1970s.[1] It was further developed alongside the participatory approaches of activists like Freire, and first took root in the education sector. The increasing demands and active participation of Indigenous leaders, some of them former bilingual education students, and a growing interest in cultural pluralism theory and practice pushed its adoption forward.[2] By the mid-1990s, interculturalism had a rights' orientation. Indigenous languages and cultures were no longer considered inferior but rather valuable resources.[3]

A subset of interculturalism is intercultural education, often referred to as IBE – Intercultural Bilingual Education.[4] IBE insists that learning be rooted in one's own culture, language, values, world view, and system of knowledge. At the same time, the learner should be open to and appreciative of other knowledge, values, cultures, and languages since the ultimate aim of intercultural education is learning to live together. Diverse systems of knowledge, lifestyle patterns, cultures, and languages are viewed as complementary rather than segregating or oppositional. During my research year in Bolivia, IBE and interculturalism had emerged as a cross-cutting component in the research and development programming of a growing number of NGOs, government ministries, and multilateral institutions within the country.

Of particular relevance to the themes in this book is the fact that interculturalism values two kinds of knowledge: the intimate insider knowledge of community process and the knowledge of the outside opportunity structure.[5] It goes a step further than mainstream participatory process-es that, in their application at least, are too often unidirectional. In the lat-ter, the outsider uses participatory tools to understand the insider but the reverse is rarely the case. The insider is rarely afforded a close look at the operations and ways of being of the outsiders' world. Interculturalism, in contrast, looks at both realities. It also moves beyond a simple review of the power relationship between distinct cultures to look at the diverse subcultures within more homogenous groups, such as the youth and adult subcultures of an otherwise ethnically homogeneous cultural group.[6] The following passage by Peruvian socio-linguist and educator, Luis Enrique López, captures the broader Latin American interest in an inter-culturalism framework especially well:

> We need this concept to analyze and design action to promote
> dialogue, dynamic interaction and relationships between societies
> that, however socially, culturally and ethnically distinct, need to share
> space and practical, everyday living in an atmosphere of mutual
> understanding and respect ... That is why this concept is seen to be
> critical to the construction of a new democratic project in Latin
> America, based on the principle of inclusion of indigenous societies
> that until recently were excluded from the national agenda.[7]

Interculturalism is thus fundamentally a political concept that not only considers cultural and ethnic diversity but also the structure of social rela-tions and the distribution of wealth and power.[8] There is also a very prag-matic argument for interculturalism. Interaction between the outsider and insider is built on a negotiated agenda and process that will help both the outsider and insider to avoid conflict or a stalemate. Every attempt is made to appreciate competing interests, distinct perspectives and experi-ences, and the long-term benefits of designing a path forward that is acceptable and just for all concerned. Power imbalances and competing interests are thus acknowledged from the start. Through dialogue and interaction that is structured to be accessible, efforts are made to mitigate imbalances and redistribute power. The interaction is by definition anchored in a spirit of cooperation. Interculturalism essentially grafts cooperative conflict resolution methods onto its conceptual framework.[9] Successful interculturalism practitioners, like successful mediators, appre-ciate the importance of listening carefully to the other's perspective when navigating through very tricky cross-cultural waters.

At the time of my research and arguably since, the application of *inter-culturalidad*, like much popular development theory, has not measured up to its promise. Adoption has too often been hesitant, ambivalent, or devoid of a wholehearted understanding of its meaning and value. Even those singing the praises of interculturalism face challenges practising what they preach. Opposing priorities, funding constraints, donor-driven timelines, inadequate resources for teacher education, and difficulties in reconciling alternative world views, values, and educational approaches present very real challenges for the effective integration of the concept into development programming. And try as they might, many of the Westerners involved also fail to drop the paternalistic thinking of Western advantage. They continue to speak an incomprehensible language to those inexperienced in their ways of understanding and behaving. There are, of course, also those agencies and individuals that intentionally use the progressive language of interculturalism to implement programming that is essentially assimilationist in nature.[10]

One of the more fundamental problems with the application of interculturalism has been the tendency to confuse it with biculturalism, a focus on the notion of two distinct cultures rather than on the interrelationship between them.[11] When interculturalism becomes biculturalism dressed in more inclusive language, one culture usually ends up overpowering the other. Intercultural research and planning methods have likewise tended to ignore the reciprocal learning needed for sustainable and just change. In practice, as suggested, local issues have been emphasized in a one-sided investigation of Indigenous ways of knowing. Few and far between are programs that assist Indigenous communities to understand the broader social, economic, and political forces that they are up against so they can make informed decisions about their alternatives and negotiate on more solid footing.

Another clear sign of the continuing gap between intercultural theory and practice that I observed in Bolivia was the absence of Indigenous leadership on the decision-making bodies that governed intercultural programs. For example, the Bolivian staff with the United Nations Fund for Population Activities (UNFPA) that I interviewed for my study, while presenting a very eloquent and sincere defence of their agency's integration of intercultural principles and education into their field programs, could not come up with the name of a single Indigenous leader on the program's governance board.[12] Frolian Condori, president of an Indigenous organization promoting the Quechua peoples' rights – el Consejo Educativo de la Nacion Quechua (CENAQ) – had this complaint when I met with him: "Donor organizations," he said, "consider round table consultation meetings sufficient.[13] The Quechua people, on the other hand, want to have an equal voice within the key decision-making bodies."[14]

Many of the Bolivian and Latin American round tables and networks that I have encountered have boasted a participatory, intercultural framework for community or regional planning. But they rarely began at the scale required to build the trust needed for trust to blossom. Even when the legitimate representatives of those on the margins sit at the table (not always the case), the much higher representation of participants from the dominant society or organization is enough to overwhelm. They do not feel connected and thus are unable to participate in meaningful ways. Being offered the opportunity to speak up is simply not the same as having the informed confidence to speak out. Unless existing power structures based on hierarchical relations are addressed head on, the interaction will continue to favour the dominant society.[15]

The literature on interculturalism that I reviewed for my book generally did not address the issues of program scale, scope and timing, all of which are critical to the building of cultural understanding and trust. Attention to the scale and breadth of a desired interaction, as resilience studies demonstrate time and again can make or break its success. Small tangible victories create an opening for the resolution of more difficult challenges. An effective intercultural process will build understanding and trust piece on manageable piece under terms that consider the number of actors suitable for such negotiation and the possible gap in understanding at the start.

Finally, although not directly commented on in the mainstream development literature I reviewed, interculturalism also corresponds with Indigenous beliefs about the connection and interdependence of all living and non-living matter on earth. There is a co-management, co-responsibility, principle at its centre that distinguishes it from a strict focus on the rights and demands of the marginalized. About Indigenous views of *interculturalidad*, Grimaldo Rengifo of one of Peru's leading NGO authorities on Indigenous knowledge systems, PRATEC, wrote, "We bring interculturalism into the conversation by balancing the diverse modalities of relationships between humans and nature."[16]

I propose the following guidelines for an approach to insider-outsider interaction that I have called Intercultural Reciprocity. If it is welcomed and taken seriously, a respectful partnership may be possible.

- Strategic interaction focusing on long-term rather than short-term gains.
- Analysis of power imbalances and commitment to power sharing.
- Programming that is at a manageable scale to initiate the relationship.
- Openness to change and compromise.
- Valuing diverse knowledge systems and the use of accessible and interactive research and planning tools
- Two-way education that seeks to understand the insider knowledge of community process and the knowledge of the outside opportunity structure
- Intra-cultural education and dialogue to ensure the less powerful are informed and thus have greater leverage; that the more powerful understand the benefits of cooperation.
- Consensus decision-making, shared governance, and shared accountability
- Cooperation on a strategic vision of mutual benefit
- Establishing strategic alliances with broader social movements.

Chimpa Rodeo and Mojón Demographic Data

Chimpa Rodeo, Bolivia, Demographic Data (14 of 33 families or 42%), July 2000

Families	Adults		Children		Language spoken		Valley migration		Permanent relocation to city (no. persons)	Wife's village/municipality
	M	F	M	F	Quechua	Spanish	Temporary (avg no. of mos.)	Full-time (no. persons)		
Family 1	2	2	2	4	9	2	3	2	0	Sauce Mayu/Ravelo
Family 2	1	1	2	2	5	1	6	0	0	Lequecha/Ravelo
Family 3		2	1	4	7	4	2	0	0	Chimpa Rodeo/Ravelo
Family 4	2	2	4	1	9	5	1	1	0	Ura Rodeo/Ravelo
Family 5	1	5	1	1	7	2	0	0	2	No response
Family 6	1	1	2		4	3	0	0	0	Valley/Chuquisaca
Family 7	3	1	2	2	8	5	2	0	1	Lequecha/Ravelo
Family 8	1	2	1	2	6	2	2	0	0	Pajly/Ravelo
Family 9	1	2	4	1	8	6	0	0	2	Ravelo/Ravelo
Family 10	2	2			4	1	1	0	0	Valley/Chuquisaca
Family 11		1	2		3	2	0	0	0	Ura Rodeo/Ravelo
Family 12	2	2	6		9	2	2	0	0	Chimpa Rodeo/Ravelo
Family 13	3	2	2	1	8	5	4	1	2	Chimpa Rodeo/Ravelo
Family 14	1	3	6	2	12	3	1	0	2	Chimpa Rodeo/Ravelo
Total	20	28	35	20	99	43	24(2.1)	4	18	

Mojón, Bolivia, Demographic Data (11 of 46 families or 24%), August 2000

Families	Adults		Children		Language spoken		Valley migration		Permanent relocation to city (no. persons)	Wife's village/municipality
	M	F	M	F	Quechua	Spanish	Temporary (avg no. of mos.)	Full-time (no. persons)		
Family 1	1	2		1	4		5	0	0	Mojón, Ravelo
Family 2	1	2	4	1	8	3	5	0	0	Moroto, Ravelo
Family 3	3	2	1	3	9	2	5	2	0	Pichacani, Ravelo
Family 4	1	3	3	1	8	2	5		3	Mojón, Ravelo
Family 5	4	1	1	3	9		5		1	Tana Pacaje (valley)
Family 6	1	1	5	2	9	2	10	9	0	Mojón, Ravelo
Family 7	3	2	1	1	7	1	5	0	0	Chokochuro (valley)
Family 8	4	3	2	2	9	4	5	2	0	Kisca Cancha, Ocuri
Family 9	2	3	1	1	7	3	4	0	0	Mojón, Ravelo
Family 10	1	1		2	4	1	5	0	0	Quellu Casa, Ravelo
Family 11	1	1	2	1	5	1	3	0		Antora, Ravelo
Total	22	21	20	19	71	19	57 (5.2)	13	4	

Chimpa Rodeo and Mojón Infrastructure and Animals

Chimpa Rodeo, Bolivia, Infrastructure and Animals, (14 of 33 families or 42%) July 2000

Families	Household amenities			Thatch roof	Tile roof	Animals						
	Latrine	Tap/sink	Greenhouse			Cattle	Sheep	Goats	Pigs	Chickens	Horses	Mules
Family 1		X	X	X		4	30	9	2	7		
Family 2	X	X			X	4	15	3	7	7	1	2
Family 3	X	X	X	X		8	26	10	5	7		
Family 4	X	X		X		8	37		3	4		4
Family 5		X		X			20			3		1
Family 6	X	X			X	5	25	10	4	6		
Family 7		X			X	7	30	7	5	2		1
Family 8	X	X			X	8	30		6		1	
Family 9		X		X		4	20		10			
Family 10	X	X	X	X		6	25	5	1	5		
Family 11	X	X		X			25		2			1
Family 12	X	X		X		10	30		5	5	2	
Family 13		X		X		2	10		1			
Family 14		X		X		2	30					2
Totals	8	14	3	10	4	68	353	44	51	46	4	11

Mojón, Bolivia, Infrastructure and Animals, (11 of 46 families or 24%) August 2000

| Families | Household amenities | | | | | Animals | | | | | | |
	Latrine	Tap/sink	Greenhouse	Thatch roof	Tile roof	Cattle	Sheep	Goats	Pigs	Chickens	Horses	Mules
Family 1	X	X		X		3	20	10	2	2		3
Family 2	X	X		X		3	20	10	3	3		2
Family 3	X	X		X			15		4	4		1
Family 4	X	X		X		2	30		2	4		2
Family 5	X	X		X			6		3	3		
Family 6	X	X		X				6	1	4		1
Family 7	X	X		X		4	8	8	3	1		2
Family 8	X	X		X		1	10	10	2			2
Family 9	X	X		X		5	30	10	1	1		1
Family 10	X	X		X		1	10			2		
Family 11	X	X		X								
Totals	11	11		11		19	149	54	21	24		14

Chimpa Rodeo and Mojón
Field Crops Produced

Chimpa Rodeo, Bolivia, Field Crops Produced (14 of 33 families or 42%), July 2000

F	P	W	O	B	T	C	Ok	I	FB	PL	Q	PE	VF	CH	R	F
1	X		X		X	X	X	X		X	X			X	4	1
2	X	X	X	X	X	X	X		X	X	X	X	X	X	3	3
3	X	X	X		X	X	X				X		X	X	4	3
4	X	X	X	X	X		X		X	X		X		X	4	2
5	X	X	X		X		X		X		X			X	3	2
6	X	X	X	X	X		X			X				X	3	2
7	X	X	X	X	X	X	X		X	X	X			X	3	2
8	X	X	X	X	X		X							X	4	0
9	X	X	X		X		X		X					X	5	0
10	X	X	X	X	X		X			X				X	5	1
11	X		X		X		X		X					X	3	1
12	X	X	X	X	X		X	X	X	X	X			X	3	3
13	X	X	X	X	X		X		X					X	3	1
14	X	X	X	X	X		X				X			X	4	2
	14	12	14	8	14	4	14	2	8	7	7	2	2	14		

P: potato; W: wheat; O: oat; B: barley; T: tarwi; C: corn; Ok: oka; I: Izaño; FB: fava bean; PL: papa lisa; Q: quinoa; PE: peas; VF: valley fruit; Ch: chuno; R: rotation cycle (# of crops before return to original); F: years of fallow.

Mojón, Bolivia, Field Crops Produced (11 of 46 families or 24%), August 2000

F	P	W	O	B	T	C	Ok	I	FB	PL	Q	PE	VF	CH	R	F
1	X	X		X	X	X	X		X	X		X		X	5	5
2	X	X	X			X	X			X				X	3	5
3	X	X	X	X	X	X	X		X	X		X		X	2	1
4	X	X	X	X	X	X	X		X	X				X	2	5
5	X	X	X		X	X			X			X		X	2	1
6	X	X	X			X									2	1
7	X	X	X	X	X	X	X		X	X		X		X	3	5
8	X	X	X			X	X		X	X	X	X		X	4	6
9	X	X	X	X	X	X	X		X	X				X	5	1
10	X		X		X	X								X	2	1
11	X	X	X	X	X	X	X		X	X		X		X	3	3
	11	10	10	6	8	11	8	0	8	8	1	6	0	10		

P: potato; W: wheat; O: oat; B: barley; T: tarwi; C: corn; Ok: oka; I: Izaño; FB: fava bean; PL: papa lisa; Q: quinoa; PE: peas; VF: valley fruit; Ch: chuno; R: rotation cycle (# of crops before return to original); F: years of fallow.

Notes

PROLOGUE

1 Freire 1997, Foreword.
2 Goodale 2009.
3 This person, I was later told by his colleague, was eventually fired from his job.
4 Two and a half years later, out of the blue, I received a call from a London School of Economics doctoral student who had dug up my report. She told me that the funder had eventually launched the project. "You would be pleased to hear," she said, "that this time they proceeded along lines you had recommended in your report."
5 Servicios Multiples de Tecnologias Apropiadas (SEMTA), an organization that worked at an altitude of over 4,000 meters. I learned a lot about facilitating community leadership from SEMTA over my ten years of interaction with them (see: http://www.blogger.com/profile/09954954109376728477).
6 I think of George Bernard Shaw's words about this matter and hope that I have not become quite so skeptical: "Hegel was right when he said that we learn from history that man can never learn from history."
7 Silvia Rivera Cusicanqui's 1990 critique of NGOs in Northern Potosí is particularly harsh. I should also note that, during her professional career, she has sometimes used only the first of her last names (Rivera) as well as both.
8 *Coyllas* and *cambas* are slang terms used to refer to: highland migrants who move to the Amazon basin; and the original lowlanders, respectively.

CHAPTER ONE

1 In Healey 2001, 65.
2 Puente Rodriguez 2010, 125.

3 See Powers 2006; Zimmerer 1996; Programa de Autodesarrollo Campesino 1996,11; FAO 1995, 4.

4 Cepeda (1995) conducted genetic testing of the tubers to determine their distinctiveness. As I learned from my conversation with Miguel Holle of the International Potato Centre (CIP), morphological differences usually contribute to reports of diversity that are inflated by up 50%. The importance of morphologically different varieties should not be underestimated however. A genetically identical plant might in one location express an insect resistance and in another location not. The key factor is the plasticity of the variety or its ability to grow well over changing environments (Dr Melaku Worede, personal communication March 2007).

5 See Nicole Bezençon 1994,1.

6 See Nash 1979; Frank 1966; Wallerstein 1974; Watkins 1977.

7 Tristan Platt 1982, 28.

8 See Powers 2006, 260.

9 In conversation with IPTK staff 15 March 2000; see also Platt 1982, 14; Bezençon 1994.

10 Permanent migration to urban slums or rainforest settlements was also on the rise, with the population growth at negative 1.25 % (Municipal Development Plan, Ravelo 1997, 19).

11 See Goudsmit 2008; NOVIB 1998, 16; Cusicanqui-Rivera 1992, 153; Platt 1982, 18–21; Uriost 1981, 167.

12 Among the most convincing are Escobar 1997, 1995, 1991; Fergusson 1994; and Sachs 1992.

13 For a thoughtful definition of agency, and more particularly as it relates to the Andes, see Stillar 2009.

CHAPTER TWO

1 In Chambers 1992, 14.

2 See Nash 1975; 1974; Asad 1973; Hymes 1969; Berreman 1969; 1966; Nader 1969; Gough 1968; Marquet 1964; Tax 1953.

3 Joan Vincent (1990) contends that there were a number of late nineteenth-century anthropologists who offered incisive critiques of European domination. But, as Gledhill (1994, 3) points out, referencing Vincent, these "strands of an anthropological approach to politics were not those that became hegemonic in the discipline after 1940."

4 See Kathleen Gough 1968; Kulchynski 1993; Malinkowski 1930.

5 See Purcell 1998.

6 The various methodologies that have been developed to undertake this more participatory approach are generally grouped under the category of Participatory Action Research (PAR). See Fals Borda 1991a, 4. This dialogical research process was conceived precisely to assist individuals and groups without the power to control the research process. PAR researchers are openly ideological and passionate in their ambition to promote more inclusive and democratic knowledge production.

7 In a publication, subtitled *The Making and Unmaking of the Third World*, Arturo Escobar (1995,15) admonishes development anthropologists for having "overlooked the ways in which development operates as an arena of cultural contestation and identity construction." The development discourse they have helped to establish, he insists, "has created an extremely efficient apparatus for producing knowledge about, and the existence of power over, the Third World" (7). Quoting Asad (1973), he asks, "does not development today, as colonialism did in a former epoch, make possible 'the kind of human intimacy on which anthropological fieldwork is based, but ensure that intimacy should be one-sided and provisional' even if the contemporary subjects move and talk back?" (14). Not surprisingly, Escobar (1997) questions the development anthropologist's right to practice his or her trade within Indigenous communities, at least under the current terms of reference, i.e., funded by mainstream institutions intent on normalizing a deficit model of development in an effort to maintain Western dominance in the world order. Escobar and others theorizing on deficit development approaches have influenced my thinking on this subject. His ironic tendency to homogenize anthropologists, however, has made me wonder whether he has himself essentialized extremely complex relationships. Also see Shepherd 2010.

8 See Goodale 2009, 4.

9 See Chambers 1994; Hall 1992; Fals Borda 1991; Ryan and Robinson 1990.

10 Sometimes also called participatory learning and appraisal (PLA). See Chambers 1995.

11 Barrett 1996, 111.

12 See Choque 1999.

13 Interestingly, when my IPTK colleague and I visited with this young farmer, a leader who had participated in some of IPTK's training programs, there was a friend present from Sucre who discouraged participation. He suggested that the work of outside researchers generally was of little direct benefit to the researched, a point not easily refuted. This farmer eventually demonstrated considerable interest in the research, as evidenced by his participation in the

PRA session, his willingness to allow me to interview his father, one of the most senior residents of the hamlet, and his request that I photograph his wedding. On this last matter, my services as a photographer proved especially popular throughout the year. On each return to the village, I brought copies of my latest photos. There was always a scramble to see them. There were no mirrors in these villages.

14 Lather 1986, 67.

15 Ibid.

16 Miriam (1998) in Ellerby 2000, 27 has identified a helpful list of characteristics for qualitative research that capture the possibilities and parameters of the process I followed. These include: an overall interest in understanding the meaning people have constructed; taking the inductive – from the particular to the general – approach to knowledge generation; focusing on gaining the emic, or insider's perspective; the acknowledgement of the researcher's own perception in the identification of meaning; and the centrality of the researcher as a primary instrument for data collection and analysis. These last two points are especially relevant to the connectionist perspective on knowledge generation and transmission that I hold, to be discussed in chapter 5.

17 See Lusted 1986 in Giroux 1987, 18.

18 Goodale 2009, 13/19.

CHAPTER THREE

1 San Martin 1997, 90.

2 Chimpa Rodeo, together with a neighbouring hamlet, Ura Rodeo, formed a larger community – Rodeo Huayllas – with both sharing a common chapel and one union local, whose elected official or *dirigente* generally alternates between each hamlet. Their geographical separation from each other, however, influenced a somewhat distinct identity. Historically, in fact, under the Indigenous *ayllu* system of social organization to be described later in this chapter, the residential settlements were generally in small hamlets. Hamlets were in turn linked together in a larger, minimal *ayllu* called *cabildo* (Platt 1982, 44). During my 2011 return to Chimpa Rodeo, I discovered that the two hamlets had indeed separated, each now having their own governance structures and *dirigentes*. Mojón also consists of two hamlets, Mojón *Baja* and Mojón *Alta* (lower and upper Mojón); but the geographical spread is negligible and the residents function as one tightly knit unit.

3 Before the Agrarian Reform of 1953, hacendados controlled 90% of arable land and exploited 50% of the population in serf-like conditions. Healey 2001, 17.

4 Tarwi not only fixes nitrogen, but grows well in marginal soils. It also has a greater nutritional value than either soyabeans or peanuts. Healey 2001, 103.

5 One farmer I met in a neighbouring community had sufficient land to fallow some of his fields for as long as ten years, the ideal he suggested for a full restoration of the land's fertility and productivity. Don Irineo, personal communication, August 2000.

6 Platt 1982, 14.

7 UNICEF's construction of household latrines, launched and completed within six months after my departure, resulted in a small extension of the road but no significant improvement.

8 Mamani 1999.

9 Thorwaite cited in Mamani 1999, 32.

10 Mamani 1999, 32.

11 Bolivia is in fact a country that contains every world climate and terrain. See Powers 2006, 29.

12 Collins 1988, 116 describes this Andean-wide system especially well. In an earlier article (1986, 652–3) she also rightly takes issue with Andeanists who described the Andean household through Western constructs, imposing a Eurocentric grid on the Andean reality. There is a tendency, she further argues, to neglect or ignore productive relationships that can divide, rather than unify, family members. Or to miss extrahousehold relationships that can be more central to social and biological reproduction than those within the household. The families within my more limited study, however, did not prove to be exceptions to the dominant highland pattern of a multi-generational household living within a cluster of small buildings on their homestead.

13 My journal entry in chapter 7 offers a description of my participation in a wedding ceremony. Also see ASUR 2002 for a good description of Jalq'a marriage traditions.

14 For an excellent description of the rules at hand in neighbouring Macha, see Platt 1982,42.

15 See Webster in Collins 1988,11.

16 See Femenias 2005; Collins1988; Harris 1985; and Lambert 1977.

17 Carter's (1977) original research on this issue is very instructive.

18 "Llamero" is the name given to the Jalq'a's Indigenous neighbours in the

remaining municipalities of Chayanta. Because many live above 3,600 metres where llamas thrive and are shepherded, the identity, Llamero, seems to have stuck. See Platt's (1976) excellent ethnography.

19 On the Llamero marriages see Platt 1976, 26.

20 Cereceda 1998, 19.

21 See Cereceda et al. 1998, 30–1 and Healey 2001, 267 and 1992, 32.

22 For a fascinating account on women's clothing and embroidery as an asser-tion of power and a "politics of belonging" see Femininas 2005. See also Ras-nake 1988 on art forms as an example of cultural resistance.

23 Cereceda et al. 1998, 17.

24 In 2000, extension workers estimated that there were still at least 25% in tra-ditional dress within Mojón. It has not been possible to confirm this esti-mate, since a good number of families were away in the valley.

25 A for-profit second-hand clothing retail store that collects used clothing through local charities.

26 A decade later, this clothing has not changed.

27 See Femenias 2005, 28–9.

28 *Oca* is a small tuber, shaped a little like a carrot that tastes a little like squash, only sweeter. It is highly nutritious, not unlike many of the Andes' unique crops.

29 My husband and I were invited to try the procedure in Ravelo on a bright June day. I took off my shoes, rolled up my pant legs and stepped onto the pile of slightly frozen potatoes. Much like skating the first time, within min-utes, I was splayed on the ground, the object of a good laugh. With my pride a little bruised but not much else, I picked myself up with a sheepish grin. Hav-ing observed his wife's foolhardy confidence, Pat was considerably more care-ful when he stepped on the pile. He managed to stay on his feet. My story travelled far and wide. Having at least attempted the task, I won another pinch of respect from my new friends, or at least that is what I would like to think.

30 I received a copy of this legend from an IPTK colleague shortly before my departure from the field. He had clipped it from an agricultural magazine published in Sucre but had not noted publication information, only the name of the person who recounted it in the magazine: R.L. Salazar. I was thus unable to confirm the extent to which the people of Chimpa Rodeo and Mojón knew of this legend. I include it here because my IPTK informant was convinced of its authenticity as a highlander legend and because its story fits well with the creationist mythology of the people of this region. The translation is mine.

31 Bolivians are not alone, however, in the increased levels of assault as a result of binge drinking. There is evidence of tremendous spikes in wife assault after drinking binges during public celebrations in my own home country, Canada. This is apparently the case with one of Canada's largest agricultural fairs and festivals, the Calgary Stampede. My stepdaughter, Sarah Mooney, employed in the childcare field in Calgary, recounted this disturbing fact after her discussion with a lawyer working within Calgary social services system.

32 See Diaz-Olavarrieta et al. 2007, S46.

33 See Burman 2011 and Van Vleet 2008 for detailed and thoughtful insights into the complex question of gender relations in the Andes.

34 Pape (2008) offers a very convincing rebuttal to the notion of a welcomed gender complementarity and stresses that women surveyed do not see their exclusionary practices as at all acceptable.

35 See Wiest 1998 on this phenomenon in Mexico.

36 These are reported figures, not verified through applied testing. They do correspond fairly well, nevertheless, to the area's census data cited in various local reports. See IPTK 2000; 1999a; 1997; NOVIB 1999; PAC1996.

CHAPTER FOUR

1 See Juan San Martin 1997, 90.

2 Unpublished transcription of a story recounted by 75-year-old Don Vincente of Chimpa Rodeo on 1 August 1998. This translation from Spanish into English is mine.

3 See Nash 1977, 136. Also see Varese 1996, 124 and Scott 1990. Scott argues that people who are deprived in society often resist the oppression through the construction of their own "hidden transcripts."

4 For further information on *El Tio*, see Jaurez 2000; Godoy 1985; and Nash 1977.

5 See Harris 1982 in Rasnake 1988, 178.

6 See Escobar 1995.

7 The practical agency of the Jalq'a farmer calls to mind practice theory. Influenced by the scholarship of Pierre Bourdieu (1972), this theory seeks to explain the dialectic between human activity and the systems humans operate within (Ortner 1984, 148; also see Rahman 1999 and Gledhill 1993). See also van der Ploeg's (1993) critique of Bourdieu's view of Indigenous knowledge as practice that is devoid of theory.

CHAPTER FIVE

1 Merchant 1990, 677.

2 Naydler 1996, 3.

3 Berkes 2008 in Pretty 2010, 3 asks us to consider that the division commonly
   made between nature and culture is hardly universal, but rather reflects
   industrialized thought that seeks to control and manage nature. See also
   Berkes, Folke, and Colding 2003, 5.

4 Frederich Engels is an unexpected surprise among them.

5 See Naydler 1996, 93. Also see von Bertalanffy 1968 in Berkes et al. 2003.

6 Berkes et al. 2003, 5.

7 Ibid.

8 Holling 1996, 33; Pimm 1984, 325.

9 Berkes and Ross 2012, 2; Gunderson et al. 2010; Gunderson 2000, 425;
   Holling 1996, 31–3; and Pimm 1984.

10 Berkes and Ross 2012, 2.

11 Swedish Ministry of the Environment 2002, 146.

12 Ibid. A note of caution is warranted for those wanting simply to superim-
   pose ecological resilience on social resilience. If we are to avoid the biological determinism and reductionist thinking this concept attempts to bury, it
   makes more sense to consider social resilience as having borrowed concepts
   from ecological resilience to help us to understand the human dimension.
   See Adger 2000, 351.

13 Berkes et al. 2003, 14.

14 Swedish Ministry of the Environment 2002, 147.

15 Human-induced climate change and climate extremes also influence forest
   fires or insect outbreaks, of course.

16 Berkes et al. 2003, 14; Gunderson 1995.

17 Berkes 2007, 284.

18 Gunderson et al. 2010, xx.

19 Berkes et al. 2003, 15.

20 MacKenzie 2009.

21 See Adger 2000, 351.

22 Levin 1999, 198–206.

23 See Wilbanks and Kates 1999.

24 In the year 2000, and arguably still today, in Bolivia or, for that matter more
   broadly within the Andes, the term resilience was not a significant part of
   the development discourse I encountered. Resilience does not even translate
   well into Spanish. When I used it with many of my Latin American col-

leagues, they first interpreted the word as resistance, which is, of course, a kindred word. The concept that was deeply in vogue in 2000 within Latin America was interculturalism. Interculturalism represents an approach to interaction between and within cultures that does, however, share some characteristics with resilient principles. Its proponents stress the importance of our inter-relationships and mutual learning. They also insist on the power sharing needed for more equitable engagement and development. A critical review of its basic tenets is given in Appendix 3.

CHAPTER SIX

1 See Burchard 1976, 411; Martinez 1994b, 21.

2 Martinez 1994b, 23.

3 Pacheco 1994; 1996; Barragán 1994.

4 See Rasnake 1988. His manuscript on the subject of Andean resistance to cultural domination, and more particularly on their maintenance of symbolic configurations and complex modes of organization among select ethnic groups is a must read. The paradox, Rasnake argues, is that while Andean peoples did not accept the "symbolic universe" of their "conquerors," they did accept the burden of the state.

5 *Ayllus* were initially very useful to state authorities anxious to collect tributes from their Indigenous inhabitants. Between 1831 and 1847, for example, the Bolivian State earned 37.5 % of its income from these "tributes" or head taxes. Sanchez-Albornoz 1978, 98 in Rasnake 1988, 61. Beginning in the eighteenth and accelerating in the nineteenth century, *ayllus* were increasingly denied political or economic authority, ensuring therefore "the dominion of the hacendados or large landowners and as managers of state apparatus, the nation state." The most comprehensive and clear explanations that I discovered about the *ayllu* system were in Platt 1976; Rasnake 1988; Cusicanqui-Rivera 1990, and Goodale 2009.

6 See also Choque and Mamani 2001; Cereceda 1998, 7–8; Martinez 1994b, 18; Harris 1985; Godoy 1986, 723; Platt 1982 and 1976.

7 The atlas was commissioned by the now defunct Farmer Self-Development Program in Potosí (PAC), supported by European Union funding. Informally, PAC officials reported that the program was discontinued in 1999 because the Bolivian government was not contributing the counterpart funding needed to access these European funds.

8 Pachero 1996, 227 referencing Platt 1987 and Saignes' 1986.

9 See Pacheo 1994, 46–9.

10 Martinez 1994b, 2/18; see also Cereceda 1998, 7–8.

11 Martinez 1994, 7.

12 Cereceda 1987 in Pacheo 1998, 45.

13 Cereceda 1998, 9.

14 See Harris's work on the Laymi (1985, 327); Cusicanqui-Rivera 1990 and 1992; Goodale 2002 and 2009. Cusicanqui-Rivera 1990 offers a stinging critique both of the union movement and NGO role in undermining the ayllu and traditional Indigenous governance systems for modernization of limited benefit. I will take this issue up in a subsequent chapter.

15 I was first introduced to this idea in June Nash's (1979,122) compelling masterpiece on Bolivian miners, *We Eat the Mines and the Mines Eat Us.*

16 Recent works about identity within the new post-MAS Bolivia have been especially insightful. See, e.g., Mark Goodale 2009.

17 See Isbell 1978, 81. According to Tristan Platt (1992, 135), what matters in the anthropological quest to pinpoint genealogy and identity is not simply the genealogical origin of cultural elements but also the changing fields of social meaning in which they are embedded.

18 See Rasnake 1988, 3.

19 Murra 1972. See also Platt 1976; Harris 1985.

20 Murra 1984.

21 Weather in the Andes can change in hours and even in minutes; it is not the average that is measured but rather the extreme. See Rengifo Vasquez 2011.

22 See Netting 1971, 11 in Burchard 1976, 403.

23 See Puente Rodriguez 2010, 126; Dandler and Sage 1985, 128. See also Brush et al. 1980.

24 Traditionally, the leader of each minimal *ayllu* distributed the *mantas* among the households of a hamlet. In some instances, the same fields have remained in the system over generations. In other cases, decision-making about the particular fields under the manta system involved consensus-based community meetings to identify the manta fields. This was the case in Mojón. See Platt 1982, 45; Cusicanqui-Rivera 1992.

25 See Cusicanqui-Rivera 1992, 92. The concept of the community justice ethic among subsistence peasant farmers is treated thoughtfully in James Scott's (1977) book about the moral economy of peasant societies. Where Scott sees risk aversion among subsistence peasants, however, I see risk management. Scott also links risk aversion to a lack of innovation suggesting that subsistence survival – relentless and unforgiving – creates a fear of innovation. I would differ on this matter. The ability to innovate and take measured risks is

critical to survival on always demanding and ever-changing landscapes. As this chapter argues, the ecological complementarity practices of Andean peoples were highly innovative in a context of significant ecological complexity. To resist the offerings of modernity that are not suited to your livelihood is not resisting change in itself, as seems to be suggested in Scott's analysis.

26 Murra 1967b, 343 in Burchard 1976, 428–9.

27 Cusicanqui-Rivera 1992; Platt 1982, 45.

28 See Sanchez 1982, 158.

29 Platt (1982, 78) claims that the respective regimes were repeatedly foiled in their efforts to recruit a permanent labour pool.

30 See Sanchez 2002 for an insightful review of this experience.

31 See Choque 1999.

32 See Rengifo 2000; AGRUCO 1998; San Martin 1997.

33 See Urioste 1988,167. This legislation allowed for the territorial claims of Indigenous peoples. It was nevertheless painfully slow in its implementation, inspiring a new breed of mestizo "cowboy" squatter eager to slice off a handsome share of the pie.

34 As Murra (1984,119) observed, "It is remarkable that, in spite of the pressure exercised against everything Andean and those who created them during the 450 years of colonial and republican regimes, we still encounter among highland peasants a preference for locating their fields in complementary fashion, on several different ecological tiers, sometimes located several days' walk from the centre of population. There is well-documented, contemporary evidence of sizeable groups who have managed to maintain their ethnic self-awareness, along with access to their outliers in the lowlands."

35 Also see Murra 1985b.

36 See Platt 1982

37 On deep ecology, see Nazarea 1999, 104 and Merchant 1992.

38 Cited in Burchard 1976, 428.

39 In conversation with Don Iriñeo, an IPTK expert farmer and employee. He showed me his fields that were under such fallow.

40 Drawing insights from Mental Health, Developmental Psychology, and Community Development theories of resilience, Berkes and Ross (2012,10) have developed a graphic representation of community resilience that compliments this representation.

41 See Klein (1984), as well as Diamond (1997) and Flannery (1996).

42 "Almost every culture," Pearson declares, "has restrictions, religiously or socially sanctioned, on the use of certain plants, animals, or limitations on

hunting and gathering activities ... during certain periods" Pearson 1989 in Muchena and Vanek 1995, 509.

43 Pierotti and Wildcatt 1999, 193.

CHAPTER SEVEN

1 Colucci-Grey et al. 2005, 229.
2 See http://plato.stanford.edu/entries/connectionism.
3 See http://www2.lse.ac.uk/researchAndExpertise/Experts/m.e.bloch@lse.ac.uk.
4 See Quinn 2009, 3.
5 Fillmore 1975; Rosch 1977; and E.E. Smith 1988.
6 Smith, Sera, and Gatuso 1988, 372 in Bloch 1994, 277.
7 Bloch 1994, 277. Quinn (2009, 3) defines schemata as clusters of associations – synapses firing together—built up from experience. The tendency of schemata to be filled in when only a part of them were reactivated was due to the capacity of synapses to be activated by associated synapses – a property known as synaptic plasticity.
8 Bloch 1994, 277.
9 Here Bloch is acknowledging the work of linguist Bowerman (1977).
10 Ibid, 278.
11 See Borofsky 1987; Lave 1988; 1990; Anderson 1983; and Dreyfus and Dreyfus 1986.
12 Bloch 1994, 279.
13 Ibid.
14 Ibid, 280. Cognitive anthropologists Strauss and Quinn (1994, 286), who also favour a connectionist theory of cognition, underscore the non-linear, flexible, and fluid nature of this process. "We think of knowledge," they remark, "not as sets of rule-like sentences stored in a central memory repository but rather as links among a widely distributed network of many little processing units that work like neurons ... Learning can occur without explicit teaching and ... such learning is compatible with flexible responses to new situations."14 See also Strauss and Quinn 1997.
15 See Bates and Elman 1993.
16 Hill and Mannheim 1992, 382.
17 Ibid, 381. "Knowledge," Hill further notes in Hill and Irvine 1993, 17, "is a social phenomenon, an aspect of the social relations between people."
18 Bloch 1998, 46.
19 Agrawal 1999, 179 notes: "At the very moment that Indigenous knowledge is proved useful to development through the application of science, it may,

ironically, be stripped of those very characteristics that could even potentially mark it as Indigenous. Researchers promoting the preservation of Indigenous knowledge through 'memory banking' programs that feature community-based Indigenous knowledge documentation might want to consider the trade offs." The emphasis on documentation also might shift the focus away from work to conserve the actual holders of that knowledge and their applied, dynamic and *sometimes* improvisational practices. Although well intentioned, it seems akin to the funding of a botanical encyclopedia versus support for a threatened community in the rainforest. See Nazarea 1998; Kothari 1997; Warren and Rajasekaran 1993.

20 Richards 1993, 67.

21 Lest I be accused of over-generalization myself, it is important to note that as with any community or social grouping, among Indigenous farmers, there are the gifted, the capable, the mediocre, and those who depend on the others to get by. See also Rahman 1999a; Gledhill 1993; Ortner 1984.

22 Connectionism bears a strong resemblance to another theory about human cognition and the epistemology of knowledge – constructivism, inspired by the studies of Lev Vygotsky (1929) as well as child psychologist Jean Piaget (1952),22 and educational psychologists Jerome Bruner (1990). They described the learners they studied as situated, active knowledge constructors. Constructivism, like connectionism, suggests that learners construct meaning through experiences with the real world. They do not learn facts and theories in isolation from the rest of their lives but rather in relationship to what else they know and what they believe. Learning is thus social and engaged, with each of us constructing our own rules and mental models that we use to make sense of our experiences. Knowledge acquisition, it follows, can be facilitated, but not taught. There are different branches of constructivism, the two dominant being cognitive constructivism and social constructivism. But proponents of each of these schools of thought agree that learning is a search for meaning and meaning requires understanding of the whole as well as parts. What distinguishes constructivism from connectionism is the belief, by proponents like Vygotsy (1929) at least, that language and learning are inextricably linked. Without one, you don't have the other. For scholars who have studied the non-verbal character of Indigenous knowledge transmission, Bloch's emphasis on apprenticeship, non-verbalized, non-linear, memory-based, and perceptual learning for the transmission of knowledge is more compelling.

23 Cajete 2000, 259.

24 Leavitt 1991, 277.

25 De Voogt 1996, 7. De Voogt is the first to have documented the rules of the game. Also see 2003, 63 for details.

26 De Voogt 1996, 7.

27 See Barnhardt 2003, 62.

28 Ibid. Barnhardt posits that new sciences, like the science of resilience, with their focus on complexity and the study of non-linear, dynamic systems may in fact be helping Western scientists to recognize the order in Indigenous phenomena that were previously considered chaotic and random. See also Bernhardt 2005, 13. "Until recently," Bernhardt writes, "there was very little literature that addressed how to get Western scientists and educators to understand Native world views and ways of knowing as constituting knowledge systems in their own right, and even less on what it means for participants when such divergent systems coexist in the same person, organization, or community. It is imperative, therefore, that we address these issues as a two-way transaction ... Non-Native people ... need to recognize the coexistence of multiple world views and knowledge systems, and find ways to understand and relate to the world in its multiple dimensions and varied perspectives."

29 Ross 1996.

30 Ibid, 115.

31 Ibid.

32 Ibid, 116.

33 See Davidson Hunt and Berkes 2010.

34 Ibid, 229.

35 Ibid, 232.

36 See Stairs 1994; 1991.

37 Stairs 1991, 281.

38 Dorais circa 1990, 299. Also see Dorais (2010), *The Language of the Inuit*, for a still more comprehensive overview of this subject.

39 Stairs 1991, 282.

40 Stairs 1994, 68.

41 Leavitt 1991, 274; see also Ohmagari and Berkes 1997 on Cree knowledge transmission.

42 Ibid, 273.

43 Pierotti and Wildcat 1999, 192.

44 Cosmovision, originally a Spanish word referring to a people's cosmological vision, has emerged as concept used by English-speaking researchers of Indigenous knowledge. Haverkort and Hiemstra (1999) define it to be the way a certain population perceives the world or cosmos. It also includes

assumed relationships between the spiritual, natural and the social world. Given the spiritual, other world dimension of Indigenous thought, cosmovision arguably may be considered a more accurate word than the Western term, world view, which is usually used by westerners to capture this concept.

45 Slikkerveer 1999, 171; detailed accounts of this cosmovision can be found in the work of: Proyecto *Andino de Tecnologias Campesinas* (PRATEC) 2011; *Agroecologica Universidad* Cochabamba (AGRUCO) 2011 and 1998; KAWSAY 2010; CREAR et al. 1991.

46 See Warren and Rajasekaran 1993, 38.

47 Rist, San Martin and Tapia 1997. Also see San Martin 1997.

48 See Bolliat et al. 2012.

49 According to Berkes, Folke, and Gadgil (1993, 151), modern scientific knowledge, with its accompanying world view of human beings apart from and above the natural world, has been extraordinarily successful in furthering human understanding and manipulation of simpler systems. However, neither this world view nor scientific knowledge has been particularly successful when confronted with complex ecological systems. It is within this context that traditional ecological knowledge is of significance. Also see Berkes, Folke, and Colding 2003, 2 and Colucci-Gray et al. 2006.

50 Planning systems featuring logical frameworks such as results-based management (RBM), as Barnhardt (2005, 11) reminds us, are heavily influenced by the need for applied competency. In Western terms competency is often assessed based on predetermined ideas of what a person should know, which is then measured indirectly through various forms of "objective" tests. Such an approach does not address whether that person is actually capable of putting that knowledge into practice. In the traditional Native sense, competency has an unequivocal relationship to survival or extinction – if one fails as a caribou hunter, the entire family is in jeopardy. One either has or does not have requisite knowledge, and it is tested in a real-world context.

51 Sillitoe 1998, 230.

CHAPTER EIGHT

1 Van der Ploeg 1993, 224.

2 Farmers in this region produce potatoes from their tuber root rather than from seed. However, they commonly use the word *semilla* or seed when referring to the planting of potatoes. Thus, when the word seed is used in this context here, it should be assumed to refer to a tuber.

3 Altieri 2002.

4 Interview with former PROSEMPA employee 5 May 2000; and local resident, June 2000.

5 Interview with ex-PROSEMPA worker, 5 May 2000. In their study of potato production in Bolivia, Dandler, and Sage (1985, 135) report that, unlike officials in Santa Cruz and Chuquisaca, conscientious planners in the Department of Potosí had actually managed to keep imported varieties out of the seed markets. This does not appear to have been the case in the Province of Chayanta, however. What these authors may have failed to consider was the stronger link Northern Potosí farmers had with markets and exchange mechanisms in neighbouring Chuquisaca. Indeed, several of the farmers in the municipality of Ravelo hold valley lands in Chuquisaca. In any case, my informants, including a worker with the National Potato Seed Program, insisted that Argentinean tubers arrived in Ravelo with a vengeance.

6 See Puente Rodriguez 2010, 126.

7 See van der Ploeg 1993, 223.

8 Like crown corporations.

9 Puente Rodriguez 2010, 128 has a very good overview of PROINPA's history and more recent potato research.

10 My research into their approaches and relationships with the Jalq'a of Chimpa Rodeo (they were not in Mojón at the time) was less comprehensive. When I first arrived, I had, in fact, toyed with the idea of leaving them out of my research. It was soon clear to me, however, that I could not do justice to the Jalq'a story in this region without a treatment of their presence and influence as well.

11 The link between the renewal of local vegetation and sustainable forestry seems not to have been well understood.

12 See Cott 2002, 53; see also Albo 2002 on the significance of the LPP.

13 NOVIB 1999, 17.

14 Courses include legal rights education, literacy training, and cultural dance and sports programming for children and youth.

15 NOVIB 1999, 34.

16 NOVIB 1999.

17 See IPTK 1999c.

18 During the organization's early history, IPTK frequently risked government sanctions, including those affecting the personal safety of its leaders.

19 See Gorski 2008, 518 for a discussion on how the broader neo-liberal governance in Latin America in this period favoured a view of the challenges at hand emphasizing deficits to justify inequality.

20 IPTK 1997, 4.

21 Indeed, Platt appears to have stayed in CENPRUR residences in Ocuri at one point during his research period and prefaced an IPTK-sponsored study on the *ayllu* governance system in the region. See Pacheco 1996.

22 This was also the case with the "greening" of the region through the planting of Eucalyptus trees, which require a great deal of water. IPTK staff members did their share of such reforestation in the region, being careful, they told me, to plant them on hillsides in ways that would not seriously drain the water table in this semi-arid region. Farmers who witnessed their rapid growth and utility as firewood, building materials, and medicine, planted them on their homesteads and near their fields, draining precious water from their soils.

23 See Puente Rodriguez 2010.

24 In conversation with Dr Awegechew Teshome, plant genetic resources specialist, 15 May 2012.

25 See Dandler and Sage 1985, 130.

26 On Indigenous soil management systems in Bolivia see Ettema 1994.

27 Informal interview, July 2000.

28 Interview 31 July 2002.

29 Kohl 2003, 153.

30 Conversation with a former field program coordinator, July 2002.

31 Conversation with the former Ravelo program field coordinator, Sucre, July 2000.

32 Veltmeyer and Petras (2007) consider the LPP to have represented a purposeful 'politics of accomodation' strategy, heavily influenced by the United Nations Development Program. It was designed, they argue, to curb the growing power of social movements. Also see Kohl's 2003 and Van Cott 's 2002 critical but more favourable reviews.

33 Interview with former extension worker in Ravelo, 6 July 2002.

34 PAC 1999.

35 The agrochemical arm of Novartis soon after merged with Syngenta.

36 Syngenta 2003, 1.

37 Ibid.

38 Bayer 2003a, 1.

39 Ibid.

40 Bayer 2003b.

41 Bayer 2003

42 Paraphrased from a conversation in July 2000.

43 ANED was an ecumenical social credit institution founded in June of 1978 by

11 social development agencies. Supported in the year 2000 in part through the ethical investments of Northern donors. See ANED 2011, available at: http://www.aned.org/quienes_somos_es.html.

44 Scott (1990) coined this phrase to capture the notion of being silenced in the face of greater power.

45 Rahman1999b,179. Rahman references Scott (1990) on the issue of hidden transcripts.

46 IPTK 1999d, 49.

CHAPTER NINE

1 Interview with an IPTK field staff member, November 2000.

2 Albo 2002, 84.

3 Arcienega and García 1999, 49.

4 Ribera 1992, 18.

5 Ibid.

6 See Albo 2002, 92 and Platt 1982, 19.

7 Urioste 1988.

8 Paraphrased from comments made during an informal interview, 2 May 2000.

9 Interview with a former Field Program Coordinator, July 2000.

10 Collins 1986, 654.

11 Illich 1986, 654.

12 For a quick overview of RRA and its roots see HD.gov (USA) 2009. Also see Crawford 1997 for a more detailed review on behalf of the United Nations Food and Agriculture Organization (FAO).

13 Informal interview, July 2000.

14 Participatory Rural appraisal (PRA) was designed to build on the lessons learned, and mistakes made, within Rapid Rural Appraisal processes. PRA is located in a stronger analytical framework and requires facilitators with more in-depth training. See Chambers 1995.

15 Gardiner and Lewis 1996, 44, referencing Pottier 1993.

16 CIPCVA 1994, 1/2.

17 Ibid.

18 Albó 2002 and 2000, 28.

19 See McGovern 1999. "Modern social science procedures," she argues, "are mechanisms for understanding aspects of reality by focussing attention on [just] particular aspects of reality. But by zooming in on that particular process, other expressions of that reality can be marginalized or excluded." See also Nazarea 1998 and 1999.

20 See Hanson 1985; Hunn 1999.

21 This may well not have been the case for all, but it had certainly been the case for that particular IPTK staff person when a serious motorcycle injury had sidelined him without a regular salary for an extended period of time. He was forced into the city and into a day labourer's role. Interview 6 July 2000. En route to IPTK's office in Sucre, I regularly passed the morning gathering of unemployed people nervously gathered in the hope that someone would need an *albanil* (day construction worker) or a maid that day.

22 AIPE 1999, 25.

23 PAC 1996.

24 See van der Ploeg 1993, 222. This deterioration of the crops' genetic vitality is the subject of considerable research. Puente Rodriquez's 2010 doctoral dissertation outlines efforts underway, including the possibilities and drawbacks of biotechnology and plants genomics. His discussion of their political and cultural ramifications is especially thoughtful. As will be discussed in the chapter on alternatives, the support of participatory plant breeding (PPB) that brings scientists and farmers together to cross local varieties with varieties that express additional preferred characteristics is an encouraging alternative to the biotech seed approach. In-situ plant varietal selection (PVS) is another strong option, as is the distribution for in-situ experimentation of farmers' varieties from national and international gene banks.

25 Paraphrased quote from interview with a CENPRUR graduate in Ravelo, 6 July 2000.

26 Interview 13 June 2000 with Holle, CIP, Lima, Peru.

27 See Carr 's work (1977, 244) on the Dasanetch of Ethiopia in Merchant 1990, 677.

CHAPTER TEN

1 FHI 2002.

2 Conversation with CARE USA Bolivia Director, Potosí, Nov. 2002.

3 Ravelo Municipality's Year 2000 Annual Report, 2001.

4 Centro de Estudios Sociales 1994, 144.

5 Chagas is caused by the parasite *Trypanosoma cruzi*, which is transmitted to animals and people by insect vectors that are found only in the Americas (mainly in rural areas of Latin America where poverty is widespread). Chagas disease (*T. cruzi* infection) is also referred to as American trypanosomiasis. (Centers for Disease Control 2010). The disease is transmitted through the feces of infected insects that then tend to feed at night, while the victim

is asleep. The response to the infection can vary from swelling of the face, eye, or other parts of the body at the site of invasion, to a fatal outcome due to heart failure years later. Young children are particularly at risk.

6 Conversation with a Rodeo school official, 5 Sept. 2002.

7 FHI 2002.

8 Interview with a FHI staff person, Sucre, 27 Sept. 2000.

9 Ibid.

10 Posted on an FHI field-station wall, Aug. 2000.

11 The translation is generally "creator of the world."

12 Interview with a FHI staff person, Sucre, 27 Sept. 2000.

13 Ibid.

14 Informal interview, 5 Sept. 2000. I remember wondering if she understood that Bolivia was one of the top ten mega-biodiversity hotspots on this planet.

15 Centro de Servicios Agropecuarios Técnicos, Chuquisaca 1998, 3.

16 Both also graciously received me in their residence in Pata Rodeo on lonely nights when I had no place to stay.

17 Without a translator, I would not have been able to understand the Quechua dialogue beyond a few phases and expressions. But the presence of the American assistant who also spoke very little Quechua forced the local nurse to translate quite regularly.

18 See Swartley's 2002 critique of development professionals in the agriculture and environment fields who did not apply a critical lens to their review of traditional ecological knowledge and farming systems. As within all farming systems and all kinds of development work, enthusiasts can indeed get it wrong. While evidence favouring TEK and agro-ecology approaches is clear and mounting, Swarthley is right is calling for rigour in the assessment of local practices.

CHAPTER ELEVEN

1 Grafton 1992, Introduction.

2 In Downing 1987, 41.

3 Citation of Godoy 1992 in Psacharapoulus and Patrinos 1994, 15.

4 Members were scholars from City University of New York (CUNY), Purdue University, University of Colorado, University of Sussex, England, Georgetown University Medical School, Chinese University of Hong Kong, Amsterdam Free University.

5 Wickens and Sandlin 2007, 277.

6 Hinzen 1994, 215.

7 Ibid., 217.
8 UNESCO 1988, 1 in Robinson-Pant 2004: 14.
9 Lind 2008, 11
10 UNESCO 2010 Media Release, International Literacy Day.
11 UNESCO, 1996, 15.
12 UNDP 1997,11.
13 UNDP 2010.
14 See Wickens and Sandlin 2007, 277.
15 Godoy 1992 in Psacharopoulus and Patrinos, 1994, 15.
16 See Altieri 1999, 292. Wickens and Sandlin 2007, 275 go so far as to suggest that if we analyze policy documents about literacy that are emerging from these agencies carefully, particularly those from UNESCO and the World Bank, we cannot help but conclude that their programs represent a form of neo-colonialism.
17 See De la Piedra 2009, 110 and Robinson-Pant 2004, 1.
18 Katmandu Post, 12 June 1997.
19 See also Graff 1994 in Aikman 1999, 21.
20 BBC News 2008.
21 See Robinson-Pant 2004, 15.
22 Wickens and Sandlin 2007; Street 2008; 2002, 1993; Graff 1994 and 1986; Reder 1994; Roburn 1994; Kelder 1996; Aikman 1999; McGovern 1999.
23 Hinzen 1994, 214.
24 Ibid., 219. This excerpt from a newspaper article praising the results of an NGO literacy program in Nepal differs little from the UNESCO and Bolivian testimonial cited above: "Kahili Gurung, who has completed the literacy class, says she was living in the darkness until six months ago; but now she has been encouraged to move forward after she has been able to read and write."
25 Ibid., 221.
26 Robinson-Pant 2004, 12.
27 See Graff 1986, 61. Robinson-Pant 2004, 1 contends that the high dropout rates from women's literacy programs suggest that the assumed link between literacy and development can be disputed.
28 Graff 1986, 61.
29 Robinson-Pant 2004, 11.
30 See Luke 2003.
31 Robinson-Pant 2004, 7.
32 Stephen Reder 1994,3; also see Kelder, 1996; Giroux, 1987; Walsh, 1991.
33 Kelder 1996, 3.

34 For post-modern critiques see Escobar 1999, 1995, 1994; Illich 1999; McGovern 1999; Rahnema and Bawtree 1997; Sachs 1992; Rockhill 1987.

35 Kelder 1996, 3; see also Lithman (circa 1990, 6–10) for an interesting take on the Occidental interest in literacy education.

36 Giroux 1987, 3.

37 Luke 2003, 132.

38 See Lind 2008.

39 Tufte 1990 in Ellerby 2000, 21.

40 Goody and Watt 1968, 30.

41 Ibid., 49.

42 Ibid., 22.

43 Ibid., 49.

44 Ibid., 30.

45 Ibid., 48.

46 Ibid., 68.

47 Shearwood 1987, 632.

48 Goody and Watt 1968, 57.

49 Ibid., 57.

50 Goody 1994, 254. Goody and Watt's emphasis on the dichotomy between oral and literate societies placed them in an illustrious camp. Although adamant about the need to recognize the values of different knowledge systems, structural anthropologist Claude Lévi-Strauss considered the merging of myth and history into one, and the consequent absence of historical knowledge, as one of the distinctive features of *la pensée sauvage*. "Primitive" peoples, Lévi-Strauss further suggested, are less prone to engage in analytical reasoning that might question the foundations of their knowledge. Other intellectual powers behind such theory include Walter Ong as well as David Olson. In oral cultures, Ong proposed, the spoken word shapes sound as well as thought processes and the present moment takes precedence over the past. Writing and reading are solitary acts fostering the interior development of thought. Echoing Goody and Watt, he further advanced that with the objectification of thought in written language and the development of analytical thought, a skeptical approach to truth and knowledge was created. Olson wrote that there "seems little doubt that writing and reading played a critical role in producing the shift from thinking about things to thinking about representations of those things."

51 See Scribner and Cole 1981. Their research with the Vai peoples of Liberia found few differences on a variety of cognitive measures between those able and those unable to write the Vai script. In reviewing their research, Olson

(2007, 3) argues that differences did emerge when the Vai participated in longer term, formal education. Still, it is not the engagement and interactive learning Olson emphasizes but rather the fact that, as he puts it: "schooling is essentially a literate enterprise." Capturing thought on paper, he insists, leads to deeper levels of analysis. See also Street 1994; Bloch 1994, Borofsky 1994; Vayda1994; Graff 1986; Heath 1986a.

52 See Maurice Bloch's (1998, 152) "Literacy and Enlightenment" for an insightful and new dimension to the critique of Goody's "great divide" theory. Based on fieldwork in Japan, Bloch explores how the relationship of the spoken language, writing, and thought are different with different types of writing systems. These differences argue against any broad generalization about 'literacy" and its link to critical thinking.

53 Street 1993, 23. See also Heath and Street 2008, 8.

54 See Borofsky 1994, 345.

55 Ibid., 345.

56 See also Vadya 1994, 320.

57 Street 1993, 41.

58 Lamola 1992.

59 Reijntjes et al. 1992, 4.

60 See Altieri 1999, 293.

61 Van der Ploeg 1993 borrowing Mendas' (1970) concept.

62 Van der Ploeg 1993, 209.

63 See Gadgil et al. 1993, 151.

64 De la Piedra 2009; Wickens and Sandlin 2007; Robinson-Platt 2004; Luke 2003; Street 2002; Kasten 1998; Osborne 1996; Thaman 1994; Lafrance 1994; Watahomigie and McCarty 1994; Dick et al. 1994; Fleras 1993; Standing Committee on Aboriginal Affairs 1990; Hampton 1989.

65 Giroux 1987, 2.

66 Freire 1973, 48.

67 See Arts in Education 2002.

68 Friere 1970, 58.

69 Lusted 1986 in Giroux 1987, 18.

70 Freire and Macedo 1987.

71 Freire in Roburn 1994, 1.

72 Freire 1970, 50.

73 Ibid, 108.

74 Street 1993.

75 There is interesting research to suggest in fact that within the Andean world, communities have long participated in the literate conventions of the

dominant society by having select members with reading and writing skills serve as their interlocators and intepreters. See Rappaport 1994, 97.

76 Graff 1986, 64.

77 Robinson-Pant 2004; Street 2002; Osborne 1996; McLaughlin 1994, Reder 1994; Kater 1984; Graff 1886; Ferdman and Weber 1994; Heath 1986a and 1986b; Ogbu, 1987.

CHAPTER TWELVE

1 Platt 1976,12.

2 UNICEF 2002.

3 Ibid.

4 See UNICEF 2002a, 6.

5 For a comprehensive review of interculturalism, a concept that helped to shape intercultural work in Bolivia (as elsewhere) see Appendix 3.

6 UNICEF 2002b, 2.

7 It should be noted that this was not the first substantive attempt at reform aimed to incorporate Indigenous world views. In the 1940s, the Bolivian government sought, albeit unsuccessfully, to spread across the country's rural areas the model that had been developed a decade earlier by teachers Elizardo Pérez and Avelino Siñani at the famous *escuela-ayllu* of Warisata. The intent was to provide a curriculum especially geared toward the needs of the Indigenous peoples of the Bolivian highlands. See Brienen 2002, 616.

8 The Ministry of Education, Culture and Sports 1999, 10.

9 Teacher training, Ravelo municipal offices, 21 October 2000.

10 UNICEF 1993a.

11 Informal conversation with IPTK staff person, Ocuri, April 2000.

12 Albó 2000, 9.

13 Ibid., 87.

14 Centro de Estudios Sociales [CENDES] 1994, 141.

15 In cooperation with the Bolivian government's National Education Secretariat and the Social Investment Fund or *Fundos de Inversión Social* (FIS).

16 CENDES 1994, 142.

17 Ibid., 236.

18 Ibid., 257–61.

19 CENDES 1994, 257.

20 Ibid., 260–1.

21 Translation was required, since the La Paz native holding the regional pro-

gram coordination position was an Aymara speaker and had very limited Quechua. Trainers were otherwise all native Quechua speakers.

22 UNICEF 2002.

23 "Whole language" is an approach to the teaching of reading and writing that builds on the idea that there needs to be meaning in the learning process. It grew out of dissatisfaction with a purely phonetic approach. See: http://jan.ucc.nau.edu/~jar/Reading_Wars.html.

24 Conversation with a literacy coordinator, July 2000.

25 UNICEF 2002.

26 The exception was a fascinating and very determined grandmother who took her practice reading and writing materials with her when shepherding her sheep. Two years is possibly a short period for assessment purposes. But *Yuyay Japina* had a fixed duration of two years in each community. No follow-up activities were built into the program, so the chances of moving beyond this level of skill were very slim.

27 Informal interview, 2 May 2000.

28 Interview with UNICEF Regional Program Director, 1 August 2000.

29 Ravelo Literacy Promoters Workshop, 17–21 July 2000.

30 Interview with a UNICEF Program Director, La Paz, 14 December 2000.

31 As opposed to "emic," which relates to deeper cultural norms and beliefs.

32 Bloch 1994, 277; Smith 1988; Rosch 1977; Fillmore 1975.

CHAPTER THIRTEEN

1 Frank 1986, 1.

2 When I read the article shortly after its publication, I thought: "That's gutsy!" It was a full decade later that I found out that Leonard Frank was a pseudonym.

3 This problematic, James Ferguson (1994, xiii) writes, sees debtor Third World nation states and starving peasants as sharing a common "problem" that both lack a single "thing": "development."

4 See the G8's New Alliance for Food Security and Nutrition. See also Patel 2010; Off 2010; *Globe and Mail* 2008; *San Francisco Chronicle* 2008; *Washington Post* 2008.

5 For a review of studies and perspectives of this nature, see the website of the Consultative Group on International Agriculture Research (CGIAR): www.cgiar.org.

6 See Altieri and von der Weid 2011; Lappe 2011.

7 Smit et al. 1996 estimate that 15–20% of the global food output is grown in cities; in Redwood 2008.

8 In conversation with the ETC Group (June 2012). This cost was verified with representative of the Consultative Group on International Agricultural Research (CGIAR) and with staff at the Gates Foundation.

9 See Heinrich Boll Stiftung and ETC Group 2102 and Fuglie et al. 2011.

10 Monsanto 2013.

11 Parrott and Marsden, 2002 and Safe 2005 in Vanloqueren and Baret 2009, 978.

12 See Vanloqueren and Baret 2009 on the drawbacks of a singular privileging of high tech in research and development.

13 See Kaskey, J in *Businessweek* 8 September 2011.

14 CBC News 2011.

15 See Wale et al. 2011; Altieri 2009; Herren et al. 2009; Pretty 2006.

16 Pimbert 2008, 9.

17 See Naerstad 2010, ETC Group 2009 and Altieri 2009, 104–5. If we include the food produced or provided by fisherfolk, hunters and gatherers, and pastoralists, in addition to that of small-holder farmers in rural and urban centres, this system may well feed up to or more than 70% of our planet's people.

18 Van der Ploeg 2008, iv.

19 Ibid.

20 Altieri 2009, 103.

21 Price increases abruptly halted in 2009 as a result of falling commodity prices, restricted availability of credit, and a sudden fall in energy prices. However, fertilizer prices resumed their climb in 2011 and continued to increase in 2012 in response to high energy prices and strong worldwide fertilizer demand driven by rising crop prices. Agriculture and Agri-Food Canada 2012, 1–2.

22 In a session I attended within the recent United Nations conference on sustainable development (Rio + 20), the newly elected Prime Minister of Bhutan delivered a keynote address that pledged his country's full intention to transition to 100 % organic and biodiverse food production within the near future.

23 The Ad hoc Advisory Group to the Madrid Conference on Food Security. "Small Holder Food Production and Poverty Reduction" Report, 26 January 2009, 13.

24 See the New York Times: http://topics.nytimes.com/top/reference/times topics/organizations/g/gates_bill_and_melinda_foundation/index.html.

25 ETC Group March/April 2007. Research conducted by Canada's ETC Group notes that the Gates-Rockefeller alliance will spend $43 million to breed 200 "non-GE" African plant varieties and $20 million to upgrade national agricultural research around the continent. In a departure from the original Green Revolution, AGRA will also give $37 million to the sellers (to buttress village- or district-level agribusiness suppliers) and $24 million to the buyers (to pay for farmers' access to the sellers' "improved" seeds and inputs.) That is a total of $61 million to subsidize the flow of new technologies. Another $26 million will go to provide a monitoring and evaluation facility in Nairobi – bringing the total to $150 million for the "seed" round of the first phase.

26 Speech 23 February 2012, to the International Fund on Agricultural Development (IFAD), Rome, Italy.

27 ETC Group 2009,15.

28 Private conversation with Dr Melaku Worede, former Ethiopian national Gene Bank director and International Scientific Advisor to USC Canada.

29 See, e.g., the New Alliance for Food Security and Nutrition 2012.

30 According to USDA researchers, as of 7 November 2011, imported poultry was 30–40% cheaper than locally produced chicken (Rawdon and Ashitey 2011).

31 The NGO GRAIN has more accurately called this phenomenon "land grabs." See http://www.grain.org/article/entries/3995-land-grabbing-in-latin-america. For a concise case study of trade and land issues that are influencing agricultural policy in Africa see Joan Baxter 2010, 1. See also Frederick Haufman's insightful, albeit highly cynical, look at factors – beyond food availability – that explain hunger.

32 See Olivier de Schutter, 2010.

33 RAFI 1995, 4.

34 See Brush 1994 in Correa 2000, 240.

35 Principe 1989 in United Nations Conference on Trade and Development (UNCTAD) 2000, 6.

36 Posey and Dutfield 1996, 34.

37 King et al.1996, 168.

38 UNCTAD 2000, 6.

39 UNCTAD 2000.

40 UNCTAD 2000: 6.

41 RAFI 1995:7. Even so, as Posey (1990,15) pointed out, less than 0.001% of the profits from drugs that originated from traditional medicines have ever gone to the Indigenous peoples who led researchers to them.

266 Notes to Pages 181–90

42 The Protocol on Access and Benefit Sharing (ABS) of the United Nation's International Convention of Biological Diversity (CBD), adopted in Nagoya in November of 2011, does, at long last, formally recognize the contributions of Indigenous peoples and local communities, in theory at least. The terms of this voluntary protocol, however, are far weaker than many civil society organizations and Indigenous peoples' movements had hoped for. Ratification by member states has also been painfully slow.

43 There are plenty of individual examples of private or corporate profits stemming from Indigenous "intellectual property," details of which can be found in other publications. See, e.g., The ETC Group's website: www.etc.org; Brush and Stabinsky (eds) 1996; and Roht-Arrianza 1996, particularly her examples from Madagascar and Ethiopia.

44 See the Millennium Ecosystem Assessment 2005, 3.

45 Up to 22% of the wild relatives of peanuts, potatoes, and beans are expected to disappear by 2055, hit by a changing climate. FAO Media Release 25 March 2010.

46 Ibid.

47 Posey 1999, 164.

48 Nash 1979.

49 On resistance and accommodation among Latin American Indigenous people more broadly, see Varese 1996 and Dove 1996.

50 NOVIB, 1999, 6.

51 Picard 2002, A1.

52 Berkes, Colding, and Folke 2003, 2.

53 And as Agrawal (1999, 179) reminds us, even when genuine attempts are made to champion and conserve Indigenous knowledge systems, the principles of Western science are often used to explain it. In this "scientization" of Indigenous knowledge, the knowledge is easily sanitized, robbed of its original context, meaning, spiritual dimension, and value.

54 Chambers 1983.

55 In Bühler 2002, 6.

CHAPTER FOURTEEN

1 In conversation with Colleen Ross, September 2011. Colleen also takes a lead role in La Via Campesina's work on biodiversity conservation. She has also been the farmer who brings me my fresh produce thanks to my Community Shared Agriculture share with her farm, Watatah Downs, in Iroquois, Ontario,

2 Netting 1993, 334.

3 Sadly, we are today witnessing the hungry eyes of the children of Ethiopia's neighbours, Somalia being one vivid example. Again, civil strife has played a major role in these famines.

4 More recent research has discovered that it is the control of moisture versus temperature that is most important to longer-term seed storage. See Visser 2011.

5 See Teshome 1996. Teshome's research clearly demonstrated a strong correlation between farmer's diversity assessments and those of their scientist counterparts. "Intraspecific variation closely accorded with both folk and numerical taxonomies; as farmers increase their selection criteria, diversity at the field level increases to meet their diverse needs and requirements ... farmers' knowledge of storability corresponded with laboratory estimates of resistance to pest infestations."

6 I debated the merits of highlighting this program by way of introduction to the concept of ecological agriculture. The academic in me worried about bias. Whether as natural scientists or social scientists, however, don't we all start with questions based on our particular experiences and then research the answers through lenses that are tinted with our own perceptions and assumptions? The Seeds of Survival story is the one I know best. So I have included my first-hand account.

7 In conversation with Jamal Mohammed, Wollo, Ethiopia, 2005.

8 Leaders of the Philippines South East Asian Regional Initiatives for Community Empowerment (SEARICE) and India's Green Foundation, e.g., both cite their Ethiopia SOS training experience as the inspiration for the agricultural biodiversity approach their organizations promote. Personal communications with the executive directors, 2011 and 2008.

9 Altieri 2009, 103. Miguel Altieri is credited with having labeled the science "agro-ecology."

10 USC Canada's Honduras program partner works with farmers to collect (although carefully not to deplete) valuable micro-nutrients from the forest floor as a kind of mulch that adds to soil fertility.

11 See Holt-Gimenez. 2006.

12 See Humphries et al. 2006. Humphries, it should be noted, also deserves much credit for her pivotal role in launching and nurturing the pilot that led to USC Canada's partnership with FIPAH and their Seeds of Survival program today. There have also been some very positive social and gender equality benefits as well. The CIALs' collaborative initiatives on food security have functioned as gender equality "communities of practice," enhancing

women's status both within the household and within the public arena. See also Humphries et al. 2012.

13 Holt-Himenez 2001 in Altieri 2009, 108.

14 Noteworthy groups include but are hardly limited to Brazil's Agroecology and Family Agriculture Association that has since 1983 championed agro-ecology as a means to strengthen local family farming and sustainable rural communities. In South Asia, activists like Vandana Shiva, with her Navdanya network of seed keepers and organic producers across 16 states has been instrumental in building this movement.14 When it comes to both well-refined policy work and on the ground programming, the Southeast Asia Regional Initiatives for Community Empowerment has played a key leadership role. The now-retired global network – Community Biodiversity Development and Conservation (CBDC) – with its range of research, government, and non-governmental members from Southern and Northern countries, also helped to advance biodiversity-based ecological agriculture in important ways, as have the Andean members of the COMPAS Endogenous Development and Biocultural Diversity Network, including Bolivia's AGRUCO.

15 ETC Group 2013, cover.

16 According to La Via Campesina's' European farmer representative, Paul Nicholson, in a speech at Yale University, 14 September 2013.

17 See Pimbert 2010 for a description of a very innovative form of assisting farmers to understand the bigger picture through citizen juries and village courts. As part of his work on food sovereignty with the International Institute for Environment and Development, Pimbert played a leading role in designing and promoting this innovative public engagement tool.

18 On the historical role of international trade on local food systems see Evans and Rimas 2010.

19 UNCTAD 2013.

20 Herren et al. 2009; see also Pretty 2006.

21 See De Schutter 2010 and 2011 and a presentation to a Yale University conference on Food Sovereignty, 14 September 2013.

22 E.g., the Food and Agriculture Organization (FAO), the International Fund for Agricultural Development (IFAD) and Bioversity International – the plant genetic resources research institute of the Consultative Group on International Agricultural Research (CGIAR) – and the Oxfam and Action Aid families, to name a few.

23 McMichael's (2006) thoughtful article on the conflict between food security and food sovereignty also effectively links the debate to social movement building, the attempt to democratize the food world, and the politics of the Left. See also Wittman et al. 2011; Patel 2008; Pimbert 2010; and Caouette 2010.

24 On the conflict between the concept of food security and food sovereignty see Schanbacer 2010.

25 The farmer-led civil society action that effectively stopped the inclusion of agriculture within the World Trade Organization's (WTO) regulatory framework is a prime example of the power of the food sovereigntists' response. See Roberts 2013, 88; Friedmann 2011, 169; and Patel 2103 and 2009.

26 On 14 and 15 September 2013, Yale University, in collaboration with San Francisco's Food First, and The Hague' International Institute of Social Studies (ISS) held a conference that exposed these debates. Papers are available at: http://www.yale.edu/agrarianstudies/foodsovereignty. Of particular relevance to this theme are the Bernstein, McMichael, Clark, and Schanbacher papers. Also see Fabricant 2012, 108.

27 On the question of transitioning to more sustainable technique, see the collaborative publication of the More and Better Network called: *Agricultural Transition: A Different Logic*. Hilmi 2012.

28 See Bernstein 2009.

29 See Cooke and Kothari 2001; Gledhill, 1994.

30 See Nyéléni 2007 – Forum pour la Souveraineté Alimentaire, 23–27 Février 2007, Sélingué, Mali. http://www.nyeleni.org/.

31 The unofficial claiming of a public space, like the strips of land in the centre of boulevards, to plant a garden.

EPILOGUE

1 Executive Director of PIANGO, a pan-South Pacific network of NGOs, made this remark during a keynote address for the Canadian Council for International Cooperation annual general meeting, 26 May 2011.

2 My employer at the time, Canadian Lutheran World Relief, agreed to partner with IPTK on this new approach.

3 Of all the villages in the municipality, Yurubamba, with its more fertile valley lands and commercial production, is probably the one that has most inspired the "*los paperos*" nickname.

4 See Goodale 2009, 160.

5 Morales is the second Indigenous president in all of Latin America.

6 See Cusicanqui-Rivera 1990, 98 and Goodale 2009. Susan Healing's (2006) doctoral research into the cultural resilience and identity of Bolivia's Indigenous peoples offers especially thoughtful analysis into the question of the way exclusion can breed resistance and resilience.

7 On 20 April 2011, Bolivia marked the International Day of Mother Earth

with the world's first legislation that grants to all nature rights equal to humans. See: http://www.ens-newswire.com/ens/apr2011/2011-04-20-01.html. But in the government's continued support for agri-business and production monocultures in crops like soy, and their blind eye on the entry of genetically modified seeds that tie the country to powerful corporate interests, serious contradictions have surfaced. Not long after my return from Bolivia in April 2011, food sovereignty was written into a new law entitled the Law of Productive, Communal, and Agricultural Revolution. Included in this new legistation, however, is both the idea of national seed security through the production of the country's own seeds and a reference to the promotion of biotechnology that many civil society actors believe will allow for the full-fledged entry of genetically modified organisms into the system. The National Council of Ayllus and Markas of Qullasuyu (CONAMAQ) denounced the law for "playing games with the multinationals that dedicate themselves to genetically modified plants and non-organic fertilizers." See Fabricant 2012, Battaglia 2011, and CONAMAQ 2011.

8 Wittman et al. (eds) 2011, 55.
9 Puente Rodriguez 2010, 134.
10 See Simmarro and Antolin 2012, 549. Veltmeyer and Petras (2007) point to 2007 national income figures that demonstrate widely disproportionate returns for investors and entrepreneurs. See also Fabricant (2012, 1) for a critical review of the role of the landless peasant movement – a Bolivian MST – in bringing Morales to power, Morales's and their purposeful politicization of indigeneity to effect change, and the limitations of a social movement state.
11 Critics contend that the highway would do little for Bolivians, but only benefit Brazil as a route to the Pacific. Brazil's development bank, BNDES, has pledged hundreds of millions in loans and the road would be built by OAS, a Brazilian construction firm. Protests in the fall of 2011 forced a government retreat on this project. See Survival International October 2011; BBC News Aug. and Sept 2011. In a very recent book, Vice-President Alvaro Garcia Linera (2012) offers a very detailed retort to the critics of Bolivia's action on this matter. Some critics, he contends, are not fully conversant with the complex history of this region or the challenges. Other critics are part of a predictable counter-revolution. See also Fabricant 2012, 9.
12 Puente Rodriguez 2010, 125.
13 See Postero 2010; Schiwy 2011.
14 See Powers 2010.

APPENDIX TWO

1 Cepeda 1996, 1.
2 Barrett 1996, 123.
3 Sjoberg and Nett 1968 in Oakley 1995, 35.
4 Oakley 1995, 58.
5 See Ojeda and Retolaza 1999.
6 See Sanchez 2002.

APPENDIX THREE

1 López 2001, 18.
2 See López 2010, 8.
3 Ruiz 1984 in López 2010, 9.
4 There has been a more recent shift to labeling it as intercultural education for all. See López 2010, 9.
5 I have taken the idea of insider intimate knowledge and outside opportunity structure from Lockhart 1984. He does not talk about interculturalism but offers a very insightful analysis of the insider-outsider dialectic in Native socio-economic development programs in Canada. It struck me as very useful to "interculturalism" theory.
6 López 2001.
7 Ibid., 28.
8 See Speiser 2010.
9 Jean Paul Lederach's (1995) work on conflict transformation across cultures is particularly instructive: "Conflict is connected to meaning and meaning to knowledge, and knowledge is rooted in culture. People act on the basis of the meaning things have for them. Meaning is created through shared and accumulated knowledge. People from different cultural settings have developed many ways of creating and expressing as well as interpreting and handling conflict ... Understanding conflict and developing appropriate models of handling it will necessarily be rooted in, and must respect and draw from, the cultural knowledge of people."
10 See Aikman's excellent review (1999) of interculturalism within Latin America and more particularly within the Peruvian Amazon. López's more recent (2009) update on the state of the interculturalism question in Latin America, including Bolivia, is also a worthwhile reference. Gorski's 2008 look at the gap between the theory and practice of intercultural education likewise offers important insights into this matter.

11 Ibid.

12 Sucre-based interviews with UNFPA's intercultural and communications program managers, October 2000.

13 Aminur Rahman's (1999a, 92) study of Bangladesh's Grameen Bank credit
program for women sheds light on this issue. One participant in a workshop designed to facilitate borrowers' ability to enhance their social status
and exercise greater control over their lives, had this to say: "Sir and *apa*
(male and female speakers) were from the city and they were very educated
people. They talked and talked. Many times I could not understand what
they were talking about. Other times they were talking about things which
we already know."

14 Paraphrased from an interview in Spanish on 11 December 2000.

15 A final key actor left out of the decision-making and planning process
when it comes to the promotion of interculturalism with the education system was the public school teacher. In spite of the widely recognized role
that teachers play in creating the conditions for successful learning, teachers
were not, for example, at the centre of nations' ambitious intercultural education reforms, at least not in a substantive way. They were offered materials, professional development through short-term in-service training workshops and some advisory support. Rarely did they have a major voice in the
shaping of the materials or curriculum. During my encounter with the
teachers in Mojón and Ravelo schools, it was also clear many did not fully
understand the concepts thrust on them. For a thorough overview of the
rural teacher and intercultural education in Bolivia, see Speiser 2010.

16 Rengifo 2000,13. See also Rengifo 2005.

References

Adger, W. Neil. 2000. "Social and Ecological Resilience: Are They Related?" *Progress in Human Geography* 24(3): 347–64.

AGRA Watch. 2010. "Gates Foundation Invests in Monsanto: Both Will Profit at Expense of Small-Scale African Farmers." Seattle: Community Alliance for Global Justice, August: 1.

Agrawal, Arun. 1999. "On Power and Indigenous Knowledge." In D. Posey, ed. *Cultural and Spiritual Values of Biodiversity*. London: Intermediate Technology Publications, 177–184.

– 1995 "Indigenous and Scientific Knowledge: Some Critical Comments." *Indigenous Knowledge and Development Monitor* 3(3) December. Online journal: http://app.iss.nl/ikdm/ikdm/ikdm/3-3/articles/agrawal.html.

Agriculture and Agri-Food Canada. 2012. "Canadian Farm Fuel and Fertilizer: Prices and Expenses." *Market Outlook* 4(1) (March): 1-8.

Agroecologica Universidad Cochabamba (AGRUCO). 2011. Internet source: http://www.agruco.org/agruco/index.php.

AGRUCO. 1998. *Plataforma Para El Dialogo Intercultural Sobre Cosmovision y Agricultura*. Cochabamba: COMPAS.

Aguirre, J. 1999. "Reseñas: Cultura escrita en sociedades tradicionales." Internet source: http: //www.ucm.es/info/especulo/numero5/goody.htm.

Aikman, S. 1999. *Intercultural Education and Literacy: An Ethnographic Study of Indigenous Knowledge and Learning in the Perúvian Amazon*. Amsterdam: John Benjamins Publishing Company.

Albo, Xavier. 2002. "Bolivia: From Indian and Campesino Leaders to Councillors and Parliamentary Deputies." In R. Sieder (ed) *Multiculturalism in Latin America: Indigenous Rights, Diversity and Democracy* Institute of Latin American Studies. Hampshire, England: Palgrave Macmillan, 74-102.

– 2000. *Iguales aunque Diferentes*. La Paz: UNICEF

Allen, C. 1988. *The Hold Life Has: Coca and Cultural Identity in an Andean Community*. Washington: Smithsonian Institution Press.

Altieri, M. 2009. "Agroecology, Small Farms, and Food Sovereignty." *Monthly Review*, July-August 2009: 102–12.

– 2002. "For An Agriculture That Doesn't Get Rid Of Farmers." NACLA *Report on the Americas* 35(5): 29–34.

– 1999. "The Agroecological Dimensions of Biodiversity in Traditional Farming Systems." In D. Posey (ed) *Cultural and Spiritual Values of Biodiversity*. London: Intermediate Technology Publications, 291–7.

– 1995. *Agroecology: The Science of Sustainable Agriculture*. Boulder, CO: Westview.

– and F. Funes-Monzote. 2012. "The Paradox of Cuban Agriculture" *Monthly Review* 63(8): 23–33. Internet source: http://monthlyreview.org/2012/01/01/the=paradox-of-cuban-agriculture

– and J.M. von de Weid. 2011. "Prospects for Agroecologically Based Natural-Resource Management for Low-Income Farmers In The 21st Century." Internet source: http://www.fao.org/docs/eims/upload/207904/gfar0048.pdf

– and A. Yurjivic. 1995. "The Latin America Consortium on Agroecology." In D. M. Warren et al. (eds) *The Cultural Dimension of Development*. London: Intermediate Technology Press: 458–68.

– and L. Merrick. 1987. "*In-situ* Conservation of Crop Genetic Resources through Maintenance of Traditional Farming Systems." *Economic Botany* 41(1): 86–96.

Anderson, J. 1983. *The Architecture of Cognition*. Cambridge, MA: Harvard University Press.

Arcienega, M. and P. García. 1999. "El Mercado Complemento: Intercambio en la Provincia Chayanta, Norte de Potosí." Sucre: CIPRES/ IPTK internal document.

Arensberg, C.1954. "The Community Study Method." *The American Journal of Sociology* 60: 109–24.

Arnstein, S. 1969. "Ladder of Citizenship Participation." *Journal of the American Institute of Planners* 35: 216–24.

Asad, T. 1973. "Introduction." In T. Asad (ed) *Anthropology and the Colonial Encounter*. Atlantic Highlands, NJ: Humanities Press: 9-24.

Asch, M. 1982. "Dene Self-Determination and the Study of Hunter-Gatherers in the Modern World." In E. Leacock and R. Lee (eds) *Politics and History in Band Societies*. Cambridge: Cambridge University Press.

ASUR Foundation. 2000.. "Arte Indígena." Sucre: brochure.

Battaglia, N. 2011. "Bolivia Enacts Law of Productive Revolution." *The Argentina*

Independent. On-line edition: http://www.argentinaindependent.com/current affairs/newsfromlatinamerica/bolivia-enacts-law-of-productive-revolution/

Barnhardt, R. and A.O. Kawagley 2005. "Indigenous Knowledge Systems and Alaska Native Ways of Knowing." *Anthropology & Education Quarterly* 36: 8–23.

– 2003. "Culture, Chaos, and Complexity: Catalysts for Change in Indigenous Education." *Cultural survival Quarterly* 27(4) winter: 59–75.

Barragán, R. 1994. *Indios de arco y flecha?: Entre la Historia y la Arqueologia de las Poblaciones del Norte de Chuquisaca (Siglos XV–XV)*. Sucre: Ediciones ASUR.

Barrett, S. 2009. *Anthropology: A Student's Guide to Theory and Method, 2nd edition*. Toronto: University of Toronto Press.

– 1984. *Anthropology: A Student's Guide to Theory and Method*. Toronto: University of Toronto Press.

– 1984. *The Rebirth of Anthropological Theory*. Toronto: University of Toronto Press.

Bates E. and J. Elman.1993. "Connectionism and the Study of Change." In M. Johnson (ed), *Brain Development and Cognition: A Reader*. Oxford: Blackwell Publishers: 623–42.

Baxter, J. 2010 "Protecting Investors, But What About the People? Dissecting the Contradictions of Agricultural Research Investments in Sierra Leone. *Pambazuka News:* 480.

Bayer 2003a."Folidol". Internet source: www.bayercropscience.com.au/products/resources/Folidol%20M%20500.pdf

Bayer 2003b. "Tamaron". Internet source: www.bayercropscience.cl/msds/tamaron600sl.pdf

BBC News. 2011. "Bolivia Amazon Road Protesters Break Police Blockade." *BBC Worldwide:* Homepage 24 September 2011. http://www.bbc.co.uk/news/world-latin-america-15048897.

BBC News. 2011. "Indigenous Bolivians March against Amazon Road." *BBC Worldwide*: Homepage 15 August 2011. Internet source: http://www.bbc.co.uk/news/world-latin-america-14536163.

BBC News. 2008. "Bolivia declares literacy success." *BBC News*: 21 December 2008. Internet source: http://news.bbc.co.uk/2/hi/americas/7794293.stm.

Bebbington, A. 1992. "Grassroots Perspectives on 'Indigenous' Agricultural Development: Indian Organizations and NGOs in the Central Andes of Ecuador." *The European Journal of Development Research* 4(2): 132–67.

Beerer, D., T. Carlson, and S. King. 1995. "Shaman Pharmaceuticals: Integrating Indigenous Knowledge, Tropical Medicine, Modern Science and Reciprocity into a Novel Drug Discovery Approach." Internet source: http://netsci.org/Science/Special/feature11.html.

Berkes, F. 2009. "Revising the Commons Paradigm." *Journal of Natural Resources Policy Research* 1(3): 261–64.

– 2008. *Sacred Ecology: Traditional Ecological Knowledge and Resource Management.* 2nd edition. New York: Routledge.

– 2009. "Indigenous Ways of Knowing and the Study of Environmental Change." *Journal of the Royal Society of New Zealand* 39(4) December: 151–6.

– and H. Ross. 2012. "Community Resilience: Toward an Integrated Approach." *Society & Natural Resources: An International Journal* 26 (1): 5-20.

– , G.P. Kofinas, and F. S. Chapin III. 2009. "Conservation. Community and Livelihoods: Sustaining, Renewing and Adapting Cultural Connections to the Land." In F.S. Chapin III, G.P. Kofinas, and C. Folke (eds) *Principles of Ecosystem Stewardship: Resilience-based Resource Management in a Changing World.* New York: Springer-Verlag.

– , J. Colding, and C. Folke, (eds). 2003. *Navigating Social-Ecological Systems: Building Resilience for Complexity and Change.* Cambridge: Cambridge University Press.

– and C. Folke. 1998. "Ecological Practices and Social Mechanisms for Building Resilience and Sustainability." In F. Berkes and C.Folke (eds) *Linking Social and Ecological Systems: Management Practices and Social Mechanisms for Building Resilience.* Cambridge: Cambridge University Press: 414–36.

Bernstein, H. 2009 "Agrarian Question from Transition to Globalization." In A. H. Akram-Lodhi (ed) *Peasants and Globalization: Political Economy, Rural Transformation and the Agrarian Question.* New York: Routledge: 239–61.

Berreman, G. 1969. "'Bringing It All Back Home': Malaise in Anthropology." In D. Hymes, (ed) *Reinventing Anthropology.* New York: Pantheon Books: 83–98.

– 1966. "Anemic and Emetic Analyses in Social Anthropology." *American Anthropologist* 68: 346–54.

Bertalanffy, L. 1968. *General Systems Theory: Foundations, Development, and Application.* New York: George Braziller.

Berthoff, A.E. 1991. "Forward." In P. Freire and D. Macedo (eds) *Literacy: Reading the Word and the World.* South Hadley: Bergin & Garvey Publishers.

Bezençon, N. 1994. "Cambio y Persistencia en el Norte de Potosí: Estrategias Domesticas De Las Familias Productores de Papa en la Zona de Ravelo." Sucre: PROINPA, unpublished manuscript.

Bloch, M. 1998. "Cognition and Ethnography." In M. Bloch *How We Think They Think: Anthropological Approaches to Cognition, Memory and Literacy.* Boulder, CO: Westview.

– 1994. "Language, Anthropology and Cognitive Science." In R. Borofsky (ed) *Assessing Cultural Anthropology.* Toronto: McGraw-Hill: 276–82.

Bolivian Ministry of Education, Culture and Sports. 1999. *Compendio de legislación sobre la Reforma Educativa y leyes conexas.* La Paz: Ministerio de Educación y Cultura.

Boillat, S., E. Serrano, S. Rist., and F. Berkes. 2012. "The Importance of Place Names in the Search for Ecosystem-Like Concepts in Indigenous Societies: An Example from the Bolivian Andes." *Environmental Management,* DOI 10.1007/s00267-012-9969-4 13 November.

Borofsky, R. 1994. "On the Knowledge and Knowing of Cultural Activities." In R. Borofsky (ed) *Assessing Cultural Anthropology.* Toronto: McGraw-Hill: 331–46.

– 1987. *Making History: Pukapukan and Anthropological Constructions of Knowledge.* Cambridge: Cambridge University Press.

Bourdieu, P. 1972. Outline *of a Theory of Practice.* Cambridge: Cambridge University Press.

Bowerman, M. 1977. "The Acquisition of Word Meaning: An Investigation in Some Current Concepts." In P. Johnson-Laird and P. Watson (eds) *Thinking Readings in Cognitive Science.* Cambridge: Cambridge University Press.

Brienen, M. 2002. "The Clamour for Schools: Rural Education and the Development of State-Community Contact in Highland Bolivia, 1930–1952." *Revista de Indias* LXII 226: 615–50.

Bronner, S. 1993. "Of Critical Theory and Its Theorists: Introduction." Internet source: http: //www.uta.edu/huma/illuminations/bron1.htm.

Brokensha, D., M. Warren, and O. Werner (eds). 1980. *Indigenous Knowledge Systems and Development.* Latham: The University of America Press.

Bruner, J. 1990. *Acts of Meaning.* Cambridge, MA: Harvard University Press.

Brush, S. 1989. "Rethinking Crop Genetic Resource Conservation." *Conservation Biology* 3(1):19–29.

– and D. Stabinsky (eds). 1996. *Valuing Local Knowledge: Indigenous People and Intellectual Property Rights.* Washington, D.C.: Island Press.

– and D. Guillet. 1985. "Small Scale Agricultural Production in the Central Andes." *Mountain Research and Development* 5(1): 19–30.

– , J. C. Heath, and Z. Humán. 1980. "Dynamic of Andean Potato Agriculture." *Economic Botany* 35(1): 70–88.

Bühler, U. 2002. "Participation 'with Justice and Dignity': Beyond 'the New Tyranny." *Peace Studies Journal,* University of Bradford, Internet source: http: www.peacestudiesjournal.org.uk/docs/Participation.PDF.

Burchard, R. 1976. *Myths of the Sacred Coca Leaf: Ecological Perspectives on Coca and Peasant Biocultural Adaptation in Peru.* Bloomington: Indiana University at Bloomington, Department of Anthropology, PHD Dissertation.

– 1975. "Coca Chewing: A New Perspective." In V. Rubin (ed) *Cannabis and Culture.* Chicago: Aldine: 463–81.

Burger, J. 1990. *The Gaia Atlas of First Peoples*. Toronto: Doubleday.

Burman, A. 2011. "Chachrawarmi: Silence and Rival Voices on Decolonization and Gender Politics in Andean Bolivia." *Journal of Latin America Studies* 43: 65–91.

Cabitza, M. 2011. " Will Bolivia Make the Breakthrough on Food Security and the Environment?" *Guardian* June 20.

Cabitza, M. 2011. "Bolivia Law Aims to Protect Food Sovereignty." Poverty Matters Blog, *Guardian* 29 June.

Cabixi, D. 1999. "Voices of the Earth: Brazil – Daniel Matenho Cabixi." In D. Posey (ed) *Cultural and Spiritual Values of Biodiversity*. London: Intermediate Technology Press, 132–4.

Cajete, G. 2000. *Native Science: Natural Laws of Interdependence*. Santa Fe: Clear Light Publishing.

– 1998. *Look to the Mountain: Ecology of Indigenous Education*. Skyland, NC: Kivaki Press.

Calhoun, C., E. Li Puma, and M. Postone. 1993. "Introduction: Bourdieu and Social Theory." In C. Calhoun, E. Li Puma, and M. Postone (eds) *Bourdieu: Critical Perspectives*. Chicago: University of Chicago Press.

Caouette, D. (ed). 2010. "Au-delà de la crise, La Souveraineté alimentaire: repenser l'agriculture." *Possible* 34(1–2), été.

Carr, C. 1977. *Pastoralism in Crisis: The Desanetch and Their Ethiopian Lands*. Chicago: University of Chicago, Department of Geography.

Carter, D. 1997. "Recognizing Traditional Environmental Knowledge." IDRC *1997–1998. Annual Report: Biodiversity Conservation Theme: Document 9*. Ottawa: International Development Research Centre.

Carter, W. E. 1977. "Trial Marriage in the Andes?" In R. Bolton and E. Mayer (eds) *Andean Kinship and Marriage*. Washington: American Anthropological Association, 77–216.

CBC News 2011 "Herbicide-Resistant Superweeds Overpowering Crops." CBC *News* 7 Oct. Internet source: http://www.cbc.ca/news/technology/story/2011/10/07/technology-superweeds-roundup-ready.html.

CBD (International Convention on Biological Diversity) Alliance. 2010. "Agricultural Biodiversity Feeds the World." *Top 10 for Cop 10 Briefing Paper* October. Internet source: http://undercovercop.org/wp-content/uploads/2010/10/briefing8_top10forCOP10_ENG.pdf.

Centro des Estudios Sociales (CENDES). 1994. *La Alfabetización en Bolivia: Situación Actual y Perspectivas*. La Paz: Centro de Estudios Sociales.

Centro de Ingeniería en Proyectos Regionales Económicos y Sociales (CIPRES) and Instituto Politecnico Tomas Katari (IPTK). 1997. *Plan de Desarrollo Municipal, Sección Ravelo 1997–2001*. Sucre: CIPRES-IPTK.

Centro de Servicios Agropecuarios Técnicos. 1998. "Organizarse: Una Guía para Campesinos Agricultores" Sucre: Peace Corps and USAID.

Cepeda, R. 1996. "Potencial Varietal De Solanum Tuberosum (Solanum Tuberosum Ssp Tuberosum Y Solanum Tuberosum Ssp Andigenum) En La Microcuenca De Ravelo Provincia Chayanta Del Departamento De Potosí." Unpublished thesis in partial fulfilment of an agricultural engineering degree. Sucre: Faculty of Agricultural Sciences and Forestry, University of San Francisco Xavier.

Cereceda, V., J. Dávalos and J. Mejía. 1998.. *Los Diseños de los Textiles Tarabuco y Jalq'a*. Sucre: Antropólogos del Surandino.

Chaboravarthi R. 2000. "Neem Patent Revoked by European Patent Office." Kuala Lumpur, Malaysia: Third World Network, 11 May.

Chambers, R. 1995 "Paradigm Shifts and the Practice of Participatory Development." In N. Nelson and S. Wright (eds) *Power and Participatory Development: Theory and Practice*. London: Intermediate Technology Publications, 30–42.

– 1994a. "The Origins and Practice of Participatory Rural Appraisal." *World Development* 22(7): 953–69.

– 1994b. "Participatory Rural Appraisal (PRA): Challenges, Potential and Paradigm." *World Development* 22(10): 1437–53.

– 1992. "Rural Appraisal: Rapid, Relaxed and Participatory." Brighton: University of Sussex, International Development Studies Discussion Paper 311.

– 1983 *Rural Development: Putting the Last First*. Harlow: Longman Publishers.

Chisholm, L. 1990. "Action Research: Some Methodological and Political Considerations." *British Educational Research Journal* 16(3): 249–57.

Choque, A. 1999. "Diagnostico de Sauce Mayo." Sucre: IPTK, unpublished manuscript.

Choque, M.E. and C. Mamani. 2001. "Reconstitución del Ayllu y derechos de los pueblos indígenas: El movimiento indio en los andes de Bolivia." *Journal of Latin American Anthropology* 6(1): 202–24.

Collins, J. 1988. *Unseasonal Migrations: The Effects of Rural Labor Scarcity in Perú*. Princeton: Princeton University Press.

Collins, J. 1986. "The Household and Relations of Production in Southern Perú." *Comparative Studies in Society and History* 28: 651–71.

Colucci-Gray, L, E.C. Giuseppe Barbiero, and D. Gray. 2006. "From Scientific Literacy to Sustainability Literacy: An Ecological Framework for Education." *Wiley InterScience*. Internet source: www.interscience.wiley.com.

Committee on Genetic Vulnerability of Major Crops. 1972. *Genetic Vulnerability of Major Crops*. Washington: National Academy of Sciences.

Consejo Nacional de Ayllus y Marcas del Qullasuyo (CONAMAQ). 2011. *Manifesto Por La Defenza de la Vida en Defenza de Madre Tierra Por Un Modelo Economico*

Del Ayllu (Comunitario) Sin Trasgenicos (Organismos Geneticamente Modificado).
   La Paz, June.
Convention on Biological Diversity. 2010. Access and Benefit Sharing Informa-
   tion Kit. Internet source: http://www.cbd.int/abs/information-kit/.
Cooke, B. and U. Kothari. 2001. *Participation: The New Tyranny?* London: ZED
   Books.
Córdova, M.E.O. 2006, La interculturalidad: ¿Proceso que pertenece sólo para los
   indígenas? Internet source: http://intercultural-idad.org/
   numero03/2_08.htm.
Cossío, C. and L. Tomaselli (eds).1990. *Educación Bilingue Intercultural: una expe-
   riencia educativa.* Quito: International Development Research Centre (IDRC).
CREAR, PRATEC & CEBIAE (eds). 1991. *Educación y Saber Andino: Sistematización de
   Experiencias Institucionales.* Iquique, Chile: Ediciones El Jote Errante.
Cusicanqui, S. Rivera. 1992. *Ayllus y Proyectos de Desarrollo en el Norte de Potosí.*
   La Paz: Ediciones Aruwiyiri.
Cusicanqui, S. Rivera. 1990. "Liberal Democracy and Ayllu Democracy in
   Bolivia: The Case of Northern Potosí." *Journal of Development Studies* 26(4):
   97–121.
Dangler, J. and C. Sage. 1985. "What Is Happening to the Andean Potatoes? A
   View from the Grass-roots." *Development Dialogue* 1:125–38.
Davidson, A. 1993. *Endangered Peoples.* San Francisco: Sierra Club Books. David-
   son-Hunt, I. and F. Berkes. 2010. "Journeying and Remembering: Anishinaabe
   Landscape Ethnoecology from Northwestern Ontario." In L.M. Johnson and
   E.S. Hunn (eds) *Landscape Ethnoecology: Concepts of Biotic and Physical Space.*
   Oxford: Berghahn Books: 222–40.
Delgado, F. 1993. *La Agroecologia en las Estrategias del Desarrollo Rural.* Cusco:
   Centro de Estudios Regionales Andinos Bartolomé de las Casas.
De La Peidra, M. "Hybrid Literacies: The Case of a Quechua Community in the
   Andes." *Anthropology and Education Quarterly* (40)2: 110–128.
Densmore, F. 1974. *How Indians Use Wild Plants For Food, Medicine and Crafts.*
   New York: Dover Publications.
De Schutter, O. 2011. *Report Submitted by the Special Rapporteur on the Right to
   Food.* New York: United Nations General Assembly, Human Rights Council,
   20 December: A.HRC/16/49.
– 2010 "Responsibly Destroying the World's Peasantry." Internet Source:
   http://www.project-syndicate.org/commentary/deshutter1/English.
– and G. Vanloqueren. 2011. "The New Green Revolution: How Twenty-First
   Century Science Can Feed the World." *Solutions* 2(4): 33–44.

De Voogt A. 2003. "Muyaka's Poetry in the History of Bao." *Bulletin of the School of Oriental and Africa Studies* 66(1): 61–5.

– 1996 "Indigenous Problem-Solving and Western Methodology: The Case of Bao." *Indigenous and Development Monitor* 4(3): 7–9.

Diaz-olavarrieta, C., S. Garcia, B. Feldman, A Polis, R. Revollo, F. Tinajeros, and D. Grossman. 2007. "Maternal Syphilis and Intimate Partner Violence in Bolivia: A Gender-Based Analysis of Implications for Partner Notification and Universal Screening." *Sexually Transmitted Diseases* 34(7): S42–S46.

Di Castell, S., A. Luke, and K. Egan. 1986. *Literacy, Society and Schooling: A Reader*. Cambridge: Cambridge University Press.

Dick, G., D. Estell, and T. McCarty.1994. "Saad Naakih Bee'enootiilji Na'alkaa: Restructuring the Teaching of Language and Literacy in a Navajo Community School." *Journal of American Indian Education*, Spring: 31–45.

Dorais, L.J. 2010. *The Language of the Inuit: Syntax, Semantics, and Society in the Arctic*. Montreal: McGill-Queen's University Press.

Dorais, L.J. (circa 1990). "Language, Culture And Identity: Some Inuit Examples." Département d'anthropologie, Université Laval (unpublished manuscript). Internet source: http://www2.brandonu.ca/library/cjns/15.2/dorais.pdf

Dove, M. 1996. "Center, Periphery and Biodiversity: A Paradox of Governance and A Developmental Challenge." In S. Brush and D. Stabinsky (eds) *Valuing Local Knowledge: Indigenous People and Intellectual Property Rights*. Washington, D.C.: Island Press.

Downing, J. 1987. "Comparative Perspectives on World Literacy." In D. Wagner (ed) *The Future of Literacy in a Changing World*. Toronto: Pesgamon Press, 40–61.

Dreyfus, H. and S. Dreyfus. 1986. *Mind over Machine: The Power of Intuition and Expertise in the Era of the Computer*. New York: The Free Press.

Duin, B. and K. Wilcox. 1994. "Indigenous Cultural and Biological Diversity: Overlapping Values of Latin America Ecoregions." *Cultural Survival Quarterly* 18(4) Fall/Winter. Internet source: http://www.culturalsurvival.org/our publications/csq/article/indigenous-cultural-and-biological-diversity-overlapping-values-latin-am.

Dyck, N. and J. Waldram. 1993. *Anthropology, Public Policy and Native Peoples in Canada*. Montreal: McGill-Queen's University Press.

Easterly, W. 2008. "Can the West Save Africa?" Working Paper No.14363, Cambridge, MA: National Bureau of Economic Research.

Ellen, R. 1998. "Comments on Paul Sillitoe's 'The Development of Indigenous Knowledge." *Current Anthropology* 39(2) April: 238–9.

Ellerby, J. 2000. "Spirituality, Holism and Healing Among the Lakota Sioux: Towards an Understanding of Indigenous Medicine." Masters Thesis, University of Manitoba.

Evenson, R., D. Gollin, and V. Santaniello (eds). 1998. *Agricultural Value of Plant Genetic Resources*. Wallingford: CAB International.

Evenson, R. 1996. "Economic Valuation of Biodiversity for Agriculture." In Pan American Health Organization (ed) *Biodiversity, Biotechnology, and Sustainable Development in Health and Agriculture: Emerging Connections*. Washington, D.C.: PAHO: 153–66.

Escobar, A. 1997. "The Making and Unmaking of the Third World through Development." in M. Rahnema (ed) *The Post-Development Reader*. London: ZED Books.

– 1995. *Encountering Development: The Making and Unmaking of the Third World*. Princeton: Princeton University Press.

– 1991. "Anthropology and the Development Encounter: The Making and Marketing of Development Anthropology." *American Ethnologist* 18(4): 658–82.

ETC Group. 2013. Poster: "Who Will Feed Us? The Industrial Food Chain or the Peasant Food Web?" http://www.etcgroup.org/content/poster-who-will-feed-us-industrial-food-chain-or-peasant-food-webs.

– 2009. "Who Will Feed Us: Questions for the Food and Climate Crisis." *Communiqué* 102: November.

Etienne, M. and E. Leacock. 1980. "Introduction." In M. Etienne and E. Leacock (eds) *Women and Colonization: Anthropological Perspectives*. New York: Praeger.

Fabricant, N. 2012. *Mobilizing Bolivia's Displaced: Indigenous Politics and the Struggle over Land*. Chapel Hill: University of North Carolina Press.

Fals Borda, O. 1991a. "Some Basic Ingredients." In O. Fals Borda and M. Rahman (eds) *Action and Knowledge: Breaking the Monopoly with Participatory Action-Research*. London: Intermediate Technology Publications: 3–34.

– 1991b. "Remaking Knowledge." In O. Fals Borda and M. Rahman (eds) *Action and Knowledge: Breaking the Monopoly with Participatory Action-Research*. London: Intermediate Technology Publications: 147–64.

– 1979. "Investigating Reality in Order to Transform It: The Colombia Experience." *Dialectical Anthropology* IV March: 33–55.

Femenias, B. 2005. *Gender and Boundaries of Dress in Contemporary Peru*. Austin: University of Texas Press.

Ferdman, B., R. Weber, and A. Ramirez (eds). 1994. *Literacy across Language and Cultures*. New York: State University of New York Press.

Ferguson, J. 1994. *The Anti-Politics Machine: Development, Depoliticization and Bureaucratic Power in Lesotho*. Minneapolis: University of Minnesota Press.

Fillmore, C. 1975. "An Alternative to Checklist Theories of Meaning." *Proceedings of the First Annual Meeting of the Berkley Linguistic Society*: 123–31.

Financial Express [The]. 2005. "EPO Revokes neem patent rights," 10 May.

Firth, R. 1981. "Engagement and Detachment: Reflections on Applied Social Anthropology to Social Affairs." *Human Organization* 40(3): 193–201.

– 1938. *Human Types*. London: Thomas Nelson and Sons.

Flannery, T. 1996. *The Future Eater: An Ecological History of the Australasian Lands and People*. London: Secker and Warburg.

Fleras, A. 1993. "Preschooling with a Cultural Difference: A Maori Language Education Program in New Zealand." In K. McLeod et al. (eds) *Aboriginal Languages and Education: The Canadian Experience*. Oakville: Mosaic Press.

Food for the Hungry International. 2002. "Bolivia: Tibet of the Americas." Internet source: www.fhi.net/countries/countriesphp3?countryid=3.

Foucault, M. 1980. *Power/Knowledge*. New York: Pantheon Books.

Fowler, C. and P. Mooney. 1990. *Shattering: Food, Politics and the Loss of Genetic Diversity*. Tucson: University of Arizona Press.

Frank, A.G. 1966. "The Development of Underdevelopment." *Monthly Review* 18(4) September: 17–31.

Frank, L. 1986 "The Development Game." *Granta* 20 Winter: 31–243.

Fraser, E. and Rimas, A. 2010 *Empire of Food: Feast, Famine, and the Rise and Fall of Civilizations*. New York: Free Press.

Freire, P. 1997. "Preface." In S. Smith, D. Willms and N. Johnson (eds) *Nurtured by Knowledge: Learning To Do Participatory Action Research*. Ottawa: International Development Research Centre.

– 1973. *Education for Critical Consciousness*. New York: Continuum.

– 1970. *Pedagogy of the Oppressed*. New York: Continuum Publishing Company.

– and Macedo, D. 1987 *Literacy: Reading the Word and the World*. South Hadley: Bergin & Garvey Publishers.

Friedmann, H. 2011. "Food Sovereignty in the Golden Triangle Region of Ontario." In H. Whittman, A. Desmarais, and N. Wiebe (eds) *Food Sovereignty in Canada: Creating Just and Sustainable Food Systems*. Winnipeg: Fernwood Press.

Fuglie, K., P. Heisey, J. King, C. Pray. K. Day-Rubenstein, D. Schimmelpfennig, S. Ling Wang, and R. Karmarkar-Deshmukh. 2011. "Research Investments and Market Structure in the Food Processing, Agricultural Input, and Biofuels Industries Worldwide, ERR 130." United States Department of Agriculture, Economic Research Service: December.

Gadgil, M., F. Berkes, and C. Folke. 1993. "Indigenous knowledge for biodiversity conservation." *Ambio* 22: 151–6.

Garcia Linara, A. 2012. *Geopolitics of the Amazon: Patrimonial-Hacendado Power and Capitalist Accumulation.* La Paz, Bolivia: Edificio de la Vicepresidencia del Estado Plurinacional.

Gardner, K. and D. Lewis. 1996. A*nthropology, Development and the Post-Modern Challenge.* London: Pluto Press.

Gari, J.A. 2000. *The Political Ecology of Biodiversity: Biodiversity Conservation and Rural Development at the Grassroots.* Abstract of unpublished PHD dissertation, Oxford University.

Gates, W. 2012 "Prepared remarks by Bill Gates." Unpublished remarks, Rome: IFAD Offices, 23 February.

Gaventa, J. 1993. "The Powerful, the Powerless and the Experts: Knowledge Struggles in an Information Age." In P. Park et al. (eds) *Voices of Change: Participatory Research in the United States and* Canada. Toronto: Ontario Institute for Studies in Education (OISE).

Giroux, H. 1987. "Introduction: Literacy and the Pedagogy of Political Empowerment." In P. Freire and D. Macedo (eds) *Literacy: Reading the Word and the World.* South Hadley: Bergin & Garvey Publishers.

Gledhill, J. 1994. *Power and Its Disguises: Anthropological Perspectives on Politics.* London: Pluto Press.

Global Bird Management Corp. "Common Bird Transmitted Diseases: American Trypanosomiasis and pigeons: (Chagas Disease) 2003. Internet source: http://www.birdmanagement.com/diseases2.html

Globe and Mail. 2008. "Climate Change," 14 October. Internet source: http://www .theglobeandmail.com/servlet/story/RTGAM.2008.1014.wunclimatechange14/ BNStory/International.

Godoy, R. 1992. "The Effects of Rural Education on the Use of the Tropical Rain Forest by the Sumu Indians of Nicaragua: Possible Pathways, Qualitative Findings, and Policy Options." Cambridge, MA: Harvard Institute for International Development.

– 1986. "The Fiscal Role of the Andean Ayllu." *Man* 21: 23–41.

– 1985. "Mining: Anthropological Perspectives." *Annual Review of Anthropology* 14: 199–217.

Gonzales, T. and M. Gonzalez. 2010. "From Colonial Encounters to Decolonizing Encounters. Culture and Nature Seen for the Andean Cosmovision of Ever: The Nurturance of Life as Whole." In S. Pilgram and J. Pretty (eds) *Nature and Culture: Rebuilding Lost Connections.* London: Earthscan, 83–95.

Goodale, M. 2009. *Dilemmas of Modernity: Bolivian Encounters with Law and Liberalism.* Stanford: Stanford University Press.

Goodale, M. 2002. "Legal Ethnohistory in Rural Bolivia: Documentary Culture and Social History in the *norte de Potosí.*" *Ethnohistory* 49(3) Summer: 583–609.

Goody, J. 1994. "Culture and its Boundaries: A European View." In R. Borofsky (ed) *Assessing Cultural Anthropology*. Toronto: McGraw-Hill: 250–60.

– and I. Watt (eds). 1968. "The Consequences of Literacy." In J. Goody and I. Watt (eds) *Literacy in Traditional Societies*. London: Cambridge University Press: 7–69.

Gorski, P. 2008.. "Good Intentions Are Not Enough: A Decolonizing Intercultural Education." *Intercultural Education* 19(6): 515–25.

Goudsmit, A. 2008. "Exploiting the 1953 Agrarian Reform: Landlord Persistence in Northern Potosí, Bolivia." *Journal of Latin American and Caribbean Anthropology* 13(2): 361–86.

Gough, K. 1968. "New Proposals for Anthropologists." *Current Anthropology* 9(5) December: 403–35. Also appeared as "Anthropology and Imperialism." *Monthly Review* 19(11): 12–27.

Graff, H. 1994. "Literacy, Myths and Legacies: Lessons From the History of Literacy." In L. Verhoeven (ed) *Functional Literacy: Theoretical issues and educational implications*. Amsterdam: John Benjamins, 37–60.

– 1986. "The legacies of literacy: continuities and contradictions in western society and culture." In S. Di Castell, A. Luke, and K. Egan (eds) *Literacy, Society and Schooling: A Reader*. Cambridge: Cambridge University Press: 61–86.

Grafton, A. 1992. *New Worlds, Ancient Texts: The Power of Traditions and the Shock of Discovery*. Cambridge: Belknap Press of Harvard University.

Gramsci, A. 1968. *The Modern Prince and Other Writings* (translated by L. Marks). New York: New World Paperbacks.

Gray, A. 1999. "Indigenous Peoples, their Environment and Territories: Introduction." In D. Posey *Cultural and Spiritual Values of Biodiversity*. London: Intermediate Technology Publications: 61–6.

Green, E. 1986. "Themes in the Practice of Development Anthropology." In E. Green (ed) *Practising Development Anthropology*. Boulder, CO: Westview, 1–9.

Grenier, L. 1998. *Working with Indigenous Knowledge: A Guide for Researchers*. Ottawa: International Development Research Centre.

Grillo, R. 1985. "Applied Anthropology in the 1980s: Retrospect and Prospect." In R. Grillo and A. Rew (eds) *Social Anthropology and Development Policy*. London: Tavistock, 1–36.

Gunderson, L. 2000. "Ecological Resilience – In Theory and Application." *Annual Review of Ecology and Systematics* 31: 425–39.

– , C. Allen, and C.S. Holling (eds). 2010. *Foundation of Ecological Resilience*. New York: Island Press.

– , C. Holling and S. Light (eds). 1995. *Barriers and Bridges to the Renewal of Ecosystems and Institutions*. New York: Columbia University Press.

Hall, B. 1992. "From Margins to Center? The Development and Purpose of Participatory Research." *The American Sociologist,* 23 (4) Winter: 15–28.

Hamilton, R. "Introduction." In R. Hamilton (ed) *The Art of Rice: Spirit and Sustenance in Asia.* Los Angeles: Fowler Museum at UCLA.

Hampton, R. 1989. "Using Insights from the Native Literate as a Tool in the Linguist's Bag." *Notes on Literacy* 57:41–6.

Hanson, B. 1985. *Dual Strategies, Dual Realities: The Future Path of Aboriginal People's Development.* Saskatoon: Hanson.

Harris, O. 1985. "Ecological Duality and the Role of the Centre: Northern Potosí." In S. Masuda, I. Shimada, and C. Morris (eds) *Andean Ecology and Civilization: An Interdisciplinary Perspective on Andean Ecological Complementarity.* Tokyo: University of Tokyo Press, 311–35.

Harris, O. 1982. "Labour and Produce in an Ethnic Economy, Northern Potosí, Bolivia." In D. Lehmann (ed) *Ecology and Exchange in the Andes.* New York: Cambridge University Press, 70–96.

– 1978. "Complementarity and Conflict: An Andean View of Male and Female." In J. La Fontaine (ed) *Sex and Age as Principles of Social Differentiation.* London: Tavistock.

Harrison, K.D. 2007. *When Languages Die: The Extinction of the World's Languages and the Erosion of Human Knowledge.* Oxford: Oxford University Press.

Haverkort, B. and W. Hiemstra (eds). 1999. *Food for Thought: Ancient Visions and New Experiments of Rural People.* London: Zed Books.

– 1996. "COMPAS: Intercultural Dialogue on Cosmovision and Agricultural Development." *Indigenous Knowledge and Development Monitor* 4 (2) August: 23–4.

Healey, K. 2001. *Llamas ,Weavings and Organic Chocolate: Multicultural Grassroots Development in the Andes and Amazon of Bolivia.* Notre Dame, IN: University of Notre Dame Press.

– 1992 "Back to the Future: Ethnodevelopment among the Jalq'a of Bolivia." *Grassroots Development,* 16 December: 22–32.

Healey, S. 2006. "Cultural Resilience, Identity and the Restructuring of Political Power in Bolivia, Bali, and Indonesia." Paper submitted for the 11th Biennial Conference of the International Association for the Study of Common Property, Bali, Indonesia, 23 June:1–23.

Heaney, T. 1993. "If You Can't Beat 'Em, Join 'Em: The Professionalization of Participatory Research." In P. Park et al. (eds) *Voices of Change: Participatory Research in the United States and* Canada. Toronto: Ontario Institute for Studies in Education (OISE).

Heath, S. 1986a. "The Functions and Uses of Literacy." In S. Di Castell, A. Luke, and K. Egan, (eds) *Literacy, Society and Schooling: A Reader.* Cambridge: Cambridge University Press, 15–25.

– 1986b. "Critical Factors in Literacy Development." In S. Di Castell, A. Luke, and K. Egan (eds) *Literacy, Society and Schooling: A Reader.* Cambridge: Cambridge University Press, 209–29.

– and B. Street. 2008. *Ethnography: Approaches to Language and Literacy Research.* New York: Teachers College Press.

Hedican, E. 1995. *Applied Anthropology in Canada: Understanding Aboriginal Issues.* Toronto: University of Toronto Press.

Hermann, M. 2002."Native Potatoes from the Andes: New Health Foods and Gourmet Delights." International Potato Center (CIP). Internet source: www.cipotato.org.

Herren, H., B McIntyre, J Wakhungu, and R. Watson. 2009. *International Assessment of Agricultural Knowledge. Science and Technology for Development* (IAASTD): A Synthesis of the Global and Sub-Global IAASTD Report. Washington, DC: Island Press.

Heinrich Böll Stiftung and ETC Group. 2012. "Who Will Control the Green Economy?" Unpublished paper presented to the United Nations General Assembly's Interactive Dialogue: "Harmony with Nature," 18 April.

Hill, J, and B. Mannheim. 1992. "Language and World View." *Annual Review of Anthropology* 21: 381–406.

Hilmi, A. 2012. *Agricultural Transition: A Different Logic.* Oslo: More and Better Network.

Hinzen, H. 1994. "Policy and Practice of Literacy: Experiences and Interpretations." *Adult Education and Development,* Institute for International Cooperation on the German Adult Education Association 43: 213–31.

Hobart, M. 1993. "Introduction: The growth of ignorance." In M. Hobart (ed) *An Anthropological Critique of Development: The Growth of Ignorance.* London: Routledge. Hoggan, K. "Neem Patent Revoked." *BBC News* 11 May.

Holling, C.S. 1996. "Engineering Resilience versus Ecological Resilience." In P.C. Schulze (ed) *Engineering within Ecological Constraints.* Washington, DC: National Academy of Engineering, National Academies Press, 31–44.

Holt-Gimenez, E., M. Altieri, and P. Rosset. 2006. "Food First Policy Brief No. 12: Ten Reasons Why the Rockefeller and the Bill and Melinda Gates Foundation Will Not solve the Problems of Poverty and Hunger in Africa." San Francisco: Food First, 1–10.

– 2006. *Campesino a Campesino: Voices from Latin America's Farmers' Movement.* San Francisco: Food First.

– 2001. "Measuring Farms Agroecological Resistance to Hurricane Mitch." *LEISA* 17: 18–20.

Hornberger, N. 2000. "Bilingual Education Policy and Practice in the Andes: Ideological Paradox and Intercultural Possibility." *Anthropology and Education Quarterly* 3(2): 173–201.

– 1994. "Synthesis and Discussion: Conditions for Collaborative Change." *Journal of American Indian Education*, Spring: 61–3.

Horton, D. and H. Fano. 1985. *Potato Atlas*. Lima: International Potato Centre (CIP).

Howard, P. 2010. "Culture and Agrobiodiversity: Understanding the Links." In S. Pilgrim and J. Pretty (eds) *Nature and Culture: Rebuilding Lost Connections*. London, UK: Earthscan, 163–84.

Humphries, S., L. Classen, José Jiménez Freddy Sierra, Omar Garalldo, Marvin Gómez. 2012. "Opening Cracks for the Transgression of Social Boudaries: An Evaluation of Farmer Research Teams in Honduras." *Elsevier World Development* 40 (10): 2078–95.

Hunn, E. 1999. "The Value of Subsistence for the Future." In V. Nazarea (ed) *Ethnoecology: Situated Knowledge/ Located Lives*. Tucson: University of Arizona Press.

Hymes, D. 1972. "The Use of Anthropology: Critical, Political, Personal." In D. Hymes (ed) *Reinventing Anthropology*. New York: Pantheon, 3–82.

Illich, I. 1999. "Development as Planned Poverty." In M. Rahnema and V. Bawtree (eds) 1999. *The Post Development Reader*, London: ZED, 94–103.

– 1971. "A Constitution for Cultural Revolution." In I. Illich, *Celebration of Awareness*. London: Calder and Boyas. Internet source: www.cogsci .ed.ac.uk/~ira/illich/texts/const_revolution/const_revolution.html

International Center for Ethnobiology. 2008. "Declaration of Belem." Internet source: http://www.ethnobiology.net/_common/docs/ DeclarationofBelem.pdf.

Instituto Politecnico Tomas Katari (IPTK). 2000. "Plan Estratégico 2000–2010." Sucre: internal document.

– 1999a. "Proyecto Apoyo Municipio Productivo de Ravelo 1999–2002." Sucre: internal document.

– 1999b. "Información Institucional." Sucre: internal document.

– 1999c. "Informe de Actividades del AIPE 96–99." Sucre: internal document.

– 1998.. "Centro de Profesionalización Rural (CENPRUR): Planes de Estudio." Sucre: internal document.

– 1997. "Informe de Actividades: Plataforma NOVIB." Ravelo: internal document.

International Institute for Sustainable Development (IISD). 2001. *Locating Energy for Change: An Introduction to Appreciative Inquiry*. Winnipeg: Author.

International Potato Centre (CIP). 2002. "Potato." Internet source: www.cipotato.org/potato.

Inter-Parliamentary Union and UNESCO. 1996. *The Parliamentary Vision for Education, Culture and Communication on the Eve of the 21st Century*. Final Document of the Inter-Parliamentary Conference on Education, Science, Culture and Communication on the Eve of the 21st Century, Paris, 3–6 June.

Isbell, B.J. 1978. "To Defend Ourselves: An Analysis of Andean Kinship and Reciprocity within a Ritual Context." *In* R. Bolton and E. Mayer (eds) *Andean Kinship and Marriage*. Washington: American Anthropological Association, 81–105.

Jackson, T. 1993. "A Way of Working: Participatory Research and the Aboriginal Movement in Canada." In P. Park et al. (eds) *Voices of Change: Participatory Research in the United States and* Canada. Toronto: Ontario Institute for Studies in Education (OISE).

Juarez, G. 2000. "El culto al 'tio' en las minas bolivianos." *Cuadernos hispanoamericanos* 597: 25–32.

Kaskey, J. 2011. "Attack of the Superweed." *Businessweek*, September 8: Companies and Industries. Internet source: http://www.businessweek.com/magazine/attack.

Kasten, E. (ed). 1998. *Bicultural Education in the North: Ways of Preserving and Enhancing Indigenous Peoples' Language and Traditional* Knowledge. New York: Waxmann.

Kater, A. 1984. "Culture, Education and Indigenous Learning Systems." In K Epskamp, (ed) *Education and the Development of Cultural Identity: Groping in the Dark*. The Hague: The Centre for the Study of Education in Developing Countries, 20–7.

Kathmandu Post Staff Writer. 1997. "Literacy Classes for Women." *Kathmandu Post*, 12 June.

Kaufman, F. 2009. "Let Them Eat Cash: Can Bill Gates Turn Hunger into Profit?" *Harper's Magazine*, June, 51–9.

Kelder, R. 1996. "Rethinking Literacy Studies: From the Past to the Present." Proceedings of the 1996 World Conference on Literacy. Internet source: http://www.litserver.literacy.upenn.edu/ILI/ilproc/ilprocrk.htm.

Kemp, E. (ed). 1993. *The Laws of Mother: Protecting Indigenous People in Protected Areas*. San Francisco: Sierra Club Books.

King, S., Carlson, T. and K. Moran. 1996. "Biological Diversity, Indigenous Knowledge, Drug Discovery and IPR." In Brush, S. and D. Stabinsky (eds) *Valuing Local Knowledge: Indigenous People and Intellectual Property Rights*. Washington, DC: Island Press, 167–85.

Kleinman, A. 1996. "Bourdieu's Impact on the Anthropology of Suffering." *International Journal of Contemporary Sociology* 3(2): 203–10.

Knudtson, P. and D. Suzuki. 1997. *Wisdom of the Elders.* Toronto: Stoddart.

Kohl, B. 2003. "Democratizing Decentralization in Bolivia: The Law of Popular Participation." *Journal of Planning and Research* 23: 153–64.

Kothari, B. 1995. "From oral to written: the documentation of knowledge in Ecuador." *Indigenous Knowledge and Development Monitor* 3(2). Online journal: http://app.iss.nl/ikdm/ikdm/ikdm/3-2/articles/kothari.html.

Kulchyski, P. 1993. "Anthropology in the Service of the State: Diamond Jenness and Canadian Indian Policy." *Journal of Canadian Studies,* 28(2): 21–51.

Laird, S. 1999. "Forests, Culture and Conservation." In D. Posey (ed) *Cultural and Spiritual Values of Biodiversity.* London: Intermediate Technology Publications.

Lambert, B. 1977. "Laterality in the Andes." In R. Bolton and E. Mayer (eds) *Andean Kinship and Marriage.* Washington: American Anthropological Association, 1–27.

Lamola, L. 1992. "Linking the Formal and Informal Sectors in Plant Genetic Resources Conservation and Utilization." CEISIN Thematic Guides.

Lather, P. 1986. "Issues of Validity in Openly Ideological Research: Between a Rock and a Soft Place." *Interchange* 17(4): 63–84.

Lave, J. 1990. "The Culture of Acquisition and the Practice of Understanding." In J. Stigler, R. Shweder, and G. Herdt (eds) *Cultural Psychology.* Cambridge: Cambridge University Press, 309–27.

Lave, J. 1988. *Cognition in Practice.* Cambridge: Cambridge University Press. Leavitt, R. 1991. "Language and Cultural Content in Native Education." *The Canadian Modern Language Review* 47(2): 277.

Lederach, J.P. 1995. *Preparing for Peace: Conflict Transformation Across Cultures.* Syracuse: Syracuse University Press.

Levin, S. 1999. *Fragile Dominion: Complexity and the Commons.* Reading, MA: Perseus Books.

Levin, S. et al. 1998. "Resilience in natural and socio-economic systems." *Environment and Development Economics* 3: 225–36 .

Lewis, H. 1993. "Traditional Ecological Knowledge: Some Definitions." In N. Williams and G. Baines (eds) *Traditional Ecological Knowledge: Wisdom for Sustainable Development.* Canberra: Centre for Resources and Environmental Studies, Australian National University, 8–12.

Lewis, V. 1996. "Introduction: Farmers, Herders and Fisherfolk Safeguarding Biodiversity for Food Security." In P. Mulvany (ed) *Dynamic Diversity Booklet.* London: Intermediate Technology Group.

Lilongula, R. 1999. "Voices of the Earth: Solomon Islands – Ruth Lilongula." In D. Posey (ed) *Cultural and Spiritual Values of Biodiversity.* London: Intermediate Technology Publications, 162–4.

Lind, A. 2008. *Literacy for All: Making a Difference.* Paris: UNESCO.

– 1985. *Adult Literacy in the Third World: A Literature Review.* Stockholm: Institute of International Education.

Lithman, G. circa1990. "Universalizing Essentialism: The Properties of Literacy and the Understanding of Literacy Program [*sic*]." Stockholm: Centre for Research in International Migration and Ethnicity and the University of Stockholm Social Anthropology Department. Unpublished manuscript.

Lui, C.H. and R. Mathews. 2005. "Vygotsky's Philosophy: Constructivism and Its Criticisms Examined." *International Education Journal* 6(3): 386–99.

Lockhart, A. 1985. "The Insider-Outsider Dialectic in Native Socio-Economic Development: A Case Study in Process Understanding." *The Canadian Journal of Native Studies* 2(1): 159–68.

López, L.E. 2009. "Reaching the Unreached: Indigenous Intercultural Bilingual Education in Latin America. Background paper prepared for the Education for All Global Monitoring Report." Paris: UNESCO.

– 2001. "Interculturalidad, educación y gestión del desarrollo: Documento de trabajo." *Interculturalidad y Desarrollo: Lecturas de apoyo.* Lima: Escuela Para el Desarrollo.

Luke, A. 2003. Literacy and the Other: A Sociological Approach to Literacy Research and Policy in Multilingual Societies. *Reading Research Quarterly*, 38(1): 132–41.

Lusted, D. 1986. "Why Pedagogy?" *Screen* 27(Sept–Oct): 4–5.

Lyons, O. 1999. "All My Relations: Perspectives from Indigenous Peoples." In D. Posey (ed) *Cultural and Spiritual Values of Biodiversity.* London: Intermediate Technology Publications, 450–52.

Maffi, L. 2010. "Biocultural Diversity: The True Web of Life." *NatGeo News Watch*, 29 June. Internet source: http://blogs.nationalgeographic.com /blogs/news/chiefeditor/2010/06/biocultural-diversity-the-true-web-of-life.html.

– 1999. "Linguistic Diversity." In D. Posey (ed) *Cultural and Spiritual Values of Biodiversity.* London: Intermediate Technology Publications.

– 1998. "Linguistic and Biological Diversity: The Inextricable Link." Internet source: http://cougar.ucdavis.edu/nas/terralin/paper003.html.

Maguire, P. 1993. "Challenges, Contradiction, and Celebrations: Attempting Participatory Research as a Doctoral Student." In P. Park et al. (eds) *Voices of Change: Participatory Research in the United States and* Canada. Toronto: Ontario Institute for Studies in Education (OISE).

Malinowski, B. 1930. "The Rationalization of Anthropology and Administration." *Africa* 3(4): 405–29.

Mamani, J.C. 1999. "Relación de Reprocidad en el Trabajo Agropecuaria en 13 Comunidades de la Segunda Sección de la Provincia de Chayanta." Unpublished thesis in partial fulfilment of an agricultural engineering degree. Sucre: Faculty of Agricultural Sciences and Forestry, University of San Francisco Xavier.

Maquet, J. 1964. "Objectivity in Anthropology." *Current Anthropology* 5(1) February: 47–55.

Martin, P. 1984. "Prehistoric overkill: the global model." In P. Martin and R. Klein (eds) *Quaternary Extinctions: A Prehistoric Revolution.* Tucson: University of Arizona Press, 354–403.

Martínez, G. 1994a. "Prologo." In D. Pacheo, *Machas, Tinkipayas y Yamaras: Provincia Chayanta (Norte Potosí).* Sucre: CIPRES.

– 1994b. "Prologo." In R. Barragán, *Indios de arco y flecha?: Entre la Historia y la Arqueologia De Las Poblaciones Del Norte de Chuquisaca (Siglos XV–XV).* Sucre: Ediciones ASUR.

Maybury-Lewis, D. 1992. *Millennium: Tribal Wisdom and the Modern World.* New York: Viking.

McGill University. 2011. "Definition of Development Anthropology." Posted on the Department of Anthropology website. Internet source: http://www.mcgill .ca/anthropology/graduate/.

McGovern, S. 1999. *Education, Modern Development, and Indigenous Knowledge: An Analysis of Academic Knowledge Production.* New York: Garland Publishing.

McLaughlin, D. 1994. "Critical Literacy for Navajo and Other American Indian Learners." *Journal of American Indian Education,* Spring: 47–59.

Mead, M. 1979. "Anthropological Contribution to National Policies During and Immediately After World War II." In W. Goldschmidt (ed) *The Uses of Anthropology 11.* Washington, D.C.: American Anthropological Association, 145–57.

Mendras, H. 1970. *The Vanishing Peasant: Innovation and Change in French Agriculture.* Cambridge: Cambridge University Press.

Merchant, C. 1992 *Radical Ecology: The Search for a Liveable World.* New York: Routledge.

– 1990 "The Realm of Social Relations: Production, Reproduction, and Gender in Environmental Transformations." In B. L. Turner, W. Clark, R. Kates, J. Richards, J. Mathews, and W. Meyer (eds) *The Earth as Transformed by Human Action.* Cambridge: Cambridge University Press.

Mies, M. 1986. *Patriarchy and Accumulation on a World Scale: Women in the International Division of Labour.* London: Zed.

Mino-Garces, F. 1982. "Enfoques Teóricos sobre Alfabetización Bi-Cultural: el Programa MACAC, Ecuador." *América Indígena:* 221–7.

Molero Simarro, R. and M.J. Paz Antolin. 2012. "Development Strategy of the MAS in Bolivia: Characterization and an Early Assessment." *Development and Change* 43(2): 531–56.

Monsanto 2012 "Corporate Profile." Internet source: http://www.monsanto.com/investors/Pages/corporate-profile.aspx.

Mooney, P. 2001. "The ETC Century: Erosion, Technological Transformation and Corporate Concentration in the 21st Century." In *Development Dialogue* 1(2): Entire Journal. Uppsala: Dag Hammarskjöld Foundation.

– 1992. "Towards a Folk Revolution." In D. Cooper, R. Velve, and H. Hobbelink (eds) *Growing Diversity*. London: Intermediate Technology Press.

Moore Lappe, F. 2011. *EcoMind: Changing the Way We Think To Create The World We Want*. New York: Nation Books.

– 1985. *Diet For A Small Planet:* Ballentine Publishers.

Mucha, J. and J. Vanek. 1995. "From Ecology through Economics to Ethno-science; Changing Perceptions on Natural Resource Management." In D.M. Warren, J. Slikkerveer, and D. Brokensha (eds) *The Cultural Dimensions of Development*. London: Intermediate Technology Press, 5: 5–11.

Murphy, R. 1971 *The Dialectics of Social Life: Alarms and Excursions in Anthropological Theory*. New York: Basic.

Murra, J. 1985a. "'El Archipiélago Vertical' Revisited." In S. Masuda, I. Shimada, and C. Morris (eds) *Andean Ecology and Civilization: An Interdisciplinary Perspective on Andean Ecological Complementarity*. Tokyo: University of Tokyo Press, 15–20.

– 1985b. "The Limits and Limitations of the 'Vertical Archipelago' in the Andes." In S. Masuda, I. Shimada, and C. Morris (eds) *Andean Ecology and Civilization: An Interdisciplinary Perspective on Andean Ecological Complementarity*. Tokyo: University of Tokyo Press, 3–14.

– 1984 ."Andean Societies." *Annual Review of Anthropology* 13: 119–41.

– 1967. "La Visita de los Chupachu Como Fuente Etnológica." In J. Murra (ed) *Visita de la Provincia de León de Huánuco en 1952, Iñigo Ortiz de Zúñiga (1)*. Huánuco, Peru: Universidad Nacional Hermilio Valdizan.

Myr, L. 1998. "Biodiversity Conservation and Indigenous Knowledge: Rethinking the Role of Anthropology." *Indigenous Knowledge and Development Monitor* 6(1) March: 13–15.

Nader, L. 1969. "Up the Anthropologist – Perspectives Gained from Studying Up." In D. Hymes (ed) *Reinventing Anthropology*. New York: Pantheon Books, 284–311.

Naerstad, A. (ed). 2010. *A Viable Food Future*. Oslo: Norwegian Development Fund.

Nash, J. 1979. *We Eat the Mines and the Mines Eat Us: Dependency and Exploitation in Bolivian Tin Mines*. New York: Columbia University Press.

- 1977. "Myth and Ideology in the Andean Highlands." In J. Nash, J. Corradi, and H. Spalding (eds) *Ideology and Social Change in Latin America*. New York: Gordon and Breach.

- 1975. "Nationalism and Fieldwork." *Annual Review of Anthropology* 4: 225–45.

- 1974. "Ethnology in a Revolutionary Setting." In G. Huizer and B. Manheim (eds) *The Politics of Anthropology*. The Hague: Mouton, 353–70.

Naydler, J. 1996. *Goethe on Science: An Anthology of Goethe's Scientific Writings*. Edinburgh: Floris Books.

Nazarea, V. (ed). 1999. *Ethnoecology: Situated Knowledge/Located Lives*. Tucson: University of Arizona Press.

- 1998. *Cultural Memory and Biodiversity*. Tucson: University of Arizona Press.

Nelson, N. and S. Wright. 1995. *Power and Participatory Development: Theory and Practice*. London: Intermediate Technology Publications.

Netting, R. 1971. "The Ecological Approach in Cultural Study." *Addison Wesley Modular Publications* 6: 1–30.

New Scientist Editorial Team, 2001. "The Greener Revolution." *New Scientist* 3 February.

The New York Times. 2010. "The Bill and Melinda Gates Foundation." 29 January. Internet source: http://topics.nytimes.com/top/reference/timestopics/organizations/g/gates_bill_and_melin da_foundation/index.html.

Niemeijer, D. 1995. "Indigenous Soil Classification Systems: Complications and Considerations." *Indigenous Knowledge and Development Monitor* (1) January: 20–1.

Niezen, R. 1999. "Aboriginal Self-Determination and the Cree Pursuit of Northern Flood Agreement Implementation." In J. Chodkiewicz and J. Brown (eds) *First Nations and Hydro Electric Development in Northern Manitoba: The Northern Flood Agreement: Issues and Implications*. Winnipeg: University of Winnipeg Press, 83–92.

NOVIB. 1999. "Informe de la Misión de Evaluación." Sucre: NOVIB internal evaluation report.

- 1998. "Desarrollo Sostenible en los Andes: Conceptos y Metodología." Sucre: internal document.

Oakley, A. 1995. "Interviewing Women: A Contradiction in Terms." In D. Marsden and P. Oakley (eds) *Evaluating Social Development*. Oxford: Oxfam: 30–61.

Ochoa, C. 1990 *The Potatoes of South America: Bolivia*. Cambridge: Cambridge University Press.

Ogbu J. 1987. "Opportunity Structure: Cultural Boundaries and Literacy." J. Langer (ed) *Language, Literacy and Culture: Issues of Society and Schooling.* Norwood: Alex. Publishing Corporation.

Ohmagari, K. and F. Berkes. 1997. "Transmission of Indigenous Knowledge and Bush skills Among the Western James Bay Cree Women of Subarctic Canada." *Human Ecologist* 25(2): 197–222.

Ojeda, S. and I. Retolaza. 1999. *Herramientas son para construir: medio y fin de las técnicas participativas para un desarrollo comunitario.* La Paz: Centro de Información para el Desarrollo.

Olson, D.R. 2008. " Footnotes to Goody: On Goody and His Critics." Internet source: http://barthes.ens.fr/articles/Olson08.pdf. Originally delivered as a conference paper, "Ecritures: sur le traces de Jack Goody." At ENSSIB, 24–6 January, Lyon, France.

O'Neil, J., J. Kaufert, P. Leyland, and W. Koolage. 1993. "Political Considerations in Health-Related Participatory Research in Northern Canada." In N. Dyck and J. Waldram (eds) *Anthropology, Public Policy and Native Peoples in Canada.* Montreal: McGill-Queen's University Press.

Ong, W.J. 1982. *Orality and Literacy.* London: Methuen.

Ortner, S. "Theory in Anthropology since the Sixties." *Comparative Studies in Society and History* 26(1) January: 126–66.

Osborne, B. 1996 "Practice into Theory into Practice: Culturally Relevant Pedagogy for Students We Have Marginalized and Normalized." *Anthropology and Education Quarterly* 27(3): 285–314.

Pacheo, D. 1996 *Poblamiento étnico provincia Chayanta (Siglos XIX y XX)* Sucre: IPTK-CIPRES.

– 1994 *Machas, Tinkipayas y Yamaras: Provincia Chayanta (Norte Potosí)* Sucre: CIPRES.

Pape, I.S.R. 2008. "This Is Not a Meeting for Women: The Sociocultural Dynamics of Rural Women's Political Participation in the Bolivia Andes." *Latin American Perspectives* 35 (6): 41–63.

Paredes Bermejo, S. 2009. "La Interculturalidad: proyecto por construir." *Diario Los Andes, Perú.* Internet source: http://www.losandes.com.pe/Education/20090816/25877.html.

Park, P. 1993. "What Is Participatory Research? A Theoretical and Methodological Perspective." In P. Park et al. (eds) *Voices of Change: Participatory Research in the United States and Canada.* Toronto: Ontario Institute for Studies in Education (OISE).

Patel, R. 2013. "The Long Green Revolution." *The Journal of Peasant Studies* 40(1): 1–63.

– 2010. *The Observer*, "Mozambique's food riots – the true face of global warming" Sunday, 5 September 2010 http://www.guardian.co.uk/commentisfree /2010/sep/05/mozambique-food-riots-patel.

– 2009. "What Does Food Sovereignty Look Like?" *The Journal of Peasant Studies* 36(3): 663–706.

– 2008. *Stuffed and Starved: The Hidden Battle for the World Food System*. New York: Melville House Publishing.

Perrings, C. 1998. "Resilience in the Dynamics of Economic Environmental Systems." *Environment and Resource Economics* 11(3–4): 503–20.

Petras, J. 2008. "Social Movements and Alliance Building in Latin America." *The Journal of Peasant Studies* 35(3): 476–528.

Piaget, J. 1952. *The Origins of Intelligence in Children*. New York: International Universities Press.

Picard, A. 2002. "Today's Fruits, Vegetables Lack Yesterday's Nutrition." Globe and Mail 6 July: A1.

Pickard, G. 2010. "Green Revolution and Hunger: The Failings of the Green Revolution Put Hunger back on the Priority Agenda." *UN Post*, 17 June : Front Page.

Pierotti, R. and W. Wildcat. 1999. "Traditional Knowledge, Culturally-Based World-Views and Western Science." In D. Posey (ed) *Cultural and Spiritual Values of Biodiversity*. London: Intermediate Technology Publications, 192–8.

Pilgrim, S. and J. Pretty. 2010. "Nature and Culture: An Introduction." In S. Pilgrim and J. Pretty (eds) *Nature and Culture: Rebuilding Lost Connections*. London: Earthscan, 3–20.

Pimm, S. 1984. "The complexity and stability of the ecosystem." *Nature* 307(5949): 321–6.

Pires, A. "What's Lost When Languages Are." *Science* 328 April: 431.

Pimbert, M. 2010. Towards Food Sovereignty: Reclaiming Autonomous Food Systems. Oxford: International Institute for Environment and Development.

Platt, T. 1992. "Writing, Shamanism and Identity or Voices from Abya-Yola." *History Workshop Journal* 34: 135–43.

– 1982. "The Role of the Andean *ayllu* in the Reproduction of the Petty Commodity Regime in Northern Potosí (Bolivia)." In D. Lehmann (ed) *Ecology and Exchange in the Andes*. New York: Cambridge University Press, 27–69.

– 1976. *Espejos y Maíz: Temas de la Estructura Simbolica Andina*. La Paz: CIPCA.

Posey, D. (ed). 1999. "Introduction: Culture and Nature – The Inextricable Link." *Cultural and Spiritual Values of Biodiversity*. London: Intermediate Technology Publications.

- 1998. "Comments on Paul Sillitoe's 'The Development of Indigenous Knowledge." *Current Anthropology* 39 (2): 242–243.
- 1990. "Intellectual Property Rights: And Just Compensation For Indigenous Knowledge." *Anthropology Today*, 6(4) August: 13–16.
- and G. Dutfield. 1996. *Beyond Intellectual Property: Toward Traditional Resource Rights for Indigenous Communities and Local Communities.* Ottawa: IDRC.

Postero, N. 2010. "Morales's MAS Government: Building Indigenous Popular Hegemony in Bolivia." *Latin American Perspectives* 37(3): 18–34.

Powers, W. 2006. *Whispering in the Giant's Ear: A Frontline Chronicle from Bolivia's War on Globalization.* New York: Bloomsbury Publishers.

Pozzi-Escot, I. 1990. "Balances y Perspectivas de la Educación para Poblaciones Indígenas en el Perú: 1990." *Allpanchis* 35/36(II): 393–434.

Pretty, J., A. Noble, D. Bossio, J. Dixon, R. Hine, F. Penning de Fries, and J. Morison. 2006. "Resource Conserving Agriculture Increases Yields in Developing Countries." *Environment, Science and Technology* 40(4): 1114–19.

Principe, P. 1989. "Valuing the Biodiversity of Medicinal Plants." In O. Akerele, V. Heywood, and H. Synge (eds) *The Conservation of Medicinal Plants.* Cambridge: Cambridge University Press.

Programa de Autodesarrollo Campesino (PAC). 1996. "Program Review Potosí." European Union unpublished manuscript.

Proyecto Andino de Tecnologias Campesinas (PRATEC). 2011. Internet source: http://www.pratecnet.org.
- 2009 *Climate Change in Andean Communities: Facts, Perceptions and Indigenous Adaptations.* Lima: PRATEC.

Psacharopoulos, G. and H. Patrinos. 1994. *Indigenous People and Poverty in Latin America.* Washington: World Bank.

Puente Rodriguez, D. 2010 *Redesigning Genomics—Reconstructing Societies: Local Sustainable Biotechnology Development.* Amsterdam: self-published with the support of The Netherlands Graduate School of Science, Technology and Modern Culture (WTMC) and the Vrije [Free] University Amsterdam.

Purcell, T. 1998. "Indigenous Knowledge and Applied Anthropology: Questions of Definition and Direction." *Human Organization* 57(3): 258–72.

Quinn, N. 2009. "Remarks," Society for Psychological Anthropology 2009 Lifetime Achievement Award. Asilomar, California: Society for Psychological Anthropology, 28 March.

Quiroga, T. 1999. *Bolivia – Un mundo de potencialidades: Atlas estadístico de Municipios.* La Paz: INE, MDSP-VPPFM, Cosude.

Quiroz, C. 1996. "Local Knowledge Systems Contribute to Sustainable Development." *Indigenous Knowledge and Development Monitor* 4(1) April: 5.

- 1994 "Biodiversity, Indigenous Knowledge, Gender and Intellectual Property Rights." *Indigenous Knowledge and Development Monitor* 2(3) Special Issue: 12–14.

Rahman, A. 1999a. *Women and Microcredit in Rural Bangladesh: An Anthropological Study of Grameen Bank Lending.* Boulder, CO: Westview.

- 1999b. "Rhetoric and Realities of Microcredit for Women in Rural Bangladesh: A Village Study of the Grameen Bank Lending." PHD Dissertation, Faculty of Graduate Studies, University of Manitoba.

Rahnema, M. 1999. "Introduction." In M. Rahnema and V. Bawtree (eds) 1999. *The Post Development Reader,* London: ZED.

- and V. Bawtree (eds). 1999. *The Post Development Reader,* London: ZED.

Rappaport, J. 1994. *Cumbe Reborn: An Andean Ethnography of History.* Chicago: University of Chicago Press.

Rapport, D. and L. Maffi. 2010 "The Dual Erosion of Biological Diversity and Cultural Diversity: Implications for the Health of Ecocultural Systems." In S. Pilgrim and J. Pretty (eds) *Nature and Culture: Rebuilding Lost Connections.* London: Earthscan, 103–19.

Rasnake, R. 1988 *Domination and Cultural Resistance: Authority and Power Among an Andean People.* Durham: Duke University Press.

Ravelo Municipality 2001. *Annual Report for 2001.* Ravelo, Bolivia: Municipal pamphlet. Reder, S. and K. Wikelund. 1993. "Literacy Development and Ethnicity: An Alaskan Example." In B. Street (ed) *Cross Cultural Approaches to Literacy.* Cambridge: Cambridge University Press: 176–197.

Reder, S. 1994. "Practice Engagement Theory: A Sociocultural Approach to Literacy Across Language and Culture." In B. Ferdman, R. Weberand and A. Ramirez (eds) *Literacy Across Language and Cultures.* New York: State University of New York Press: 33–69.

Redwood, M. (ed). 2008. *Agriculture in Urban Planning: Generating Livelihoods and Food Security,* International Development Research Centre (IDRC). Ottawa: Earthscan.

Reijntjes, C., B. Haverkort, and A. Waters-Bayer 1992 *Farming for the Future: An Introduction to Low External Input and Sustainable Agriculture.* London: Macmillan.

Rengifo, G. (ed). 2011. *Small-Scale Agriculture in the Peruvian Andes.* Lima: PRATEC.

- 2005. "The Educational Culture of the Andean-Amazonian Community." INTERculture *148: 1–36.*

- 2000. *Niños y Aprendizaje en los Andes.* Lima: PRATEC

- 1991 "Notas Sobre El Saber Campesino Andino." In CREAR, PRATEC, CEBIAE (eds) *Educación y Saber Andino*. Lima: IDRC and COTESU, 33–51.

Rhoades, R. and A. Bebbington. 1995. "Farmers Who Experiment: An Untapped Resource for Agricultural Research and Development." In D. M. Warren et al. (eds) *The Cultural Dimension of Development*. London: Intermediate Technology Press, 296–307.

Richards, P. 1993. "Cultivation: Knowledge or Performance?" In M. Hobart *An Anthropological Critique of Development: The Growth of Ignorance*. London: Routledge, 61–78.

Rist, S., J. San Martin, and N. Tapia. 1999. "Andean Cosmovision and Self-sustained Development." In B. Haverkort and W. Hiemstra (eds) *Food For Thought: Ancient Visions and New Experiments of Rural People*. London: Zed.

Roberts, W. 2013. *The No Nonsense Guide to World Food: New Edition*. Ottawa and Toronto: New Internationalist and Between the Lines.

Robinson-Pant, A. 2004. "The 'Illiterate Woman': Changing Approaches to Researching Women's Literacy." In A. Robinson-Pant, Women, *Literacy and Development: Alternative Perspectives*, 14–35.

- 1996 "PRA: A New Literacy." *Journal of International Development* 8(4): 531–51.

Roburn, S. 1994. "Literacy and the Underdevelopment of Knowledge" in *Akwe;kon Journal*, Ithaca: Akwe;kon Press, Internet source: http://cug.con cordia.ca/~mtribe/mtribe94/native_knowledge.html.

Rockhill, K. 1987. "Gender, Language and the Politics of Literacy." *British Journal of the Sociology of Education* 8(2): 153–67.

Roht-Arrianza, N. 1995–96 "Of Seeds and Shamans: The Appropriation of the Scientific and Technical Knowledge of Indigenous Peoples." *Michigan Journal of International Law* 17: 919–65.

Rondon, M. and E. Ashitey. 2011. "Ghana" Accra: Global Agriculture Information Network, USDA Agricultural Service, 10 July. Internet source: http://gain.fas.usda.gov/Recent%20GAIN%20Publications/Poultry%20and%20 Products%20Brief%20Annual_Accra.

Rosch, E. 1977. "Classification of Real World Objects: Origins and Representations in Cognition." In P. Johnson-Laird and P. Watson (eds) *Thinking Readings in Cognitive Science*. Cambridge: Cambridge University Press.

Ross, R. 1996. *Return to the Teachings: Exploring Aboriginal Justice*. Toronto: Penguin.

Rural Advancement Foundation International. 1998. "Quinoa Patent Dropped: Andean Farmers Defeat US University." *RAFI Genotype*, 22 May:1–3.

- 1995. *Conserving Indigenous Knowledge: Integrating Two Systems of Innovation*. New York: United Nations Development Program.

- 1993. "Biopiracy: The Story of Natural Cotton in the Americas." RAFI *Communiqué*, November.

Rusten, E. and M. Gold. 1995. "Indigenous Knowledge Systems and Agroforestry Projects in the Central Hills of Nepal." In D. M. Warren et al. (eds) *The Cultural Dimension of Development*. London: Intermediate Technology Press, 88–111.

Ryan, J. and M. Robinson. 1990. "Implementing Participatory Action Research in the Canadian North: A Case Study of the Gwich'in Language and Cultural Project." *Culture* X(2): 57–71.

Sachs, W. (ed). 1992. *The Development Dictionary: A Guide to Knowledge as Power*. London: Zed Books.

Sahlins, M. 1972. "The Original Affluent Society." In *Stone Age Economics*. Chicago: Atherton-Aldine, 1–39; reprinted in M. Rahnema and V. Bawtree (eds) 1999. *The Post Development Reader*. London: ZED, 3–22.

Sampar. P. 2001. "Last Words." *World Watch Institute*. May/June: 34–40.

Sample, I. 2009. "World Faces 'Perfect Storm' by 2030, Chief Scientist Warns." *The Guardian*, 18 March.

Sanchez, R. 1982. "The Andean Economic System and Capitalism." In D. Lehmann (ed) *Ecology and Exchange in the Andes*. New York: Cambridge University Press, 157–90.

Sanchez, L. 2002. "Who Are the Oppressed." Smith College, Center for International Education website. Internet source: www.umass./cie/beyond_friere.

San Martin, J.1997. UK'AMAPI: *en la búsqueda del enfoque para el desarrollo rural autosostenible*. La Paz: AGRUCO.

Schaefer, T. 2009. "Engaging Modernity: The Political Making of Indigenous Movements in Bolivia and Ecuador, 1900–2008." *Third Word Quarterly* 30(2): 397–413.

Schanbacer, W.D. 2010. *The Politics Of Food: The Global Conflict between Food Security and Food Sovereignty*. Santa Barbara, CA: Praeger.

Schibner, S. and M. Cole. 1981. *The Psychology of Literacy*. Cambridge: Cambridge University Press.

Schiwy, F. 2011. "Todos Somos Presidentes: Democracy, Culture and Radical Politics." *Cultural Studies* 25(6): 729–56.

Science Daily. 2010. "Virulent New Strains of Ug99 Stem Rust, a Deadly Wheat Pathogen." http://www.sciencedaily.com/releases/2010/05/100526134146.htm.

Scoones, I., M. Melnyk, and J. Pretty, (compilers). 1992. *The Hidden Harvest: Wild Foods and Agricultural Systems*. London: International Institute for Environment and Development.

Scott, J. 1990. *Weapons of the Weak: Everyday Forms of Resistance*. New Haven: Yale University Press.

– 1976. *The Moral Economy of the Peasant: Rebellion and Subsistence in Southeast Asia*. New Haven: Yale University Press.

Selener, D., N. Endara, and J. Carvajal 1999. *Participatory Rural Appraisal and Planning Workbook*. Ecuador: International Institute for Rural Reconstruction.

Shearwood, P. 1987. "Literacy among the Aboriginal Peoples of the Northwest Territories." *The Canadian Modern Language Review* 43(4) May: 630–42.

Shepherd, C.J. 2010. "Mobilizing Local Knowledge and Asserting Culture: The Cultural Politics of In-Situ Conservation of Agricultural Biodiversity." *Current Anthropology* 51(5), October: 629–54.

– 2005. "Imperial Science: The Rockefeller Foundation and Agricultural Science in Peru." *Science as Culture* 14(2): 113–37.

Shimida, I. 1985. "Introduction." In S. Masuda, I. Shimada, and C. Morris (eds) *Andean Ecology and Civilization: An Interdisciplinary Perspective on Andean Ecological Complementarity*. Tokyo: University of Tokyo Press, xi–xxxii.

Shiva, V. and I. Dankleman. 1992. "Women and Biological Diversity: Lessons for the Indian Himalaya." In D. Cooper, R. Velvé, and H. Hobbelink (eds) *Growing Diversity, Genetic Resources and Local Food Security*. London: Intermediate Technology Publications.

Shiva, V. 1991 "The Green Revolution in the Punjab." *The Ecologist* 21(2): 57–60.

Shulze, P. (ed). 1996. *Engineering within Ecological Constraints*. Washington, DC: National Academy of Engineering.

Sieder, R. (ed). 2002. *Multiculturalism in Latin America: Indigenous Rights, Diversity and Democracy* Institute of Latin American Studies. Hampshire, England: Palgrave Macmillan.

Sillitoe, P. 1998. "The Development of Indigenous Knowledge: A New Applied Anthropology." *Current Anthropology* 39(2) April: 223–235.

Simpson, L. 1999. "The Construction of Traditional Ecological Knowledge: Issues, Implications and Insights." Unpublished PHD Dissertation, Faculty of Graduate Studies, University of Manitoba.

Sjoberg, G. and R. Nett. 1968. *A Methodology for Social Research*. New York: Harper and Row.

Slikkerveer, L. 1999. "Ethnoscience, 'TEK' and Its Application to Conservation." In D. Posey (ed) *Cultural and Spiritual Values of Biodiversity*. London: Intermediate Technology Publications, 169–74.

Smith, E.E. 1988. "Concepts and Thought." In R.J. Sternberg and E.E. Smith (eds) *The Psychology of Human Thought*. Cambridge: Cambridge University Press.

Smith, L., M. Sera, and B. Gattuso. 1988. "The Development of Thinking." In R.J. Sternberg and E.E. Smith (eds) *The Psychology of Human Thought*. Cambridge: Cambridge University Press.

Smith, S., D. Willms, and N. Johnson. 1997. *Nurtured By Knowledge: Learning to do Participatory Action Research*. Ottawa: IDRC.

Sobrevila, C. 2008. *The Role of Indigenous Peoples in Biodiversity Conservation: The Natural But Often Forgotten Partners*. Washington, DC: The International Bank for Reconstruction and Development, The World Bank.

Speiser, S. 2010. "Becoming an Intercultural Primary School Teacher: Experiences from Bolivia." *Intercultural Education*, 11(3): 225–37.

Stairs, A. 1994. "Indigenous Ways to Go to School: Exploring Many Visions." *Journal of Multilingual Development*, 15(1): 63–76.

– 1994. "The Cultural Negotiation of Indigenous Education: Between Microethnography and Model Building" *Peabody Journal of Education*. 69(2) Winter: 155–74.

– 1991. "Learning Process and Teaching Roles in Native Education: Cultural Base and Cultural Brokerage." *The Canadian Review of Modern Languages* 47(2): 280–294.

Standing Committee on Aboriginal Affairs. 1990. *You Took My Talk: Aboriginal Literacy and Empowerment*. Ottawa: Queens Printer, December.

Starn, O. "I Dreamed of Foxes and Hawks": Reflections on Peasant Protests, New Social Movements and the Rondas Campesinas of Northern Perú." In A. Escobar and S. Alvarez (eds) *The Making of Social Movements in Latin America: Identity, Strategy and Democracy*. Boulder, CO: Westview.

Stillar, B. 2009. "The Social Agency of Things? Animism and Materiality in the Andes." *Cambridge Archaeological Journal* 19(3): 367–77.

Strauss, C. and N. Quinn. 1997. *A Cognitive Theory of Cultural Meaning*. Cambridge: Cambridge University Press.

Strauss, C. and N. Quinn. 1994. "A Cognitive/Cultural Anthropology." In R. Borofsky (ed) *Assessing Cultural Anthropology*. Toronto: McGraw-Hill: 284–96.

Street, B. 1994. *Cross Cultural Approaches to Literacy*. Cambridge: Cambridge University Press.

– 1993. "Culture is a Verb: Anthropological Aspects of Language and Cultural Process." In D. Graddol, L. Thompson, and M. Byram (eds) *Language and Culture, Papers from the Annual Meeting of the British Association of Applied Linguistics*. Cleverdon: Multilingual Matters, 23–43.

Stockholm Resilience Centre. 2011. *Research for Governance of Social-Ecological Systems*. Internet source: http://www.stockholmresilience.org/download /18.5004bd9712b572e3de6800017246/org-src+2010+webb.pdf.

Survival International. 2011. "Bolivia Cancels Controversial Road Plans – Survival International." *Survival International – The Movement for Tribal Peoples. Survival*, 25 Oct. Internet source: http://www.survivalinternational .org/news/7827.

Swartley, L. 2002. *Inventing Indigenous Knowledge: Archaeology, Rural Development, and the Raised Field Rehabilitation Project in Bolivia.* New York: Routledge.

Swedish Ministry of the Environment. 2002. *Stockholm Thirty Years On: Progress Achieved and Challenges Ahead in International Environmental Cooperation.* Stockholm: Ministry of the Environment.

Syngenta. 2002. "Ridomil Gold Copper Fungicide." Internet source: http://www.syngentacropprotection-us.com/prod/fungicide/ridomilgold copper/index.asp?nav=WORKERSSAFETY.

Tax, S. 1953 *An Appraisal of Anthropology Today.* Chicago: University of Chicago Press.

Thaman, K. 1993. "Culture and the Curriculum in the South Pacific." *Comparative Education* 29(3): 249– 62.

The New Alliance for Food Security and Nutrition. 2012. Internet source: http://www.whitehouse.gov/the-press-office/2012/05/18/fact-sheet-g-8-action-food-security-and-nutrition.

Thurston, O. and J. Parker. 1995. "Raised Beds and Plant Disease Management." In D. M. Warren et al. (eds) *The Cultural Dimension of Development.* London: Intermediate Technology Press: 140–6.

Titiloa, O. and D. Marsden. 1995. "From Ecology through Economics to Ethnoscience: Changing perceptions on natural resource management." In D. M. Warren et al. (eds) *The Cultural Dimension of Development.* London: Intermediate Technology Press, 499–504.

Trapnell, L. 1984. "Mucho Mas Que una Educación Bilingue." *Shipihui* 84(30): 239–46.

UK Food Group. 2010. *Securing Future Food: Towards Ecological Food Provision.* London: UK Food Group Briefing, January.

United Nations Children's Fund (UNICEF). 2002. "Programa Subregional Andino de Servicios Básicos Contra La Pobreza (PROANDES)" Internet source: www.unicef.org/bolivia/pp/p6.htm.

– 1993a *Cultura 1.* La Paz: UNICEF.

– 1993b *Lengua 2.* La Paz: UNICEF.

United Nations Conference on Trade and Development (UNCTAD). 2013. Trade and Environment Report: *Wake up before it is too late: Make agriculture truly sustainable now for food security in a changing climate.* Geneva, 18 September. http://unctad.org/en/pages/PublicationWebflyer.aspx?publicationid=666.

– 2000. Trade and Development Board, Commission on Trade in Goods and Services, and Commodities, Expert Meeting on Systems and National Experiences for Protecting Traditional Knowledge, Innovations and Practices. Geneva, 30 October – 1 November 2000. [TD/B/COM.1/EM.13 /2 22 August 2000.]

United Nations Development Program (UNDP). 2010. *Human Development Report 2010 – 20th Anniversary The Real Wealth of Nations – Pathways to Human Development.* New York: Oxford University Press.

– 1997. *Governance for Sustainable Human Development: A UNDP Policy Document* New York: United Nations Development Program, January.

United Nations Educational, Scientific and Cultural Organization (UNESCO). 2010. International Institute for Educational Planning (IIEP) Media Release "Literacy: An Essential Foundation for Development" Paris: UNESCO, 8 September.

– 1996. *Medium-Term Strategy, 1996–2001.* Paris: UNESCO.

United Nations Food and Agriculture Organization (FAO). 2010. Commission on Genetic Resources for Food and Agriculture. *The Second Report on the State of the World's Plant Genetic Resources for Food and Agriculture. Synthetic Account.* Rome: FAO.

– 2010. Media Release. "World deforestation decreases, but remains alarming in many countries: FAO publishes key findings of global forest resources assessment." Rome: Communications Department, 25 March.

– 2010. Media Release. "Crop biodiversity: use it or lose it: FAO launches 2nd State of the World's Plant Genetic Resources for Food and Agriculture report." Rome: Communications' Department, October 26.

– 2009. *The International Treaty on Plant Genetic Resources for Food and Agriculture* (ITPGRFA). Rome: FAO.

– 1996. Report on the State of the World's Plant Genetic Resources for Food and Agriculture. Rome: FAO.

– 1995. *La Papa en la Década de 1990: Situación y perspectivas de la economía de la papa al nivel mundial.* Rome: FAO Programa de manejo Postcosecha y Comercialización.

United Nations News Center. 2010. Media Release. "UN report paints grim picture of conditions of world's indigenous peoples." New York: UN News Center, 14 January.

United Nations Secretariat of the Permanent Forum on Indigenous Issues. 2010. *State of the Worlds' Indigenous Peoples* New York: UN Publications. Internet source: http://www.un.org/esa/socdev/unpfii/documents/SOWIP_web.pdf.

United Nations University Institute of Advanced Studies. 2010. "The Ayllu System of the Potato Park, Cusco, Peru." unias: Satoyama Initiative. Internet source: http://satoyama-initiative.org/en/case-studies/americas/agriculture/ayllu.

Urioste, M. 1988. *Segunda Reforma Agraria: campesinos, tierra y educación popular*. La Paz: Centro de Estudios para el Desarrollo.

Usher, P. 1993. "Northern Development, Impact Assessment, and Social Change." In N. Dyck, and J. Waldram (eds) *Anthropology, Public Policy and Native Peoples in Canada*. Montreal: McGill-Queens University Press.

Vadya, A. 1994. "Actions, Variations and Change: The Emerging Anti-Essentialism View in Anthropology." In R. Borofsky (ed) *Assessing Cultural Anthropology* New York: McGraw-Hill, 320–9.

Van Cott, D.L. 2002. "Constitutional Reform in the Andes: Redefining Indigenous State Relations." In R. Sieder (ed) *Multiculturalism in Latin America: Indigenous Rights, Diversity and Democracy*. Institute of Latin American Studies. Hampshire, England: Palgrave Macmillan, 45–73.

Van der Pleog, J. 2008. *The New Peasantries: Struggles for Autonomy and Sustainability in an Era of Empire and Globalization*. London: Earthscan.

– 1993. "Potatoes and Knowledge." In M. Hobart (ed) *An Anthropological Critique of Development: The Growth of Ignorance*. London: Routledge: 209–28.

Vanloqueren, G. and P. Baret. 2009. "How Agricultural Research Systems Shape A Technological Regime That Develops Genetic Engineering But Locks Out Agroecological Innovations." *Research Policy* 38: 971–83.

Van Vleet, K.E. 2008. *Performing Kinship: Narrative, Gender, and the Intimacies of Power in the Andes*. Austin: University of Texas Press.

Varese, S. 1996. "The New Environmental Movements of Latin American Indigenous People." In Brush, S. and D. Stabinsky (eds) *Valuing Local Knowledge: Indigenous People and Intellectual Property Rights*. Washington, D.C.: Island Press.

Von Liebenstein, G., J. Slikkeveer, and D.M. Warren. 1995. "ciran: Networking for Indigenous Knowledge." In D.M. Warren et al. (eds) *The Cultural Dimension of Development*. London: Intermediate Technology Press.

Vygotsky, L.S. 1929. "The Problem of the Cultural Development of the Child, II." *Journal of Genetic Psychology*, 36: 414–34.

Waldie, P. 2011. "World Food Prices Hit New High, Raising Fears of Another Crisis." *Globe and Mail*, Thursday 6 January: A1.

Waldram, J. 1993. "Some Limits to Advocacy Anthropology in the Native Canadian Context." In N. Dyck and J. Waldram (eds) *Anthropology, Public Policy and Native Peoples in Canada*. Montreal: McGill-Queens University Press.

Wale, E. 2012. "Introduction: Setting the Scene for grpi Economics." In E. Wale,

A. Drucker and K. Zander (eds) *The Economics of Managing Crop Diversity On-Farm*. London: Earthscan.

Walsh, C. (ed). 1991. *Literacy As Praxis: Culture, Language, and Pedagogy*. Norwood, NJ: Ablex.

Walsh, S. 2010. "A Trojan Horse of a Word? 'Development' in Bolivia's Southern Highlands: Monocropping People, Plants and Knowledge." *Anthropologica* 52(2): 241–58.

– 2003. "Western 'Capacity Building' among Bolivian *Paperos*: The Marginalization of a Stewardship of Choice." In J. Oakes et al., (eds) *Native Voices in Research*. Winnipeg: Aboriginal Issues Press.

– 2003. "Development Assistance among Jalq'a Paperos in Potosí, Bolivia: From Trojan Horse Toward Strengthened Resilience." PHD Dissertation, Faculty of Graduate Studies, University of Manitoba.

Warren, D.M., J. Slikkerveer, and D. Brokensha (eds). 1995. *The Cultural Dimension of Development*. London: Intermediate Technology Press.

– and B. Rajasekaran. 1993. "Putting Local Knowledge To Good Use." *International Agricultural Development* 13(4): 8–10.

Watahomigie, L. and T. McCarty. 1994. "Bilingual/Bicultural Education at Peach Springs: A Hualapai Way of Schooling." *Peabody Journal of Education*, 69(2) Winter: 26–42.

Watkins, M. 1977. *Dene Nation: The Colony Within*. Toronto: University of Toronto Press.

Wallerstein, I. 1974. *The Modern World System: Capitalist Agriculture and the Origins of the European World Economy in the Sixteenth Century*. New York: Academic Press.

Webster, S. 1977. "Kinship and Affinity in a Native Quechua Community." In R. Bolton and E. Mayer (ed) *Andean Kinship and Marriage*. Washington, DC: American Anthropological Association, 28–42.

White, S. C. 1996. "Depoliticizing Development: The Uses and Abuses of Participation." London: Oxfam U.K unpublished manuscript.

Whittman, H., A. Desmarais, and N. Wiebe (eds). 2011. *Food Sovereignty in Canada: Creating Just and Sustainable Food Systems*. Winnipeg: Fernwood.

Wickens, C. and J. Sandlin. 2007. "Literacy For What? Literacy For Whom? The Politics of Literacy Education and Neocolonialism in UNESCO- And World Bank-Sponsored Literacy Programs." *Adult Education Quarterly* 57(4): 275–92.

Wiest, R. 1998. "A Comparative Perspective on Household, Gender and Kinship in Relation to Disaster." In E. Enarson and B, Hearn Morrow (eds) *the Gendered Terrain of Disaster*. New York: Praeger.

Wilbanks, T. and R. Kates. 1999. "Global Change in Local Places: How Scale Matters." *Climate Change* 43: 601–28.

World Resources Institute. 2005. *Millennium Ecosystem Assessment: Ecosystems and Human Well-Being* Washington, DC: World Resources Institute.

Worm, Boris, Edward B. Barbier, Nicola Beaumont, J. Emmett Duffy, Carl Folke, Benjamin S. Halpern, Jeremy B. C. Jackson, Heike K. Lotze, Fiorenza Micheli, Stephen R. Palumbi, Enric Sala, Kimberley A. Selkoe, John J. Stachowicz, and Reg Watson. 2006. "Impacts of Biodiversity Loss on Ocean Ecosystems." *Science* 314, 3 November: 787–90.

Zimmerer, K. 1996 *Changing Fortunes: Biodiversity and Peasant Livelihood in the Perúvian Andes*. Berkeley: University of California Press.

Index

Aboriginal peoples. *See* Indigenous peoples

acculturation, 39, 58, 187; vs. interculturalism and resilience, 162–3, 228. *See also* clothing; colonialism; Indigenous peoples; interculturalism; resilience

AGRA (Alliance for a New Green Revolution for Africa), 177–9, 265n25

Agrarian Reform Act, 21, 121, 243n3. *See also* INRA

agribusiness, 265n25. *See also* agroindustry; biotechnology

agricultural extension agents. *See* extension workers

agro-ecology, 176, 193, 195, 201, 209, 258n18. *See also* Agroecology and Family Agriculture Association; AGRUCO; food sovereignty; organic farming; Seeds of Survival; smallholder farming; Southeast Asia Regional Initiatives for Community Empowerment

Agroecology and Family Agriculture Association, 268n14

agro-industry, 176, 179. *See also* agribusiness; Green Revolution; Monsanto

AGRUCO (Agroecologica Universidad Cochabamba), 253n45, 268n14

aid. *See* development assistance

Alaskan Native Hunters, 93–4. *See also* connectionism

Algonquin, 94. *See also* connectionism

Alliance for a New Green Revolution for Africa. *See* AGRA

All Saints Day, 61

All Souls Eve, 54, 59–61

Andes: crops of, 244n28; ecosystems of, 35; gender complementarity in, 43–4; local governance in, 72; Peruvian, 37; weather patterns of, 248n21

ANED (Asociación Nacional Ecuménica de Desarrollo), 255n43; partnership with IPTK on credit scheme, 115, 132, 140–1. *See also* Grameen Bank; credit; IPTK; micro-credit

Anishinaabe language: and spatial patterning, 94–5. *See also* Algonquin; Inuit; Mi'kmaq

Annan, Kofi, 178

anthropology: as child of imperialism, 25, 240n3; and connectionism, 88, 92; and development work, 26, 52, 241n7; interactive methodologies of, 25–6, 32; and knowledge mining, 15, 25; and language translation, 27–8; research ethics of, 27. *See also* Benchmark Household Surveys; donut-style research; field research methods; Indigenous peoples; PAR; PRA; triangulation; Trojan-Horse aid; validity checks

Asociación Nacional Ecuménica de Desarrollo. *See* ANED

ASUR (Foundation for Anthropological Investigation and Ethno Development), 73, 215; and development of Indigenous weaving and textiles, 205

ayllu, 21, 72–4, 242n2; and aid organizations, 141; IPTK stances towards, 120–1; and land management, 76–8, 81; and the state, 131, 247n5, 269n7; and the union, 75–6, 123, 248n14. *See also* Agrarian Reform Act; Chimpa Rodeo; ecological complementarity; Indigenous peoples; Land Reform Act; Jalq'a; Mojón; National Council of Ayllus and Markas of Qullasuyu

Aymara: language of, 15, 71, 162, 168, 262n21; people, 36, 164, 208

ayni, 78, 82. *See also* Chimpa Rodeo; Mojón

Baffin Island, 95

Bao, 92–3, 95–6, 171. *See also* connectionism

Barabaig, 10–11

Barrios, Frans, 101, 119

Bayer, 114, 175. *See also* agro-industry; biotechnology; Green Revolution; monoculture

Benchmark Household Surveys, 31, 216–18; and potato plant diversity data, 218–21; and quantifiable data, 218; research methods and, 26–7, 30. *See also* Chimpa Rodeo; field research methods; IPTK; Mojón

Bill and Melinda Gates Foundation, 177, 265n25. *See also* AGRA; Rockefeller Foundation

biodiversity: of Bolivia, 17, 210, 258n14; conservation of, 131, 135; and culture, 183; and ecological agriculture, 194–5, 201–2, 209, 267n8, 268n14; factors in decline of, 132–3; in mainstream policy development, 176; and new Green Revolution, 179; and Western approaches to development, 22, 107, 129, 140, 170, 174. *See also* AGRA; CBDC; ecological complementarity; Green Revolution; IBCR; monoculture; PGRC; organic farming; resilience; small-holder farming; Seeds of Survival

Biodiversity Conservation and Research. *See* IBCR

biopiracy, 180–4. *See also* bioprospecting

bioprospecting, 180, 182, 265n41. *See also* biopiracy; biotechnology

biotechnology, 257n24, 269n7; companies, 175, 179. *See also* Bayer; Green Revolution; monoculture; Monsanto; Novartis

Bloch, Maurice, 88, 92; on language